Managing Health Benefits in Small & Mid-Sized Organizations

Managing Health Benefits in Small & Mid-Sized Organizations

Patricia Halo, CEBS

AMACOM

American Management Association

New York • Atlanta • Boston • Chicago • Kansas City • San Francisco • Washington, D.C.
Brussels • Mexico City • Tokyo • Toronto

Special discounts on bulk quantities of AMACOM books are available to corporations, professional associations, and other organizations. For details, contact Special Sales Department, AMACOM, an imprint of AMA Publications, a division of American Management Association,
1601 Broadway, New York, NY 10019.
Tel.: 212-903-8316   Fax: 212-903-8083

This publication is designed to provide accurate and authoritative information in regard to the subject matter covered. It is sold with the understanding that the publisher is not engaged in rendering legal, accounting, or other professional service. If legal advice or other expert assistance is required, the services of a competent professional person should be sought.

Library of Congress Cataloging-in-Publication Data

Halo, Patricia.
    Managing health benefits in small & mid-sized organizations / Patricia Halo.
      p.   cm.
    Includes bibliographical references and index.
    ISBN 0-8144-0457-X
    1. Insurance, Health—United States.   2. Small business—Employees—Insurance requirements—United States.   I. Title.
HG9396.H325   1999
658.3′254—dc21   99–10715
                                     CIP

Printing number

10 9 8 7 6 5 4 3 2 1

To my grandfather, John L. Miklethun, former insurance commissioner of the state of North Dakota and former state senator, who taught me a love of books and learning, and, by example, how to be an elected official of integrity; and to my mentor and adviser, Isaac Goodfriend, former insurance committee chair of the Rockland County Legislature, who guided me toward a career of usefulness and purpose

Contents

CHAPTER 3   Health Plan Review   33

A series of guidelines and worksheets to assist you in evaluating your organization's needs and in understanding health plan and industry situations that can prompt your review and possible action.

CHAPTER 4   How to Find and Select Services   51

How to select a plan using a checklist of requirements, and how to prepare comprehensive specifications for coverage and administration. Two procedures to help you gather information and bids on a range of products and services to meet your organization's health plan needs.

CHAPTER 5   Plan Design and Providers   69

How to identify and compare health plan options that will meet the needs of your organization and its employees. Use of networks, coverage limitations, and eligibility issues as they are relevant to plan design.

CHAPTER 6   Financing Your Health Plan   101

This chapter examines the issue of risk—to what degree you wish to be at risk and to what degree you expect your administrator, providers, or carrier to be at risk.

It helps you to quantify the philosophy of your organization regarding employee cost sharing and discusses risk-sharing features for your plan.

CHAPTER 7 Employee Communication and Cooperation 120

Requirements of law, good management, and common sense are guides to follow when you communicate health plan information to employees. How to get cooperation in limiting abuse of your health plan.

CHAPTER 8 Wellness and Case Management Services 142

Specific programs for early detection, treatment, coordination of services, and appropriate referral. Initiatives to help lower cost for your health plan and to result in healthier and more productive employees.

CHAPTER 9 Monitoring Your Health Plan 178

Periodic benchmarks and management strategies to help keep your plan on track and to identify problem areas. How to monitor insurers, administrators, in-house staff, and outside specialists. Detailed reports that help you measure and compare costs, plan performance, administrative and organizational influences, and employee reactions to any changes. How to report the results.

CHAPTER 10   Legislation and Your Health Plan   211

A synopsis of legislation that guides and affects health coverage and health care issues. An overview and a reference that can help with compliance and understanding of legal requirements.

CHAPTER 11   Getting the Most From Your Consultant, Agent, or Broker   239

Help with understanding the services provided by health insurance professionals and their unique ability to assist you. Worksheets to help you compare services and their costs when you need a health plan adviser.

CHAPTER 12   Self-Funding   263

A discussion about the concept of self-funding and its potential advantages for your organization. Worksheets to help you consider self-funding your health plan and to project its impact on your organization.

CHAPTER 13   Opportunities for the Smaller Organization   292

A presentation of the unique characteristics of smaller organizations and the role of the health plan for them. A series of tips for smaller employers to reduce cost and improve health plan services, including how to negotiate with a carrier or MCO and how to decide whether to self-fund or whether to participate in association plans or other pools.

APPENDIX   Resources   311

A listing of resources, including my choices for the top reference books, periodicals, Web sites, wellness resources, advisory organizations, and consulting companies for health plan needs.

Glossary   315

A concise listing of terms and provisions.

Bibliography and Suggested Readings   331

Index   343

Preface

When I first was asked to work on a health insurance consulting project, my immediate reaction was "how boring." It hasn't worked out that way during my past nineteen years as a benefits specialist. Anything but. Health benefits has been a dynamic, growing field, one that presents major opportunities for employers, health care industry professionals, and ordinary people to make a difference in the cost, the availability, and the quality of health care services.

About four years ago I found myself wanting to chronicle my experience as a benefits specialist. My thought was to describe the development and use of good plan management techniques and to share my insights, gained not only from nineteen years as a health care consultant but from my experience as a small employer who realizes firsthand how few expert services are available to guide us through the health insurance industry.

In my experience, employers seem to choose among three basic approaches to selecting an employer-sponsored health plan. First, some assume the sales representative who outlines products for them is interested in the well being of their business and is capable of meeting their needs. If so, their involvement in health plan decisions might be delegated and limited to a review of costs. I'd call this approach "let the insurance company do it for me."

Some employers decide to learn about health insurance and how to identify and select appropriate services in order to make an informed choice. They might, with the help of staff from their organization, determine the best alternatives and then select the one that meets their organization's needs. This is the "do-it-yourself" approach.

A third approach is to hire a benefits professional on staff or as a consultant to conduct reviews, make recommendations, and assist with decisions. The employer's selection will rely upon the professional's experience, compatibility with company staff, and range of expertise. I refer to this as the "let-the-hired-gun-do-it" approach.

This book offers a fourth possibility, one that can be valuable regardless of the approach you as an employer have taken. This text can supplement the information you get from the company representative, a hired professional, your staff, and your own research and experience.

At a given time, you can use the chapters you need and the related resources found in the illustrations and the Glossary. By so doing, you can fine-tune your plan, find answers to your benefits and insurance questions, monitor the professionals who work on your behalf, and improve your health plan management and its operation. This hybrid approach to the challenge of plan management can work for you regardless of the size of your organization. It puts you in the driver's seat, but doesn't require that you do it all.

Over the past two decades, I have been asked by employers to review plan performance, reduce costs, expand services, and comply with regulations. To do that successfully, benefits managers must have the cooperation and support of employee groups. As a manager responsible for health plan decisions, you will want to keep in mind that it literally takes two to tango.

Often, employees become the strongest advocates of review and adjustments to a health plan. Given consistent and appropriate information, for instance, employees will follow rising plan costs and identify trends of inappropriate use. Once they recognize the dissipation of limited dollars, they are more likely to be supportive of various activities to improve plan performance.

Perhaps nothing needs to be done with your health plan. It still is important to employee morale and employee understanding to involve workers in the review process and to communicate openly with them about your thinking. This is true even if standard renewals are your goal.

The bottom line is that health plan funds are not infinite—and, increasingly, plan costs are paid by employees. Learning how to control costs yet protect benefits is a major goal for enlightened employees and managers.

Throughout the text, the problems of rising costs, increased regulation, employee resistance, and employer limitations are presented, along with a series of charts and explanations that allows you to apply the concepts and data to your organization. An overview of today's health insurances issues and an insurance primer are included. They can be useful whether you are a novice to the field or an experienced benefit manager.

The needs of your particular organization are important. These can be identified by using the specific methods and worksheets provided to guide your review and examination of your present health coverage and your organization's needs. The book is based on the theory that doing rather than discussing will help you develop useful solutions.

Your concerns about administration, plan design, financing, new developments in the health insurance field, from your perspective as a small or mid-sized employer, are addressed in chapters devoted to these topics.

For many years I developed, managed, and championed self-funded health plans for employers with 500 to 10,000 employees. My work in that niche of the health insurance business is reflected in the examples and narrative of my chapters on self-funding (Chapter 12) and on smaller employers (Chapter 13).

This book has been written to be easy to use. I assume that while you are not an insurance professional you are informed of standard business practices as an owner, employer, or manager. You may wish to glance at the Table of Contents or the Glossary to find the topic area of greatest use to you. My concept is to provide a convenient reference for you to keep on hand as your benefit plan, your organization, and your needs change. If I lapse into what seems like great detail on what you perceive to be a minor point, please stick with the discussion to its conclusion. Detailed analysis and discussion rest on one important lesson I have learned in the last nineteen years—small issues in health plans can grow to gigantic proportions in a nanosecond.

Health insurance language and paperwork can be real obstacles for employees and employers alike. It sometimes seems as if it's part of a deliberate plot; your employees may even complain that it is part of the carrier or employer game plan to reduce cost. The importance of making health coverage understandable and easier to access is evident. My hope is to encourage simpler writing about health insurance by example, with the plain language used here.

If you are challenged by the task of managing your company's health benefits, you are on the right track. The field of health insurance is constantly changing, even though it is change that can be forecast and often managed, and it therefore presents a challenge. In this book I trust you find a friend and adviser, one who can guide you safely as you review, analyze, evaluate, select, and monitor your health plan.

My goal for this book is that you find it useful.

Acknowledgments

I want to thank those who have made this book possible and who have enriched my life in the process. First and foremost are my children, Z and Tyler, who are involved with my business and integral to my well-being and peace of mind. Next, are my friends and colleagues who have encouraged me to pursue writing and my career in insurance: William Eli Kohn, Frank Borelli, Don Rubin, Steve Lovell, Marie Wallace, Mary Ann Harnett, Richard Saitow, Bob Gerald, Harold Luckstone, Stanley Rubenzahl, Al Cardillo, Jerry Rosenbloom, and Anne Poor.

A special thanks goes to two of my friends. Ray O'Connell was the first to see an outline of this book a few years back and was kind enough to remember it at an opportune time. Susan Conry, my graphics and design advisor of many years, labored with me through hundreds of illustrations and technical charts to cull the best for each chapter.

Thanks to the supportive folks at AMACOM who have caused the book to blossom from my concepts and early efforts into a volume that we hope will be useful to many—Adrienne Hickey, Jacquie Flynn, Mike Sivilli, and Vanessa Vazquez; and to Bernice Pettinato of Beehive Production Services.

CHAPTER 1

The Big Picture

■ HEALTH PLANS TODAY: A CHALLENGE

Change is often unwanted, and usually challenging. In the field of employee health benefits, however, it is a matter of course. How do changes in the health insurance industry affect a small or mid-sized business? Does the change involve a shift in responsibility or expectation that makes it more costly or more difficult for your business? How can you, as a small- or mid-sized-business manager, best respond to ensure stability for your organization and employees?

These questions should concern you, whether you are a small-business owner, benefit manager, risk manager, supervisor, or employee—in short, if you are anyone who works and needs health benefits. When you consider the cost of health benefits and the business necessity to provide them, these questions about health coverage are of the utmost importance.

Today's health benefits climate developed over the past sixty years. This summary of its development will help you to put your health plan needs into perspective and to recognize change that has occurred.

■ BENEFIT RELATIONSHIPS

Who provides benefits, and to whom, in today's workplace? In the early 1900s employees and the general public were expected to arrange and pay for their own health care costs. During the 1930s and 1940s, the rise of labor unions and the creation of insurance programs and supportive legislation established benefits, including health insurance, as an employee right. For nonunion employers, the need to provide employer-sponsored health plans arose to meet competitive standards and growing employee expectations. Health benefits have become increasingly important to employees. By 1993, a Gallup poll surveyed Americans and found that 20 percent had passed up a job opportunity solely because of some dissatisfaction with the health benefits offered.

Today, legislation, accepted business practices, employment contracts, and employee needs have combined to result in government- and employer-sponsored plans that are available to more and more people. Currently, about 174 million Americans have health insurance. According to the *Executive Report on Managed Care*, 70 percent of Americans are covered by private health insurance through their employers. Concurrent with the growth of health coverage has been a shift from private insurance to coverage provided from public sources.

	Calendar Year			
	1965	*1980*	*1993*	*1994*
National total in billions	$41.1	$247.2	$892.3	$949.4
Source of Funds	**Percent of Total**			
Private	75.0	57.6	56.6	55.7
Public	25.0	42.4	43.4	44.3

EXHIBIT 1-1. National health care costs. (Source: Health Care Financing Administration, Office of the Actuary; data from the Office of National Health Statistics.)

Since 1975, according to the Health Care Financing Administration (HCFA), private coverage for health care costs has declined, rapidly from 1965 to 1980 and more slowly from 1980 to the present. The percentage of health care expenditures paid from public sources increased during the same time period, from 25 percent in 1965 to 42.4 percent in 1980, and continues to increase, as shown in Exhibit 1-1.

Furthermore, the National Center for Health Statistics reports on the decline of private insurance for Americans under age 65, from 77.2 percent in 1984 to 71.3 percent in 1995. It is clear that private health insurance declined as public programs grew, in part, to replace them.

Medicare and Medicaid

Medicare and Medicaid pay some health care costs for certain categories of Americans and are sponsored by the federal government. They are supported and administered, in part, by state and local government.

Medicaid is provided to those who are below a certain income level on the premise that available health care throughout life promotes good health and therefore means less cost to society for premature death and for chronic or catastrophic illness. Medicaid is paid for with federal taxes and is administered locally at the county level by departments of social services. Recent changes in Medicaid have included the mandate by federal and state legislation that Medicaid recipients be offered health maintenance organizations (HMOs) or managed-care plans. This mandate seeks to encourage more consistent health services for low-income patients by having a primary care physician monitor and direct care when the Medicaid member is in need of services.

HCFA reports in 1999 that in 1997 more than 38 million Americans were enrolled in the federal Medicare program, which covers the aged and disabled and those with end-stage renal disease. Projections indicate that the Medicare enrollment in 1998 will increase by more than one million, to 33.8 million aged Americans, 5.3 million disabled, and nearly 300,000 persons with end-stage renal disease. Among the Medicaid population are 100,000 recipients who are blind and 5.9 million who are disabled. The total combined cost for Medicare and Medicaid in 1996 was $351 billion, more than one third of the nation's total health care costs.

The number of Americans over age 65 is expected to increase from 53.1 million in 1995 to 92.2 million in 2025. This will put added financial stress on the national health programs for the elderly and disabled, Medicare and Medicaid.

The Uninsured and the Underinsured

Reuters reported in 1998 that more than 47 million Americans remain without coverage, and tens of millions more are estimated to be underinsured. Historically, the number of people without health coverage grows in periods of economic decline. Health insurance is expensive and is out of reach for those who are out of work or struggling financially.

Controversy about how to pay for the uninsured and the underinsured has raged for years. The gist of the issue has to do with current medical practices and with existing legislation that guides health care services. The fact of the matter is that when people are acutely sick, they receive services. Doctors write off the cost or bill higher amounts to those who pay, while hospitals and emergency rooms are required by law to treat those with urgent medical conditions. It is not an ideal situation and often leaves the uninsured and the underinsured without preventive care and nonurgent care for routine illness, which, typically, is about 20 percent of health care costs.

To pay for the uninsured and the underinsured, hospitals are often allowed to charge uncollected debt to a fund administered by state government. In many states, the funds provided to hospitals come from special taxes and dedicated fees charged to insured and self-insured health plans or from a combination of federal and state tax dollars allocated for charity payments to hospitals. For example, the state of New Jersey estimates its charity care costs for 1998 to be $300 million. Some states, such as Florida, California, and New York, face a higher burden of cost as visitors and non-residents use charity services at local hospitals. Taxpayers pay for this usage through federal, state, and local taxes that contribute to health care clinics and hospitals. So, the simple answer is that we all pay now for about 80 percent of the cost of care for the uninsured and underinsured.

Legislative Directions

One outcome of the erosion of private coverage, the shift to public programs, and the increasing focus on the uninsured and underinsured is the move for legislatures to encourage private employer coverage. Federal and state legislatures recognize the importance of health insurance provided by an employer as a condition of employment. The growth and expansion of such plans removes the burden from government to offer and provide coverage for employed persons.

Despite legislative intent and action, there has been no recent growth in private plans. Instead, the value of employer-sponsored benefits has decreased since 1985, and there has been a steady erosion of health coverage and pensions as a component of compensation, as noted in Exhibit 1-2, developed by the Harvard University economist James Medoff. This graph reflects another transfer of responsibility—away from the employer and toward the employee as the employer increases wages and decreases benefits, expecting the employee to be responsible for health care and retirements needs.

In recent years, legislation has required coverage for more employees and for pre-existing conditions and has improved portability, or the ability to take benefits from one job to another; continuation of coverage; expanded benefits for family leave and the disabled; patient rights to services and appeals; liability for health plan denials; and mandated coverage for mental health and other treatments. Each legislative change has a cost impact on employer-sponsored health plans and discourages expansion of such plans.

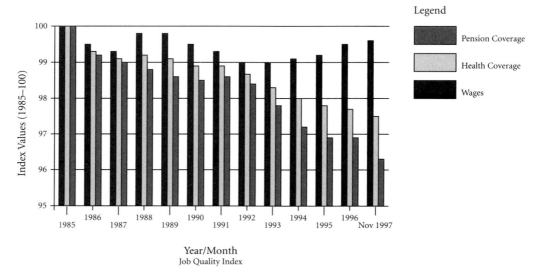

Legend

Pension Coverage

Health Coverage

Wages

Index Values (1985–100)

Year/Month
Job Quality Index

EXHIBIT 1-2. Steady erosion of health profits. Components of compensation due to changes in U.S. job mix (1985–Nov. 1997). (Sources: Netscape, IC Policy Online, May 8, 1997; Employee Benefit Research Institute; James Medoff, Meyer Kestenbaum Professor of Labor and Industry, Harvard University.)

An Aging Workforce

In addition to legislative requirements, the burden of tax-supported programs, and trends in expanded coverage, employers should be concerned with the aging of the workforce and how it will affect health plan costs and needs. Life expectancy is going up in the United States, and so is the age of the average employee, with the normal retirement age raised gradually for those born in 1943 and later from 65 to 66 or 67 years for the first time since the Social Security Act was passed in 1938. A significant increase in the number of aged Americans is projected to occur over the next fifty years. What will be the effect on health insurance plans and on employers? How will an increase in the number of older employees affect health insurance costs? Will the importance of health benefits increase as the workforce ages? Are different benefits appropriate for an aging workforce?

There is clear evidence of increased cost of claims for each decade of employee age in employer-sponsored health plans. Increased cost is expected as employees age and feel the effects of less than healthy lifestyles, the process of aging, and inherited chronic and catastrophic disease. As employees reach fifty-five to sixty-five years of age, their costs are the highest of all employee age cohorts. This information may be adjusted as more employees work beyond sixty-five years of age.

In the past, Medicare has become, at sixty-five years, the primary provider for health care even for people who were working and covered by other health plans. That is no longer the case, with Medicare having become the secondary provider for those who are employed past retirement age. This means that the employer-sponsored health plan, as the primary source of coverage for older workers, has experienced a marked increase in costs for this group of employees. Your health plan will feel the effect of these added costs, and older workers will require stability in their health plan to assure them of coverage when they need it.

You might explore voluntary supplemental coverages for older workers to meet their needs without increasing your costs. Long-term care policies, home care and nursing home benefits, comprehensive drug benefits, hospice care, and services for chronic illness are high on priority lists of older employees and can be offered as a self-pay option to them.

To combat the impact of an aging workforce, your priorities might include early-detection and intervention programs for catastrophic disease, support services to guide and counsel employees on the efficient use of health care dollars, and disease management services to assist those with chronic health problems. These initiatives will help contain the rising cost of health benefits for older workers and are a humanitarian and positive way to respond to their increased health care needs.

Employers as Plan Sponsors

What makes employer-sponsored plans the right way to go? Why can't employees be given a lump sum and allowed to purchase their own plans? There are some natural cost-saving and efficiency factors that make employer-sponsored health plans desirable. Practical matters of enrollment, evaluation of eligibility, payment of premiums, and notification of plan changes and procedures are all more easily accomplished at the work site, where employee records are available and where employees can be reached.

Group plans are more efficient as an economy of scale, with enrollment and eligibility completed at one time and place, communications uniformly distributed, and collection of premium centralized. Coverage provided as a term of employment also offers simpler reporting and monitoring. Tax incentives and other government actions are geared to the employer-sponsored plan and would be more difficult and costly to effect on an individual basis.

For both practical and financial reasons, it is likely that legislation will continue to increase employer responsibility for employee health and well-being. Given this trend, how can you, as a small or mid-sized employer, comply with legislation and yet limit your exposure to unwanted risk? The key to your success in this effort lies in plan design and implementation.

■ PLAN DESIGN AND TYPES OF BENEFITS

Modern health plans were developed in the 1940s and 1950s to cover hospitalization and serious illness—in short, as insurance against catastrophic loss. The goal of health insurance was to keep employees from being bankrupted or devastated by the financial burden of serious illness.

Today, that has changed. Health plans are viewed as a benefit of working, and coverage often includes a wide variety of optional and nonurgent services. Some examples are coverage for alternative therapies, drugs of all types, well care, counseling, routine screening, at-home care, nursing homes, and dental and vision services. The health plan has evolved from insurance against occasional major loss to comprehensive benefits that enhance health and are designed to be used on a regular basis.

Basic areas of coverage for a health plan include hospitalization and major medical and prescription drugs. Within these categories is a wide range of possibilities.

Predesigned Coverage

Employers select health coverage to meet specific needs, and sometimes they need to blend a unique package of coverage and services to do the job. However, even with unique needs, there's no need to reinvent the wheel. Most health plans can be purchased with set benefits and coverage and with standard enrollment, eligibility, and terms of coverage. Each plan developed and sold by an insurance carrier or HMO is a separate product, often one of many offered by the same company. These individual products must be approved by the state department of insurance before they can be sold to ensure that they meet state requirements for coverage.

States differ in their requirements and in their mandated benefits. So, if yours is a multistate organization, you may have health plans that differ in services and coverage according to location, even if you use the same carrier. Most HMOs and managed-care insurance plans are regional and therefore are limited to one area where they are approved to provide medical services. This may result in your offering different plans at each location and in dissimilar employee options among locations.

If your employees are transferred among locations, or if there is a perception that one location is preferable because of its health plan, you may want to consider adjustments. Careful attention to the details of coverage and conditions at each location is important to the small and mid-sized employer. You want to know what you are buying and that the coverage will meet your employees' needs.

Coverage Variations

The following examples will give you an idea of some standard plan design features, each of which has a cost impact and an effect on your employees.

- *Deductible:* An out-of-pocket expense paid annually by each member in the health plan before his or her coverage begins. It can be large or small, ranging from $50 a year to $5,000 a year. It may be waived if a network doctor, facility, or service is used.
- *Copayments:* Another out-of-pocket cost that affects employee use and appreciation of the health plan. It is paid at the time of service and is usually a flat amount, typically from $2 to $50, depending on the type of service provided. If several services are provided, more than one copayment may be required.
- *Coinsurance:* Employee share of costs, usually 10–50 percent of the acceptable medical fee. This is paid to the doctor or facility by the employee and is limited to some maximum dollar amount per year. A higher coinsurance, such as 30 percent, may be required for out-of-network use, while a lower percentage or no coinsurance may apply to network services. Coinsurance for major medical services is commonly referred to as 80–20 coverage, indicating the payment responsibility of the plan (80 percent) and the employee (20 percent) based on usual and customary charges. Coinsurance can also apply to plans where actual charges are the basis for payment, instead of usual-and-customary fee schedules.
- *Usual, customary, and reasonable fees:* Medical services paid according to a schedule or an average, usual fee paid for the same service in a given area. Usual, customary, and reasonable (UCR) payments are developed by zip code, so a doctor may get paid at one level in his primary office and at a different level at another office. One carrier or plan may pay at 85 percent of the UCR schedule, and another plan or carrier may pay at 70 percent of UCR. You will want to determine how fees paid to doctors and other providers compare between health plans. In networks the doctor is paid under a contract that can be based on fee for service, capitation (a monthly amount per patient, regardless of how often the patient is seen or what treatment is provided), or a combination of the two.

■ *Hospitalization coverage:* Payments for inpatient stays, paid on a per-diem rate, according to charges, or on the basis of a diagnosis-based global fee. State regulations and agencies may regulate discounts for hospital services. Variations in plan design include total number of days of inpatient hospital stay allowed (120–365 days a year); limited access to hospitals based on preadmission certification and preapproval of surgery and treatment; discharge planning requirements; and advance negotiated fees. Special conditions may exist for certain types of hospitals, such as mental health facilities, transplant centers, and specialty care centers. Limits may apply for outpatient and ambulatory services by a hospital, including emergency room use.

■ *Doctors and other providers:* Services may be provided by individual physicians and group practices, or by a smaller or larger network of providers. Patients may be required to obtain approval from the plan, a managed-care service, or a primary care physician before receiving care or specialist services. Approved care may be kept to a certain number of visits or services, and care may be limited to only one geographic area, except for medical emergencies. Limits on certain types of treatment, such as alternative therapies and chiropractic and physical therapy services, may be included.

■ *Drug coverage:* Payments may be restricted to generic drugs, limited to a yearly maximum, available only from limited pharmacies or mail-order sources, and subject to preapprovals and ongoing evaluation of need. Other variations include elimination of drug coverage, a separate drug copay, coverage only by reimbursement, coverage for the employee only, and coverage only for drugs for short-term, acute illnesses.

■ *Riders:* These allow small and mid-sized employers to make a basic plan available to all employees, with riders for added benefits available for purchase by individual employees who wish to purchase richer coverage. Vision, prescription drug, dental, enhanced major medical, and long-term care riders are often available.

■ *Voluntary benefits*: Increasingly common today, these benefits are paid for by the employee who selects additional coverage or services. They might include life insurance, disability and long-term-care coverage.

Enrollment, Eligibility, and Payment Variations

Plans can vary in their terms and conditions for enrollment, eligibility, and payment. Until passage of the Employee Retirement and Income Security Act of 1974 (ERISA), employers faced few requirements except for union welfare plans regulated under the Taft-Hartley Act and plans defined by union contracts. Today, an employer-sponsored health plan has specific rules and regulations about employees or retirees who are excluded, about excluded coverage or benefits, and about those who lose coverage for any reason. Times have changed, with employers losing substantial control over who is and is not covered and the conditions under which benefits are provided.

■ *Open enrollment and initial enrollment:* Eligible employees must enroll for health plan coverage within certain time limits, no less than once yearly. They may opt to change health plans annually, if more than one choice is available to them. Time limits are set within which an eligible employee must enroll; or otherwise, the employee must wait for the next open enrollment period.

■ *Eligibility:* New hires and transferred employees may have a waiting period prior to becoming eligible for plan coverage. This practice eliminates unnecessary expense and paperwork for employers when employees leave within three to six months of employment. Restrictions on eligibility may exclude retirees, dependents, part-time employees, dependents covered by other plans, commission-based employees, and independent contractors and professional consultants.

- *Payment restrictions:* Limits on time periods during which employees may file claims, procedures and requirements for submitting claims information, and rules about other sources of payment are all considered when a claim is made. Subrogation and coordination of benefits are potential sources for payment of medical services. Subrogation is the obligation of an employee to reimburse the health plan if payment has been received for medical costs as a result of the settlement of a lawsuit. Coordination of benefits provides that, when other family members have coverage for your employee or for themselves, your health plan costs can be limited by the responsibility of these other plans.

- *Right to appeal:* Health plans are required to set forth the appeal process to be followed when a claim is denied. Some plans allow for verbal and written appeals within thirty days, while others allow up to six months; some have a panel of medical staff, some have an employee-management committee, and some have claims and administrative staff with medical consultants. Written instructions on the appeal process must be provided to everyone in the plan.

■ FLEXIBILITY OF PLAN DESIGN

As a small or mid-sized employer, you may wonder if you can find a health plan tailor-made for your group and whether you can alter a plan to better meet your needs. Remember, some aspects of the health plan—enrollment, eligibility, continuation of coverage, and service aspects related to premium payments, employee communications, selection of the administrator and plan management—are normally designed by you. Often, you and your staff are responsible for some of these activities and can control how they work to meet your objectives.

You do not control coverage when you purchase an insurance plan. It is important for you to make a careful selection of coverage and service levels that meet your employees' needs from those plans available to you. The plans from which you select need to gain approval from the state insurance departments and so cannot be randomly altered. On the other hand, changes in the health insurance industry have resulted in a greater variety of plans from which to choose, which makes it easier for you to find an appropriate plan for your organization.

If you decide to self-insure some or all of your benefits, you have wide latitude in coverage levels, although they must still remain within limits that are acceptable to your employees, to the insurance industry, and to the medical community. There are few insurance department controls on self-insured plans.

■ HEALTH CARE SERVICES

Your selection of a health plan may automatically determine the quality of care provided to your employees. For instance, the plan you select will determine whether your employees use a network only, a combination of in-network and out-of-network services, and have unlimited access or restricted access on approval for health care services. Patient care and its quality are a concern for you as an employer who provides a health plan. Ultimately, your goal is satisfied if you have healthy employees who understand and appreciate the value of the health plan you provide.

This introduction to health care services covers important concepts that you can use every day to better manage your health plan, and its benefits.

Limits to Access

If a plan limits access to doctors, hospitals, or other services, does that necessarily sacrifice good care? If the plan is careful to include quality providers, it may not. But, in this era of managed care, will the average employee covered by a plan be able to seek the best specialist in any geographic area? Chances are, no.

Have we seen quality of care improve or decline with the limitations placed on employee choice of doctor or hospital? Managed-care network membership seems to be increasingly consolidated, with carriers and HMOs making it harder for doctors and facilities to join. It may be that the network concept is fully established, and adequate providers already belong. Or it may be that new, lower-cost arrangements, with limited doctors and single facilities, are more profitable for the HMO or carrier. This tightening of network membership further limits access to services for health plan members.

An example of this is the trend among HMOs to contract with one facility in a densely populated suburban area for diagnostic x-rays, despite the availability of convenient network services throughout the area. Members of these HMOs are now required to travel to a single, often distant, facility for diagnostic x-rays. They are no longer able to use other network facilities for these services. As a consequence of this barrier to care, members will be less likely to seek services before they exhibit serious symptoms. This means that illness will be detected at a later stage and be more costly to treat, with less likelihood of success. A gloomy note, but true.

"Penny-wise and pound-foolish" comes to mind. Remember, the carrier or HMO is not guaranteed that you will continue to purchase coverage from it, and so its focus is on keeping down short-term expenses and on reducing risk. This is diametrically opposed to your goals as the employer. You are more often concerned with the long-term health and well-being of your employees and wish to ensure that they receive quality health care when they need it.

Recent statistics show that the United States spends more money on health care than any other country in the world; yet it does not have the lowest death rates for surgeries, illnesses, or treatments, or for newborn deaths or incidence of catastrophic illness. It appears that we are not doing as good a job as we might, despite the tremendous amount of money we spend on health care. We need to improve both quality of care and access to care as an important part of improving our outcomes.

Physician Autonomy

A controversial subject, physician autonomy became a burning issue with the advent of nonmedical and medical monitoring of physician decisions. Both insurance carriers and HMOs have requirements for review and monitoring of medical services and claims.

Doctors traditionally opposed having someone who does not know the patient and who is not liable for the outcome determine what treatment is allowed. They raise questions about whether admission to a hospital or use of a new diagnostic test or costly procedure is frowned upon or denied by the carriers on the basis of cost alone, without proper attention to the quality of care or medical necessity.

Carriers and HMOs penalize doctors financially if they use higher-cost services compared to an average. Doctors have complained that this oversight and monitoring inhibits their practice of medicine in the best interest of the patient. Insurance industry control over the practice of medicine based on cost justification is currently the subject of state and federal legislation that addresses gag clauses in managed care contracts.

Given their impact on physician autonomy, why do doctors join networks? Advantages to the doctor include more patients, less paperwork, and easier filing and acceptance of claims. For the patient, use of a network means lower out-of-pocket costs for quality medical care.

Doctors and Abuse of the Health Care System

As with any profession, some doctors do not live up to the highest standards. In recent years, as a response to publicized fraud and abuse of the health care system, state legislation has been proposed and passed to monitor and regulate doctors who refer patients to facilities and services in which the doctors have an ownership or interest. There is a firm and prompt censure of doctors who are found to misuse Medicare and Medicaid by overbilling or inaccurately billing these tax-supported programs. A recent study by Blue Cross-Blue Shield revealed that 65 percent of the cost of fraudulent claims is attributable to physician overcharges.

Over $189.4 billion was spent in 1994 on physician services, as shown in Exhibit 1-3. This translates to $700 per person in the United States. Some regulation and monitoring is clearly appropriate.

Self-Regulation

Substantial self-regulation of doctors is built into the health care system. Doctors are highly trained and credentialed; they must meet rigorous education and experience requirements in order to be licensed and go through a review process to be admitted to practice in a hospital and peer review to retain hospital privileges. Some board certifications require that doctors stay up-to-date on treatment and practice guidelines.

In addition, doctors are insured for malpractice to protect them and their assets from mistakes; the cost of this coverage depends upon their track record. When they are sued by a patient, their cost of malpractice insurance will increase; if more lawsuits occur, malpractice coverage will cost them more than they can afford. Eventually, they may not be able to purchase it at all, and loss of coverage will cause them to lose hospital privileges.

	National Total (billions)	Per Capita Amount	Private	Public
			(as a percent of total)	
Total	$949.4	$3,510	55.7	44.3
Personal health care	831.7	3,074	56.5	43.5
Hospital care	338.5	1,251	41.0	59.0
Physician services	189.4	700	67.9	32.1
Nursing home care	72.3	267	42.1	57.9
Other personal care	231.5	856	74.3	25.7

EXHIBIT 1-3. National health expenditures by type. Data are as of calendar year 1994. (Source: Health Care Financing Administration, Office of the Actuary; data from the Office of National Health Statistics.)

Most carriers and HMOs require proof of medical malpractice insurance for a doctor to maintain network status.

These checks and balances of licensing, hospital privileges, and malpractice insurance cause the medical profession to be self-regulating to a large extent.

Oversight of Doctors

Doctors' decisions are supervised in many ways by insurance carriers and HMOs. They require doctors to update credential files and to provide current licenses, board certifications, and proof of malpractice insurance. Requiring approvals for care that extends over time, preadmission approvals for hospitalization or testing that the doctor feels is necessary, denials for treatment options that are costly, and second-guessing in general—these are ways in which doctors believe insurance companies interfere. It is this medical management and interference with patient treatment that doctors oppose.

Examples of governmental oversight of physicians include government requirements for practice, inspections of facilities and equipment, use of accreditation agencies, and monitoring of patient care by public agencies. Departments of health and insurance in most states and, often, county and local agencies are responsible for monitoring health care quality and delivery of services by physicians. Doctors complain of the red tape caused by these regulations, inspections, and the accreditation process.

Can some oversight of physicians be helpful? If regulatory systems provided more support, guidance, and convenience to doctors and their staff, the concept of oversight might be more successful. Doctors' desire to make unhampered decisions about patient treatment will not go away. Insurance companies will continue their efforts to ensure that they are paying for appropriate care, and government will continue to safeguard public health and well-being through regulations and enforcement.

The impact of these competing forces is felt by everyone who sees a doctor, who needs to file a health claim, who is responsible to employees for health plan services, or who provides health plan services. It is helpful to understand the perspective of each—the doctor, insurance plan, and government agencies. This triumvirate directly affects the quality of patient care, physician autonomy, and covered services.

Alternative Therapies

What effect will the growing acceptance among health plans of the hands-on therapies of acupuncture, chiropractic, and massage have on cost and patient care? Therapies for nutrition, stress reduction, and healing are approved by some plans and are rapidly gaining acceptance among consumers. Major health insurers such as Aetna/USHealthcare, Blue Cross-Blue Shield, and Oxford Health Plans have already begun to offer plans with basic coverage of such therapies, or offer coverage through riders. Some states already include chiropractors, nutritionists, and others in mandated coverage regulations, thereby including them as part of required coverage in insurance contracts.

Recently, it was reported in the national media that one in every three visits to a health care provider in the United States was made to an alternative therapy provider. It is clear that most Americans, including, most likely, your employees, welcome the opportunity to seek nontraditional care. An important point is that such care is far less costly than traditional medicine. Equally important is that such therapies, especially in the cases of chronic and catastrophic illness, do not claim to replace traditional treatment and providers.

We are seeing a trend, as alternative care providers grow in popularity and increase in numbers, in favor of care that enhances and promotes health and well-being. This is a major change from the earlier health insurance philosophy of providing care only when someone is sick.

■ HIGHER COSTS AND THEIR EFFECTS

If your premium is competitive, isn't it the best you can do? As a small or mid-sized organization, what can you do to control costs better? Every time a news story features the rising cost of health benefits, these questions come up, and the answers can affect your health plan and your organization.

Although health care cost increases have slowed, they still far outpace inflation. Taking a look at the history of these increases can yield some useful insight. In the 1980s, health care costs rose between 10 percent and 20 percent each year, nonstop. A New York State municipal health plan that cost $79.00 each month in 1979 increased in ten years to more than $250.00 monthly, and in 1998 it cost $582.00 monthly. With all other things constant, this rate of increase can make you pause and look for ways to control cost.

Are these increases typical or a fluke? In 1965 health care expenditures represented 5.7 percent of the Gross National Product and cost about $202 per person in the United States. By 1994 they accounted for 13.7 percent of the Gross National Product and cost $3,510 per person. A comparably dramatic increase appears to be occurring in 1998. The projected trend for health care coverage for 1998 and the actual percentage changes for 1997 by plan type and coverage are shown in Exhibit 1-4. Projected increases for 1998 were 13 percent for traditional fee-for-service plans, 9.4 percent for preferred-provider organizations (PPOs), 6 percent for point-of-service (POS) plans, and 4.8 percent for HMOs. An increase up to 12.7 percent in retail prescription drug costs was anticipated.

	1999 Projected (%)	1998 Projected (%)
Medical		
Nonnetwork fee-for-service plans	12.0	13.0
Preferred provider organizations	9.4	9.4
Point-of-service plans	7.8	6.0
Health maintenance organizations	6.8	4.8
Dental		
Nonnetwork fee-for-service plans	8.3	9.3
Network fee-for-service plans	6.9	6.4
Prepaid network	4.0	3.5
Prescription Drug		
Retail	16.6	12.7
Mail order	15.0	13.2

Note: Data for actives and retirees under age 65.

EXHIBIT 1-4. Medical, dental, and prescription drug trends: 1999 projected vs. 1998 projected. (Source: *The Segal Trend Survey, 1998.* Reprinted by permission of The Segal Co., © 1997. All rights reserved.)

Employees are directly affected by such increases when their contribution to health coverage premiums is based on premium costs. On average, employees pay 20 percent of premium cost in a traditional plan, and 16 percent of premium cost for HMOs, according to a 1997 Towers Perrin study. The percentage of cost paid by retirees, who may be least able to afford it due to their fixed incomes, has risen continuously over the past decade. An indirect effect on employees occurs when the fixed cost of a health plan rises—employers cut back on wages and other benefits or cut back on the health plan itself to stabilize their expenses.

Cost-Control Approaches

Rapid increases in health plan costs cause a ripple effect, felt mostly by benefits managers and by employees covered by health insurance. Someone has to pay, as benefits managers balance dollars and services, and employees bargain or lobby for improvements and lower contributions. Cost-curbing initiatives began in the 1980s as a reaction to health care inflation, and continue today. The following general approaches are used to curb the costs of health plans.

Cost Shifting

Major shifts of cost occur regularly in health plans from the employer to the employee, and from government-sponsored programs to employers and individuals. Cost shifting does little to control rising health care costs; it merely changes who pays for them.

Examples of such shifting are increased employee deductibles, copayments, and other out-of-pocket expenses. Fixed maximums for annual and lifetime coverage also limit the plan's responsibility. Through these mechanisms, the burden of rising costs is increasingly transferred to those covered and away from the employer.

Cost shifting has also occurred in government programs such as Medicare. Cost was shifted to participants when Medicaid instituted an annual $100 deductible for major medical costs and hospital coinsurance payments for inpatient stays. Medicare has also shifted cost to employers as stated earlier, through changed coverage rules; a working person and his or her nonworking spouse past normal retirement age are covered by the employer's plan before Medicare. Medicare offers no prescription drug coverage and therefore shifts that cost also to the retiree, who is expected to pay for drugs when needed.

More employees and retirees are required to contribute substantially to health plan monthly costs; many are not covered at all once they leave employment, except by self-paying; and the number of years to earn full coverage in retirement has increased. All of these examples of cost shifting are found today in most health plans.

Eligibility Controls

Employers can limit eligibility, or who is allowed to be in the health plan, to control cost. New employees may have waiting periods before becoming eligible, with 60 to 180 days now common. Classes of employees may be ineligible to join the health plan (i.e., part-timers, retirees), and dependent coverage may be eliminated or paid in full by the employee. These are typical changes in eligibility requirements that reduce cost to the employer and restrict who is covered.

Benefits Limits

Coverage and plan benefits can be reduced or eliminated to limit cost. Examples include restrictions:

- On payments for specific diseases and conditions
- For some services
- In the total amount to be paid
- On who is paid to provide care
- On how care is approved by the health plan
- On payments for preexisting conditions

Coverage may be excluded or limited for some illnesses, such as AIDS, mental illness, and Alzheimer's, and for emergency room services when used for nonlife threatening conditions or for hospital admission prior to obtaining advance approval by the health plan. Requiring use of generic drugs and of discounted physician and outpatient services are further examples of limitations on plan benefits.

Coverage can also be changed to pay a higher percentage of the cost for doctors and facilities in point-of-service (POS), participating-provider-organization (PPO), or hospital-provider-organization (HPO) networks. Such networks are established to help reduce plan costs through discounted payments for medical services by doctors and other providers. Your employees may pay less out of pocket, and your plan can reduce claim cost when providers accept lower fees.

Administrative Savings

Plan management can be held accountable to reduce operating costs. New administrative services have been developed by specialists such as insurance carriers, third-party administrators, pool managers, benefits consultants, and benefits managers. A wide range of services is now available to manage the issues of subrogation, high-cost-claim review, periodic reenrollment, negotiated discounts, case management savings, and coordination of benefits. These have become cost-control hot buttons. Administrative costs to provide these services are considered a negotiable item by employers and are carefully examined.

Electronic capability, or using computers to manage health plans, is of growing importance in cost control. New techniques to identify and track high-cost claims and to increase network referrals and utilization is an example of how electronic tracking can improve cost-effective administration.

High-Cost-Claims Control

Wellness and preventive health programs and case management services can produce cost savings. Their primary goal is to target chronic and catastrophic illness and to reduce its drain on the health plan. A standard equation applicable to most health plans is that fewer than 20 percent of plan members account for 80 percent of plan cost. This 20 percent includes plan members who have catastrophic or chronic illness; they are the employees who rely upon the health plan to avoid financial disaster. Your control of plan use and cost by these employees is crucial.

Wellness and preventive health programs that result in early diagnosis for cancers, heart disease, diabetes, osteoporosis, and other costly, long-term illnesses demonstrates effective cost control. Most early-detection programs have components that include education about the disease, notification of findings to the patient and a physician, and follow-up to counsel the patient toward meaningful treatment or behavioral change. Employers frequently offer lower health plan contributions and incentive payments to encourage plan members to participate and to reward them for positive results.

Lifestyle changes such as smoking cessation, stress reduction, better nutrition, and increased exercise are encouraged by some worksite programs. Less likely to show direct health plan savings, these programs are geared toward encouraging healthier habits. The concept is to reduce risk factors such as smoking, obesity, and a sedentary lifestyle that are linked to the development of high-cost illnesses such as heart disease, diabetes, and cancer.

Managed-care services can help with high-cost claims through case management and utilization review by nurses to guide care for those with catastrophic or chronic illnesses such as heart disease, cancers, asthma, and diabetes. Disease management, patient education and counseling, and referral to appropriate doctors and facilities are some of the specific services provided. This activity helps eliminate and reduce unnecessary testing, some doctor visits, and duplicative care. Case management has helped to control cost by guiding plan members to lower-cost services, reducing unnecessary services through coordination of care and patient counseling, and encouraging patients to follow the treatment recommended by their doctors.

Cost reports on case management show a return on investment that ranges from $1 to $10, while wellness intervention programs show returns of $2 to $12 for each dollar spent. There can be major differences in the wellness and case management services available to you. A complete discussion of how to select these services for your health plan appears in Chapter 8.

Financing the Health Plan

Creative methods have been developed to finance health plan costs. Some typical examples are:

- Self-insurance or self-funding for employers and employer groups
- Creating groups of employers who pool resources to buy coverage for less money
- Negotiating for lower-cost insurance based on a plan's historical costs
- Committing to using a particular lower-cost network for health care services
- Scheduling premium payments to lower short-term costs or to guarantee premiums

Self-funded employer plans usually benefit from improved cash flow and reduced administrative costs. They may achieve lower claim costs if the plan is carefully designed and managed.

Plans for pools, union welfare funds, and associations have the advantage of the power of numbers to spread the risk of high-cost claims and administrative charges. Such plans may offer improved services to keep members happy and are often membership oriented.

Some employers may be able to select health plans where their premium each year is directly based on the actual health care costs of their employees. Others select lower-cost network options for health care services, such as POS, PPO, or HMO plans.

Insurance carriers offer a variety of plans that weight plan premiums later in the year, allow for a catch-up of premium at year-end, or guarantee premiums over a period of time. Flexible financing of premium payments makes coverage more affordable for seasonable businesses and for employers with cash flow problems.

Each financing alternative has potential advantages and limitations. You should analyze your needs to select the best choice for your organization. For help with this, refer to chapters 3 and 6, which deal with health plan review and with financing your health plan, respectively.

Indirect Costs

The training of doctors, or graduate medical education (GME), is one factor in health care costs. Some states train a higher-than-average number of doctors who will not practice in the United States once they complete graduate medical education requirements. This is especially true for large cities, such as New York and Los Angeles, where medical students from overseas train at teaching hospitals affiliated with medical schools in those cities. This training, which provides doctors for many other countries, is a cost burden for such hospitals. That cost is passed along in higher hospital costs, which may be covered by payments from state and federal taxes.

To convey some idea of the magnitude of this expense for resident and nonresident doctors, the New York State budget provided a subsidy to teaching hospitals of $1.385 billion in 1998 for graduate medical education.

Technology also influences cost increases. More diagnostic tests are done today than ever before in the history of our health care system, and these tests are vastly higher in cost than earlier, less accurate versions. One need only consider MRIs, bone densitometry, CAT scans, the PSA test for prostate cancer, and transplant technology.

It has been reported that 40 percent of diagnostic testing is unnecessary, duplicative, or so poorly done that it needs to be repeated. An improvement in patient education and counseling prior to such testing can result in more cost-effective use of diagnostic services. Coordination of care between different physicians who are treating the same patient can also reduce unnecessary testing.

Major technological advances have improved the treatment and outcomes for premature babies and for transplant patients. New procedures and successful techniques for transplantation have increased the frequency and reduced the cost of transplant operations. The average cost of a heart and lung transplant is one-third of the cost five years ago. Premature babies are now surviving and living healthy lives, and advances in genetic research promise improved outcomes in the future.

The cost of new technology continues to affect health insurance plans. To counter the wider use of these services, some plans eliminate or restrict coverage for transplant services, and others offer programs to identify problem pregnancies earlier to reduce the incidence of caesarean and premature deliveries, with their higher costs.

■ ADMINISTRATIVE ISSUES

Until the 1980s, most health plans were provided by insurance carriers as indemnity or insured products, with the rules, procedures, and terms of coverage dictated by them. In the past two decades, however, major changes have resulted in new organizations, such as HMOs and PPOs, and in the establishment of self-funded or self-insured plans. Traditional insurance accounts for fewer than one-third of health plans today.

Earlier, we noted that the government has stepped in, *increasingly* since the 1970s, to regulate health insurance and to offer expanded social programs such as Medicare, Medicaid, and Social Security and Workers Compensation health coverages. How can the small or mid-sized employer benefit from a different plan administration, from a switch to a new type of organization or plan, and from the use of appropriate government programs to benefit employees?

Insurance Carriers and HMOs

The organizations that provide insurance coverage are a primary element in the struggle to provide quality health plans at an affordable cost. These organizations allocate health care resources among those covered; they get paid to do it; and the system works to some degree. Members tend to blame them when they say no or delay payment and to praise them when they cover staggering costs for major surgery or lingering illness that could drain personal resources.

Health insurance was designed to cover high costs, not to pay for every medical cost. Our expectations of what should be covered have changed since hospitalization and major medical coverages were first developed in the 1940s.

We have seen the growth of HMOs over the past twenty years. Until recently they were federally protected by legislation that guaranteed them the right to offer coverage at worksites with more than fifty employees in any county in which they were licensed. This legislation was created by Congress in 1984 on the premise that HMOs would provide quality care, offer preventive medicine, and lower the cost of care. There has been progress toward these goals, although some disagree with a philosophy that limits access to services. Despite their critics, HMOs now provide coverage to over 67 million people, more than one half of those with private health coverage in the United States.

Merger Mania

One current development is the frequent mergers between insurance carriers and HMOs, with the merged conglomerates offering more types of plans. It is not uncommon for health plan vendors such as Aetna/USHealthcare, GHI, Blue Cross-Blue Shield, CIGNA, and Mutual of Omaha to offer a dozen choices to employers. These might include limited-network plans such as POS and PPOs, along with several traditional or indemnity plans and straight HMOs. Open-access plans that allow more freedom of choice are the latest variety, allowing members to select a specialist without the primary doctor's permission. Each of these plans has its own identity, including medical provider networks, and its own terms of coverage. The variety alone can create problems.

From an employee's viewpoint, it is confusing, at best, to have new plan names, benefits booklets, and frequent coverage or provider changes. The burden rests with employers and benefits managers to be careful in how often they make such changes, to consider the way any change will affect employees, and to fully explain new plans to employees. A good rule of thumb is to change health plans no more than every three years, depending on satisfaction level and cost issues.

Health Care Liability and Patient's Rights

Health care is a business. Recent legal decisions have ruled that liability for medical decisions rests with carriers and HMOs, who require preapprovals and who often withhold approval on what is perceived as financial grounds. In response, many states have passed legislation that holds the carrier or HMO accountable for the effect of such decisions.

Some states have passed patient rights and consumer legislation that require HMOs and carriers to be held liable if a patient dies or suffers because of treatment decisions that were made by the HMO or carrier. There is a federal initiative to pass consumer rights legislation that would create a uniform standard for liability. Linked with this legislation are requirements to make specialists more accessible to patients. Over time, the result of such legislation should be an improvement in the quality of approval decisions by health plans.

In the meantime, it is wise for you, as the employer, to fight on behalf of the plan member for services that are ordered by the member's doctor. There have been cases where the plan sponsor or employer has been sued for damages resulting from denial of services by a health plan offered by the employer.

■ MARKET FORCES AND THEIR EFFECTS

What particular problems exist for the employer based on the number of employees covered by a health plan? How do the costs of small employers compare to those of larger organizations? What can the mid-sized organization do to take advantage of strategies often used by large employers?

Problems of Size

Size affects nearly everything in a health plan and can make plan changes difficult for the small and mid-sized employer. Large employers may have union and institutional issues that drive up cost and coverage levels, but they also have the advantage of size to spread the risk and to negotiate rock-bottom rates and service contracts.

As a mid-sized organization, you will need to pay attention to the details to have a cost-effective health plan for employees. You may have some of the advantages of size, when compared with the small business organization, such as the options to self-fund or to request a premium based on claims history. If you are a small employer, a business of ten employees or more, you are a prime client for your insurance professional because so many larger organizations of 100 employees or more are now self-funded for health benefits. As a consequence, you are sought after by the insurance professional who can shop the market for you and provide a range of cost and service options.

Organizations with fewer than 5,000 employees are more likely to be directly affected by market forces than larger employers. For instance, smaller companies are more likely to be regional or local, making them more susceptible to regional and local economic fluctuations. Thus, if unemployment is high in a given area, it may directly reduce the volume of sales or income for a mid-sized employer located there, which in turn makes fixed expenses, such as wages and health insurance, harder to meet.

Buying Power

Market forces within the insurance industry also affect a small or mid-sized organization to a greater degree than a large employer, primarily because those organizations have less bargaining clout with insurance carriers or HMOs. If it is a "hard" market where insurance costs are rising or less negotiable due to large losses within the industry, the smaller company will quickly feel the brunt in higher premiums. The larger organization, on the other hand, is generally either experience rated or self-insured, which helps keep plan expenses closer to the claims costs of employees and does not require payment toward insurance industry losses.

You should request and maintain records from your health plan on your experience (claims payments made on behalf of your employees). If your experience is good, meaning your costs are less than the premium you paid, it may be possible for you to negotiate a lower premium. This can help insulate you from undeserved premium swings.

Business Necessity

The primary goal of your organization is to stay in business and to realize a profit from services or products sold. If you are a nonprofit organization, your goal is to provide your service cost-effectively to satisfy a social need. In either case, you operate within the business conditions of competition, operating costs, and available resources.

Competition is a strong influence on you as a small or mid-sized organization because you are less likely to be diversified, with several products or services in different industries. You may need to compete for employees within your industry or your geographic area. This type of competition is directly related to your health plan. If your employees are highly trained or technical and professional staff, or if there is a limited labor market at your location, you may be pressured to offer a richer health insurance plan to attract and retain employees.

You also have less depth of staff (fewer people at any given level or job position) and therefore less ability to transfer trained employees from one location to another than the larger employer. Furthermore, your investment in each employee for recruitment, training, and compensation is proportionately higher than it would be for a larger employer.

If your bottom-line costs have a direct impact on your ability to compete and your business operates with a narrow profit margin, health plan costs are even more important to control. You may have to juggle the need to keep additional employees on staff with the need to provide an affordable health plan within your budget. To keep operating costs down, you might reduce employee hours and thus control the cost of wages. It is harder to control health plan premiums that continue each month; they cannot be reduced to meet your short-term needs.

Business necessity issues of operations, costs, and resources require that you exercise care when selecting your health plan. Remember, it is costly and requires staff and funding resources. Furthermore, switching health plans may upset operations. A related issue is your relationship with employees. Depending on employee contracts and the labor environment, you may need several years to negotiate a change in health plans. If you recognize the issues that are specific to your organization, your management of your health plan will be more controlled.

Retiree Issues

You may feel the effect of an aging workforce on your health plan in some direct ways. Health costs for older workers are much higher than those for younger workers, and retiree health insurance may be prohibitively expensive. As noted earlier, your cost of claims or experience will be higher when the average age of your health plan member is older, resulting in higher premiums for everyone. Nonetheless, retiree coverage may be an accepted business practice in your industry or geographic region, and so you may be expected to provide it.

You must take care to have clear-cut and definitive policies in place on retiree coverage. Recent court rulings required that employers provide retiree coverage that adheres to the written descriptions of health plan coverage presented in benefit booklets and the verbal representations by personnel staff. These rulings point out the importance of established procedures, precise training and instructions for personnel staff, and written explanations of how retiree health insurance will be handled.

Limits on Resources

As a small or mid-sized organization, you have more limited financial and personnel resources. Thus, there will be added pressure on your organization when the economy has a turndown or if new regulations are required. You are also less likely to have an adequate reserve of capital to cover fixed costs during a declining economy. Similarly, your staff and your available expertise for implementing new regulations may be limited. You may therefore opt to augment your staff by hiring a consultant or rely upon insurance company representatives to inform you and keep you in compliance with changing requirements. The need for this expertise is highlighted by recently passed federal laws such as the Consolidated Omnibus Budget Reconciliation Act (COBRA), the Americans with Disabilities Act (ADA), and the Family Medical Leave Act. Each of these laws required notifications and established procedures for employers with fifty to 5,000 employees. A complete review of legislation is presented in Chapter 10.

■ SUMMARY

The overall answer to your health plan needs will grow out of your exercise of good judgment. You are encouraged to consider the large picture when you examine your health plan. Understand the individual needs and traits of your organization, and apply the basic insurance concepts that are introduced in Chapter 2. It is commonly said that information is power, and this is especially true as you proceed in the technical and complex discipline of health benefits. You can avoid pitfalls and problems in your health plan management by using the guidelines and information provided in this book.

CHAPTER 2

A Health Plan Primer

■ INSURANCE BASICS

Like most technical and complex activities, insurance and health benefits follow a series of principles and have their own language. Once you understand relevant insurance principles and have an overview of legislation that affects health plans, you'll be better able to follow the twists and turns that occur with your health plan. In this chapter, you can review the differences in the types of plans available, helpful resources, and health plan choices. This information is basic to understanding the issues that might influence your health plan decisions and your organization.

■ INSURANCE PRINCIPLES

The Law of Large Numbers is an insurance principle that directly affects small and mid-sized organizations. It states that when the risk of loss is spread among a larger number, the risk to each individual is less. "Safety in numbers" or "spreading the risk" are other phrases used to describe the law of large numbers. The larger the group, the more predictable and stable its costs will be. An understanding of this term can go a long way toward helping you make sense of health insurance and wellness issues that require your attention. The Law of Large Numbers is based on the projection of probabilities, or what will probably happen in the future, judging from known facts that can be taken into account.

The size of a group is related to its financial stability. For example, according to the American Cancer Society's Cancer Facts & Figures 1997, the cancer incident rate for all sites for each 100,000 of population is 469 for white males and 346 for white females. It is possible to project the anticipated cost of cancer claims in a group of 100,000, with variations for age, gender, ethnicity, and geographic location, all of which have an impact on the incidence of cancer. It is harder to do this for smaller groups, and once a group is very small, say, fifty people or less, it is impossible to apply average incident rates. They simply don't hold.

Let's examine how the Law of Large Numbers applies in the case of cancer claims. If a group of 100,000 white males has a premium based on average incidence, the cost of 469 cancer claims is spread among all 100,000 employees. If fewer cancers occur in the year, premiums will accumulate at year end and so prove to be higher than needed. If more than 469 cancers occur in the year, premiums may be too low to cover costs, and a premium increase will be required for the next year. Remember that cancer claims are only one type of high-cost claim, used as an example here.

How will the annual cost of cancer claims affect each individual in the 100,000 member group who pays premiums? Minimally, because the incidence can be projected fairly accurately with such a large group, and the cost is spread over a large number of plan members.

The impact of a higher-than-average number of cancer cases will be greater for members of the smaller organization, unless they are part of a larger insurance pool. For example, suppose that in a workforce of fifty males there are three cancer cases in one year. These cases represent a cancer incidence rate of 6 percent for the small group, or more than twelve times the average. No small organization by itself could pay such high cancer costs, even with an increase in premium. However, the impact of the costs can be reduced if the small organization is part of a larger group, such as a group health insurance plan or a pooled plan with other small organizations. Then the cost of so many cancer cases in one year is spread among the entire group.

To put the large and the small organization into perspective for this example, the employer with 100,000 males would have to have not 469 but 5,628 cancer cases in one year to have the same cancer incidence rate of 6 percent as given for the small organization with fifty males and three cancer cases. Such a high rate is highly improbable.

Insurance works because it is based on the Law of Large Numbers. The larger pool of premium dollars assures payment of claims for the small number of members with high costs.

The Law of Large Numbers is based on what is likely and probable. Once the number is smaller, likelihood and probability are harder to determine, and the total amount of funds available to pay high cost claims is also limited. The idea is to have the many share the risk of the few.

Underwriting is the function of estimating probable loss for a group or a plan and goes hand in hand with the Law of Large Numbers. For each insurance product offered, a great deal of thought and calculation has gone into the premium cost for the coverage and services provided.

The set of facts and estimations used to calculate premium and to project costs is known as *actuarial assumptions*. Among the factors considered is the probable use of benefits among any group of plan members. Estimates of use are computed on averages, so the plan must be sold to an average population of members in order to perform as the underwriters project. By *average* we refer to known incidence rates for disease and mortality and the impact of age, gender, ethnicity, and location on these incidence rates. An average group would fit a profile for so many males, so many females, the number of members in certain age cohorts, and a mix of ethnic backgrounds. To improve the accuracy of projections, adjustments are made by underwriters for each variance from an average in categories such as these.

Underwriters project and estimate loss for employer groups who apply for coverage. They examine the demographics, claims history, and losses of an employer before the coverage is written and before the group is accepted as a risk. Insurance companies indemnify, or guarantee, the losses of those who are covered. Underwriting is the function of estimating what those losses will be.

For each chronic or catastrophic disease, there is a substantial cost. As a result, these illnesses have a major and direct impact on a group's total health care cost. If the age, gender, or ethnic background of a group varies from an average mix and skews toward one that indicates a higher risk for these illnesses, the underwriter will project higher costs for the group.

Other underwriting considerations include the availability of services in a given area and their relative cost. There may be variations in coverage that need to be considered, such as for plans that allow for extensive routine care, well care, or special coverage that increases cost because the plan is "richer" than most. Underwriters develop probable cost, given the characteristics of the group, such as the proportion of males to females and the number of members in different age cohorts.

Underwriters are the watchdogs for the insurance industry; they make sure that enough premiums are collected to pay claims for each insurance product sold. The problems the underwriter faces vary, depending on the size of the employer.

If an employer is large enough to be experience rated, usually with more than 500 employees, the underwriter will examine a three-year claims history of the organization, the benefit levels provided, and facts about the covered members that indicate higher than average use—age, gender, ethnicity, and type of work, for example. Smaller organizations might also be experience rated, depending on their location, industry, and available insurance plans.

The purpose of being experience rated is to lower cost. The carriers often are willing to tie premiums to the actual costs incurred for health care services. If you are seeking an annual premium, the underwriter would develop your cost of claims so that the carrier could quote a premium to you that includes an accurate estimate of claims, plus administrative and other costs.

Mid-sized organizations might benefit from underwriting, too. If you have a younger, healthier workforce, or effective wellness and early-detection programs to reduce the cost of catastrophic claims, your experience will reflect it. Good claims experience, even for mid-sized organizations, can translate into lower premium and administrative costs. If the employer has a stabile workforce with few changes and relatively low turnover, and if there are no major changes anticipated in business activities, there is reason for the underwriter to assume that claims will continue to be lower than premiums. It is appropriate for you, as a mid-sized organization, to seek reduced premiums when you are armed with a low-cost claims history for three years.

The underwriter's task is to determine the level of risk for the carrier, HMO, or pool when it agrees to provide your employees with health coverage. The issue of risk and how it affects your health plan, premiums, claims payments, benefits, and long-term needs is at the heart of the matter.

Risk is something we know about. How risky a life you lead usually depends on your ability or capacity to lose. By definition, when something is risked there is a possibility and a probability of loss. If you gamble, you might understand the odds of placing bets and throwing dice without any guarantee that you will win.

In insurance, the carrier, HMO, or pool is gambling that your employees will cost less than the premium you pay. If you are self-funded, you are gambling that the cost of your health plan will be less than your budget, which can be less than the cost of the same benefits in an insured plan. Your comfort level with risk is an important consideration.

Standard ways to deal with risk are to **transfer** it to someone else, to **avoid** it, to **control** it, or to **reduce** it. The field of risk management has grown tremendously in the past fifteen years, as a result of the need to handle risk in organizations of all sizes. One area of risk is your health plan.

Transfer of risk means you have someone else assume it. A typical approach is to purchase insurance in which the carrier accepts your risk in exchange for a profit. You might decide to transfer a part of your risk, all of it, or none of it. Some of your decision will be based on how much you can afford to lose, some will be based on how much you are inclined to gamble, and some will be based on how you perceive the opportunity to win.

To transfer the risk of your health plan, you might purchase an insured plan from a carrier or HMO. Another, more subtle transfer is to shift the costs of coverage to employees, to other plans, and to government social programs, which may pay for some coverage.

Avoiding risk means you do not undertake it. For example, you could eliminate coverage and services or limit who can belong to your health plan. You might be inclined to avoid risk that is high cost and catastrophic, such as coverage for transplants, AIDS, in vitro fertilization, or long-term rehabilitation therapies.

Controlling risk refers to your ability to identify risk and then to implement activities that help you limit its cost to and its effect on your organization. A prime example of this approach in a health plan is to implement early diagnosis and intervention services for chronic and catastrophic illnesses such as cancer, cardiac disease, and diabetes. Disease management services for employees who have such illnesses is another step toward controlling your cost and your risk.

Reducing risk means that you take on a risk to a limited degree. In your health plan risk reduction can be seen in limiting the number of visits to certain providers, using a limited network of providers with lower cost, setting maximum amounts payable for certain illnesses annually, during a lifetime, or for specific services.

Risk management of health plans relies upon all of these approaches, usually in some combination. Ultimately, your mix of techniques will reflect the resources of your organization and your philosophy about your role and your organization's role in providing an employee health plan.

Adverse selection is another insurance term that is relevant to your health plan. Remember the example of the organization with fifty male employees and three cancer cases in one year? That may have been the result of providing health benefits to an organization with a much higher-than-average number of older, sicker employees. When this happens, it is called adverse selection. We recognize that insurance is based on the Law of Large Numbers and underwriting, both of which depend on average incidence of use and cost per person. When the averages are skewed, due to unusual extremes of age, physical condition, gender, ethnicity, or claims history, it doesn't work. Basically what happens is that the projection of risk and cost is wrong because averages don't apply.

The term "adverse selection" also has to do with consumer selection of one health plan over another, and some argue that unnatural limitations on consumer selection cause adverse selection. This application of the term relates to the negative impact of government regulation on a plan's overall risk or cost that results when high-risk individuals select it for coverage. The increased cost due to adverse selection is not the result of any improvement or change in quality or access. When older, sicker members choose one health plan, they drive its cost and utilization to levels higher than expected. Similarly, there is greater-than-average risk when such plan members are accepted, since they are likely to cost the plan far more than an average employee.

The concept has to do with balance and with free markets. If every plan accepts a certain number of high-risk members, then all plans will be affected to the same degree. However, when one plan, due to its cost of premium, benefits provided, government regulation, or other reason, attracts more members who are older or sicker, it increases that plan's cost and use. When this occurs, it is said that the plan suffers from adverse selection.

A related but opposite occurrence happens when healthier, younger employees opt for one plan over another. This might have the positive effect of a lower risk, resulting in below average costs for that plan. If your workforce is in this category, you might shop for the best buy in a plan suitable to your low-risk group.

Market forces and competition between carriers and HMOs also affect your choices and follow certain patterns. The insurance industry creates large pools of money to cover the risk of those who purchase coverage. They cover risks such as health care needs, property damage, loss of income, and disaster costs. When losses are high in one area, it may affect another. For instance, if there are large industry losses due to hurricanes, earthquakes, and other natural disasters, there is a ripple effect on health insurance, because, for the large carriers, there is one pool of money that is drawn upon to pay for losses. Therefore, large losses in the area of liability insurance or property and casualty insurance can cause tighter markets in another area. A tighter market means that the insurance industry has less money than needed, so premiums are higher.

Legislative requirements and precedents set by legal actions, for example, might increase the amount of anticipated losses, making higher profits from health insurance a necessity. In some cases, economic conditions affect premium increases, as when interest rates change, causing insurers to earn less on investments.

When there is ample capital available, and no major trends of losses in the insurance industry, the market is more competitive, and prices are generally lower. This is called a *soft* market. When money tightens up and there are fewer insurers who aggressively seek health insurance business, premiums may go up as competition lessens. This is referred to as a *hard* market. The impact of regulations, the economy, changes in the health care industry, and regional or local trends affect the health insurance market.

■ TYPES OF PLANS

Traditional or indemnity plans are often called *fee-for-service*, since they are based on payment of an established fee for a service rendered by a physician or facility. Services are identified by number codes assigned to each medical procedure, called CPT codes, and the rate of payment is established by geographic area, often by zip code. There are organizations, such as the Health Insurance Association of America, that develop and publish these fee schedules on a quarterly basis so as to keep abreast of rising costs. Insurance carriers and HMOs may develop their own payment schedules, based on contractual agreements or standard fees charged in an area. Often, claims-paying organizations purchase a fee schedule from a national group such as HIAA and implement their fees at a percentage of the schedule.

This type of plan usually offers a choice of physician, facility, or other provider to the member. A percentage of cost is paid by the member in the form of an annual deductible, copayment, or coinsurance. It is understood in such plans that a percentage of the total allowable cost is the member's responsibility. Most often, there are annual maximums, maximum amounts payable for certain types of service, and lifetime maximum amounts to each plan member. Indemnity coverage is based on a philosophy of reimbursing or covering a member for necessary health care services chosen by the plan member.

There have been predictions that traditional indemnity coverage is dying. In my opinion, that is not the case. There are swings in the health insurance business, as with every other business, and the swing lately has been to more, not less, freedom of choice for plan members. The name may change, but the concept remains. It takes on strange forms, sometimes, as you will see with some of the other types of plans described here.

Increasingly, in recent years the traditional plan has added point-of-service features and a network of providers to its indemnity approach. A plan member using the point-of-service option has a limited, often lower, out-of-pocket expense but only for a fixed group of providers. This plan option requires a flat copayment at the time of service, instead of a deductible or coinsurance, when a lower-cost network provider is used. It often is coupled with traditional coverage, including freedom of choice under fee-for-service terms for nonnetwork providers.

Participating provider organizations are networks of providers who offer a full range of services to plan members at discounted rates. Sometimes a PPO plan limits covered services to those provided by the network, and PPO fees can be similar to insurance premiums when they are quoted to cover all member health care costs.

Out-of-pocket expense to the plan member can follow the point-of-service or indemnity model, meaning it can be a flat amount or a percentage of the fee charged. There is usually a monthly fee to the employer for access to the PPO network if it is purchased as an adjunct to the health plan. You may wish to contract for access to a PPO to reduce the cost of medical services, if the network lists physicians and facilities used by your employees. The fee for PPO access may easily be offset by the discount for services.

In some cases, the PPO is made available for certain facilities or providers only with traditional coverage for all other services to plan members. For example, there are hospital PPOs that can limit the expense of inpatient hospital stays but have no impact on drug or major medical coverage.

HMOs or health maintenance organizations are of two types, by federal legislation: group or staff models and individual practice associations. HMOs developed more fully with Kaiser Health Plans in California in the 1940s to provide health care to Kaiser employees on the job and then expanded to offer health care services to others. The concepts of preventive care, well care, and comprehensive health services coordinated by a primary care physician stem from these efforts.

An HMO is an insurer, too. These organizations are licensed by the federal and state governments and are given the opportunity to provide services on a county-by-county basis. They are primarily regional as a result of this regulatory approval process, although several are now consolidating and offer services that cover several states. They are paid a monthly premium for providing comprehensive health care services.

HMOs feature networks of physicians and facilities contracted to them at rates that are often deeply discounted. Their payment to primary care physicians and facilities can be a blend of **capitation** (a flat fee paid each month for each HMO enrollee who selects the physician as his or her primary-care physician), or on a fee-for-service basis. There may be incentives and disincentives built into the HMO contract, making some provider choices of services more or less profitable. The formulas developed by the HMOs for these payments are complex and do not usually affect a particular group of employees.

The **provider service organization** (PSO) is a newer development. It is generally composed of hospitals in a given region that create a network of physicians, facilities, and ancillary care services. The PSO is then marketed to large employers in the area as a quality discounted network and sometimes provides coverage on an insured basis. Utilization and costs for covered health care services are projected and budgeted, with premiums developed for each group.

This development of a premium rate involves the process of underwriting, the Law of Large Numbers, the acceptance of risk by the PSO, and the employer's trust in this one group for plan member health care. The PSO is able to contract with other facilities and networks to offer care outside its region. Since PSOs are in the early stages of development, they should be considered local or regional.

There are pros and cons to all types of plans. Any health plan is a trade-off among cost, benefits provided, administrative services required, and quality medical services. Employees select health plans primarily on the basis of cost, as suggested by their growing selection of HMOs over the past ten years. HMOs are under fire in the press whenever services are denied or when high profit margins are reported in the financial pages. Annual reports about HMO and insurance carrier complaints are recorded by state insurance departments as shown in Exhibit 2-1. Nonetheless, recent surveys indicate growing consumer

HMO	Complaint Ratio	Upheld Complaints	NY Premium (in millions)
1. Kaiser Foundation Health Plan of NY	0.000	0	$ 39.0
2. Blue Choice	0.004	3	701.3
3. Empirce B.C. & B.S. Healthnet	0.010	3	292.8
4. Rochester Area HMO (Preferred Care)	0.010	2	193.2
5. Health Care Plan, Inc.	0.016	3	184.7
6. MDNY Healthcare, Inc.	0.021	1	46.7
7. Community Health Plan	0.031	8	255.6
8. HMO-CNY, Inc.	0.034	2	58.8
9. Vytra Healthcare Long Island, Inc.	0.034	6	519.4
10. Independent Health Association, Inc.	0.035	18	519.4
11. Health Services Med. Corp. of Cen. NY[a]	0.036	5	140.0
12. Healthsource of New York/New Jersey	0.038	3	79.3
13. Capital District Physicians' Health Plan	0.045	13	289.6
14. United Healthcare of Upstate N. Y, Inc.	0.052	2	38.7
15. MVP Health Plan, Inc.	0.064	25	392.4
16. Community Blue	0.066	19	286.5
17. Aetna Health Plans of NY Inc.	0.079	9	114.0
18. United Healthcare of New York, Inc.	0.080	9	112.6
19. Physicians Health Services of NY, Inc.	0.092	16	173.0
20. HIP Health Maintenance Organization	0.125	129	1,030.5
21. HMO Blue	0.143	8	56.1
22. Prudential Health Care Plan of NY, Inc.	0.149	15	100.6
23. Healthsource HMO of New York, Inc.	0.181	5	27.6
24. U.S. Healthcare, Inc.	0.208	197	946.9
25. NYLCare Health Plans of NY, Inc.	0.254	33	129.7
26. CIGNA Healthcare of New York, Inc.	0.255	19	74.4
27. Oxford Health Plans (NY), Inc.	0.358	742	2,072.0
28. Wellcare of New York, Inc.	1.174	96	81.8
Total	0.162	1,391	$8,611.4

[a] Excludes HMOs with less than $25 million in NYS premium and those first licensed in 1997. Also excludes Medicare and Medicaid business.

EXHIBIT 2-1. A complaint listing is published each year by state insurance departments for HMOs and carriers licensed by the state. (Source: New York State Department of Insurance, 1988.)

acceptance of the restrictions of managed-care plans such as HMOs, PPOs, and PSOs. Increasing consumer satisfaction levels have been documented that show that the HMO is now better accepted than the PPO and is approaching the satisfaction level of fee-for-service plans (see Exhibit 2-2). One factor that affects employees' acceptance of HMOs is whether their doctor is in the network. Oxford Health Plans, a large HMO based in Connecticut, has reported that it has a network of more than 50,000 providers in the northeastern states where it provides services. The primary complaint about HMOs is the essence of their design—that care is not as accessible as members might want.

The hybrid plan is the plan most chosen today. Indemnity plans have added POS and other network variations during the 1990s, and HMOs have added POS and traditional indemnity options, called Open Access, to their list of available products. Insurance carriers and HMOs are merging, and groups of HMOs and PSOs are pooling and consolidating in every part of the United States.

This frantic business activity spawns new configurations of health plans from which you can choose the best option for your organization. It is likely that the health plan of

Market	Number of Plans Profiled by Type			Top Ranked Plan and Type
	HMO	POS	FFS/PPO	
Atlanta	5	3	4	Blue Cross Blue Shield of GA (FFS)
Baltimore–Washington	6	3	5	a
Boston	6	3	0	Harvard Pilgrim (HMO)
Chicago	5	3	4	HMO Illinois (HMO)
Cleveland–Akron	3	2	3	QualChoice (HMO)
Dallas–Fort Worth	6	3	2	United HealthCare (POS)
Dayton–Springfield	3	1	3	Tie—Health Maintenance Plan (HMO) Tie—United HealthCare (HMO)
Grand Rapids–Muskegon	5	1	2	Priority Health (HMO)
Hartford	3	2	1	ConnectiCare (HMO)
Houston–Galveston	4	4	1	United HealthCare (HMO)
Indianapolis	3	1	4	Premium Preferred Network (PPO)
Kansas City	7	1	1	CIGNA HealthCare (FFS)
Lansing	3	0	2	Physicians Health Plan (HMO)
Memphis	2	1	2	Baptist & Physicians (FPO)
New York City Area	5	3	2	Oxford Health Plans (HMO)
Northern New Jersey	5	2	4	Blue Cross Blue Shield of NJ (FFS)
Philadelphia	1	2	2	a
Phoenix	3	2	1	CIGNA HealthCare (PPO)
San Francisco Bay Area	5	3	1	a
Southeast Michigan	6	5	6	Care Choices (HMO)

aNo single plan scored significantly above other plans in this market, or, the major plan(s) in the market are not adequately represented.

EXHIBIT 2-2. Satisfaction levels by plan type by region. (Source: The MEDSTAT Group *Quality Catalyst* Program, 1998 enrollee study; copyright © 1998 the MEDSTAT Group, Ann Arbor, MI.)

your choice will be a hybrid plan with some of the best features of each type now available and that each year, with open enrollment and renewal, you will gradually see a transition to the hybrid plan through selections you and your employees make.

■ LEGISLATIVE OVERVIEW

Since the 1930s there has been a slow revolution in health benefits in the United States, with occasional flareups in recent years. It began with the Social Security Act, passed in 1938, which provided the first government-sponsored benefit program. By World War II, labor leaders were lobbying the federal government to expand the Social Security program and to do something to offset wage freezes by allowing benefits to be determined by collective bargaining. In 1947 the National Labor Relations Board declared health benefits to be bargainable, and the Taft-Hartley Act established union welfare funds to provide benefits.

At the same time, there was a widespread development of Blue Cross-Blue Shield plans, using a nonprofit association plan, which were the first provider networks and hospital discount programs. Health care and medical services stabilized, and there was little legislative action in the 1950s and 1960s, until in 1965 the Medicare and Medicaid programs were instituted to cover Americans who were disabled, aged, or poor.

In 1974 Congress passed the Employee Retirement and Income Security Act, or ERISA. This legislation followed on the heels of an economic situation in which several large national employers went out of business without the funds to pay for promised health benefits and pensions for their workers. ERISA was landmark legislation that called for all employer-sponsored benefit plans to be funded properly, reported, and disclosed. Accountability and responsibility for the plan sponsors, plan funding, and employee rights were clearly set forth in this legislation.

A series of laws passed in the 1980s and 1990s has expanded and refined the rules and regulations under which health plans must operate. The federal government has passed laws that require employers to provide health insurance to terminated employees, to employees on leave for family matters, to employees who have preexisting conditions, and to employees who continue working after normal retirement age, for example. Other benefits have also been mandated, such as family leave, longer hospital stays for maternity care, end-stage renal disease services, payment for immunizations, and, in some states, coverage for mammography, well-child care, prenatal care, and prescription drugs. A detailed listing of such legislation is given in Chapter 10.

The role of government on all levels in the provision of health benefits is increasing. Broad federal legislation is now pending on patient rights, physician gag clauses, privacy of medical records, and access to specialists.

Fundamentally, insurance is regulated by the states, with the federal government setting broad guidelines and sometimes enacting provisions to be implemented nationally. In recent years, there has been greater involvement on the part of regulators at the federal, state, and local levels.

The federal government establishes, with the help of Blue Cross-Blue Shield, which services are to be covered by the Medicare and Medicaid programs. They determine which services are considered experimental, among other things. One effect of such decisions is to set a standard for other plans nationwide on what treatments and services should be covered. If Medicare adopts a policy of funding preventive services such as colorectal exams, mammography, or well-care visits, it puts pressure on the insurance industry to follow suit. This is especially true since Medicare and Medicaid services can now be provided by HMOs and other health plans, which must include the mandated care and which compete directly for enrollees with Medicare under the newer MediChoice for Medicare Part C coverage.

State government enacts legislation to implement federal law locally. They also regulate the insurance industry and health care services through their departments of health and insurance, which have enforcement powers. Most mandated benefits are legislated at the state level, as are requirements for licensing, funding, and rate increases. Regulations that cover services, credentialing, and fees for hospitals, home health care, and ancillary medical facilities are the province of state government. Funding for charity care and graduate medical education is distributed to hospitals from fees, surcharges, and taxes collected by the states.

Local government can influence health care services and provides public health services and enforcement of state and federal regulations. For example, the county health department inspects hospitals and other health care facilities, testing equipment to ensure it is acceptable. The county departments of social services provide health plan choices to the poor, disabled, and aged and often provide mental health and substance abuse services. County health departments provide public clinics, education and counseling, and intervention programs for disease. Public health nurses may provide home health care, and the county health department may enforce regulations for home health agencies. Decisions to expand hospital facilities, or to certify new facilities, are made with the review and recommendation of local and state health officials.

■ BASIC EMPLOYER CHOICES

Full Insured Plans

Assumption of risk is a variable that will affect your choice of a health plan. If you opt for an insured plan, one where you pay a set premium and there are no other fees or charges, you will assume little or no risk. Nothing is foolproof, however. If your employees are older, or if several of them have chronic or catastrophic illness, you have some risk even with insurance coverage. You can assume that your premiums will be affected by the health costs of your employees, no matter how big or small your organization is. The old saying that "there is no free lunch" is true in health insurance. Your health care costs will catch up with you, sooner or later.

Association Plans and Pools

If you are a small or mid-sized employer and have access to an association plan or other pool for insurance, you may be able to reduce your cost and transfer some or most of your risk for health coverage. Such plans have rules about risk and underwriting. Your membership may be contingent on a review, based on the demographics and claims history of your employees. If your risk level is high, you may be asked to pay an excess fee to join the pool, or you may be rejected. If your risk is low, you may be eligible for an advance or periodic discount when you join the association pool. There are usually periodic reviews of your claims cost that affect your future premiums and may result in a year-end fee assessment.

The concept of the pool is to share resources to cover the risk of many, similar organizations. Pools and association plans are usually available on an industry basis so that they are less likely to experience adverse selection because some variables such as employment status and socioeconomic demographics are more predictable and common. Typically, if you opt for such a plan and it is not contributory, you will be expected to have all of your eligible employees enroll in it. This helps prevent adverse selection because younger, healthier employees do not have the choice of enrolling in another employer-sponsored plan, and your sicker, older employees are not the only ones drawn to the pooled plan. These plans often have outstanding member services, good communications, and professional plan management.

Ineligible Employees

Underinsured and uninsured employees present a special challenge. Your health plan eligibility rules may limit enrollment to those who are full time, perhaps after a waiting period. You may find, therefore, that, because of plan eligibility requirements, or your part-time work force, you have a sizable population of employees who are uninsured or underinsured. You will then want to review plan design issues. You may offer short-term or long-term disability and workers' compensation to such workers to meet their health care needs outside of your health plan.

Government Programs for Eligible Employees

One way you can transfer risk is to review available government programs. There are subsidy programs available in many states that will defray some of the cost of employer-sponsored benefits for eligible employees, and the Medicare and Medicaid programs may be suitable for some who are disabled or who earn low wages. New child health insurance programs may cover dependent children for some employees at lower income levels. You will want your personnel and benefits staff to be up-to-date on these provisions and on how to counsel disabled employees regarding Medicare and Medicaid options for chronic disability.

Other Plans and Self-Payment

Another source of coverage can be spousal or dependent coverage that is available from another plan. Your office might provide counseling and reminders to encourage your employee's use of other plans. You might also consider plan provisions that allow employees who are ineligible for company-paid insurance to purchase limited or full coverage on their own. You should review your policies from time to time to be sure that your eligibility requirements are still appropriate for your needs.

Self-Funding

Self-insurance or self-funding offers a range of choice to you. If you are a small or mid-sized employer who offers hospitalization, major medical, and drug coverage, you might explore the concept of self-funding some of these benefits, or all of them. Additional benefits such as vision and dental might also be self-funded. Self-funding calls for the establishment of a fund from which health care claims are paid. Most often, claims are paid by an outside administrator who may also offer discount network services.

Careful attention to the demographics of your workforce, your claims history, and any changes you can anticipate are essential to the decision of whether to self-fund. The stability of your workforce, available financial and staff resources to make such a commitment, and ready access to needed administrative and plan management services are other considerations. Your motivation to self-fund your health plan or some part of it might stem from your need to control rising costs, to take advantage of cash-flow savings, to better manage plan activities and administration, to offer unique benefits or services, or to be more aware of the cost and use of your benefits.

■ HELPFUL RESOURCES

There are lots of places you can go to find more information about the concepts and topics covered in this chapter. First of all, you can review the table of contents to see which chapters focus in depth on each of these areas. You can rely upon your insurance professionals, on your personnel or benefits staff, and on outside consultants. Your broker, agent, consultant, or service vendor can provide valuable guidance, support, and expertise.

Lawyers, accountants, and actuaries might provide specialty assistance to you for specific questions on health insurance, health benefits, employee communications, legal issues, and financial implications.

Your trade or industry associations may offer insurance seminars, conferences, or assistance. Many associations offer 800-numbers to answer your business questions, and some have specific programs for helping with health plan questions and choices.

Publications and the Internet are good sources for impartial information that you can access conveniently. Publications are available from your local library, by subscription, or as handouts at meetings and conferences. You will find a listing of my favorite trade publications for general insurance information and specific health plan news and useful websites in the Appendix.

■ SUMMARY

My goal in this chapter is to see that you are prepared to follow the logic and suggestions contained in the rest of this book, as well as to manage your health plan every day at work. Knowing the basic principles of insurance and understanding the thinking upon which those principles are founded are important to give you depth of knowledge. From this point on, you will have a healthy awareness of the reasoning behind developments in the health care business and how different aspects are connected. Your ability to make wise choices and to forecast the outcome of some of your own choices should be improved.

CHAPTER 3

Health Plan Review

■ REVIEW OPTIONS

There are several reasons to review your health plan on an annual, biannual, or occasional basis. These include:

- To perform a standard review
- To explore new services
- To revise your plan after instituting organizational changes

Regardless of the reason, your decision will affect every employee and the organization as a whole. The guidelines provided in this chapter can help you avoid some of the problems that can occur from the review process.

You may choose simply to compare the costs of similar plans and leave it at that. Or, you may need to conduct a more thorough review of health plan options and services appropriate for your organization. Even a simple review of your plan can cause ripples among employees, not to mention the concern it might raise with the broker, agent, consultant, and insurance carrier who currently serve your organization.

As a matter of course, you should review your health plan at least every three years. If you routinely do so already, you should compare your usual procedures with those outlined here.

A Guideline for Health Plan Review

1. *Alert top management, appropriate supervisors, your staff, and employee representatives that you are beginning the review process.* Early notice can be formal or informal, depending on the size of your organization and your management style, and can help you avoid common complaints such as "You're trying to take something away," "We can't afford to make any changes now," and "Why make waves?" These negative responses might result if you proceed but keep everyone in the dark.

2. *Assemble and review the documents relevant to the health plans you now provide.* Include the latest copies of benefit booklets, notices, and descriptions of material modifications; currently effective employee contracts; copies of contracts with your health insurer or administrator and those with other service providers; and information about the demographics of your employee group. A form for recording typical demographic data is illustrated in Exhibit 3-1.

(text continues on page 37)

Socioeconomic

Dept/Location	Age Cohorts <21	22–40	41–65	>65	Gender M	F	Insurance Ind	Fam	Employee Status Act	Ret	P/T	F/T	Income <20M	21–35M	36–55M	>55M	Education <HS	HS	Col	Adv	Ethnicity White	Afr/Am	His	Asian	Other	Bargaining Unit
Elementary #1																										
Elementary #2																										
Elementary #3																										
Elementary #4																										
Elementary #5																										
Elementary #6																										
Jr Hi School																										
Sr Hi #1																										
Sr Hi #2																										
Retirees																										

Column one can be used to separate data by department, location, bargaining unit.

Age cohorts can be broad or narrow, with most organizations interested in <21 yrs., >65 yrs., and two or three groups in between.

Gender can affect health plan use, benefits needed, and wellness program planning.

Insurance status (individual, family, or no coverage) is important as it affects total lives covered by the plan, and cost issues.

Active or retired data are important to maintain, with retirees data either kept separately or by location.

Part-time and full-time workers will affect plan enrollment and may be important for plan review.

Type of work can be relevant to richness of benefit design, as can socioeconomic information. It can also help identify problem areas of coverage.

Ethnicity can point up early detection needs for specific illnesses, help project higher or lower than average incidence of certain illnesses, and in some cases help with planning for communication on health plans to a diverse work force.

Some Examples on How to Use These Data:

Example 1. A typical workforce will have a proportion of Individual to Family coverage of 35:65. Once the proportion varies from average, for instance, if the proportion becomes closer to 50:50 and the over-65-yrs age cohort increases, your plan costs and utilization will be expected to rise. It is logical to conclude that retirees and/or older workers have opted for individual coverage to replace or supplement Medicare. The high cost of such a plan member is disproportionate to the individual premium charged, and so overall costs will exceed premium by an amount related to the number of older workers enrolled for individual coverage.

Example 2. If the individual enrollments are higher than average, but the age cohort increase is in 21–40 yrs., combined with an increase in the socioeconomic factors of less education and lower income level, you might assume that younger, unmarried employees who are just starting out have enrolled, and normally will have lower health care needs and therefore costs. This influx of healthy, younger employees will help reduce the cost to your plan.

Example 3. If your retiree population exceeds 20% of your covered members, your costs will be higher than projected for an average demographic of employees. You might note if the retirees are over 65 yrs. or under as an indicator of whether Medicare might pick up the bulk of their health care costs, leaving your plan supplemental. If they are under 65 yrs. and not covered elsewhere, you will experience high utilization and costs until they are at an age where Medicare will cover them.

EXHIBIT 3-1. Demographic data illustration by location. (Source: Halo Associates.)

The following list of survey topics is a guide that can be personalized to help you get feedback from employees about the health plan(s) you offer. For best results, it should be used for one type of plan (HMOs, indemnity, PPOs, POS, or other MCOs) and for each geographic location.

You should consider how you intend to use the results before you finalize a survey.

General topic areas are overall satisfaction, physician quality, access to care, preventive services, convenience, and complaint handling.

Survey Topics

General experience with plan

- Overall satisfaction with plan
- Overall satisfaction with quality of medical care
- Perceived effect on well-being
- Re-enrollment intentions
- Likelihood to recommend plan

Satisfaction with Financial Responsibilities

- Overall satisfaction with member share of costs
- Contribution to premium
- Copayments or coinsurance
- Out-of-network expense

Reported Use of Services

- Primary-care physician
- Specialists
- Out-of-network services
- Hospital
- Preventive care

Reason for Selecting Plan

- Affordability
- Choice of doctors
- Coverage
- Convenience

Satisfaction with Plan Specifics:

- Primary-care physicians
  Variety and number of locations
  Accessibility and office hours
  Quality of doctors and staff
  Communication (telephone, in person)
- Specialists
  Same as above
- Administration and customer service
  Overall satisfaction with services
  Out-of-network experience
  Hospitals
  Pharmacy benefits
  Preventive medical services

Demographics of respondent, including age, income, health status, number of dependents

Uses for the survey results include the following:

1. Help improve the quality of care and service to members
2. Reduce costs
3. Strengthen employee relations

In preparing an employee satisfaction survey, be sure to maintain objectivity and comparability. That means you should keep surveys separate for each type of plan offered and not mix surveys for members of HMOs and employees covered by indemnity or other types of plans. The satisfaction levels by type of plan will vary tremendously; if you mix them you won't have an accurate measurement to help you evaluate satisfaction. You should also keep geographic locations separate. What may be a problem in one location may not be in another. Last, you should ask questions so that the responses might result in action.

Your reasons for doing the survey can include gaining information to help you change health plan options by eliminating those plans where satisfaction level is low or adding lower-cost plans of the type that has the highest satisfaction level. Or you might aim to improve service by sharing the results with your health plan administrator so that it can address areas of weakness. You also might wish to demonstrate your concern about employees and improve their awareness of the value of their health plan.

EXHIBIT 3-2. Employee satisfaction survey topics. (Source: Halo Associates.)

3. *Seek input from managers, personnel and benefits staff, employee representatives, and the current health insurance professionals who service your account. Typical questions cover:*

- Member satisfaction with administrative and claims services
- Cooperation and support services provided to your organization and staff
- Any perceived changes in access to care or coverage
- Additional services or coverage of interest
- Planned changes within your organization
- Anticipated changes with the insurance company or plan now in use
- Other competitive plans and services

One comprehensive way to get good feedback on your health plan is through a satisfaction survey of your workforce, including managers. Typical survey topics are listed in Exhibit 3-2. You will want to keep questions straightforward and specific, yet allow adequate space for other comments and feedback. You don't want to imply or convey that major benefit improvements or changes are planned, unless that is the case. A sample satisfaction survey appears as Exhibit 3-3.

The sample survey should be used as a guide and should be personalized or fine-tuned to meet your organization's needs. Remember, it will most likely be your staff who will have to tally and evaluate survey responses, so their input in its preparation is important. Benefit staff may also be aware of specific issues that concern employees. Survey responses can guide your health plan review decisions and also be of interest to top management when change is recommended.

4. *Evaluate the three-year premium cost and claims cost history of the health insurance you provide to employees.* Request your claims history or experience from your health insurance professionals. This information will allow you to measure the bang for the buck, or how much of your premium dollar is spent on your employees and their families. Remember to request that administrative and other fees, which are often lumped together with claims costs, be provided separately.

Your review of these costs and your claims history ought to be done well in advance of the plan review. Allow at least two months to receive it and another month to review it. You should request these reports a minimum of six months in advance of the plan termination date. This will enable you to digest the information, implement a review, and complete a specification and bid process. You will not lose the opportunity to act if you allow two to three months to decide on making a change. Many carriers require a minimum of thirty to sixty days to implement a health plan for a new group, depending on its size. Often your current plan will require the same amount of time for cancellation.

5. *Prepare specifications that meet your needs.* If you require a simple comparison, the major categories are covered in the following section on conducting a standard review. If your needs are more complex, please refer to Chapter 4 for specific guidelines.

Consider your organization's requirements, such as:

- Monthly management reports
- Quarterly or rolling lag reports
- Assistance with enrollment of new employees and reenrollments
- Services to help you better meet the requirements of legislation

Consider whether you need additional communications or periodic mailings about health plan services to keep employees and retirees better informed. These items may be

(text continues on page 40)

Please complete the following questions and add any comments you may have. Our goal with this survey is to determine whether or not the benefit plan(s) which we provide to employees and their families is meeting your needs. We are also committed to a high quality of service for plan administration and other services. Your feedback can help us evaluate these services.

You can help us by completing your survey and returning it to: _____
(name, title, address of person or department who will tally the survey results)

Please rate the general area covered for each question by circling a number (5 = highest and 1 = lowest rating)

Add your comments for each section. Use the back of the paper for additional remarks.

I. **Benefits.** Please let us know how well you feel your coverage for health benefits meets your health care needs.

1   2   3   4   5

Comments:
_____
_____
_____
_____

II. **Plan Procedures.** Please indicate how acceptable you feel the plan procedures for filing and following up on claims, obtaining approvals, receiving explanations of benefits, plan booklets, and other documents are.

1   2   3   4   5

Comments:
_____
_____
_____
_____

III. **Administrative Services.** Please rate the services you have received from the plan administrator, including claims payment and notifications, response to claims inquiries or problem claims, accessibility of network and nonnetwork doctors, hospitals, and facilities, and your general satisfaction level with all such services provided by the current administrator.

1   2   3   4   5

Comments:
_____
_____
_____
_____

EXHIBIT 3-3. Health plan satisfaction survey. (Source: Halo Associates.)

IV. Enrollment/Eligibility Services. Please indicate your satisfaction with staff and health plan services provided to you for enrolling or changing enrollment in your health plan and for providing information on your eligibility for coverage.

1   2   3   4   5

_____
_____
_____
_____

V. Dispute Resolution. How well do you think the plan handles disputed claims and coverage issues on your behalf?

1   2   3   4   5

Comments:

_____
_____
_____
_____

VI. Cost. How fair is the out-of-pocket cost to you for health plan services, whether it is a part of the premium, deductible, copayment, coinsurance, or services not covered?

1   2   3   4   5

Comments:

_____
_____
_____
_____

VII. Importance of Health Plan. Indicate by your rating how important health coverage is to you and your family.

1   2   3   4   5

Comments:

_____
_____
_____
_____

(optional section)

Please indicate how much out-of-pocket expense you incurred last year for health care services. $ _____
How much do you think your employer spent for health coverage on your behalf last year? $ _____

Please add any additional comments on any issue related to your employee health plan or benefits here:

_____
_____
_____

Thank you for participating in this survey. We value your response.

needed by your organization, depending on your size and the sophistication of your in-house staff. Many small and mid-sized organizations have internal benefits newsletters and notices and a staff that is accustomed to handling enrollment and eligibility questions and generating plan reports. Your resources can be supplemented by services available to you from your health plan vendor.

The cardinal rule in specifications is to ask . . . you might receive. Remember, during this process all of your bidders are putting their best foot forward. You might stumble on new services for reporting, communication, and plan management, at no added cost. Pleasant surprises are often a perk of this routine activity.

6. *Keep a level playing field.* You should give all vendors a fair chance to be selected. Do not convey or imply that you are inclined to stay where you are and make no changes, yet feel obliged to go through the process. Keep in mind the cost and effort that a submission entails on the part of vendors and the fact that you will need legitimate bids in the future.

Even if you are convinced that your current benefits and administration are fine, remember that lower costs are frequently the result of the bidding process. You may receive a lower quote from your current service vendor—whether an administrative company, broker, agent, consultant, HMO, or insurance plan.

7. *Involve others in your decision.* Your review will be easier and more assured of success if you don't proceed in a vacuum. It is not sufficient to alert management, staff, and employee representatives only at the beginning of the review. There are many ways to get others involved with your review of the health plan and to win support for any decisions that result—whether you ask the boss to take a look at final candidates, invite a friendly employee representative to sit in on presentations, or establish a more structured committee to evaluate the plans you have short listed.

■ STANDARD REVIEW

A standard review is the orderly and scheduled process of evaluating and analyzing your health plan. It can include writing specifications and soliciting bids and should ensure that your health benefits and plan services are appropriate to meet the needs of your organization and that they are competitively priced, within your ability to pay. It does not imply any urgency. However, if you have not gone to bid on your health plan for three years or longer, now is the time.

There are four basic areas included in a standard review of health plans: experience, service capabilities, coverage, and cost. You can refer to the Plan Review Scorecard in Chapter 4 for specifics to consider in each area.

Experience

Your health plan vendor, whether an HMO, carrier, administrator, or other service, should be expected to have at least a minimum number of years of experience, usually five to ten. You should verify credentials and experience and obtain client references. The vendor's range of experience and track record within the health care industry is a benchmark for assessing its ability to serve your organization.

Service Capabilities

Your review will include services provided to employees, retirees, and their families, and support services for your organization and staff. Among the services to review are their capabilities for electronic reporting, on-site and off-site service representatives, staff training and facilities, discount and network services, plan materials for your employees, and their claims review and complaint procedures.

Coverage

Most states have mandates for specific coverage, basic health plan models, and various enriched plans approved for sale. Basic plans generally provide coverage for hospitalization and major medical expenses and usually offer prescription drug coverages. Individual states may have mandates that require medical coverage for mammography, immunizations, well-child care, mental health care, and chiropractic care, for example. Additional benefits are available through the purchase of riders or by the selection of a richer plan that offers extended or enhanced benefits.

An example of coverage that varies from plan to plan is a benefit for birth control pills, which may be excluded from one plan, included but subject to copayment in another, and covered in full by another. Other examples of coverage that often varies are coverage provisions for dental and vision care, alternative therapies, and wellness services. Deductibles or copayments vary, as well.

The main thing is that you compare apples to apples and then consider the bells and whistles of added coverage and riders. It is a good idea to set up a comparative graph, such as shown in Exhibit 3-4, which will help you with the process.

Cost

You may find cost the most important comparison for your organization. If you have completed this review so far, your cost comparison will have validity because you will be aware of differences in experience, services, and coverage that affect cost. You will want to be advised of any startup costs and any variable administrative fees tied to claims cost or plan performance, as well as any communications or materials charges, fees for document preparation, or special fees for reports or optional services.

If you are buying an insurance product from a carrier or HMO, you should request a premium illustration that reports the specific costs included in the total premium quoted. A sample premium illustration is shown in Exhibit 3-5. It can take the mystery out of your premium and provides a breakdown of costs for premium taxes, high-risk pooling charges, any surcharges, and retention, or profits. The premium illustration may vary in content and format from state to state.

■ EXPLORING NEW SERVICES

If you have not shopped the health plan market lately, or if your company is in a period of growth and change, you may want to use the review process to find out about new, available services, especially those that can reduce cost, improve service, or make your job easier. The health care industry has new services resulting from technological improvements, industry trends, and the need to be competitive that can make a periodic review useful.

For instance, during the past ten years, there has been a major development in disease management services that are available to your employees who are chronically ill. Typically, there may be a toll-free number for employees to call, special literature or printed materials that can be sent to them, and a case management nurse who can counsel and

Type of Coverage/Issue	Plan A	Plan B	Plan C	Plan D
Hospitalization				
# inpatient days				
Hospital network				
Urgent care				
Pre-admit approval				
Discharge planning				
Specialty hospitals				
Transplant centers				
Long-term care				
Co-payment				
Maximum				
Restrictions				
Major Medical				
Maximum, yr.				
Coinsurance				
Copayments				
Preapprovals				
Limitations				
Network				
Nonnetwork				
Specialty				
Alternative				
At-home care				
Diagnostic tests				
Radiology				
Laboratory				
Prescription Drugs				
Maximums				
Copayments				
Coinsurance				
Reimbursement				
Brand				
Generic				
Managed pharmacy				
Mail-order service				
Chronic medications				
Pharmacy network				
Geographic area				
Additional Benefits				
Nonprescription Drugs				
Dental				
Vision				
Alternative Therapies				
Special Services				
Wellness/Preventive				
Disease Management				
Case Management				
800# Call Center				

EXHIBIT 3-4. Coverage comparison. (Source: Halo Associates.)

ABC Employer
Renewal for: 1/1/99

Group # 123456789

Base Experience Period*
10/1/97–9/30/98

A. Paid claims	1,099,868
B. Less: Large-claim subsidy	0
C. Plus: Pooling charges	26,763
D. Plus: Adjustment for claims on an incurred basis	15,235
E. Base Period Incurreds (A+B+C+D)	$1,141,866

Estimated Current Period**
1/1/98–12/31/98

F. Adjustment for changes in cost and utilization of benefits (lag—3 months)	60,519
G. Current Period Incurred Claims (E+F)	$1,202,385

Projected Renewal Period
1/1/99–12/31/99

H. Adjustment for changes in cost and utilization of benefits (12 months)	240,440
I. Expenses	191,178
J. Projected required premium (G+H+I)	$1,634,003
K. Current Premium at Base Enrollment	1,671,005
L. Rate adjustment factor	0.978***

Notes: *The carrier wants to include the most recent, full twelve months ending with the third quarter to the current year as part of the projection of costs on which a premium is calculated.

**To that, the carrier adds an anticipated three months of claims that will be incurred in the current year but paid in the coming year. This is known as the lag.

***The end result of this example is that there is an anticipated cost that is less than the current premium by .978%.

EXHIBIT 3-5. Premium illustration. (Source: Halo Associates.)

advise them. These valuable services are usually included in the cost of your health insurance. They are well received and provide support to your employees, and they can help reduce claims cost.

Another example is the electronic inquiry for claims information, dispute resolution, or claims filing. In some cases these services are provided to your benefits staff, and in others they are available for your employees at work-site stations established by your health plan vendor. In either case, they can measurably reduce the time it takes to get claim information or to have claims paid. These services can improve employee satisfaction with the health plan, reduce the paperwork required to submit and pursue payment on claims, and reduce the claims assistance workload of your staff.

Technology is moving rapidly toward providing better health care services to those in rural or hard-to-reach locations. This can be very meaningful to employers who have employees in isolated settings. If your organization needs to address this issue, you might ask your health plan vendor about on-line and telephonic medical conferencing and mobile medical services.

To take full advantage of new services, it is important to know which are available to you and at what cost. Then you can identify your needs so that you can select services that will meet them. You have an ideal opportunity, when you review your health plan, to learn about new services that may be available.

■ RESPONDING TO ORGANIZATIONAL CHANGE

Either an immediate need or a longer-term change can be the impetus for you to examine your health plan. Short-term and long-term issues that prompt organizational change fall into two categories—internal and external forces.

Internal Forces

Regardless of company size, management in all organizations is concerned with short-term and long-term internal pressure. Some examples include:

- Increase or loss of business, resulting in growth or reduction of size
- Relocation or expansion
- Investments in capital improvements
- Need for new technology and/or highly trained employees
- Changes in management or organizational structure
- Mergers, acquisitions, or changes in management philosophy

Each of these changes can be short term or long term, and each will affect your selection of health plan services. For instance, if your organization is growing or declining, relocating or expanding its facilities, your goal may be to have the health plan set a tone of stability and reassurance. On the other hand, the health plan may be less important at a time of change, with financial and staff resources allocated elsewhere. If there are reductions in the workforce or a need for capital for investment, you may need to make cost-effectiveness a priority or to maintain the status quo for a period of time. Your health plan review is directly affected by such internal pressures when you go to bid. Remember, if you plan to cut back and reduce the number of employees covered by your health plan, you need to report the expected enrollment to your insurance professionals, carriers, and HMOs so that they can project accurate premiums. Conversely, if you anticipate adding employees or having to attract and retain highly skilled employees, you should prioritize your health plan.

Growth is hard on your staff, too, and you should evaluate whether your organization is properly staffed to help you conduct a plan review and incorporate any changes at a time of organizational upheaval. During times of change, sometimes the best thing to do is to do nothing. Once the dust settles, you will have ample time to review alternatives and select new health coverage to meet the needs of your workforce. It is quite possible that, during times of restructuring or organizational upheaval, employees will see changes to their health plan as a threat.

If, during a time of change, you are charged with the goal of assessing health insurance alternatives and finding a less costly way to provide health benefits, you might conduct a search-and-information project to determine the basic issues and potential benefits. A valid report on such activities might include a suggested timetable for future implementation. This approach can be productive, yet avoid an immediate change that may be disruptive to other organizational activity. Comparative choices can be described and background information gathered for future review and decision.

Employee Agreements

Your organization may be required to go to bid periodically, purchase a specific plan or type of coverage, or expand coverage under certain conditions to comply with the provisions of a new or amended employee or collective bargaining agreement. There are countless possibilities in such a situation.

Part of your job, when a health plan must conform to an employee agreement, is to comply with its requirements when you prepare bids and specifications to provide coverage and services. An interpretation of benefit provisions and clarification of coverage requirements must be given to you in writing. Labor relations experts, legal consultants, and employee representatives are some of those upon whom you will rely for information and approvals. Your organization has no doubt established protocols to follow to ensure that no grievances will result from the way plan changes are made. If you don't know what these are, be sure to ask.

Communicating with employees about the plan review and any resulting benefit changes is your responsibility as the plan sponsor. You are accountable for distribution of notices and announcements about health plan coverage, any planned modifications to it, and other communications about the plan. A full description of requirements for plan reporting and disclosure is contained in Chapter 7.

When an employee agreement governs benefits and health plan changes, and if your review results in changes or amendments to the plan, you may be asked to prepare and distribute information for employees, subject to the written approval of an employee representative. Once the plan and any changes are approved, a positive working relationship with employee representatives is important to both employees and management. Good communication regarding the plan, following procedures that were established in advance, helps maintain that relationship

External Forces

Whether your organization has always been located in several states or is planning to relocate or expand to several states, the influence of geography and location is important to consider. Where you are located can make a difference, and multiple locations may require you to familiarize yourself with the plans available in more than one geographic area, making your job more difficult.

If one of your sites is in a rural location, your choices may be limited, and health services may be scarce. In urban settings, health plan costs may be higher for a given level or even a lower level of benefits than they are in rural areas. Transfer of employees to new locations may mean a major cost increase because of higher health plan costs or increased worker turnover resulting from dissatisfaction with the health plan available at the location.

Local and state regulations can affect your selection of a health insurance plan. As noted previously, it is state law that regulates health insurance carriers and HMOs. Fees and charges may be added by state and local government that cause the cost of a plan to vary from one area to another. Consumer protection laws for health plans also vary widely by state. A plan that enjoys a good reputation and track record in one state may not have a good record in another. Many states have grievance and appeal procedures that are provided by, or overseen by, the state.

When your organization does business in several states, you should track anticipated legislation in each state in which your employees receive health plan coverage and maintain an up-to-date file as part of your background information when considering any change. This information is available from public sources, such as industry periodicals and daily newspapers, and from benefit consultants or other insurance professionals.

Other forces outside your organization can affect your health plan review. Industry growth or decline, the removal of your competitors, the announcement of new advances or business developments, stock market fluctuations, imports or pricing changes for raw goods or other resources—all of these are part of the daily information about your business that may influence health plan decisions.

Unanticipated hikes in health insurance costs arising from economic conditions or outside influences can make you scurry around to find a better buy in health care. This may result in increased costs for health care that are disproportionate to the plan's importance to your organization. An unexpected premium increase can occur midyear for some plans or on your plan's renewal date. You should ask your benefit consultant, agent, broker, or plan service representative to keep you informed throughout the year of legislation, economic pressures, and market conditions that might mean an unexpected increase. But what if no one tells you? What do you do, with a tentative amount already budgeted, when you find that your health plan will cost 10 to 20 percent more than planned?

Several options are available to you, and they all require planning, so you are forearmed. You should be prepared with cards, individual files, and e-mail addresses of the insurance carriers, HMOs, agents, brokers, and consultants who have contacted you over the years. If you regularly update these resource listings, it will be much easier to get prompt assistance from qualified professionals when you need it.

As a parallel activity, you might learn from trade publications how the insurance market, various carriers and HMOs, and the economy are doing. Getting health benefit scuttlebutt at conferences is another good way to stay ahead of the curve, as is keeping in touch with colleagues at other organizations who are responsible for health plans.

Your public relations image within the local community is an important factor when you undertake a health plan review. If your organization has a reputation for fairness, generosity, and humanity, it is important to recognize the expectation of the surrounding community and of your employees who are members of the local community. You will be restricted in your plan choices by those expectations.

It was suggested earlier that you keep management in the loop when you consider a health plan review or change. These external influences, which are probably handled by other departments or managers, are another reason for you to involve your management and supervisory staff. You should ask appropriate managers to review your organization's short-term goals for the coming two to five years before initiating your health plan review.

■ ORGANIZATIONAL GOALS

Why does your organization provide health benefits to employees? This question is central to your health plan decisions. The following possibilities can provide an answer for your organization. How well you understand these goals can help to refine your thinking about a health plan that will work best for your organization.

Corporate Philosophy

In your organization, is there a commitment from top management and those who have ownership in your organization to the health and well-being of employees? Does that commitment include a health plan that meets employees' health care needs? If so, such a commitment might stem from a value system that makes employee welfare a top priority. It might also stem from the organization's need for technical or professional workers. Investment in their recruiting and training is a major expense, making it a priority to keep turnover low by providing a high-quality health plan. It may be that your organization wishes to maintain high morale and productivity from employees who are vital to its success and future growth. If this thumbnail sketch sounds pretty close, then corporate philosophy is probably a prime reason for your organization to provide a health plan.

If your health plan choices are driven by an enlightened corporate philosophy, what conclusions can be drawn about the type of health coverage to meet your needs? It seems logical that you might select a richer plan with little out-of-pocket cost to the employee, a wide range of possible choices of service or plan options, reasonable coinsurance or co-payments, a geographically suited area of service that has no gaps, and strong visibility through regular communication with your employees.

Competition

Keeping up with the Joneses may be your organization's goal when it considers employee health coverage. This is usually the case if you are in an industry with a tight labor market or are in a geographic area with a workforce that can be enticed away by another employer offering a better package of wages and benefits. An organization may want to provide benefits comparable to those offered by a competitor in order to assert leadership or for the corporate equality it implies. This is seen in high-tech industries, and among financial and insurance competitors. It is certain that employees are aware of differences in benefit plans between employers in a geographic area, and very often within their industry.

How is a comparison made between your health plan and the plans of your competitors? They might be compared on any of several levels, including:

- Monthly cost for individual and family coverage
- Retiree benefits
- Out-of-pocket expenses for plan members
- Extent of coverage, including accessibility of providers and services
- Communication and member support services
- Employee satisfaction levels

The primary comparison might be on cost. You should consider cost to your organization and to your employees, based on their cost-sharing through deductibles and co-payments. You can also compare plan coverage and extent of medical services. You might also compare your utilization of benefits to regional norms provided by your health plan vendor. This can reflect the suitability of your plan for your workforce.

Once you have identified where your health plan stands comparatively, you can determine whether to meet or exceed the competition's health coverage. There may be instances where you determine it is okay to fall short of health plans provided by others. In assessing your ability to attract employees, don't forget to take into account some other important factors, such as wages, working conditions, advancement opportunities, and the total package of fringe benefits that you provide to employees.

Financial Security

If your organization is motivated to provide a health plan as a means of providing financial security for employees, it may be a reflection of your workforce. For instance, it may be that your organization has older employees, perhaps key employees, who need a health plan to safeguard them from financial disaster. It may be that your organization employs lower-wage employees who could not afford health care services unless you provide them. It may be that some of your employees have had high health care costs recently and have drawn your attention to the need for comprehensive health coverage. All of these are good examples of factors that might lead you to identify financial security as a reason to provide a health plan.

If this is the case, there are some natural conclusions that can be drawn about your ideal benefit plan. Your plan would provide broad basic benefits for catastrophic illness, some employee coinsurance as services are needed, to offset cost, with a reasonable out-of-pocket maximum for the plan year and a high lifetime maximum benefit.

Depending on your budget and your location, it may be that the straight HMO plan will meet these needs by providing comprehensive catastrophic coverage at lower cost. If sophisticated medical services are available in your area, and you think they might be needed by employees, you might opt for a basic indemnity plan with a point-of-service network of specialists from which to choose. The basic, no-frills traditional plan will provide catastrophic services, while the specialist network will help keep plan costs down.

■ CREATING AN ORGANIZATIONAL PROFILE

Now that you have considered the reasons your organization provides benefits, it's time to move on to the particular characteristics that make your organization unique, with its own particular needs. Your purpose is to select health insurance that will be of the greatest value to your organization and be a good fit, too. The fewer unexplored issues, the more likely your health insurance plan will be well received and smoothly implemented, once it is selected.

Organizational Structure

Every organization can be described by its identifying features, each of which bears discussion. Let's look at your organization's individual structure. Is your organization spread out with a decentralized administration, or more tightly administered from a central office? Do you have many locations, only one, or multiple locations with specific major sites? Consider these issues when you weigh the implementation and communication issues associated with your health plan choices. For example, if you have one central location, the need to coordinate and implement health plan services may be minimal and require little support from your health plan vendor. But, if your organization has multiple locations that operate independently, it may be necessary to seek and obtain cooperation and support at each site for plan implementation, including enrollment and employee communication, which are required by law. You must also be assured that your health plan vendor is capable of providing support at each of your locations and to various staff.

Demographics

Demographics is the term for the statistical profile of a group of people, in this case the people at your company. It refers to the makeup of your workforce on several levels, some of which are relevant to health insurance coverage and costs. Demographic data include gender, age cohorts, types of work, ethnic diversity, income levels, and whether staff is part or full time, professional or blue collar, salaried or commissioned, and active or retired.

Federal regulations prohibit discrimination among employees on the basis of age, gender, ethnic background, religious observance, or lifestyle. If you have questions about how plan changes will affect any protected group of employees, be sure to have your legal adviser or benefits consultant assist you.

Demographic influences on plan design and cost can be illustrated by a few examples. Benefits studies have shown a correlation between education and income and the use of health coverage. Benefits use seems to rise with socioeconomic status. This makes some sense; use of specialized medical services increases among those who are best able to research alternatives. The effect of higher-income professional and technical employees on a health plan is to increase costs and utilization.

Certain health benefits may be inappropriately used in some cases. For example, emergency room services are frequently used by employees who don't have a family physician, usually those employees who are lower-paid and unskilled. Prescription drug costs increase when the health plan covers older employees, particularly retirees who have Medicare, which does not include any drug benefit. The incidence of repeated or frivolous diagnostic testing increases when language and cultural barriers prevent employees from understanding or following physicians' instructions.

Ethnicity may have an impact on costs and utilization, too. Certain chronic and catastrophic illnesses have a higher occurrence within certain ethnic groups. Hypertension, cardiac disease, and prostate cancer are more prevalent among African Americans, while white women have a higher rate of breast cancer, and Hispanics and Asians have higher rates of diabetes.

Age has a direct impact on costs, also. Chronic and catastrophic illness occurs more frequently with age, and the highest-cost age cohort is fifty-five years to sixty-five years, before Medicare provides coverage. A higher-than-average proportion of older workers increases health plan costs in the short term, a fact that should be taken into account when a plan is selected.

You should also consider the impact of demographics on the need for services, likely utilization, and the resulting cost. Given the widespread use of computers, even the small and mid-sized organization can store and maintain detailed demographic files on employees. Your benefit professional or an actuary can assist you with the calculation of demographic influences on cost and utilization. These are issues that directly affect your organization's management of its health plan.

Budgeting

Budget needs are part of your organizational profile and may make a difference in the type of health plan you need. Budgetary factors include how your organization experiences cash flow, business cycles that affect your sales, and the timing of revenues and expenses. Consider whether your organization is a seasonal business or a year-round business; one with definite slow and busy times during the year; one that is dependent on new-customer development or one with an established client base. Is there adequate cash flow to sustain regular, monthly premium payments? Are there other cash needs for goods, staff, facility maintenance, or expansion that might restrict the organization's ability to pay monthly health plan premiums? If so, you will have to select a plan that meets your budgetary needs.

You may select a lower-cost plan to meet budget constraints, or a plan with higher employee cost-sharing. You may select a basic plan with the option to have employees purchase additional coverage. Or, you may opt for a plan with a flexible payment structure to meet your cash flow fluctuations and income projections.

Business Style

Your organization may be aggressive and growing, or established and mature. These are the two extremes of the business spectrum. They describe certain types of businesses or industries, as well as individual organizations. Consider where your organization falls in this spectrum as an important characteristic that might affect your health plan choices.

If your business style is aggressive and growing, you may want your health plan to reflect this. It might be a good idea to provide a wide range of benefit options to give employees choices of higher deductibles with lower premium cost, or to provide increased coverage when employees earn it through seniority. If your business is more mature and established, your health plan is less likely to vary.

It is important to understand your organization's business style so that the health plan you select is in tune with it.

■ SUMMARY

This chapter has focused on how you can make the best choice of health plan and what to consider as you make your decision. You are asked to understand whether your review is based on a standard procedure, a need for new services, or some organizational change you must face, now or in the future. Your goals in providing a health plan and your reasons for plan review are reviewed in the context of your organizational profile, as well as the important environmental and individual factors that guide your selections. As a result of this process, you should be better prepared to implement your review, to explain a decision to make no change, or to introduce change to management and employees.

Health benefits can be bewildering, and there is a great temptation to take the easy way out—to get three bids from a local broker and take the cheapest one, or to review the lists of doctors who participate in several plans and then take the cheapest one with the best doctors, or to browse through the benefit options and pick a plan that seems to offer something new at a competitive price. Sound familiar? That is how many employers make health plan decisions, more or less by the seat of their pants.

Choosing a health insurance plan is more complicated than that, but it is manageable, and well worth your while for you to spend time and energy on careful plan review. You will know that you've done a good job when your health plan effectively serves your organization and its employees.

CHAPTER 4

How to Find and Select Services

What kinds of service can you expect from those who administer and manage health plans? What are the administrative fees and charges for a health plan? How can these costs be examined and reduced? Is there a standard for such costs to which a quote or bid can be compared? How can you identify companies from which to choose, and how can you compare them?

In this chapter, we describe the process of specifications and bids. We provide a sample set of specifications and a worksheet to use when comparing plans as practical guides to help you find and select services.

■ ADMINISTRATORS—A DEFINITION

Who are administrators, anyway? They are organizations that implement and manage health benefit plans. In order to identify an appropriate organization to manage your plan and to provide administrative services, you'll have to know what services to expect. Administrators provide enrollment, record keeping, plan materials, claim processing, dispute resolution, compliance with all regulations, assistance with plan cost projections, and support for plan changes. In brief, they pay claims filed by your employees in accordance with the benefits you have selected and under the terms and conditions you have chosen. They also provide service staff to assist your benefits office and your plan members.

Types of Administrators

Insurance carriers and managed-care organizations (MCOs) provide administrative services to employers who are insured. A managed-care organization may be an HMO or one of the newer breed of hospital- or physician-sponsored groups that accepts the health care risk of your group in exchange for a premium. Alternatively, an insurance carrier may provide administrative services only (ASO plan) for a self-funded health plan or for a health plan pool. You might decide to offer more than one type of plan to your employees. For example, you might offer a self-funded health plan that is traditional fee-for-service, and one or two others that are HMOs, with strict network rules and procedures. In such a situation, you will want your employees to be clear on the differences in service, benefits, and out-of-pocket cost for each option.

Third-party administrators (TPAs) are another type of organization that specializes in the management and administration of self-funded or pooled plans, although many also administer fully insured plans on behalf of insurance carriers and HMOs. These organizations are not insurance companies that underwrite costs, charge premiums, assume a risk for higher-than-anticipated claims, and are required to have massive reserves to pay claims.

Third-party administrators use someone else's money to pay claims. The claims dollars might come from the employer, a union welfare fund, or a carrier or HMO. These companies are generally mid-sized specialty organizations that are well versed in the specific tasks required for claims and plan administration. Although most often local or regional themselves, third-party administrators may pay claims on behalf of national clients.

Some plans are self-administered, meaning that the employer or fund has employees hired and trained to provide administrative services in-house. It is difficult for a small or mid-sized organization to develop or hire enough expertise to comply with changing regulations and the technical requirements of claims adjudication, notification, and dispute resolution. Most large plans that are self-administered are managed by outside consultants and experts, as well as employees.

Electronic reporting and tracking of health plan claims and data require a capital investment in equipment and trained staff that is also prohibitively expensive for a smaller employer. The federal legislation passed in 1974 and known as ERISA requires communication and reporting of health plan information to employees and establishes fiduciary requirements with strict penalties for violators to encourage compliance. This legislation makes it more difficult for an employer to self-administer and puts a burden on those that do. Self-administration, even among larger employers, is uncommon because of the changing and complex nature of health benefits.

The issue of confidentiality is added to the issues of complexity, expertise, and compliance that are part of the health care industry. Confidentiality can be a major issue for plan members and so is an issue for small and mid-sized organizations when self-administration is considered.

Multiple Plans and Administration

Whether you hire a specialist company, a large carrier, or in-house staff to provide administrative services for your health plan, you will find that having multiple plans with different administrators, all of whom vary widely in service levels and staffing, makes your job more difficult.

If it's more work, then why do employers offer multiple plans? More and more small and mid-sized employers offer several plans to employees in response to the general trend of empowering employees and involving them in benefits decisions. It is recognized that one plan may not meet the needs of all employees, given their different family and individual situations. For instance, it may not be cost-effective to provide indemnity coverage that offers wide choices of services and physicians to a younger person who is healthy. Such plans have high deductibles and coinsurance, which might discourage the younger person from seeking care for routine and preventive care. By the time the deductible is met, these services are paid for. Typically, it is routine, lower-cost care that will be most needed when an employee is younger.

By the same token, a closed HMO with limited choices and more stringent management of care and with less out-of-pocket may not be desired by older employees who may need extensive specialty services. When your workforce is mixed, with some younger and some older employees, you may want to offer more than one plan to better meet the needs of all.

What added burdens exist for you when multiple plans are offered to employees? Your usual role as the employer is to select the type of plan(s) you want, to determine eligibility requirements for your employees, to conduct enrollment, to arrange for the funds to pay premiums, to monitor and record these activities, to monitor plan performance, and to communicate with your employees about their health plan(s). Each of these tasks is more complicated when more than one plan is offered.

Your staff will have to explain each option and be sure to provide written descriptions of each available plan, including new information if any changes are made to the plan. Keeping track of who is in what plan, whether or not premiums have been paid, and any employee contributions collected, as well as overseeing employees' selection of options— each of these tasks can be confusing and burdensome to your staff.

There is a growing body of law covering employees who have sued employers to collect payment for medical services that were not covered by the option they selected or after retirement or leaving employment. You don't want your good intentions to backfire. As with most management responsibilities, the more you plan in advance, the less likely you will have problems.

If there are good reasons for you to offer several choices, be aware of the added responsibility and workload. You will want to adequately train your staff and arrange for your broker, consultant, or insurance representative to provide ongoing needed support.

■ THE SELECTION PROCESS

It's important that you know what an administrator is supposed to do for your health plan or what a carrier has to offer so that you can negotiate appropriate services and monitor the plan's performance. A health insurance plan may be the second most costly portion of your overhead, after payroll; therefore, you'll want to select a plan that is cost-effective for your organization. Employee satisfaction with your health plan is another important consideration, as is its ease of administration.

Process to Follow

1. Select whom to invite to bid, and decide how the process is to be managed in your organization.
2. Establish a timetable for each step of the process.
3. Prepare personalized specifications to meet your needs.
4. Complete the specification distribution, receive all bids, and review them.
5. Coordinate the selection process, including contract negotiation.
6. Follow an implementation checklist to get your plan(s) up and running.

Whom to Invite

You will want to invite your current health plan or administrator and to identify other providers who might offer competitive services, pricing, or coverage options. To locate other plans, you can ask your insurance professional—agent, broker, consultant, or carrier representative—for suggestions. You might also review industry listings, such as those found annually in *Business Insurance* (see Appendix). Another source is your state insurance department, which publishes information such as a list of the HMOs, other MCOs, and insurance carriers that are licensed to provide services in your area.

In the everyday routine of your activities, you can prepare for health plan review. For example, during the year you can keep a file of sales materials for other plans that are received in mailings and in person. When you exchange information at local business meetings or in your contact with colleagues in other organizations, you can discuss health plans and learn what seems to be working for others. These recommendations are likely to be objective and may be relevant to your needs.

Once you have potential health plans or providers to invite, you can refine your list to those that seem to offer the most promise. It is likely that not all providers invited to bid will submit, since the bidding process is costly, and many providers bid only on accounts that meet their marketing and sales goals, such as limiting sales to niche markets or industries or focusing on a certain geographic area.

Timetable

You will want to establish a realistic time period to prepare and distribute bids, a deadline for submission, a schedule for reviewing and short-listing those received, dates to interview finalists, and time for your selection staff or committee to meet.

Once a selection is made, your timetable should include a deadline for notifying the organization selected and those that are not selected, and a start-up date. It generally takes a new administrator or carrier sixty days to implement plan services for a new group. A number of implementation activities are described in Exhibit 4-5.

Specifications and Bids

It is up to you to establish a standard for your health plan and for its administrative services. To do so, you start by going to bid with written specifications that outline the coverage and services you will need from your administrator, carrier, or HMO. From the submissions you receive, you will be able to make informed choices about appropriate plans and services. Implementation procedures and plan management services will be included in the specifications and covered during the selection process.

Bid Specifications

Specifications should be sent out with a cover letter that invites a bid and describes the process and your needs briefly. A prospective bidder should be able to determine quickly from your invitation letter whether it is appropriate to prepare and submit a bid. See Exhibit 4-1 for a sample invitation-to-bid letter.

It may make sense for you to tailor the specifications, creating a short list for written submission and using the bulk of the questions in an interview. Much of how you proceed has to do with your style of operation, the time you have to invest in the process, and the size of your organization.

Next, your specifications should have clear instructions to guide the bidder as the submission is prepared and should name a contact person, with telephone and fax numbers and an address, for additional questions. Sample specifications are presented in Exhibit 4-2.

Receipt and Review of Bids

Submissions received in response to the specifications will provide you with detailed, written information about each plan and/or administrator. You may opt to select more than one plan, depending on your size and need.

You may also receive a standard submission that is general in nature and does not cover items and services you have requested. You will have to decide whether to include such a submission when you are ready to compare and review those received.

Keep in mind the complexities of offering more than one health plan to your employees. If more than one choice of health plan is offered, each will cover only a portion of your employees, and the administrative services received by one employee may differ from those received by another, depending on the health plan the employee has chosen. If, for

We are pleased to invite you to submit a proposal for health insurance [*third-party administration if self-funded*] for [name of organization] employees. Our health plan provides hospitalization, major medical, prescription drugs, and dental coverages to [*fill in your number*] employees and their families.

You will find the following reference materials enclosed for your use in preparing a submission in response to this Request for Proposals:

1. A copy of the Summary Plan Description

2. An illustration of premium equivalents for 1997 and 1998 for Family and for Individual coverages, including number of participants and plan experience

Your proposal should cover any startup costs, fees, and charges for services outlined in the enclosed specifications for the period May 1, 1999, through December 31, 1999 and also for January 1, 2000, through December 31, 2000.

Please note that this health plan provides health insurance (self-funded benefits) to approximately 350 active employees and their families and to 125 retirees. Coverage is fully described in the Summary Plan Description herewith enclosed. The plan provides indemnity coverage with a Point-of-Service option. At the present time there is specific Stop-Loss coverage with an attachment point of $80,000, and a bid for both aggregate and specific Stop-Loss coverage is requested. It is not required that you bid on this coverage.

Managed-care services and preadmission certification required by the Plan are also described in the SPD and should be reviewed prior to your submission. A separate managed-care firm may be sought to provide case management and other related services, and close coordination of such services with the administrator is expected.

There may be periodic changes to benefit levels, provider networks, and procedures during the term of an administrative agreement. These will be developed and approved by [*name of organization*], and you will be advised of such activities throughout the process. These may necessitate flexibility and cooperation from the administrator for the Plan.

Your submission must be received no later than March 23, 1999. It must be complete and address each area covered by the specifications. Proposals will be reviewed and a select group of firms will be invited to participate in an interview process within one week of the bid opening on March 24, 1999. You will be notified by March 27, 1999, of any scheduled interview.

We look forward to receiving your submission and ask that you call with any question you may have.

Very truly yours,

EXHIBIT 4-1. Sample bid invitation letter. (Source: Halo Associates.)

example, you offer three health plans, you will have three different sets of administrative and service staff. You will also have to function with three different procedures for enrollment, claims filing, and service approval. Each of these will have to be communicated to your employees.

You may find substantial differences among options. They can vary in the coverage they provide, in the networks of hospitals and doctors that participate in the plan, in their philosophy of service, and in their expertise in reporting, to name a few possible areas. Given the range of possibilities, having too many plan choices can present problems for a small or mid-sized organization. Sometimes more is not better.

This plan review scorecard can help you see the differences in bidders quickly and easily by summarizing their unique characteristics. It is helpful to prepare a grid comparison of bids in this way so that others who are involved in the process can readily grasp the differences among them and assist you with making a choice.

(text continues on page 60)

Please respond to these specifications in writing in accordance with the submission requirements listed below. Each question should be addressed. The submission is to be completed by the organization that will provide the administrative services requested. Answers to the following questions will cover the minimum standards for health plan (or administrative) services for the [*name of your organization*] health benefit program.

Five copies of your submission, including all addenda and/or illustrations, must be received by [*name, title, and address of person receiving bids*] no later than [*time of day and date of deadline*].

SECTION I

[The initial section of your specifications should include questions about the background and track record of the organization that is submitting a bid. There are many who believe that a choice should be based solely on reputation, experience, and track record, on the theory that this information demonstrates that the bidder can do the job and has done it well elsewhere. It is often considered a safe and cautious method of selection.]

Experience

a. How long has your company been in business?
b. Do you have other [*your industry or type*] clients and/or business related to this [*industry or type*]? Please describe.
c. Please discuss your client base, including information such as the range of size, length of relationship, and types of service(s) provided, such as self-funded plans and union welfare plans. Include the industries and geographic areas you serve.
d. Is your company specialized as a health benefits carrier or administration company for health plans, or diversified in additional health-related services and/or in unrelated fields?
e. Please describe the objectives of your organization with regard to diversification in other health-related fields and/or in unrelated fields.
f. What are your organization's standards for adequate, prompt payment and services to clients?
g. Please discuss your relationship with area medical providers, including networks, outpatient facilities, hospitals, etc., in [*your state or region*] and the surrounding area.
h. Please discuss your relationship with out-of-area medical providers, as in question g.
i. Please provide 5 references from the [*identify your area(s) of interest*] medical provider community.
j. Please list those area hospitals in [*area, e.g., Mid-Hudson or greater New York area*] with whom you have an ongoing relationship. Describe any specific problems that may have occurred within the past three years.
k. Please indicate if you have established hospital discounts or developed special arrangements with networks through which you provide hospital discounts.
l. Describe your experience with PPO/POS plans for clients for all types of medical services, including your role in their establishment, expansion, payment schedules, negotiations, and reporting.
p. Please describe how you administer the drug benefit for plans for which you are currently an administrator; identify those drug card and mail-order drug services with whom you have had experience.
q. Do you currently administer plans that provide dental coverage, including a discounted provider network? If so, describe your experience in this regard.
r. In what way do you measure participant/patient satisfaction with your services, and how is this reported to the plan sponsor?

[Whether it is the most important section to you or not, this background information should be reviewed carefully, and you should be sure to check references that are provided. You might assign a selection committee member, if you have established such a group, or a staff member to make calls to doctors, hospitals, and other clients of the bidder to ask for a reference. It is helpful to have two or three persons making reference calls to offset any possible bias for or against a bidder.

Some of the issues you are looking at in Section I are the stature of the bidder within the health plan field, its commitment to its work, its standard of excellence, and the range of experience it has had with services you need. You can eliminate questions that don't apply to your needs, for instance, those on dental or drug benefits.]

SECTION II

[This section is concerned with the physical capability of the bidder to meet your needs. The ratio of standard to special services can indicate the bidder's degree of responsiveness and perhaps the likelihood of flexibility.]

Facilities and Services

a. Please list your office location(s) and indicate the service provided at each location.
b. Detail the geographic region(s) in which you offer service to employees and retirees.

EXHIBIT 4-2. Sample of bid specifications. (Source: Halo Associates.)

c. Explain the methods of automation (reporting/processing ability) you currently have in place. Are any major changes contemplated, and/or have any major changes been made within the past two years? If so, please describe.

d. Do you provide your self-funded plan sponsors with annual 1099 reports and other provider utilization reports? Please describe.

e. Do you provide high-cost claims reports? Please attach copies of same.

f. Do you provide lag reports, and, if so, how often? Are they standard or provided only at the request of the plan sponsor?

g. Please list and attach your standard reports furnished to the plan sponsor.

i. Explain your capabilities to provide special reports.

j. Please describe your recordkeeping and billing procedures.

k. Please describe your claims payment procedures. Enclose a flow chart to identify the staff involved with the processing and adjudication of claims.

l. What are your dispute resolution procedures and methods? What recommendations do you make to your plan sponsors regarding dispute resolution?

m. Please describe your average turn-around time for payment of claims. Note the percentage of claims not included in your average, and explain why they are delayed in payment.

n. Describe your procedure for updating the addition or deletion of providers from your network. From other networks available through your organization?

o. Indicate your routine contact by telephone or other means with plan participants and/or their families related to claims administration. Include your 800-number service, with hours and staffing.

p. What training do you provide to the plan sponsor in connection with your services? Include any written guidelines used.

[This section addresses the nuts-and-bolts issues of how claims are paid and whether or not the bidder operates according to industry standards. Many of the questions are included to gauge the bidder's business practices and customer service philosophy.]

SECTION III

[Section III explores the training, experience, and structure of staff and supervision. It is people, despite computerization, who make the difference in our service industries, including health insurance.]

Staff

Please discuss the following:

a. Your dedicated and trained claims processing staff. Include your standards and requirements for hiring, for initial and ongoing training, and for routine supervision.

b. Your capability and staff available to review and give input for plan documents and written materials.

c. Medical consultants and doctors or specialists whom you employ for peer review. Include your procedures for selection and how you make referrals to them.

d. Your account and/or customer service representative policy and procedures. Include your telephone and/or initial contact staff.

e. Do you assign any additional professional or technical staff to deliver services? Please describe.

SECTION IV

[Section IV addresses the issue of insurance to cover the large, catastrophic losses that sometimes occur within a group. Stop-loss insurance can help insulate a small or mid-sized organization from one or several huge claims that might otherwise affect its annual cost. Other general information is sought, such as the bidder's financial stability and any legal problems that might affect the bidder's ability to provide services under the contract.]

General and Stop-Loss

a. Please provide reference from three current clients.

b. Expand on your flexibility to meet [*your organization's name*] needs.

c. Discuss your typical interaction with plan sponsor staff.

d. Please attach information about your credit rating and/or financial standing.

e. Please list any stop-loss carriers with whom you have an ongoing relationship, and describe your services for interfacing with the stop-loss carrier.

(continues)

SECTION V

[Section V covers a specific and important area of service—managed care, such as case management, utilization review, discharge planning, and patient advocacy. Many carriers, HMOs, and self-funded plans build requirements into the plan that call for this service. For some, it makes logical sense to separate this oversight, monitoring service from the claims administration and the plan management functions. For others, an integrated service that does it all is the best. You can tailor this section to meet your needs.]

Managed-Care Services

a. Discuss any additional managed-care services provided by your organization, and indicate whether your organization wishes to receive specifications to bid on this service, should it be sought separately in a later bid.
b. Describe your capabilities and procedures with regard to hospital billing review or auditing of hospital and provider bills.
c. What services are provided by your organization for preadmission certification? Please describe the staff assigned and their professional qualifications.
d. Discuss your concurrent review services and staffing for those services.
e. Discuss your discharge planning services and staff.
f. Discuss your ongoing case management services, if any. Include a description of your staff, procedures, and facilities for this service.

SECTION VI

[A major purpose of specifications and bidding is to compare costs between those who submit. It is important to make a comparison that is valid by having bidders provide their fees and charges in a uniform way. Variations in bids should be carefully examined.]

Scope of Services and Fees

a. Please describe the basis for your fees and charges for [*e.g., third-party administration services, fully insured health plan, administrative-services-only contract*], including any flat fees, material costs, per capita monthly rates, and any percentage fees charged. These should be clearly indicated.
b. Explain your fees for your managed-care services described herein.
c. Indicate the contract period for your fees, and additional terms available. On what basis are any additional fees or charges assessed, and how are increases determined?
d. Describe any startup fees or costs charged.
e. Discuss any fees or charges that may be applicable for Plan changes made during the contract period.
f. Are there any special fees or additional charges for administrative or procedural changes requested during the contract period?
g. Discuss your involvement and any fees or charges related to the plan ID card and other printed materials required for participant communication.
h. Discuss any fees or costs associated with your arrangements for hospital or provider discounts.
i. Provide your cost for aggregate stop-loss insurance, noting the attached illustration of total plan costs for the past two years, and plan experience; and also provide your cost for specific stop-loss insurance with an attachment point of [*indicate amount*]. Specify for each whether it is a 12/12 or 12/15 type of coverage and whether it is on a claims-made or occurrence basis, and any limitations or exclusions for such coverage.

SUBMISSION REQUIREMENTS AND DEADLINE

Please submit your bid no later than 5:00 p.m. on [*date*] to:
Name and Title
Organization Name
Full Address

One original and five copies of your bid and all supporting documents should be submitted.
If you wish to bid on the stop-loss coverage, please fax a letter of intention to [*name and fax number*] indicating the carriers you wish to be assigned. Markets will be assigned in writing to you as an authorization for bid submission purposes.

EXHIBIT 4-2. Continued

WORKSHEET #1:   Plan Review Scorecard

[You will find it helpful, when looking at submissions from several administrators, carriers or HMOs, to consider a grid approach of comparison. This can be adapted to a comparison of bids received from each of these, based on your specifications.]

Comparison Topics	Plan 1	Plan 2	Plan 3
Years in business			
Turnaround time to pay claims			
Complaint ranking			
Reputation for service			
Doctor referrals			
Hospital referrals			
Insurance adviser input			
Total enrollment			
Local total			
Medicare			
Medicaid			
State(s) of operation			
Hospital network(s)			
Doctor network(s)			
Specialists			
Wellness services			
Free, at work site			
Covered services			
Network			
Preventive services			
5-year average premium			
5-year average increase			
HEIDIS report ranking*			
Reports available			
Group utilization			
Group costs			
Utilization by benefit			
Costs by benefit			
Other			
Financials			
Rating			
Growth or decline			
Problem areas			
Legal background			
Pending cases			
Recent lawsuits			
Cost			
Individual			
Family			
Other**			
Medical cost			

(continues)

Comparison Topics	Plan 1	Plan 2	Plan 3
Plan design	_____	_____	_____
Hospitalization			
Hospital E/R	_____	_____	_____
Inpatient	_____	_____	_____
Diagnostic services	_____	_____	_____
Doctor copay	_____	_____	_____
Major medical	_____	_____	_____
Drug coverage			
Copay (generic/brand)	_____	_____	_____
Maximum	_____	_____	_____
Network	_____	_____	_____
Geographic limits	_____	_____	_____
Physical therapy	_____	_____	_____
Psychiatric outpatient	_____	_____	_____
Alternative	_____	_____	_____

*HMOs only. **Riders to each plan make design slightly different and so cost is not exactly equivalent.

Notes: _____

_____

■ ASPECTS OF ADMINISTRATIVE SERVICES

There are several types of service to consider as you evaluate bids and interview bidders. Some of the major areas are covered here. In addition, you may have specialized needs as an organization and will require the health plan or administrator you select to do more than the normal job. You should put such special requests on the table during the interview process to see whether or not they can be done and at what, if any, additional cost to your organization. (Exhibit 4-3 contains sample questions to use when interviewing the representative of an HMO. These can be adapted for other administrators.)

Plan Documents and Communication

Your administrator will provide you with materials required to operate your plan, such as identification cards, claim forms, a Summary Plan Description or benefit booklet, periodic flyers or notices about coverage changes, and marketing materials for use during enrollment of new employees. If you are fully insured, these materials may be imprinted or slightly personalized for your group, depending on how many employees are covered by the plan. If you are self-funded, your group will automatically be large enough to have personalized materials, and the unique coverage or terms of the plan may necessitate it.

You should not pay extra for any plan documents or communication materials. They are part of the cost of doing business for the administrator and should be included in your requirements when they are hired. You can save money for your organization if periodic notices, newsletters, and mailings can be provided and distributed by your health plan administrator.

HMO: _____ Date: _____

1. How are claims processed and payments made to: _____
   Primary care physicians
   Hospitals
   Specialists
   Labs/other facilities
   Employees
2. What role does managed care play in your claims payment and processing?   _____
   Preadmission certification
   Concurrent review
   Discharge planning
   Retrospective review
   Case management
3. Explain your dispute resolution process and frequency of use: _____
   Participant disputes
   Provider disputes

Reporting

1. What reports are routinely furnished to the employer?   _____
   Monthly, quarterly, annual utilization information
   Cost information, specific to group
   Breakdown of premium costs (claims, administrative)
   Information on provider profiles
   Notification of provider changes (additions/deletions)
2. What are your plans for expanded reporting, if any?   _____

Plan Design   *Rating:*

1. Describe benefits, in addition to required and/or regulated benefits.   _____
2. In what way(s) is your plan design flexible?   _____
3. Why are some hospitals included in your plan, and some not?   _____
4. How do you select, recruit, and maintain your specialty network?   _____
5. How is quality assurance monitored and ensured in your plan?   _____
6. Does your drug coverage offer only one pharmacy, or a limited number of pharmacies? Why?   _____
7. Explain your experience with provider turnover.   _____
8. Describe your credential process for providers.   _____
9. What plans, if any, do you have for changes in design?   _____

Staffing/Facilities   *Rating:*

1. Where are your primary service facilities for the [*your area*]?   _____
2. Describe your staff, their recruitment, and training.   _____
3. How are your marketing materials developed, updated, and provided?   _____
4. Do you have representatives assigned to a specific group for service, troubleshooting, etc? _____
5. What support do you expect from [*your company*]?   _____

Cost Containment and Plan Costs   *Rating:*

1. Describe how your plan contains health care cost.   _____
2. Give an illustration of premium increases in the past five years in our area.   _____
3. What services do you provide for early detection of major illness (worksite or offsite screening)? _____
4. What health promotion programs/services do you provide?   _____

Summary   *Rating:*

Financial stability   _____
Legal environment   _____
Plan design   _____

Interviewer: Please include an overall rating of the HMO. This should take into consideration your general impressions of the HMO's ability to service the plan, its stability and future in the region and the tone of the organization.

General Rating: _____

EXHIBIT 4-3. Sample questionnaire for evaluating HMOs. (Source: Halo Associates.)

Claims Payments and Adjudication

By far the most important job of an administrator is to properly and accurately pay claims on behalf of plan members. It is expected that the administrator's claims staff understands the benefits, coverage levels, terms and conditions of coverage, and standards to adjudicate or appropriately calculate the claims payment. Processing should be done in a timely manner, within ten days to two weeks for claims that are submitted with complete information and that do not require specific review based on the services provided. Training and supervision of claims staff, as well as length of time they have worked for the administrator, are indicators of the quality of work you can expect.

Establish a policy to audit claims payment and a requirement for accuracy, such as a 1 percent or less error rate on processed claims. This accuracy standard is typical in the insurance industry, and a higher error rate is often subject to a penalty fee. This is akin to a performance-based contract with your administrator and will provide an incentive for the accurate payment of claims. A similar contract can be made for prompt payment of claims, that is, within a specified turnaround time that is usual. This can exclude claims subject to medical necessity review and incomplete claims, up to a maximum percentage of total claims submitted. About 20 to 25 percent of claims require longer processing periods.

There are benefit consultants and audit companies that will visit your administrator to determine its compliance and to objectively assess any payments to which you are entitled. These insurance professionals often work on a percentage of savings, or on a per diem basis. They are well worth their cost to the employer or group. You have much to gain by such an audit, which can result in having your claims paid on a more accurate and timely basis.

Service Staff

Dedicated service staff for your organization can be arranged if you have fifty to 5,000 employees. It is preferable to have a specific person or team assigned to your plan. Dedicated staff are trained in the specifics of your plan and the characteristics of your workforce. They can eliminate complaints and the frustration of plan members who call the plan administrator for claims information and guidance (and who might otherwise find it preferable to call your benefit or management office).

You should request dedicated staff and find out about their training and their length of service with the company. If feasible, conduct an on-site visit to check on their working conditions and to see how well they handle the workload they are given. Attention to these details will help you get the best value from the administrator.

In addition to dedicated claims staff, separate customer service staff may be available to your group to provide follow-up on claims, answer questions on coverage, change of status, or eligibility, or to provide referral information to your employees.

Ask for sample surveys on customer satisfaction or the responses from your employees during service calls. An example of a satisfaction survey is presented in Exhibit 4-4. You can also include an evaluation of the administrator's responses as part of your quarterly or annual review of your plan's administrative services. These can be your basis for requesting additional services or a reduction in fees and charges. Such documentation can help you easily to monitor ongoing administrative issues raised by callers and to nip problems in the bud.

Survey—government mail order drug plan. Out of 390 people surveyed, 201 people responded as follows (on a scale of 1–5 [5 being excellent]):

Question #1 Were you served courteously and efficiently?

Grade 1	Grade 2	Grade 3	Grade 4	Grade 5
2	3	5	50	140

Question #2 Did our service meet your expectation?

Grade 1	Grade 2	Grade 3	Grade 4	Grade 5
3	2	10	53	128

Question #3 Time required to receive your medication.

Grade 1	Grade 2	Grade 3	Grade 4	Grade 5
4	5	25	68	95

EXHIBIT 4-4. Survey of government mail order drug plan. (Source: Halo Associates.)

Reports

If you are fully insured by a carrier or MCO, you will receive premium bills, as well as monthly, quarterly, or annual reports of your total claims and administrative costs. Depending on the sophistication of the plan administrator, you may receive utilization reports that identify what services and which providers your plan members use.

As a result of the National Committee on Quality Assurance (NCQA) annual filings called HEIDIS reports, or Health Plan Employer Data and Information Set, more data are now available from HMOs, which are required to file the numbers and percentages of enrollees who receive certain services for sixty performance measures. The report also provides information on member satisfaction. Although underused at the moment, the HEIDIS report is likely to be a valuable source of information for employers who want to refer to an objective overview of the HMO's performance. They are readily available on request from each HMO.

Benefit design and cost justification are two good reasons for the fully insured employer to review health plan reports. When renewal comes along, you will want to know if you have received more or less bang for your buck from the plan you purchased. Your employees may prefer a plan that offers benefits not covered by yours, and if the utilization report suggests some areas of minimal use, you might select a different plan to better meet employee needs.

Self-Insured Companies

For the self-insured, the minimum reports will include claims runs, or the monthly register of checks and/or payments drawn on behalf of claims filed by your plan members. You will also receive summary reports of claims expenses, benefit use, possibly network use, and payments made to providers.

A lag report, or the projected amount of claims left unpaid due to late filing at year end, is important information for a self-insured plan. It spells out your pending liability, which rolls along with the self-funded plan from quarter to quarter. Claims may be incurred but not filed for some time. In a self-funded plan, your total liability is an important factor to track over time so that you can properly identify the cash-flow savings to the plan. Self-funded plans also receive the 5500 reports and 1099 reports prepared by the administrator in accordance with Internal Revenue Service regulations. Samples of these reports are included in Chapter 12 on self-funding.

Whether you are buying coverage from a carrier or MCO or are self-funded, be sure to prepare a complete listing of needed reports. This way, when you are reviewing submissions and making a decision about your health insurance plan, the bidders will be well aware of your expectations. You should receive standard and special-report samples in the bidding proposals. Clarify any added fees or charges for special reports or custom designed reports. Frequently, these can be negotiated as standard during the proposal stage to eliminate additional charges for needed information. For a full description and illustrations of useful reports for monitoring your health plan, refer to Chapter 9.

Internal Support Staff

The quality and availability of staff who will assist your benefit office and management reflects the administrator's commitment to service your plan. Sales staff that shows up at a renewal or enrollment time once a year is of marginal value to your organization. When you have more frequent access, and deliveries of materials or reports, you will have opportunities to learn about new services and products and to resolve problems in a timely manner.

Require that the administrative sales or claims staff be available regularly. Ask them to attend employee meetings and to help explain to employees about a new health plan or changes to the health insurance. They can also supply adequate quantities of written materials when needed.

You can ask for quarterly sales visits, an 800-number by which to reach sales staff, and on-site training of your staff by the administrator when new coverage or enrollment materials are introduced. If enrollment can be electronically entered for ease of processing, you can request that the computer equipment and training in its use be provided by the administrator. It may be cost-effective for both of you to make this arrangement.

Plan Design Changes

Administrators work with many plans. If you are fully insured, the administrator will bring you alternatives during sales calls or at times when you request updated information on available products. Be sure you receive alternatives from several carriers and HMOs, since they differ in the riders and auxiliary coverage they offer, as well as in the networks and providers that are available.

Network and Discount Capabilities

Administrators often have arrangements with various networks that offer discounted services from hospitals, doctors, and other health care providers. Depending on the nature and extent of these discounts, they might offset a higher administrative fee. Some administrators have their own discount contracts for medical services, which ought to be taken into account when their fees and service are reviewed. You may need further discounted fees or network access developed, or you may be located in a rural area where there are few health care providers. If you are, an administrator with an independent discounted network or with a proven ability to create discounted arrangements can be useful in accessing lower-cost needed services.

Ask the administrator to provide specific references from clients and health care providers who can attest to the provider's discount capabilities and its working relationship with hospitals and doctors in the network. A quick check might yield results that will reinforce the administrator's claims of cost savings, including whether such discounts are likely to hold over time or are subject to any expiration date or change that might impact your costs. Know what you are buying, and what you are paying for—in advance.

Integration With Case Management

High-cost claims often benefit from case management. Your administrator may or may not be accustomed to cooperating with and assisting case management professionals. You need to determine the administrator's ability to work closely with an outside company to control the cost of chronic and catastrophic claims. Some administrators offer their own case management and utilization review services to reduce the cost of catastrophic claims. There are mixed viewpoints about the advantages of a one-stop shop, where administrative and case management services are combined in one organization. Some employers choose to avoid having the fox watch the hen house; others find this combination works out well.

The philosophy of the administrator should match yours closely. Your intention can be to provide patient advocacy and guidance to employees, to reduce cost or utilization of services, or to guide utilization to a discounted network. The purpose and goal of case management for your plan should be clearly defined so that you can select an administrator who is on the same wavelength you are.

Negotiate or require that the administrator provide prompt and full communication with the case management or utilization review company at no extra cost. Determine its capacity for fax, electronic, telephonic, courier, mail, delivery service, and personal communications, and determine its willingness to be open about its claims activities and procedures. You shouldn't pay extra for copies of files to be furnished, without which the case management organization cannot do its job. Nor should you allow the administrator to add costs to its fee with small add-ons that can become a nuisance and undermine efficiency or discourage enthusiasm for case management.

■ ADMINISTRATION AND COVERAGE COSTS

Several terms are used to identify charges for administrative services in an insured plan. A premium illustration, required by most state insurance departments, sets forth these fees and charges for the premium quoted to you. These charges include a projected cost of claims, overhead costs, administrative expense, claims processing charges, pooling charges, insurance taxes where applicable, retention, any surcharges assessed by state or local government, and, sometimes, morbidity or stop loss factors. Each of these fees and charges is added to make up the premium you are quoted. A sample premium illustration is presented in Exhibit 3-5.

The carrier or HMO that is providing you with an insurance quote probably had to get approval for any premium increases from the state insurance department. You might benefit by checking, before you accept a quote, to find out what increases have been requested and allowed for the bidder over the past three years or if a large increase is pending. This will give you an indication of the insurer's financial stability; any large increases or decreases are red flags to alert you to potential problems.

Maximum premiums are approved by the state for insurance carriers and HMOs. Depending on the size of your business, you might receive quotes that are substantially below the approved level when your business is up for grabs. Remember that "low-balling" or charging an artificially low premium to get an account may lead to a big increase in the second year of the contract. To offset this possibility, ask for a two- or three-year guaranteed quote. It is best to stay with one plan for three years or longer, anyway, to reduce the cost of making frequent changes and to make you a sought-after client in the marketplace.

Standard Administrative Fees

Administrative fees can vary widely, but, as a rule, your total plan management fees should not exceed 4 to 6 percent of the plan budget. Before bids are reviewed, you can evaluate past submissions and compare them. A check of administrative fees charged to other organizations in your area can be helpful, and you can ask your benefits manager to inquire about the standard administrative fee levels for brokers, agents, or consultants. Web sites and publications also provide information on current costs, and many organizations publish updated data on administrative services. Check the resources given in the Appendix.

■ COORDINATE THE SELECTION PROCESS

Be sure you have a comfort level with the representatives from the administrator who will service your account. It's important to be able to speak openly with them about benefit issues, or the needs of your organization.

Plan to visit the claims processing department of the administrators you are considering. You may find it possible to visit only one or two, but the information you will gather from such on-site meetings will be useful to your understanding of how administrators function.

Check out the financial and legal status and reputation of the administrators you consider. Through web sites and state agencies, you can check out their records of lawsuits and bankruptcies. Rating agencies, such as A. M. Best and Standard & Poor's, and your state insurance department will be able to help you determine the financial rating of an insurance carrier or HMO, as well as its complaint ranking for administrative and procedural issues.

Call references before you make a selection. Ask about former clients who are not given as references, to hear the reasons why their names have been withheld. Speak also to claims processors, customer service staff, and managers at the administrator to determine their attitude, responsiveness, professionalism, and dedication. Inquire about the turnover rate for staff and specialized employees.

■ BROKERS, AGENTS, AND CONSULTANTS

Check with your benefits professional or adviser to learn what they know about the administrators and services you are considering. If you have gotten some assistance in this process from a broker, agent, or consultant, be sure to take into account any relationship your source may have with the submitting organization that might slant or influence the recommendations or feedback that you receive. Usually, insurance professionals will fully disclose any relationship, including fees, that might result from your selection of an administrator that they recommend.

■ CONTRACT ISSUES

The basics about contracts and contract language that is provided in this section does not replace your own careful reading and review of any contract, nor does it replace your consulting with your legal adviser regarding contract language and terms.

Your agreement with the administrator should spell out all services you expect and your performance requirements, including any penalties, and how performance is to be measured. For example, you might require that 75 percent of all claims filed be paid within ten working days. This agreement would exclude the 25 percent of claims that often require resubmission because they were incomplete.

Many organizations have boiler-plate language that is difficult to understand but necessary to include and that often has to do with placing liability or responsibility on the other party. Be sure to have any language questions explained to you in plain language so that you know what you are signing. If the benefits professional or administrator or your own staff can't explain the language, don't sign the contract. In administrative contracts, as with other agreements, it is best to iron out the kinks before you sign so that you don't have to fight about it later.

It is normal to have notarized signatures on such an agreement and for the administrator to sign before you. All parties should receive a fully executed copy of the agreement.

If you are a small organization, the agreement may be a few pages of an insurance contract brought to you by your broker or agent, on which a few typed lines spell out any individual clauses, riders, terms, or conditions. Be sure to understand each of them fully before you sign, and clarify those you don't understand.

The cost of the contract for enrollees should be clearly stated, including per month charges for individual and family coverages and any additional fees or charges. Your choice of health plan administrator, whether carrier, HMO, other MCO, or third-party administrator, will make or break your health plan. Your employees will measure the quality of the plan by the quality of its administration. You will measure plan performance, too, by the reports and plan materials provided by your administrator. The cost of your plan will be directly tied to the efficiency of your plan administrator, and your compliance with legal and regulatory requirements will rely upon the ability of your plan administrator.

■ IMPLEMENTATION CHECKLIST

Implementation of a plan or administrative change can be smoothly accomplished with coordination and planning. You can use Exhibit 4-5, the implementation checklist, to ensure that the process is trouble-free. You can tailor this checklist to meet the needs of your organization; it is meant to be used as a guide to the tasks required when you change health plans or administrators.

The plan administrator is the hub around which the wheel of your benefit plan turns. You will therefore want to make a careful selection, choosing an administrator that can live up to your expectations and meet the needs of your organization and your employees.

A few rules before implementation:

- Leave enough time to do what has to be done.
- Expect problems; they are part of any change.
- Share information with those who are affected.
- Be precise with your plan administrator, carrier, and health plan adviser about what you need and when you need it.

Note the following areas of concern to ensure a smoother implementation:

Contract Arrangements

- Receive, review, and complete your contract with the carrier or plan administrator in a timely fashion. You should receive a contract and begin the process sixty to ninety days in advance of plan start-up, or within two to four weeks of plan selection.
- Ask your attorney, business manager, or health plan adviser to recommend any corrections or changes.
- Obtain approvals required of any employee representatives in advance of signing the contract.
- Check that the initial date and payment arrangements are acceptable.
- If you are required to provide employee enrollments, or a listing of covered employees, with the signed contract, allow time for completion of this information and to verify that it is accurate.
- Prepare copies of any forms needed by the administrator (e.g., state wage reports or waivers).

Approval of Materials

- Approve and receive plan materials for distribution to employees no less than forty-five days before your start-up date, or fifteen days before an open enrollment period. These materials include the Summary Plan Description (benefit booklet) and marketing and enrollment materials that further explain the plan.
- Prepare a summary sheet, or a comparison sheet if you offer multiple plans, that briefly highlights plan benefits and costs.

Staff Training

- Alert your staff and conduct an in-service training, or staff meeting at least forty-five days prior to implementation. Your agenda should focus on the health plan and how any changes will affect employees. Benefit changes, administrative changes, and cost increases or decreases are important.

Employee Notices

- Notify employees at least thirty days in advance of any change. Include a written notice, a description of the plan provided by your carrier or insurance professional, a comparison sheet, enrollment information, guidance on how to select from several options if applicable, and whom to contact with questions about eligibility.
- Carefully describe any changes in benefits, administration, or cost that will affect employees.

Plan Member Information

- Distribute identification cards, network lists, claim forms, and welcome materials (usually provided by the plan administrator or carrier) to all employees who are enrolled in the plan.
- Indicate the work site contact for plan members, and other contacts who are available for questions.
- Have adequate supplies of materials on hand for new employees, those who become eligible, and for those who do not enroll immediately.

Document Plan Activity

- Keep a tally of plan enrollment with monthly additions and deletions to provide to finance so that accurate payment can be made.
- Be aware of requirements for cancellation of coverage, including employee rights and notification procedures, and who is responsible for them.

These areas and their related activities can be more or less complicated, depending on the size of your organization, the choices available to your employees, and whether there is a strong interest in your health plan.

EXHIBIT 4-5. Implementation checklist. (Source: Halo Associates.)

CHAPTER 5

Plan Design and Providers

What is meant by plan design? How can you as a small or mid-sized organization affect the design of your health plan? Which changes will have the most positive impact on your employees? How does plan design affect your costs? How can your plan affect medical providers and the way they serve your employees?

Your health plan is only one of the benefits that your organization provides to employees. Exhibit 5-1 shows the relative cost of medical benefits as a percentage of payroll compared to other benefits often provided by employers. Medical benefits, compared to other employee benefits, account for the highest percentage.

■ INFLUENCES ON PLAN DESIGN

There are several basic elements to plan design: coverage or benefits provided, eligibility and enrollment, cost sharing, provider access, and member services. You will have different degrees of control over each of these areas; the amount will vary according to legal requirements, financial and staff resources, and what's available from carriers and MCOs in your geographic area.

Coverage and Benefits

The most important element of plan design is coverage, or the benefits themselves. Is your plan choice one that provides basic, no-frills coverage, or is it a richer plan that covers everything from well-child visits and preventive screenings to hospice care and specialty surgery? Or, do you offer multiple plans that differ in the coverage provided?

Coverage for hospitalization, physician services, outpatient prescription drugs, mental health care, and substance abuse treatment are, by far, the most common kinds of coverage provided; at least 95 percent, and in the case of the first two 100 percent, of employees who have medical coverage receive these benefits. Examples of the range of coverage offered to employees differ among the types of plans. In Exhibit 5-2, the coverage available under different insurance options—indemnity, HMO, POS, PPO—is shown for one group of workers.

As part of their marketing effort, your health plans publish synopses of their coverage, such as that shown in Exhibit 5-3. This makes it easy for you to prepare a comparison for employees of plans from which to choose. As explained earlier, insurance carriers and MCOs are required to obtain approval from the state department of insurance for health plans. As a consequence, once approved, an insured plan offers specific benefits that cannot be reduced.

Types of Benefits	1994 (%)	1995 (%)
Legally required payments	8.9	8.9
Retirement and savings	7.2	7.5
Life insurance and death benefits	0.4	0.4
Medical and medically related benefits	10.4	10.5
Paid rest periods, lunch periods, etc.	2.2	2.2
Payment for vacations, holidays, sick leave, etc.	9.7	10.2
Miscellaneous benefits	1.9	2.2
Total	40.7	42.0

EXHIBIT 5-1. Types of benefits as a percentage of payroll, all employees, 1994 and 1995. (Source: U.S. Chamber of Commerce, *Employee Benefits*, December 1996.)

Recent legislation has required that plans offer certain benefits. For example, longer inpatient stays for maternity and mastectomy care have been mandated by several states and are now required as part of approved insurance plans. Federal legislation now requires parity for mental and physical health benefits, in both annual and lifetime spending caps, for businesses with more than fifty employees, subject to an exemption for those that would see more than a 1 percent increase in premium as a result of this requirement. Chapter 10's discussion of legislation provides details on legislated benefit requirements.

For flexibility, carriers and MCOs offer several choices of approved plans and, in addition, several riders for specific enrichment options. For example, you may be offered riders for well care, for prescription drug benefits, for vision, hearing, and mental health benefits, for alternative care, or for wellness programs. Your choices among approved plans from one carrier may include different copayments or maximums for coverage, expanded access to doctors or facilities, and a broader selection of benefits.

You can compare the coverage of plans available and select any riders or options that best meet the needs of your employees. In many cases, it's like selecting menu options of one from column A and two from column B to create a unique plan for your organization. Your choices are limited to the plans approved by the state and available from carriers and MCOs licensed in your area, unless you are self-funded, in which case you can design the coverage you wish to provide. (If you are self-funded for your health benefits, Chapter 12 outlines how to fine-tune and adjust your health plan coverage.)

Flex plans, also called cafeteria plans, offer employees several options for plan types and coverage. At present, only 17 percent of all private employers offer employees a choice of plans, according to a report in the August 1998 issue of *On Managed Care*. Of those offering a choice, only 28 percent provide employees with a financial incentive to choose a lower-cost plan. Among employers with more than 500 employees, only 22 percent provide employees with comparative data about plan quality to help them choose wisely.

You should consider the administrative and communication responsibilities that you will have with a flex plan and weigh them against the potential benefits. For instance, employees may value the opportunity to choose their coverage. Most often, flex plans reduce employee cost by allowing employees to select from lower-cost options.

Plan	Indemnity Plan w/POS		HMO #1	HMO #2	HMO #3
	POS	Indemnity			
1998 Deductible	None	$250/750 max	None	None	None
Copayments: Doctors and chiropractors Outpatient service based on cost of service. Immunization for children under 19 covered. Well-child care covered by POS doctors.	$10 service, $20 max. Up to $200.00, $15 copay Over $200.00 $25 copay	20% UCR after annual deductible is met	$3	$10 $35 ER	$10 $35 ER
Drug Copayment	$3 - generic $5 brand - if no generic		20% cost of drug	$3 generic, $5 brand	$5 generic/brand if no generic is available
Primary Providers	See M.D. list	Any M.D.	See staff list	See provider list	See provider list
Monthly Rate	$226.92 Ind $529.85 Fam		$197.19 Ind $519.24 Fam	$175.76 Ind $474.15 Fam	$173.62 Ind $451.45 Fam
Biweekly Payroll Deductions:	$ 5.68 Ind $13.25 Fam		$ 4.93 Ind $12.98 Fam	$ 4.39 Ind $11.85 Fam	$ 4.34 Ind $11.29 Fam

EXHIBIT 5-2. Comparison of health insurance options. (Source: Halo Associates.)

Service Category	Plan A	What You Pay Under Your Current Health Plan?
Physician Services		
Office Visits:		
Well Baby and Child Care	No charge	
Periodic Physicals, Gynecological Exams, & Pap Tests	$10 Copayment/office visit	
Vision Exams Every 2 Years, Surgery, X-ray Services	$10 Copayment/office visit	
Laboratory & Testing Services	$10 Copayment/office visit	
Second Surgical Opinions (not required)	$10 Copayment/office visit	
Hospital Services:		
Surgery	No charge	
Anesthesiology	No charge	
Radiology	No charge	
Visits/Consultations	No charge	
Hospital		
Hospital Inpatient	No charge	
Hospital Outpatient Surgery	$10 Copayment	
Hospital Outpatient Other	No charge	
Maternity		
Physician Services	$10 Copayment	
Hospital Services	No charge	
Nursery Care	No charge	
Emergency Hospital Care		
In area (copayment waived when followed by hospitalization)	$35 Copayment	
Out of Area	No charge	
Ambulance	No charge	
Durable Medical Equipment	20% Copayment	
Mental Health		
For Short-Term, Acute, or Crisis Intervention		
Inpatient-30 day maximum	No charge	
Inpatient-Physician-20 visit maximum	50% or $40 Copayment/visit	
Outpatient	$10 Copayment/1st visit $20 Copayment/visit 2–5 50% or $40 Copayment/visit 6–20	
Substance Abuse Diagnosis and Treatment		
Detoxification	No charge	
Rehabilitation-outpatient (60 visit maximum)	$10 Copayment/visit	
Physical Therapy		
Short term only (2 months maximum)	$10 Copayment/visit	
Home Health Care	$10 Copayment/visit	
Annual Deductibles	None	
Claim Forms	None	
Lifetime Maximum Coverage	No Maximums	

EXHIBIT 5-3. Synopsis of coverage. (Source: Halo Associates.)

You should be aware of regional cost differences, like those shown in Exhibit 5-4, which compares health plans by type and region of the country. The percentage of increase or decrease in cost between 1996 and 1997 is also shown. This comparison reveals a range of difference—nearly $400 per year per employee nationally, with an average difference of about $950 per year per employee from the South to the Northeast. The cost varies among types of plans by region, too. The difference in cost of a traditional indemnity plan from Northeast to West is $1,000 a year, and that type of plan is significantly less costly in the West compared to other choices.

The downside to flex plans includes the possibility of adverse selection, if one or more of your flex plan options is a richer, indemnity-type plan. The freedom of choice in such a plan, combined with its comprehensive benefits, makes it a likely choice for those who are sicker or who require extensive medical services. A richer plan often requires a higher employee contribution and out-of-pocket cost. It can be harder to communicate flex plan benefits, because they are more complicated, and different options affect each employee in a different way. Depending on how well employees understand their options, their satisfaction will vary with flex plans, increasing when the choices meet their needs and decreasing when they don't. Your administrative cost will be higher if you fragment your group among several health plans, because you will have fewer plan members, and therefore a weaker negotiating position, in each of them.

Exhibit 5-5 shows the rate of increase in premiums for workers in various types of plans and the rate of increase in membership of each type between March 1997 and March 1998. According to KPMG Peat Marwick, the greatest growth occurred with PPO and POS plans. This may be due to the interest of employees in greater flexibility and choice offered by these plan types, compared to HMOs, which are more restrictive. The development of HMO plans that offer POS options, or access to specialist networks and other providers, will blur the lines when comparisons are made in the future.

	National	Northeast	Midwest	South	West
Total Health Care Benefits[a]					
Costs	$3,924	$4,453	$4,047	$3,505	$3,797
Percentage change	0.2%	1.9%	−4.7%	3.7%	−1.8%
Active Employees' Medical Plan Costs					
Traditional indemnity plans	$3,521	$3,967	$3,689	$3,152	$2,979
Preferred provider organizations	3,321	3,732	3,379	2,945	3,657
Point-of-service plans	3,481	3,645	3,404	3,326	3,318
Health maintenance organizations	3,165	3,560	3,362	2,832	2,927
Percentage Change, 1996–1997					
Traditional indemnity plans	−5.8%	−3.4%	−1.8%	−5.4%	−12.3%
Preferred provider organizations	0.9	2.5	1.5	0.3	−0.3
Point-of-service plans	−0.4	−0.5	3.1	−1.0	−3.7
Health maintenance organizations	0.6	−2.7	2.3	−0.1	−1.3

Note: For all employers in the United States with 10 or more employees.
[a]Active and retiree costs divided by the number of active employees.

EXHIBIT 5-4. Individual health care costs for all U.S. employers with 10 or more employees, by region. (Source: Mercer/Foster Higgins, January 20, 1998.)

Plan Type	Rate of Increase	% Enrollment
Overall	3.3%	100%
Conventional	3.3	14
HMO	2.9	30
PPO	3.8	34
POS	2.9	22

EXHIBIT 5-5. Rate of increase in premiums and percentage increase in enrollment for different types of health insurance plans. (Source: Health Research and Educational Trust, Washington, DC, 1998.)

Eligibility and Enrollment

Eligibility and enrollment are two areas of plan design where you have more control than you do over coverage, which may reflect regulations and state approvals, and plan type, which reflects developments within the insurance marketplace. You determine eligibility and enrollment policy and procedures. You can adopt plan rules that govern who is able to become a plan member and when and how he or she is able to do so. Although eligibility is established by you and not the insurance carrier, some eligibility issues are regulated. For instance, you cannot offer an employer-sponsored health plan to only a few employees. Insurance industry standards determine whether dependent children age 18 and up will be covered (until they reach a maximum of twenty-five years of age and while they are full-time students at an accredited institution). Some plans offer a cutoff age of 21 years; others, 23 years. There are also federal standards for terminated employees, survivor coverage when the covered employee or retiree dies, and requirements for those on leave, disabled, or terminated.

Choices that you might make with regard to those workers age 65 years and up who are covered under Medicare and no longer working for you include whether to discontinue coverage under your health plan, to apply different contributions or coverage to retirees, or to reimburse the retiree for Medicare Part B. It is more common in rural areas to discontinue coverage; in union environments there are more tiered plans, with different contribution levels.

Rules about employees, their spouses and dependents, and retirees are adopted by your organization as part of its personnel policies and communicated in accordance with law to those who are affected by such rules. You are the plan sponsor and so are responsible for enrollment policies and procedures. Depending on size, you may have a personnel, risk management, or benefits office with staff who arrange for health plan enrollment, or you may have one manager or staff person who handles enrollment as a small part of daily responsibilities. No matter how large or small your health plan staff is, it is important to adhere to uniform policies, establish notification routines, and publicize enrollment activities. Attention to such operating procedures will ensure that you are in compliance with federal and state law and help maintain good employee relations.

The following are typical eligibility and enrollment responsibilities you should note:

1. *Open enrollment.* If you offer more than one health plan, you must allow employees the opportunity to switch from one to the other at least once every twelve months, for a period of thirty days. Most employers who have a plan year starting January 1 offer

enrollment options in the month of October or November. You should send out a notice to all employees, post notices, and mail notices to eligible retirees. A sample notice is shown in Exhibit 5-6. The lead time of sixty to ninety days gives employees advance notice of their right to choose, and the health plan administrator and benefits office has thirty to sixty days to implement the changes selected.

Often representatives of the carriers and MCOs offered will be present during open enrollment to assist with the process. Remember, it's a marketing opportunity for them to retain current plan members and to add new members. Many insurers provide new booklets and plan explanation materials or announce plan improvements during open enrollment periods. You don't have to allow carrier and MCO representatives to participate in enrollment meetings, if it interferes with your work site activities.

You are responsible for giving adequate notice of open enrollment to employees and eligible retirees and to distribute or make readily available a supply of plan information. You should furnish an updated comparison of plans, including any contribution costs, in time for open enrollment.

2. *Year-round enrollment processes.* These need to be available for new employees, for employees who change status (e.g., get married, have or adopt a child, retire, are divorced, take a leave), or who terminate employment. How these events are handled by your office will be decided by the eligibility conditions you establish for your health plan. You will need to document any changes, additions, or deletions and furnish this information to the health plan administrator.

In this category of activity, you should conduct a biannual or annual reenrollment to update employee files. This will help you keep current on other coverage that exists for dependents, ensure the accuracy of employee information, and remove dependents who become ineligible. Your carrier or HMO should furnish enrollment cards or forms to you. A sample enrollment form is provided in Exhibit 5-7.

ANNUAL TRANSFER PERIOD—HEALTH INSURANCE

We are now in the annual health insurance transfer period. All employees and retirees who are currently enrolled in one of the health insurance plans, has the opportunity to change to a different coverage option.

Transfers between options may be made *only during the annual transfer period.* The effective date of the option change will be January 1, 1999.

The reverse side of this memo contains a comparison of health insurance options chart including total monthly premium costs and payroll deductions for 1998.

If you plan to change your present health insurance coverage to another option, your completed enrollment form must be received by 5:00 PM on December 22, 1998.

EXHIBIT 5-6. Sample transfer period notice. (Source: Halo Associates.)

MEMBER ENROLLMENT FORM
PLEASE PRINT OR TYPE AND COMPLETE ALL SPACES

PLEASE NOTE: If you are already enrolled in _____ you do not have to complete this form.

Name (Employee) _____ SEX: ☐ M ☐ F
LAST   FIRST   INITIAL

Address _____

City _____ Zip Code _____ County _____

Home Phone (___) _____ Business Phone (___) _____ Emergency Phone (___) _____

Employer _____

Department _____

Employer Address _____

City _____ Zip Code _____

Date Employed _____ ☐ Full Time ☐ Part Time ☐ Retired

Social Security # _____

Check one: ☐ Individual Coverage (Employee Only) ☐ Family Coverage (Employee and Dependents)

FOR INTERNAL USE ONLY

I.D.# _____

Group # _____

Effective Date _____

Processor _____
            Initial   Date

You must designate your choice of primary care physician for each individual.

√ Check if

Name	Date of Birth Mo./Day/Yr.	Sex	Student Over 18	Disabled	Primary Care Physicians Name	Current Patient	Internal Use Only
01 Employee _____ LAST FIRST	_/_/_	__	☐	☐	_____ LAST FIRST		
02 Spouse _____	_/_/_	__	☐	☐	_____		
03 Child _____ *Relationship to subscriber _____	_/_/_	__	☐	☐	_____		
04 Child _____ *Relationship to subscriber _____	_/_/_	__	☐	☐	_____		
05 Child _____ *Relationship to subscriber _____	_/_/_	__	☐	☐	_____		
06 Child _____ *Relationship to subscriber _____	_/_/_	__	☐	☐	_____		

NOTE: With the exception of your spouse, each dependent must be under nineteen (19) years of age unless a student waiver or handicapped waiver is attached.

*e.g., son, daughter, step-daughter, step-son, etc.

Marital Status: ☐ Single ☐ Married ☐ Divorced ☐ Widowed

Is your spouse employed? ☐ Yes ☐ No If yes, by whom _____

Spouse's health insurance carrier (if other than yours) _____

Spouse's health insurance I.D.# _____

Eligible for Medicare? ☐ Employee I.D.# _____ ☐ Spouse I.D.# _____

FOR INTERNAL USE ONLY

INSCO # _____

CONDITIONS OF ENROLLMENT

I CERTIFY that the statements made are true and complete to the best of my knowledge and belief.

I CERTIFY that I am familiar with my contract with ___ , and that I agree to abide to the terms therein.

I AUTHORIZE any licensed physician, hospital, or other health care provider to furnish ___ with such medical information about myself and eligible dependents listed on the application that may be required.

I UNDERSTAND and agree that (with the exception of emergency procedures) all services, in order to be covered by ___ , must be performed either by a Participating Primary Care Physician or authorized by prior referral from a Participating Primary Care Physician.

I AUTHORIZE my employer to deduct from my earnings the necessary contribution, if any, required of me.

I AGREE to make directly to providers of health care such copayments as are provided for in the contract with ___ .

I HEREBY AGREE TO THE ABOVE CONDITIONS OF ENROLLMENT AND APPLY FOR MEMBERSHIP

Employee's Signature: X _____ Date: _____

EXHIBIT 5-7. Sample enrollment form. (Source: Halo Associates.)

3. *Coordination of benefits.* This insurance term refers to those cases in which more than one plan covers a person and the benefits provided by each need to be coordinated so that appropriate amounts are paid. In most cases, it applies to spouses or dependent children where both spouses work and have family coverage.

In the case of children where there are two plans, one from the mother and one from the father, there is a "birthday rule" that applies. It says that the primary coverage that pays first is that of the parent whose birthday falls first in the calendar year; if the mother's birthday is in January and the father's birthday is in April, the mother's plan covers first and the father's second. This rule has an effect on your costs, since primary coverage usually pays the bulk of the health care claim.

If an employee has other coverage, the industry rule says that the primary coverage is the plan in effect where the employee is currently working or the plan in effect where the employee, if not currently working, has worked the longest or the most recently.

New portability legislation has clarified some of the issues related to employees who switch employment and take health coverage with them. It also addresses coverage for preexisting conditions. This is described in Chapter 10, on legislation.

4. *Special provisions.* Some plans try to reduce costs by including special provisions such as a requirement that any other plan available to a dependent be designated primary. Other plans have instituted a "buy-out" where employees are encouraged to waive enrollment in an employer-sponsored health plan in exchange for a cash payment. If you have an insured plan and pay the employee a portion of the waived premium cost, you can reduce your insurance premiums during the time the employee opts to remain out of the plan. Example 5-8 is an example of plan language used for a buy-out strategy.

A word of caution with regard to the buy-out concept: you are required to allow the employee who opts out an opportunity to re-enroll for coverage, on the same conditions that re-enrollment is available to all other employees. This means you could not enforce a buy-out for twelve months if your plan calls for enrollment after a three-month waiting period. If you did, the employee could collect the buy-out payment, then discover he needs health services and opt for re-enrollment in the plan mid-year, subject to a three-month waiting period. You would be stuck trying to get reimbursed for your buy-out payment, on a prorated basis.

In addition to the administrative issues, you should evaluate the buy-out concept in light of your purpose in providing health insurance—the desire to safeguard employees against catastrophic financial loss due to illness. You want to make sure in a buy-out, if it is something you wish to pursue, that the employee has coverage elsewhere, either from another plan or from a spouse or parent.

In my opinion, the efforts to completely shift coverage responsibility to a spouse's or parent's plan is short-sighted. It does little to control costs if the employee gets sick, and it has the potential for negative employee relations if the delay to re-enroll causes hardship or if the communication about buy-out rules is unclear.

5. *Eligibility.* Three categories of workers need to be considered: active employees, retirees, and dependents of each. You will want to establish a policy that is uniformly applied to each category of employee. Among active employees, you can further categorize into full time or part time, hourly workers, salaried employees, independent contractors, or commissioned employees. For each of these you can establish a different eligibility requirement. For instance, you can specify that only salaried employees who work twenty hours per week or more year round will be covered by your health plan and that all full-time hourly workers will receive benefits on the basis of hours worked, with contributions

3. HEALTH INSURANCE -
   a)
   b)
   c) Employees who are covered under another health insurance plan equivalent to the employer plan through either a spouse or relative may opt to waive coverage under the employer's insurance policy for a full year by completing the appropriate form furnished by the employer. In order to be eligible for this option an employee must certify that he or she has health insurance through another source other than the employer. The employer will pay these employees an amount equal to 50% of the net savings in premiums that would be expended on their behalf taking into account any retirement or social security that must be paid on this amount. Employees electing to waive coverage must do so by October 15 with the provisions of this section taking effect on January 1. Payment to the employee shall be made in two halves with the first half being made during the first payroll period in March and the second being made during the first payroll period in October. Reinstatement of full coverage may be made by notifying the employer in writing no later than October 15 of the succeeding year. Reinstatement will take place on January 1. In the event of an emergency causing the loss of insurance through another source the previously stated notification deadlines may be waived to the extent that there is no conflict with the requirements of the health plan administrator. If reinstatement occurs during such an emergency, the employee will repay, pro rata, any amount already forwarded to him or her.

EXHIBIT 5-8. Sample buy-out provision. (Source: Halo Associates.)

calculated accordingly each month. Commissioned workers may have to purchase coverage, when eligible, and maintain it without interruption at their own expense. It is common to exclude any independent contractors.

You can opt to provide no dependent coverage for active or retired employees or to exclude dependent coverage for retirees only or for any other category of employee. You can change eligibility rules for your plan as of a given date, with appropriate notice to all who are affected by the change. You can provide coverage broadly but require different levels of contribution as long as you apply the contribution rules uniformly to each employee group. You can carve out certain types of coverage and exclude them from your plan, as long as the exclusion applies to all plan members equally.

Your decisions about who is eligible for coverage will depend on how important health benefits are to your employees, on your financial ability to provide a health plan, and on your business strategy for attracting and retaining employees.

6. *Retiree issues.* Because of the disproportionate cost of benefits for retirees—those over sixty-five years of age account for eight times the health care costs of the average younger person—it is important to note some eligibility strategies for retirees, in particular.

Let's look at the example of carved-out coverage. Medicare has already carved out drug coverage for retirees, although those over sixty-five years of age account for 30 percent of prescription medication use and 40 percent of over-the-counter drug use, according to the Health Care Finance Administration. What this means to plan design is that your cost will be high if you offer a comprehensive retiree plan that includes drug coverage. To keep your plan affordable, you could eliminate drug coverage for retirees or, alternatively, control costs through a substantial deductible, high copayments, or a fixed benefit maximum for the year.

An alternative strategy could be to offer a separate drug plan for retirees, one that offers medications for chronic illnesses through a discounted mail-order service, limits some medications to generic drugs only, and places an annual dollar limit on coverage that you feel is reasonable. Many states offer drug programs for seniors to augment Medicare and to supplement retiree insurance plans. You should be aware of such programs in your state so that you can advise retirees on how to enroll for them.

If you intend to provide retirees with health insurance, you can compare the cost of reimbursing retirees for Part B of Medicare in lieu of providing your health plan to them. This may be a cost-effective alternative that meets your objective of safeguarding the retiree from financial disaster in the event of serious illness. If you are self-funded, you will want to have all covered retirees enroll for Part B of Medicare, since 75 percent of its medical expenditures are underwritten by the federal government, while the premium pays only 25 percent of costs. Whether self-insured or insured by a carrier or MCO, you should determine whether the Medicare Part B premium to be paid by the retiree should be automatically deducted from any required premium contribution of your plan.

7. *Waiting periods.* Using waiting periods for eligibility is another way you can control plan costs through plan design. You can establish a waiting period of 30, 60, 180 days, or longer for health plan eligibility, on top of setting restrictions for employees, retirees, and their families. You can have a waiting period for first enrollment, and another waiting period if a plan member drops out of the plan and later chooses to re-enroll. You can have a waiting period for those who do not enroll at the first opportunity but wait until later to sign up for your health plan. Exhibit 5-9 provides sample plan language for waiting periods. You can establish different waiting periods, for example, by employee group, on the basis of hire dates, or for dependents.

8. *Contributions.* Required contributions to health plan costs can be built into plan design as part of eligibility. Your plan can require a contribution, deducted from wages or paid directly to the plan, from all or some employees. Enrollment in a contributory plan is always voluntary. You can't force an employee or retiree to join a plan in which he or she is required to contribute. On the other hand, you are required to have a uniform policy of availability for enrollment. As a consequence, it is important for you to maintain good records on your notifications regarding premium contributions and on

---

When Coverage Begins.

A. Effective Date Of Benefits.   The effective date of your membership is the first day of the second month following the date of your application, provided:

- you apply within one month from the date your employment begins;

- if you apply more than one month from the date your employment begins, your membership is the first day of the third month following the date of your application.

B. Eligibility For Benefits. Benefits are available for services rendered on or after the effective date of your membership in this group except that, under Comprehensive Major Medical coverage, if a subscriber (other than a newborn child) is confined to a hospital on the day coverage would normally become effective, coverage would not begin until the day following such confinement.

EXHIBIT 5-9. An example of delay-of-benefits language. (Source: Halo Associates.)

payments received. You should maintain a written waiver of coverage from those who choose not to contribute and are therefore not enrolled.

Contributions can be different for categories of employees as long as your plan is not discriminatory and requires the same contribution from everyone in a particular class of employee. In other words, you can require a 50 percent contribution from hourly workers, a 25 percent contribution from salaried employees, and a 100 percent contribution from commissioned employees.

You need to give careful thought to this aspect of your health plan design. Contribution levels that are too high can discourage enrollment. One of the results can be adverse selection, or a move by the sicker members who require more services to enroll in your plan, while the healthier members choose to forgo health plan membership. This situation can drive your health plan cost up, result in higher premiums for everyone who enrolls, and require a proportionately higher contribution from your organization. A balance should be struck so that your organization, its employees, and its retirees receive the advantages you intend from your health plan.

In general, you should be aware of the policies and procedures followed by competitors in your industry and in your geographic area. Enrollment and eligibility are the areas in which, no matter how small an organization, you will have the greatest control over your health plan and therefore the greatest opportunity to control cost and affect how the plan is used.

■ MEDICAL PROVIDERS AND PLAN DESIGN

Health care is big business, and one that is changing. One outcome of this change is a new flexibility on the part of doctors, hospitals, and other providers. There are several options available to you as a small or mid-sized employer as a result of market conditions and change, including lower-cost opportunities for the mid-sized employer who has more than 500 employees, depending on the type of environment in which you are located.

Concepts that can help to lower cost include selection of limited network plans, direct negotiated discount contracts, adjustments to coverage to limit access, adoption of a low fee-for-service schedule for your plan, prompt payment discounts, preadmission certification requirements, and various types of review before, during, and after services are rendered.

How can you design a plan with quality medical services and good provider access without spiraling costs? How can you enlist medical providers to help control costs? Will your environment—rural, urban, suburban—have an effect? How do you purchase a discount provider network, select a plan with a better network, or set up your own network?

Types of Providers

Who is a provider, or what, you ask. Good question, because the answer is quite different today from what it might have been thirty years ago. About thirty years ago there were doctors and hospitals, the occasional laboratory or x-ray facility, usually located in the hospital, and that was that.

Today we have doctors with all sorts of designations, including primary care physicians (PCPs), specialists and subspecialists such as pediatric cardiologists or geriatric oncologists, nurse practitioners and physician assistants, chiropractors, podiatrists, and acupuncturists, nutritionists, and a host of other alternative care practitioners. There are group practices that are single or multiple specialty offices and those that partner with a health care facility to provide diagnostic or outpatient services.

Instead of the hospitals and nursing homes we had thirty years ago, we now have acute care hospitals, surgicenters, free-standing medical centers, HMO facilities, radiology centers, diagnostic laboratories, and wellness centers. Hospitals themselves often have specialty centers within each hospital, for instance, for oncology, transplants, heart surgery, osteoporosis, or diagnostic services. Merged networks of hospitals, and collaborative services are growing nationwide, as hospitals strive to compete in the health care industry.

Now mobile services bring health care professionals, diagnostic tests, and intervention services to work sites and other facilities. These new services have expanded beyond the mammography and cholesterol screening of the 1980s and early 1990s to include portable programs for the management of chronic conditions such as diabetes, osteoporosis, and cardiac disease.

Treatment centers and preventive health services for alternative therapies are growing, with hundreds of local offices and centers, staffed by practitioners and therapists in many disciplines. Typical of these are the offices and centers that offer massage of all types, aromatherapy, herbology, Reike, biofeedback, Yoga, meditation and T'ai Chi, acupuncture, and nutrition assessment and counseling, to name a few.

An overall trend since 1982, according to the Health Care Finance Administration, has been that medical treatment is increasingly provided on an outpatient basis, with fewer and shorter hospital stays. Improved emergency and surgical techniques, medications, and treatment services at home, coupled with the high cost of hospital inpatient care, have made a long stay in the hospital a rarity.

Networks

A network is a designated group of providers used by a health plan, which directs plan members to these providers and pays them at an established rate or fee. Providers outside this group are paid at a different level or not at all. For networks of doctors, this concept blossomed in the 1930s and 1940s, when HMOs used contract doctors and hospitals, sometimes owning the hospital and having the doctors as employees, to provide services to groups they covered. PPOs followed in the 1950s with panels of physicians and expanded rapidly in the 1980s into regional and national networks.

Employees experience your health plan when they receive services from doctors and other facilities. Availability of, or restrictions on, provider services are a major part of plan design. Often the type of plan you select will determine how accessible the doctors and other facilities are to meet your employees' needs. Exhibit 5-10 provides a synopsis of the features of indemnity, HMO, POS, and PPO plans with regard to provider access.

You should select the plan type that offers an appropriate degree of access, and a particular plan that includes a network, or combination of networks, that works best for your employees.

Lower cost, compared to the going rate in a community, is a distinct advantage of using a network. So is the availability of quality care to plan members when doctors are prepaid, or contracted to provide services. Networks have disadvantages, too, given that

Indemnity/Traditional	HMO (Health Maintenance Organization)	PPO (Preferred Provider Organization)	POS (Point of Service)
Select any doctor, specialist, or facility without approval or restriction, in any location	Select primary-care physician from HMO directory who then authorizes all services	Select doctors, specialists, and other services from network directory as needed	Select option for the plan, provider, or coverage level when services are needed
Select any service that is medically necessary without approval, on order from doctor	Request approval or referral from PCP for all medical services, including specialists	Select any medically necessary service without approval from network provider	Select indemnity, HMO, PPO, or other hybrid with varying services and restrictions
Give advance notice with no approval required, for hospital admission and discharge	Seek advance approval from HMO and referral from PCP for hospital services	Give advance notice, with no approval required for network hospital admission/discharge	Follow the selected plan requirements for advance notice or approvals
Advance discounts may be negotiated by carrier, or carrier may have discounts in place	HMO uses only contracted doctors/hospitals and may limit/deny services elsewhere	PPO provides access at discount to doctors/hospitals and no services elsewhere	POS has discounted contracts with doctors/hospitals where less out-of-pocket is required
Assistance with discharge planning is voluntary	Discharge planning is done by PCP approval/referral	Discharge planning in network, voluntary	Discharge planning rules follow option selected.
Case management provided by carrier, initiated by patient	All services subject to PCP and HMO case management	Case management, initiated by patient, if available	Case management provided under POS options, by plan
Coordination of care provided by patient's physician; carrier may offer support services	Coordination of care is required; provided by PCP, subject to HMO approval.	Coordination of care provided by patient's physician; PPO used for referrals	Coordination of care is provided by patient's physician, subject to POS option chosen
Bills and claims are audited by carrier for accuracy	Bills and claims are audited by HMO for accuracy	Bills and claims are audited by PPO for accuracy	Bills and claims are audited by the plan chosen
Payment to providers based on usual and customary schedules or negotiated fees/schedules	Payment to providers based on monthly capitated rate, fee schedule, contract incentives	Payment to providers is based on discount fees by contract or negotiated specialty services	Payment to providers at POS network rate by contract, or as paid by the plan selected
Little supervision/monitoring of physician/hospital services	Direct supervision and limits on physician/hospital services	Supervision/monitoring limited except fees charged	Supervision/monitoring limited patient moves from plan to plan.
Claim filing by patient/provider for each illness each year	Claim filing done by provider for other than PCP services	Claim filing by provider for all services	Claim filing by provider or patient depending on plan
Out-of-pocket includes deductible and coinsurance to an annual maximum	Out-of-pocket include copays established for physician and other covered services	Out-of-pocket includes copays for network physicians and other covered services	Out-of-pocket varies, but is higher out of POS network and for nonnetwork plans
Services provided up to a maximum per year and lifetime	Services have no maximum per year or lifetime	Services provided with and without maximums, by plan	Services are provided subject to maximums of plan chosen
Well-care services are provided by the employer separately, unless part of plan design	Well-care services for routine checkups are provided, and some others by plan design	Well-care services provided by employer or network providers as allowed in plan	Well-care services are provided by plan sponsor separately or as part of available plan options
Subject to federal and state regulations for coverage provisions, claims appeals, provider relations, disclosure	Subject to federal and state regulations for coverage, plan approval, claims appeals, provider relations, disclosure	Not subject to regulation since network access, not benefits, are provided. Plan sponsor or administrator is regulated.	Subject to federal and state regulations that apply to each plan option given. POS network not regulated.

EXHIBIT 5-10. Comparison of coverage. (Source: Halo Associates.)

most are local or regional and restrict access to specialists and facilities outside their immediate area. Specialty services are not always readily available in a limited geographic area. For example, when plan members are seriously ill they are willing to travel to special locations for unique quality services, such as transplant, burn treatment, or heart surgery. Members are not usually given the option of nonurgent out-of-area services in a plan that restricts coverage to a network. This disadvantage is gradually disappearing with changes in the local availability of new technology, the growth of national networks, and mergers between carriers and MCOs.

Advantages to providers are clear. Payment is quicker, the amount of the fee or charge is agreed in advance, acceptance of claims is automatic, subject to medical necessity and what is covered, credentialing is done at the onset, and paperwork and follow-up explanations are minimized. A particular advantage to the doctor or facility is an increase in the number of patients and a steady stream of new patients. Participation in several networks may be necessary for the doctor to keep existing patients who change from one health plan to another.

There are disadvantages, too. Many doctors feel that the network takes on a life of its own and begins to manage care or limit their choices. State legislation has been passed to prevent certain restrictions by networks. For example, some managed-care networks were found to require that doctors not tell patients of treatment options that were expensive, not covered, or unavailable within the network. In some cases, doctors were not allowed to refer patients for services without financial penalty by the network. Federal and state legislation has been proposed, and in some areas passed, to address the issue of "gag clauses" in network contracts.

The issue of patient care and physician autonomy is at the heart of the disadvantages of a system that is considered by many to be run by nonmedical staff who are focused on the bottom line of the health care business. Doctors and patients alike chaff at the restraints established by managed care organizations that concentrate on an annual profit.

Since the carrier or MCO experiences annual turnover in the health plan, its commitment to the member's health is short term and focuses on acute medical necessity in most cases. Turnover occurs when there is little affinity of the patient with the plan. About 75 percent of individuals outside Medicare and Medicaid who are covered by private insurance receive the coverage through an employer-sponsored plan. The decision about which plans to offer ultimately rests with you, the employer organization, and not with the employee. Consequently, plan members feel little loyalty or commitment toward the plan. This is not the case if the plan is self-funded or a union trust fund, where a longer-term enrollment of members in the same plan is more likely.

Network Options

Whether you like or dislike their development, networks are here to stay and can provide valuable discounts and lower your health plan costs. Some of your options include the following:

- Select a health plan that offers an extensive network.
- Select a plan administrator that offers several discounted networks.
- Add a hospital or physician network to your existing health plan to expand services and receive greater discounts.
- Require your health plan to add the physicians and facilities used by your members.

- Select several plans so that your employees can select the one with the best network for where they live and the health care needs they have.
- If self-funded, purchase an existing network for use by your members.
- If self-funded, create your own network of providers (see Exhibit 5-11 for a sample network invitation letter).

In most cases, the health plan administrator who provides a bid will furnish a network listing, which is included as an administrative service. You should be aware of any added

Re: Point-of-Service Network

Dear [provider's name]:

Thank you for your expressed interest in joining our referenced network of providers who serve participants in the [*company name*] self-funded indemnity plan.

I am pleased to write you to invite your firm to join our network, as a provider of at-home services. Please review the enclosed fee schedule, which has been developed in response to fee and payment patterns for our plan. [*Add if appropriate:* In some cases, you will note significant differences between our schedule and that submitted by you earlier.]

We anticipate that referrals to your firm and therefore utilization will increase with your joining the network. As noted on the schedule, network providers will be those recommended to our plan participants by both the managed care service organization and the plan's administrator.

We have enclosed an agreement for your review and execution. Also enclosed is a checklist of materials to be forwarded to us with the agreement. Because we are currently preparing informational materials which will be distributed to our employees during [*month*] we ask that you respond at your earliest opportunity.

I look forward to your response and to working with you. Please feel free to contact me with any question you may have.

Very truly yours,

Director of Risk Management

EXHIBIT 5-11. Sample letter of invitation to prospective network members. (Source: Halo Associates.)

costs for network use or for expanding the network to add physicians or facilities needed by your employees. (Exhibit 5-12 shows a sample contract for physicians.)

Network Selection and Organizational Needs

If you have employees in a rural area, your choices for network providers will be more limited; in an urban area, you may have several networks from which to choose who will compete for your business. On the other hand, an organization of fifty employees in a rural area will have more weight than one of the same size in an urban area.

A 1997 study by Care Data of commercial health plans showed that 15 percent of HMO members go out of network for services that are not reimbursed. When your employees go out of network and incur costs, they do not value the plan you provide. To avoid out-of-network costs, many HMOs and other MCOs offer out-of-network access to providers with a point-of-service option. Members are covered under the POS option with indemnity-like coverage when nonnetwork providers are used. HMOs also offer open-access plans, which are growing in popularity. With these, members can go to non-network specialists without a referral from their primary care physician. It is estimated by the study that 53 percent of HMO members seek open-access services. HMOs can also offer open access to a limited network of doctors in selected specialties, such as obstetrics/gynecology.

You may choose to select a plan that offers in-network and out-of-network access, for instance, if you have employees in age groups where specialty care will be more common. It is in these circumstances that your demographic information is useful. Think of your potential prenatal claims, your older members, or a demographic group that is likely to experience a high prevalence of a specific illness. For example, if you have a high number of employees who are male, over forty years of age, and African American, you can project a relatively high incidence of prostate cancer. In that case, if you have few urologists in your network and limited services for oncology, you will be more likely to have dissatisfied members whose needs are unlikely to be met.

Time Frame for Introducing Networks

Some networks require a plan year startup, whereas others allow you to begin network use at any time. You can benefit from making an orderly transition to a new network at the beginning of a plan year. Employees don't like to have changes made to their health plan or network without sufficient notice. If your health plan offers several options to employees, you should notify them two to three months in advance of making changes. A memorandum, payroll stuffer, or bulletin posted in a high-traffic area is appropriate. Some employers like to tell employees when they are considering making a change, and why. If, for instance, you received numerous complaints about the health plan, it would be advisable to alert employees that you are conducting a review that might result in improved services or changes.

It takes two or three months to fully implement a change, including the provision of identification cards and descriptive materials. Most likely it will take one or two plan years before your employees become well informed about the plan's network. You can help by providing adequate network listings and updates to members at the onset and during the year. You can get help with this activity from your broker, agent, or consultant. Remember, it's part of your health advisor's job to help you inform employees about health plan coverage and services.

(text continues on page 88)

THIS AGREEMENT is made and entered into this first day of _____ by and between the (hereinafter called " _____ "), and _____ (hereinafter called "Provider").

THAT WHEREAS, _____ is desirous of organizing and operating a Preferred Provider Organization (PPO)

AND WHEREAS, Provider is a duly licensed physician/or facility in the State of New York

AND WHEREAS, _____ wishes to utilize the services of Provider as a participant in its PPO; and Provider is willing to be such a participant

NOW THEREFORE, in consideration of the mutual promises hereinafter contained and other valuable consideration, the parties hereto agree as follows:

1. SERVICES

Provider certifies that he is duly licensed in the State of New York. Provider agrees to provide to Members of PPO (Members) the usual and customary medical services in the field of _____. Provider agrees to render health services to Members in the same manner, in accordance with the same standards and within the same time availability as offered his other patients.

2. REIMBURSEMENT FOR SERVICES

A. Providers reimbursement for services hereunder shall be in accordance with the PPO's Reimbursement Schedule which will be approximately 70% of the UCR published regularly by HIAA. The PPO schedule is subject to change according to changes made by HIAA.

B. Provider agrees to submit directly to the designated Third Party Administrator and as soon as possible claims for reimbursement for the provision of services as described in section 1 of this agreement. Provider agrees that in no event shall Provider bill, charge, collect a deposit from, seek compensation, remuneration or reimbursement from, or have any recourse against Members. This provision shall not prohibit collection of any applicable copayments and deductible in accordance with the terms of the reimbursement schedule.

3. HOLD HARMLESS

Provider agrees to indemnify and hold harmless _____ its agents, officers, owners, directors and employees from any liability arising out of Provider performing services for Members.

4. INSPECTION OF RECORDS

Provider and _____ agree that all Member medical records shall be treated as confidential so as to comply with all state and federal laws regarding the confidentiality of patient records. However, _____ or it's designated provider shall have the right upon request to inspect all reasonable times any accounting, administrative, and medical records maintained by Provider pertaining to the PPO, to any Member and to Provider's participation hereunder. Other than as provided herein, Provider shall not be required to disclose the medical records of any Member without his or her written consent.

5. TERM

This Agreement shall become effective on _____ and shall continue in effect from year to year unless terminated by either party by a written notice thereof mailed to the other party by certified or registered mail upon thirty (30) days notice prior to such termination date. Termination shall have no effect upon the rights and obligations of the parties arising out of any transactions occurring prior to the effective date of such termination. Termination shall not release Provider from his obligations to complete the treatment of Members then receiving treatment.

6. NOTICES

EXHIBIT 5-12. Sample network participation agreement. (Source: Halo Associates.)

Any notice required to be given pursuant to the terms and provisions hereof shall be in writing and shall be sent by certified or registered mail to Provider and   .

7. ENFORCEABILITY

The invalidity of unenforceability of any terms or conditions hereof shall in no way affect the validity or enforceability of any other term or provision.

8. MODIFICATION

This Agreement constitutes the entire understanding of the parties hereto and no changes, amendments or alterations shall be made unless in writing and signed by both parties.

9. NON-ASSIGNABILITY

This Agreement, being intended to secure the services of Provider shall not be assigned, sublet, delegated or transferred without written consent of   . Any purported assignment, subletting, delegation or other transfer in derogation hereof shall be deemed null and void and of no effect whatsoever.

10. RELATIONSHIP

None of the provisions of this Agreement is intended to create, nor shall be deemed or construed to create, any relationship between the parties hereto other than that of independent entities contracting with each other hereunder solely for the purpose of effecting the provisions of the Agreement. Neither of the parties hereto nor any of their respective employees, shall be construed to be the agent, employee or representative of the other.

IN WITNESS WHEREOF, the undersigned have executed this Agreement as of the day and year first above written.

Provider Name:

By:_____   By:_____

Title: _____   Title: _____

Date: _____   Tax ID#: _____

Date: _____

*Please specify information for our PPO

Name: _____

Address: _____

_____

_____

Telephone #:   _____

Specialty(s):   _____

Purchase of Network Access

To buy the services of a network, contact national or regional provider networks near you. Sources for this information are in the Appendix. Ask your consultant, broker, or agent for names of regional networks and for their recommendation, and inquire if they have a commission arrangement with a particular network.

If you wish to explore for yourself, ask each network for information on its fees and for provider listings. When you receive the information, compare the networks' fees and the suitability of their provider listings. Not only should you be able to identify and select the lowest cost network, but you should understand the services they provide. Some networks offer toll-free call centers to provide referral services to your employees. Call centers can help control your plan costs by directing plan members to discounted services.

■ ISSUES FOR HOSPITALS

Major changes in hospital reimbursement, or how much hospitals get paid by insurance companies, MCOs, and government programs for care they provide, have occurred over the past ten years. Some states have reduced payments to hospitals for charity patients or for graduate medical education costs. Many states require surcharges from other providers, such as laboratories or x-ray facilities, who in turn pass them along to the consumer or health plan. These surcharges are used to pay hospitals for charity care and for graduate medical education. Hospitals have struggled with the trend to fewer and shorter inpatient stays, and occupancy rates have been at all-time lows for the past few years. The Health Care Finance Administration forecasts that this trend will continue through 2005, as shown in Exhibit 5-13.

As a consequence, hospitals are in the business of vying for customers and trying to meet the need for more business with several initiatives—hospital mergers, hospital-based physician networks, negotiated discounts, and specialty centers.

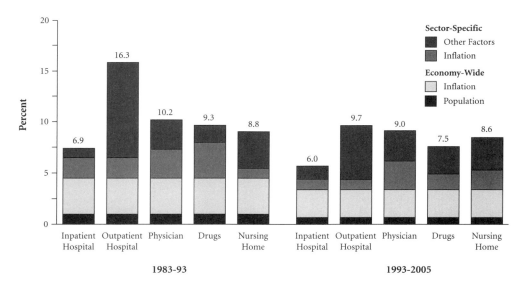

EXHIBIT 5-13. Factors accounting for average annual growth in selected types of national health expenditures: selected periods 1983–2005. Note: "Other factors" include joint effects of the factors shown. (Source: Health Care Financing Administration, Office of the Actuary; data from the Office of National Health Statistics.)

Hospital Mergers and Networks

Instead of individual hospitals, each with a personality and a unique list of admitted physicians, we are watching the consolidation of hospital services by region. From a few to scores of hospitals join forces in an HPN (hospital provider network), or the newer POS (provider service organization). Hospitals use the new entity to market services, to expand and integrate facilities and specialties, and to establish rate contracts with health insurance companies and self-insured plans. Mergers have resulted from the need to shore up hospital finances and have also had an effect on services. In some cases, a better-equipped hospital or teaching hospital initiates the merger and enlists several smaller hospitals to become part of a consolidated organization. The unique capabilities of the smaller hospitals are reinforced by the resource of the larger, better-known facility. Everyone seems to benefit.

What does this do to costs, and to health plans? Since the primary purpose is to improve the finances of the hospitals involved and to provide more cost-effective care, there are outcomes to hospital mergers that can be helpful to health plans and some that are not. On the plus side, a hospital merger can improve quality of services. The new consolidated hospital group may offer services and staff that were previously not available. A more uniform method of billing and charges may result when hospitals merge, as they consolidate some or all of their financial functions. Specialist teams may be shared by several hospitals, bringing unique quality services to new locations and, usually, closer to the patient.

On the negative side, the hospitals in a group may set rates as one unit that are substantially higher than what the local hospital was charging before the merger. There is less leverage for employers, health plans, and insurance companies to bargain with a merged group of hospitals. Rates and charges increase on the average in this situation, with a negative impact on self-funded employers, those with experience-rated health insurance, and communities that rely upon community-rated premiums.

Urban hospitals have significantly higher costs, although usually more depth of specialists and specialties. To spread those costs, city hospitals merge with suburban and nearby hospitals, helping to establish a referral network among the group that will increase volume of business and enable them to benefit from economies of scale. A side benefit is the ability to set rates that offset the losses from charity care and graduate medical education, which are usually higher for urban hospitals.

There are some obvious advantages to employer-sponsored health plans that contract with a group of hospitals. A guaranteed, credentialed network with established discounted rates is readily available, usually without network fees.

There are disadvantages, however, that go to the philosophy and focus of the institution. A hospital network is generally physician-driven. What that means is that fees will be higher in such networks, as doctors determine their own reimbursement or payment amounts. Services will be limited to those physicians who are admitted to practice at network hospitals and their associate hospitals. By definition, this limits care to the local setting.

What can you do if you have a discount arrangement in place with a hospital that is about to merge or to join a network? You can take these steps:

- Write to the hospital, noting that you expect the discount to continue and look forward to working with them, regardless of structural and administrative changes.
- Put them on notice that you expect your agreement to be "grandfathered" in so that they are more likely to honor it later.

- If it seems that the merger will encourage use of the other hospitals in the new entity, contact your nearest facility and speak to the finance office about expanded services that will result.
- Aim to have your agreement with one hospital carried over to the others.
- Maintain communication about the cost of inpatient stays, urgent care, and other expanded services they might offer.
- If your organization is small, suggest to your business association that it enter into an agreement on behalf of members with an HPN, PSO, or merged group of hospitals.

The PSO is a different type of health plan in which providers, including hospitals, other facilities, and doctors, join to provide insurance. A fixed premium is charged, and the PSO accepts the risk of providing health care to your employees, much like an insurance carrier or MCO. Your selection of the PSO will be based on the same criteria used for other plan types. Some differences will exist, since PSOs are especially encouraged in rural areas where networks are not readily developed, the population tends to be older and underserved, and medical resources are limited.

Individually Negotiated Discounts

Depending on whether your geographic area is rural, urban, or suburban, you can seek a discount for your organization. Economies of size play a part in this effort. The larger you are, the more likely the hospital will negotiate with you. If you have limited national networks to choose from in your area and are one of the larger employers in the area, you will have a good opportunity to win a negotiated discount.

In a rural setting, the hospital is often in the position of being the only such facility, or one of a limited number. It is common to see a few hospitals clustered in a rural environment, each with its own reputation, doctors, and specialty areas. The reason for the separate identities derives from the need to allocate limited resources—duplicate treatment centers aren't needed in a small community.

How can you, as a mid-sized organization, whether in a rural, urban, or suburban setting, work with local hospitals? Possibilities include the following:

- You can offer to provide the hospital with a rotating fund that will pay for emergency care services at a discount.
- You can agree to use one hospital for acute emergencies in exchange for emergency care discounts. Of course, this should be the hospital closest to your work site.
- You can agree to make prompt payments (within thirty days) in exchange for a 2 to 3 percent prompt payment discount.
- You can peg future increases in hospital expenditures for services to the Consumer Price Index, instead of to the higher medical CPI.
- You can explore the possibility of using hospital services for workers compensation injuries and/or for required workers compensation physicals at a discount. These services are often provided by individual doctors in a less uniform manner and at a higher cost.

Small organizations can follow the same concept, either with a group of employers in their area or as part of a business association.

To make a hospital discount work, you'll have to require higher copayments, deductibles, or coinsurance from employees who choose to use nonnetwork hospitals and facilities. The out-of-pocket cost and any other results of going outside the network have to be clearly communicated to employees. There should be a 15 to 20 percent differential in out-of-pocket costs for network and nonnetwork use if employees are to be encouraged to stay within the network. With the requirements for pre-admission certification in place, employees should be advised in advance that choosing a nonnetwork hospital will lead to increased cost.

Hospitals in the United States have traditionally been founded and run by boards of community members, nonprofit charity organizations, and/or religious orders. These nonprofit organizations, run by volunteer boards, are responsible in many communities for health care services and setting their cost. This is changing, especially in the western United States, with an increasing number of for-profit hospitals and hospitals owned and operated by HMOs and other MCOs, which expect to turn a profit.

Some Precautions About Hospital Networks

Your responsibility, if you select a limited hospital network, includes informing plan members of any coverage limitations so that there will be no misunderstanding when urgent medical care is needed. If your plan or carrier limits access to certain services, be sure to communicate how and under what conditions a plan member can seek a review of such a denial. If you contract with a hospital network directly, consider the impact on employee relations, as well as the cost advantages.

Hospitals have other issues to address when developing and offering risk contracts to local health plans. Most hospitals don't have the expertise and depth of resources to become insurance companies; problems with cash flow and the demands of providing twenty-four-hour care drain hospital resources. It is expensive to keep staff and equipment functioning day and night; these costs must be passed along in rates to users. When the hospital assumes risk, you have to look closely at the financial stability of the institution and at its track record at staying in the black. The high operational costs of meeting a public health need make public support of hospitals essential—and these same circumstances may be the reason that hospital assumed-risk contracts won't be cost-effective.

If you think a hospital risk contract (PSO) or limited hospital network can work for your organization, schedule a presentation by hospital representatives to gather information on costs and coverage provisions. You should include top managers and employee representatives who can pose questions about service, cost, access, and quality of care.

Hospitals as Specialty Centers

Springing up around the country, in every state and locality, are hospital outpatient centers and specialty centers within hospitals. This gradual change from the general hospital has been a reaction to the development of specialties and subspecialties. Hospitals have financial and other limits that encourage them to focus on specialty centers for growth. It is impractical for each hospital to try to attract the best physicians in every specialty and subspecialty, to maintain the latest high-cost equipment for the treatment of every disease, and to build and maintain enough space to meet every health care need.

Hospitals have responded to the specialty craze among doctors by specializing, too. The impetus to develop specialty centers within a hospital comes from medical specialists on staff who serve a certain patient population with their expertise, from board members with a personal interest, from donations from former patients and their families in gratitude for care, or from careful planning based on what other area hospitals offer and the needs of the community.

How do hospital specialty centers affect cost, and access to services? Cost is usually higher for services that rely upon higher-paid specialists and expensive equipment. Quality of care and outcomes usually improve, too. Your employees probably want specialty care and feel they deserve it, whether or not your health plan routinely provides it. State and federal legislation has been proposed that would guarantee access to specialist care without a referral from the health plan. Hospital specialty centers will benefit from this legislation, spurring their continued development.

How to Proceed

Hospitals today are accustomed to signing contracts to provide service at a discounted rate and want to know how it will benefit them. The presence of discount networks in an area limits how much negotiating hospitals are willing to do with a small or mid-sized organization.

First, you should have the facts. These include:

- How much of your utilization occurs at the hospital
- What sort of services are used, both outpatient and inpatient
- What is the frequency and length of stay for inpatient services
- What is the average cost and length of stay per admission
- What is the total amount your plan pays to the hospital annually

Second, evaluate your employees' attitude about the hospital and its services. You can survey employees through written questionnaires, ask them informally at work-site meetings, or have supervisors conduct discussion groups. Determine whether employees feel strongly that the hospital provides quality services and can meet their needs.

Third, assess the hospital's strength and weakness, including its range of available services. Include the hospital's association with specialty hospitals, its financial stability, the depth and range of medical staff, the size and extent of physical facilities, and its future growth plans. Sometimes other services are provided by the hospital. It may offer a call center for a nurse advice line, wellness programs, or return-to-work rehabilitation programs, each of which offers the potential for a collaborative relationship.

Now you are ready to meet with the hospital to discuss your needs. Prepare a game plan with several options that make sense for your organization. The most common agreements with hospitals are the following:

- A straight percentage discount off regular published charges. The basis of charges can be fixed or adjusted periodically, according to an agreed upon methodology. Discounts range from 5 percent to 30 percent, depending on competitive and negotiation factors.
- A sliding percentage discount based on increased utilization.
- A prompt-payment discount of 2 to 3 percent.
- Separate discounts for outpatient services, often as high as 40 percent.
- A discount based on prepayment or establishment of a fund on which the hospital draws as costs are incurred by plan members. This should take the cash flow and interest income advantages into account.
- Per diem charges at a flat rate, discounted.

You should, by agreement, work out the details of how utilization will be measured and over what time period. Most often, you enter into a one-year agreement that can be renewed by both parties, subject to further review. Be sure to establish an implementation checklist, and name a contact person at the hospital and one within your organization.

You should negotiate differently with specialty hospitals for mental health or chemical dependency services. Hospitals are often willing to contract with you for a discounted per diem rate in exchange for referrals. These negotiations can be conducted by case managers or plan administrators on your behalf at the time of preadmission certification. Advance discounts are usually available for as much as 50 percent of the published per diem fee from such facilities, especially if prompt payment or prepayment is part of the agreement.

■ CONTRACTS WITH DOCTORS

Contracts are signed individually by each doctor in a group and provide for one of two methods of reduced cost—a percentage discount from usual and customary fees in the area or a published discounted fee schedule, amended periodically. Payment can be made on a per capita or fee-for-service basis or be connected to a bonus or a withhold at year end. My preference is to keep it simple, with a discounted fee schedule and evaluation of physician costs monthly or quarterly.

You should review claims data to identify doctors used by plan members. To find doctors used by your plan members, review the 1099 listing of providers who were paid by your plan during the previous year. This is available from your administrator, is filed with the Internal Revenue Service annually, and shows all medical providers, with their address, often their telephone, and the amount of money paid to them on behalf of plan members. From this listing you will be able to determine those physicians and facilities that received the most money from your plan and that therefore might be most interested in keeping your members as patients. Start with these providers and send a letter, such as the one in Exhibit 5-11, to determine their interest in network participation. You should have a discount contract and fee schedule ready to distribute to network providers. (Exhibit 5-12 presents a sample network participation agreement.) These can be sent out with your first mailing to doctors on receipt of the doctor's letter of interest or response to a telephone survey.

Groups of employers, business associations, and self-funded plans are most likely to have the staff and the motivation to create a local physician network. If you form your own network, be prepared to use a benefits professional who can help establish the fee schedule and periodically review it for adjustment. Your health plan administrator will have this expertise, and his or her input should be sought; it may be possible to have the administrator create the network with minimal support from your organization. See Exhibit 5-14 for a sample of negotiated fee contract language. Be sure to have your legal adviser and your health insurance professional work with you on contract language suitable for your organization.

No matter who creates a physician network for your health plan, the providers must be credentialed, and good records maintained. Typical credential documents include the practitioner's license and resumé or curriculum vitae, a listing of all health plans, including Medicare and Medicaid, that currently accept the provider as a participant, verification of malpractice insurance in the doctor's name, a list of any board certifications, a list of all practice locations, a list of any malpractice actions pending or completed within three years, and a verification of hospital admitting privileges. These documents need to be updated when they expire, if they have an expiration date. If you maintain these records, you will need to establish a tickler file to alert your staff to expiration dates or ensure that they are updated annually if your plan administrator is responsible for doing so.

Published Rates Effective January 1	Discounted
Nursing	
RN $48/hour	$40
LPN $42/hour	$35
PRI $150 assessment	$125
Skilled Nursing Visit $125/visit	$100
Physical Therapy $150/visit - $125/follow-up visit	$125
Occupational Therapy $150/visit - $125/follow-up visit	$125
Speech Therapy $150/visit - $125/follow-up visit	$125
Social Work $150/visit - $125/follow-up visit	$125
Respiratory Therapy $150/visit - $125/follow-up visit	$125
Enterostomal Therapy $150/visit - $125/follow-up visit	$125
Nutritional Counseling $150/visit - $125/visit	$125
Intravenous Therapy	
Initial Visit $150/visit	$125
Subsequent Visit $125/visit	$100
Nursing service for continuous infusion monitoring $50/hour	$48
Home Health Aide Service	
1 Patient $15/hour	$14.50
Each additional patient - add $3/hour	$2
Personal Care Aide Service	
1 Patient $12.92/hour	$10.50
Each additional patient - add $6.46/hour	$6
Live-in $175/day	$160
Homemaker $14.50/hour	$13.50
Hospital Sitter $15/hour	$13

EXHIBIT 5-14. Sample rate schedule. (Source: Halo Associates.)

Use monthly network reports provided by your plan administrator or carrier to identify abnormal patterns of utilization. Your health plan adviser can assist with this review. Once trends of increased use are observed, a prompt call or notice to the network doctor can help control excess utilization and costs.

Sounds a bit complicated, you say. Well, it is a process. But once you have established such contracts, perhaps with the help of a benefits professional, it becomes routine to maintain it. Discounts typically range from 20 percent to 40 percent of the going rate. Depending on your size and volume, this may mean substantial savings to your health plan, without requiring your members to pay more. In fact, if they have a copayment, their share of cost will go down.

A discounted agreement, if you can negotiate one with the physicians and facilities used most often by your members, can go a long way to control rising costs. However, it doesn't answer issues related to proper use of services by your employees or to frequency of use.

■ **LIMITS TO ACCESS**

Some plans have chosen to eliminate emergency room use for nonurgent visits. A plan member might go to the emergency room, but the plan will not pay unless an admission results. Others have limited access by increasing copayments for emergency room use unless an admission to the hospital follows, thereby taking some guesswork out of the claim. Still others increase the copayment for emergency room visits regardless of admission. These provisions may be affected by pending federal legislation.

Why is it cost-effective for a health plan to limit emergency services? Emergency room services cost four to five times as much as similar services provided in nonemergency settings. Remember, the hospital keeps a staff on deck around the clock, paid full wages, and the hospital provides and maintains a complete range of equipment and facilities for use in a real emergency. These costs and overhead are passed along to emergency room users.

Typical factors used to limit access to doctors are whether fees will be paid and at what level, how much of the cost is covered, what advance requirements need to be met by the patient or plan member, and whether related services are covered. For example, plans often cover network physicians in full, subject to a minimal copayment, at rates below usual and customary, by agreement. Nonnetwork doctors may charge at usual and customary levels, but they are paid at a lower level by the plan or not at all, and the patient is billed for the remainder. When payment is made, nonnetwork services are subject to a deductible and coinsurance, usually 20 percent or more of charges.

Most network plans do not cover nonnetwork specialists without prior approval or referral from a network physician. Some plans don't cover out-of-network specialists under any conditions.

What does this mean to your health plan and your members? If your network is extensive and includes the doctors and specialists used by your members, you will have high member satisfaction and lower cost. If your network is not extensive and omits many of the doctors and services used by your members, you will have lower member satisfaction.

What about your health plan's relationship with physicians? Doctors and specialists will be satisfied if your network pays them promptly, without interference in the care given to patients, and at what they consider to be a reasonable level. They will be unsatisfied, and may drop out of the network, if payments are delayed or reduced, if managed care requirements are too stringent, or if paperwork is time-consuming.

Don't forget the mission of your health plan: to provide quality medical care to your employees that will meet their health care needs at a cost you can afford. You might be penny-wise and pound-foolish if you slash access to providers. Often, plan members will grumble, and the result may well be requests for higher wages, higher turnover rates, and lowered productivity—all of which may cost you more than any health plan savings you realize.

Preadmission Certification

Preadmission certification is the requirement that patients call and receive authorization prior to hospital admission or scheduled surgery or procedures. With a call to a preadmission number, the member advises the plan of the diagnosis, anticipated services, admission date if the patient is to receive inpatient services, and the name of the treating physician or specialist. During the call, plan members are asked about the physician or provider who will provide the service, the medical necessity of the service, and the location or facility. Some plans require approvals for diagnostic testing, too. Medical professionals usually make preadmission certification decisions, but they are not necessarily doctors or credentialed in any specialty.

Consider the possibilities if you deny coverage. Lawsuits, disgruntled employees, union grievances, and complaining doctors and other providers—these are a few of the likely effects of such an action. Denial of coverage is never to be taken lightly.

The determination of medical necessity rests with the treating physician. If a member's doctor wants the patient to have a specific service and is willing to vouch that it is medically necessary, it is difficult, and not very prudent, for the health plan to deny it. If the service is not covered, or if it is not covered at the specific facility, the plan must explain the denial. There have been many cases where a nonapproved facility provided a medically necessary service and was grudgingly covered by the health plan. It can be the smaller liability.

Hospital care is most often today acute care, and denying care may be life-threatening. Lawsuits have been won on the issue of denial of such care. Whether you are self-funded or insured, the impact of such losses will affect you. You need to be wary of limiting inpatient admissions or second-guessing medical professionals who treat your members, and consider carefully any action that might expose your organization to a lawsuit of this type.

What are the reasons for preadmission certification? What purpose does it serve, if most of the time it has to be granted? There are a couple of good reasons to require preadmission certification or approval.

Planning Cash Flow

For the insurance carrier, MCO, and self-funded employer, all of whom are concerned with having enough money on hand to pay claims, it is important to be forewarned when a large claim is about to be filed. Preadmission certification helps to ensure that this planning process occurs. From a planning standpoint, the plan administrator or carrier can evaluate the total expected cost of the claim and earmark it for follow-up. In some cases, the carrier or administrator may include the claim on a management report or notify the employer.

Be sure to communicate any preadmission certification requirement to your plan members on a regular basis so that out-of-pocket penalties can be avoided. The requirement should be printed in plain language on the identification card for the plan, in the plan booklet, and periodically in work-site newsletters, bulletins, or flyers. See Exhibit 5-15 for preadmission certification language suitable for an identification card.

Stop-Loss Impact

When an inpatient or costly service is provided to a member, it is noted for stop-loss or excess insurance purposes. For the health plan, these claims are generally 70 to 80 percent of all claim costs. Since they account for the lion's share of claims dollars, the importance of high-cost claims to the carrier, MCO, or self-funded employer is obvious.

Early identification of high-cost claims is important to control cost for a few reasons. The stop-loss carrier is a company that provides insurance above a certain level to the health plan carrier, MCO, or self-funded employer. When the stop-loss carrier is made aware of large claims ahead of time, it has a greater opportunity to win advance discounts, to help locate needed services at lower cost, and to actively manage claim costs.

Some stop-loss carriers and insurers cover high-cost claims only when services are provided at specific centers or facilities. They have arranged for their own discounts for such

This is a Managed Care Program. For full details, please refer to your Summary Plan Description. You must contact the administrator:

- prior to an elective hospital admission
- within two business days of an emergency or maternity admission
- for a psychiatric inpatient admission, and with submission of a treatment plan within 10 days
- prior to discharge or release from an inpatient stay

If you do not contact the administrator in these instances, penalties will be assessed as follows: your benefits will be reduced by a $300 penalty for no preadmission notification, and $300 for no discharge planning notification. You may not be covered for primary and/or secondary benefits, if you do not fully comply with the plan's managed care requirements.

Name

Telephone Number

Address

of Administrator

EXHIBIT 5-15. Sample language on preadmission certification for an I.D. card. (Source: Halo Associates.)

services. Transplants are a good example. A fuller explanation of stop-loss coverage is provided in Chapter 6.

For mid-sized organizations, you should receive a high-cost claim report of those claims over a set dollar limit—often $5,000 to $10,000. This will alert you to claims that might be covered by your stop-loss coverage, and that might affect your stop-loss premiums. If you are fully insured without stop-loss coverage, you can anticipate premium increases due to high-cost claims. See Exhibit 5-16 for an example of a high-cost claim report.

Advance Discounts for Services

Preadmission certification and high-cost claim identification enable the plan to arrange an advance discount for services. This may take the form of a guaranteed maximum payment amount, or the plan may pay some money up front to the facility in exchange for a discounted rate. Advance discussion between the plan administrator and the facility can clarify coverage limits and alert the facility to any services that may not be covered. The member is also advised so that any out-of-pocket expense can be known ahead of time.

Assignment of Case Management

Early notice of a high-cost procedure or inpatient stay can start wheels in motion that will continue throughout treatment. Most plans will assign a professional to help members or patients use coverage wisely to meet their medical needs. Insurers and MCOs have case management departments; self-insured employers either hire a case management firm or require their third-party administrator to provide such services. Some large self-funded plans have internal case managers who are assigned to provide patient guidance and counseling, as well as to help the patient follow plan guidelines and procedures.

HOSPITAL/MAJOR MEDICAL EXPENSE

Patient Name	ID#	Diagnosis	Prognosis
Carson, D.	12345	CVA (3/91 partial paralysis) Then fell and fractured hip 5/91	Stable—still needs therapy. Charges seem to be decreasing.
Davis, E.	67890	Rheumatoid arthritis spinal cord lesion	Improving—since 4/91 when she had surgery for removal of lesion. Claims have decreased.
Klein, S.	23456	Cystic Fibrosis	Poor—heart & lung transplant has been postponed.
Nelson, T.	56789	Coronary artery disease	Stable—had Quad bypass surgery 5/91. Seems to be doing better.
Rose, B.	78901	Colon Cancer	Poor—condition worsening. Patient on TPN feeding as of 6/91. However Medicare became primary 7/1/91.
Trent, D.	89012	Amyotrophic sclerosis Respiratory failure	Poor—only nursing charges are submitted. No change in frequency. I anticipate the same liability to continue. Major Medical.
Wang, C.	90123	Major depression Substance abuse	Poor—condition appears to be ongoing with no improvement. Anticipate more confinements. Claim paid under Major Medical.
Yale, B.	01234	Heart disease	Stable—had valve replacement 5/91. Condition seems to have stabilized.

EXHIBIT 5-16. Sample high-cost claim report. (Source: Halo Associates.)

OTHER OPTIONS FOR PLAN DESIGN

When in doubt, ask an expert. I am amazed how often a benefits manager or owner will struggle with a decision when good advice is only a phone call or fax away. For instance, if you are self-funded, your administrator should have expertise and provide advisory services to you with regard to plan coverage and services. Ask your health plan adviser or administrator to provide cost projections of contemplated coverage, to suggest language for amendments and contracts, and notices to plan members about coverage and providers. Concepts for plan design, networks, and employee services should be submitted by the administrator, and his or her recommendation on each can give you a broader perspective.

During the third quarter of each plan year, request that the administrator and other advisers, such as a benefits consultant or insurance professional, provide you with their recommendations to improve the service and cost-effectiveness of your health plan. Ask for a description of any proposed or enacted regulations and legal changes that might affect your cost, benefits, and service during the coming year. You will be receiving valuable consulting services at no cost. Exhibit 5-17 presents a model letter to request this input.

Controlling coverage, eligibility and enrollment policies, discounts, networks, and high-cost claims are all important ways to reduce cost and ensure quality care. A primary tool to control the cost of quality care is your employees or plan members. If you enlist the help of members to identify higher-than-expected costs, inappropriate costs, or duplicate billings, you can go a long way toward managing costs.

Ask your employees to review the explanation of benefits (EOB) that is sent to all members when a claim is paid, whether by the plan administrator, insurer, or MCO. You might consider a payment to members who find inaccuracies or overcharges on their EOBs. Some organizations pay the reporting member a percentage of the savings; some simply send a written thank-you to commend them. You should track reported overcharges or inaccuracies. If there are several inaccuracies reported for a certain provider, or if there are consistent inaccuracies, it is time to review whether your health plan and network are effectively managed.

The sentinel effect of your monitoring such errors will keep administrators alert and will also discourage your employees from abusing the plan. If they know that you have a policy to deal with claims errors, they will be less likely to use the plan inappropriately. This organizational approach to your plan is a healthy one for everyone involved and will improve the cost-effectiveness of the benefits plan, giving you more bang for your buck.

SUMMARY

Plan design and medical providers constitute the essence of your health plan. They determine the health care your employees will receive. No matter how careful you are or how hard you work to make your plan meet employee needs, your success in effectively managing the health plan depends on how wisely your employees use it. Encouraging and developing employee appreciation of the health plan and their appropriate use of it are the subject of Chapter 6.

Re: Health Benefit Plan

Dear [*Administrator, Consultant, Broker, Adviser*]:

We are currently reviewing our plan administration services for plan years beginning January 1, 199 . As a result, we write to ask for an update on services that are currently available, and any additional or changed services that are expected to be available beginning in 1998.

You are aware that the referenced plan currently uses _____ as the mail order drug service for about 1,000 employees, retirees and their families. As you know, over the years we have instituted some changes in our plan coverage which have increased the use of the mail order service in an effort to contain cost. With a large number of retirees in our plan, the prescription coverage is important and fully utilized. Our intention is to examine these services in areas such as the following:

- Track record on prompt dispensing and delivery of Rxs
- Customer satisfaction with services
- Utilization of 800# and on-call pharmacist
- Capabilities for drug utilization management and drug utilization review reports, and claims data for our plan
- Service representative and customer services
- Participant communication
- Cost savings capabilities
- Fees and fee structure

We would appreciate your response within the next sixty days on our mail-order drug service. If you have any questions, please do not hesitate to contact me.

Very truly yours,

EXHIBIT 5-17. Sample request for input on plan services. (Source: Halo Associates.)

CHAPTER 6

Financing Your Health Plan

After you select the health plan that you think will best meet the needs of your organization, your primary responsibility is to finance the cost. What kind of costs, relative to other payroll expenses, are we talking about? According to the annual survey conducted by the U.S. Chamber of Commerce, employers paid 41.3 percent of payroll for various employee benefits. The chart in Exhibit 6-1a shows how benefit dollars were spent in 1996, and Exhibit 6-1b presents the cost of various benefits as a percentage of payroll. Nearly one-quarter of the reported costs were for medical benefits including health insurance. It was reported that the amount of money employers spent for health insurance declined from 7.1 percent of payroll to 7.0 percent; at the same time, the share paid by the employee increased from 1.5 percent of payroll to 1.7 percent.

When you consider how you will pay for your organization's health plan, there are two areas to consider—which payment method works for your organization, and your options for shifting costs to other sources. The decisions you make about how to pay for the health plan will take into account the financial ability and benefits philosophy of your organization. You will also consider the expectations of your employees and their ability to pay a share of the cost.

Payment methods for insured and self-insured health plans fall into certain general types. Some of the most common ways to pay for health plan costs are these:

- *Monthly premiums*, paid on an annual, guaranteed basis, in predetermined amounts, for individual, family, and two-person family coverage and, sometimes, for enrollees. The employer's monthly payments are based on the number of individual, family, and other enrollments each month. These premiums might be paid in part or in full by the employer, with some share paid by the employee or covered plan member. If you are insured, the risk of loss for the plan year is the responsibility of the insurance carrier or MCO. If you are self-insured, the risk of loss is yours. The term for monthly costs is premium-equivalent and is projected by your health plan adviser in advance for the year on the basis of actuarial analysis and input. Those who are self-insured wait to project their premium-equivalent until late in the plan year, usually until the third quarter, so that current year costs include as much actual information as possible.
  - *Monthly premiums* paid on a multiyear guaranteed basis as in the preceding paragraph. For an insured plan, the risk of loss for all plan years covered by the agreement is the responsibility of the insurance carrier or MCO.
  - *Retrospective rated* premiums, in which a minimal monthly fee is charged by the carrier, on the basis of enrollment, to cover minimal claims payments, retention, and administrative and other fees. The carrier calculates additional claims cost at year-end

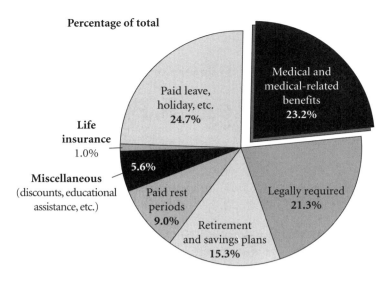

Percentage of total

Medical and medical-related benefits 23.2%

Paid leave, holiday, etc. 24.7%

Life insurance 1.0%

Miscellaneous (discounts, educational assistance, etc.) 5.6%

Paid rest periods 9.0%

Retirement and savings plans 15.3%

Legally required 21.3%

Note: Total exceeds 100% due to rounding.

EXHIBIT 6-1a. Distribution of benefit dollars. (Source: U.S. Chamber of Commerce, *Employee Benefits*, December 1997.)

	1995 (%)	1996 (%)
Legally required payments	8.9	8.8
Retirement and savings	7.5	6.3
Life insurance and death benefits	0.4	0.4
Medical and medical-related benefits	10.5	9.6
Paid rest periods, lunch periods, etc.	2.2	3.7
Payments for vacations, holidays, sick leave, etc.	10.2	10.2
Miscellaneous benefits	2.2	2.3

EXHIBIT 6-1b. Types of benefits, as a percentage of payroll, all employees, 1995 and 1996. (Source: U.S. Chamber of Commerce, *Employee Benefits*, December 1997.)

and collects a lump sum payment of what is due. Often a higher administrative fee is charged for this type of arrangement, and it is available only to stable employer groups with adequate resources.

■ The risk of loss cost is the responsibility of the employer. It can be covered for catastrophic losses by a pooling charge or stop-loss coverage. Administrative and other charges are fixed and paid monthly; when a percentage of claims is the basis for administrative fees, additional fees may be required when the year-end claims cost is available.

■ *Administrative-services-only* (ASO) fees are paid to the administrator to handle claims and provide plan management services, while claims are paid from a fund established by the employer. If funds are needed during the plan year, the employer is required to make them available. The risk of loss is assumed by the employer in exchange for the lower cost of a plan for which no retention or pooling charges are assessed. This financing method is essentially self insurance, although it is administered by an insurance carrier and has the appearance to employees of an insured plan.

- *Minimum premiums* paid as lower monthly premiums during the plan year for an insured plan; a deposit is made up front, at the end, or during the year to make up any gap between the deposit and incurred costs. This payment method is used to match the needs of organizations with variable cash flow. The risk of loss is the responsibility of the carrier or MCO.

- *Self-funded or self-insured* plans, which are established with funds from the employer to cover the cost of claims, administrative fees and services, and all plan needs. Usually a third-party administrator is hired to pay claims and manage the plan; sometimes this is done by an insurance carrier or by the employer's staff. The risk of loss is the responsibility of the employer, who often purchases stop-loss insurance to provide coverage against higher-than-projected losses. Chapter 12 includes a full discussion of the financial advantages and disadvantages of self-funding.

- *Partially self-funded* plans, hybrids in which some part of coverage may be self-funded and the balance fully insured. Hospitalization, for instance, may be insured by a carrier, and major medical coverage self-funded by the employer, while prescription drug coverage is purchased through an association plan. The combinations can vary. In one variation, the employer assumes the risk for part of the cost of each health plan member. For instance, an employer can opt to pay the first $2,000 of claims for each person covered by the plan, less any deductible due from the member. The remaining amount of the member's claims for the year is covered by the insurance carrier at a much reduced premium. The lower premium is the result of two factors—recognition of the risk the employer has opted to assume and the expectation that fewer than 20 percent of employees will submit claims of more than $2,000 during one year.

In this type of variation, the plan administrator or carrier processes and pays all claims and provides plan management services, but the employer reimburses the carrier up to the $2,000 self-insured amount.

■ THE BASIS FOR PREMIUMS

Your health plan cost, whether you are insured or self-insured, is developed from a medical plan trend factor, which can vary from carrier to carrier and among benefit consultants but is usually based on the trend components shown in Exhibit 6-2. Note that inflation, cost shifting, technological advances, utilization, and other key factors are combined for the year by plan type and result in a composite estimate of cost trends year to year. It may seem distant to you, but it is directly tied to the premium increase your insurer proposes. If you are self-insured, it directly affects the premium-equivalent projected by your health plan adviser.

If you are aware of the trend for the coming year, usually forecast four to six months in advance, you can anticipate premium increases and budget for them. Exhibit 6-3 presents a summary developed by the Segal Company of projected and actual health care cost increases, by type of coverage. You can easily compare the projected increases for the coming year to the current, actual trend and, by doing so, anticipate how your health plan selection may relate to costs.

Trend Component	Managed Care (PPO)		Managed Care (PPO with Gatekeeper)		Comprehensive Medical	
	1998	1997	1998	1997	1998	1997
Inflation (increased cost of services)	4.2	4.1	3.4	3.3	5.3	5.5
Leveraging (reduced buying power of plan deductible and coinsurance)	0.5	0.5	0.4	0.3	1	1
Cost shifting (reduced Medicare and Medicaid reimbursements)	1.1	1.2	0.9	1	1.1	1.3
Antiselection (the selection of indemnity coverage primarily by poor risks)	1	0.8	0.5	0.3	0.9	0.8
Technological advances (increasingly costly medical equipment and services)	0.5	0.4	0.3	0.2	0.5	0.6
Social shifts (population aging, AIDS, psychiatric care, and substance abuse)	0.4	0.5	0.2	0.2	0.4	0.4
Utilization (greater use of equipment and services)	1.8	2	1.8	1.7	2.8	2.7
Estimated Trend Factor	9.5	9.5	7.5	7	12	12.3

EXHIBIT 6-2. Sedgwick Noble Lowndes 1998 medical plan trend factor. (Source: Sedgwick Noble Lowndes Health Care Trend—U.S. Survey Results 1998.)

Type of Health Care Coverage	Projected Average Annual Trend, 1998 (%)	Actual Average Annual Trend, 1997 (%)
Medical		
Nonnetwork fee-for-service plan	13.0	10.2
Preferred provider organization	9.4	9.1
Point-of-service plan	6.0	N/A[a]
Health maintenance organization	4.8	−0.6
Dental		
Nonnetwork fee-for-service plan	9.3	5.6
Network fee-for-service plan	6.4	5.9
Prepaid network	3.5	3.7
Prescription Drugs		
Retail	12.7	12.9[b]
Mail order	13.2	

[a]1997 trend for POS plans is not listed because the sample size was not statistically significant.

[b]1997 prescription drug trend was not broken down between retail and mail-order programs.

EXHIBIT 6-3. Average health care costs, 1998 (projected) and 1997 (actual) by type of coverage. (Source: *The Segal Trend Survey, 1998.* Reprinted by permission of The Segal Co., © 1997. All rights reserved.)

Trade publications and other resources are listed in the Appendix to help you research trend projections and cost increases.

No matter how well you negotiate plan services, you should budget for in-house staff and organizational costs. Each of the activities of plan review will require some work by one or more of your employees. Additional costs, such as those for outside legal or consulting services, communication needs, mailing and postage, in-service training for staff and employees, distribution and storage of materials, and staff time spent responding to questions from current and, perhaps, former employees, should be part of your budget projections.

Budgeting is a key activity to manage your health plan effectively. Your ability to budget accurately for health plan costs is dependent on the information you receive and on your periodic and regular review of plan costs. Exhibit 6-4 is an example of a management report on claims cost for a self-funded plan. This report shows the cash flow inherent in claims payment and demonstrates the actual expenditures for services plan members received for the premiums paid. Using reports like this one to monitor and track your plan costs, together with a knowledge of anticipated trend increases, can help keep your budget for health plan costs on target.

When you are conducting a plan review or comparing possible changes to your plan, ask for cost projections for individual options from your health plan adviser, carrier, or administrator, who can also assist you in interpreting the short-term and long-term budget impact of the changes. For example, if you are adding a drug benefit, you should have a separate monthly premium bid that will help you see the projected cost of this new benefit to you and to your employees.

Try to recruit and train your staff with an eye on the internal support needs you expect to have. Your organization will have an obligation to pay for increased payroll and overhead costs for the duration of the plan or administrative contract. Your plan administrator might be able to assist or to reduce some of your costs by providing supplemental services and materials.

■ COST SHIFTING

When costs go up in your health plan, you may suddenly wonder why your organization is paying so much. A logical conclusion is that your employees should pay more. This is certainly the case today. In 1996 the average employee paid $525 toward a managed-care plan, compared to $272 in 1989. Employees with a traditional insured plan also paid more—$499 during 1996, compared to $238 in 1989.

Does cost shifting make sense for your organization? Does it help reduce cost? How do employees and retirees react? Can some costs be shifted easily? How can you shift costs to social programs such as Medicare or Medicaid? What is the role of other coverages, such as a dependent's coverage and a spouse's plan?

Ways to Shift Cost

Lots of questions; time for some answers. There are three basic ways to shift cost: having employees pay more, passing along costs to other programs, such as Medicare or other health plans, and requiring that medical providers absorb some cost. Despite their attractiveness in the short term, these alternatives don't really lower cost; they change only who pays.

Employees Health Benefit Plan—Financial Report 1997

Coverage	Annual Budget		January	February	March	April	May	June	Actual Expenditures July	August	September	October	November December	Total Actual	Balance	1997 Actual Average
Hospital	$ 995,909.28		$ 80,478.04	$ 68,536.23	$ 60,271.89	$ 63,196.27	$ 61,573.19	$ 83,964.20	$146,687.78	$135,366.19	$ 10,484.74	$44,634.46	$ 99,750.01	$ 854,943.00	$140,966.28	$ 71,245.25
Major Med	1,169,521.92		78,114.00	63,940.55	128,668.93	156,333.33	178,181.55	134,450.12	118,832.14	105,903.76	175,877.08	(42,868.63)	77,230.17	1,174,663.00	(5,141.08)	97,888.58
Drugs	412,620.48		48,337.82	43,606.52	31,500.43	27,098.79	54,101.07	42,052.57	31,427.24	36,843.44	42,311.01	16,490.05	51,176.06	424,945.00	(12,324.52)	35,412.08
PCS			28,674.65	16,414.68	16,574.54	16,924.50	14,451.43	22,583.85	14,727.64	14,717.73	15,841.16	16,442.07	41,112.75	218,465.00		18,205.42
Mail			19,663.17	27,191.84	14,925.89	10,174.29	39,649.64	19,468.72	16,699.60	22,125.71	26,469.85	47.98	1,062.31	197,479.00		16,456.58
Totals	$2,578,051.68		$206,929.86	$176,083.30	$220,441.25	$246,628.39	$293,855.81	$260,466.89	$296,947.16	$278,113.39	$228,672.83	$18,255.88	$228,156.24	$2,454,551.92	$123,500.68	$204,545.92
Percentage of Total Budget			8.03%	6.83%	8.55%	10.51%	12.52%	11.10%	12.65%	11.85%	9.74%	0.78%	9.72%	95.21%	4.79%	

Employees Health Benefit Plan—Financial Report 1998

Coverage	Annual Budget	January	February	March	April	May	June	Actual Expenditures July	August	September	October	November	December	Total Actual	Balance	1998 YTD Average
Hospital	$1,063,083.06	$176,724.11	$ 71,050.91	$116,529.60	$159,520.94	$119,264.70	$ 47,204.98	$103,156.28	$ 50,649.41	$ 80,957.26	$ 46,002.26			$ 971,060.45	$ 92,022.61	$ 97,106
Major Med	1,314,865.89	266,595.12	105,952.45	159,105.54	107,520.03	104,501.97	86,861.83	106,337.24	76,114.97	88,412.74	64,870.96			1,166,272.85	148,593.04	116,627
Drugs	419,638.05	78,110.80	51,735.75	35,642.06	39,961.01	43,643.61	35,472.78	55,418.02	38,042.83	37,536.19	29,025.46			444,588.51	(24,950.46)	44,459
PCS		8,602.15	16,199.10	16,414.76	16,464.18	15,499.32	22,572.36	16,989.57	15,894.86	14,858.23	16,377.44			159,871.97		15,987
Mail		69,508.65	35,536.65	19,227.30	23,496.83	28,144.29	12,900.42	38,428.45	22,147.97	22,677.96	12,648.02			284,716.54		28,472
Totals	$2,797,587.00	$521,430.03	$228,739.11	$311,277.20	$307,001.98	$267,410.28	$169,539.59	$264,911.54	$164,807.21	$206,906.19	$139,898.68	$0.00		$2,581,921.81	$215,665.19	$258,192
Percentage of Total Budget		18.64%	8.18%	11.13%	10.97%	9.56%	6.06%	9.47%	5.89%	7.40%	5.00%			92.29%	7.71%	

EXHIBIT 6-4. Two-year claims cost for a self-funded plan. (Source: Halo Associates.)

The simplest and most widely used cost shift for health plans is from the employer to the employee. It's generally done at a time when employee contracts are negotiated or when there is a cost increase that causes management to assess the organization's philosophy and goals for the employee health plan. In other words, cost is shifted to employees during times of necessity. Employee contribution levels are also established when the health plan is first designed.

How has this affected employee costs in recent years? A recently published Towers Perrin study concludes that the average employee paid about $408 annually in 1998 for employee-only medical coverage, and $1,284 annually for family coverage. Retirees younger than age 65 contributed $912 annually, while Medicare-eligible retirees contributed $540. According to an analysis of national spending trends published in *Health Affairs* (January-February 1998) by Katharine R. Levit, between 1990 and 1996 there was a cost shift of $3.6 billion to employees enrolled in employer-sponsored health plans. In another report on cost shifting, published in *Medical Benefits* (April 15, 1998), Gail Shearer notes that one of eight Americans spends more than 10 percent of his or her income on premiums and out-of-pocket costs for health insurance. She also concludes that employer contributions to health plans reduced wages about 5.5 percent for families in the $30,000–$40,000 income bracket. Hidden and direct costs for health plan coverage are being passed along to employees.

Some employers believe that family coverage is a luxury and begin to limit who can have family coverage by restricting eligibility. Examples of these attitudes are given in a May 1997 Issue Brief from the Employee Benefits Research Institute, which reported that dependent coverage declined from 35.4 percent in 1987 to 31.1 percent in 1995.

Still other employers expect employees to pay for some or all of the rising costs through increased contributions. Cost shifting to employees is held by many to be the reason for the erosion of enrollment in employer-sponsored health plans during the past ten years.

Employees nearly always react in the negative to the idea of cost shifting. After all, who wants to pay more for something that is, for most employees, intangible? Despite the recent focus on health benefits, the average employee doesn't pay much attention until he or she needs health services. On average, about half of most employees use their health plan each year. Only about 20 percent of plan members incur sizable health claims in a year. As a consequence, most employees resent increased contributions and feel as if they aren't getting their money's worth.

The cost of health insurance has increased three times faster than inflation during the past ten years. Because wage increases are usually related to the inflation index, wages don't keep up with rising health plan costs, and employees are likely to press for higher wages when asked to pay increased health plan contributions. This situation mirrors a basic spiral of inflation, in a microcosm.

Cost shifting has ramifications for utilization, and therefore ultimate cost. There is growing evidence that employees who pay high deductibles and copayments tend to shy away from seeking health care services until they are sicker than those with lower deductibles and copayments. Delayed treatment usually increases cost, because the plan member needs more extensive health services. As a result, higher deductibles and copayments can mean higher cost claims. In a fully insured plan, the carrier or MCO is the loser from delayed treatment, while in a self-funded plan it is the employer.

What happens to utilization when the employee's share of cost is increased? When the premium contribution is increased, there is some indication that increased utilization occurs as employees feel they want to "get what they are paying for." Increased contribution can also lead to lower employee satisfaction with the health plan and to a rise in complaints over the way plan benefits are provided, paid, and reported when employees feel that the premium contribution is unfair. Exhibit 6-5 presents recent developments in employer-to-employee cost shifting among retirees. The initiatives described include increased cost to the retiree in the form of higher deductibles, copayments, and contributions to premium, although other measures include moving the retiree to a lower cost plan and discontinuing retiree coverage.

What happens to enrollment in a health plan when employees are asked to pay more? A study by the AFL-CIO with the Lewin Group demonstrates that rising employee premium contributions account for 76.4 percent of workers who have lost employer-sponsored health coverage. Although, according to the Centers for Disease Control and Prevention, 83 percent of employees work for employers who offer health insurance, only 68 percent are eligible for the health plan, and only 58 percent enroll in it. (These figures are for employees of the 52 percent of employers who offer health plans to employees.) Cost shifting is a major factor in low enrollment among health plans and in the decline of employer-sponsored health plans.

Employees may resent but are less likely to openly oppose indirect cost shifting. This happens when there is a change in plan design or benefits that limits coverage. Some examples are the maximums established on certain benefits—chiropractic visits, outpatient psychiatric counseling, specialist visits or testing. Other plan provisions that shift cost indirectly are annual or lifetime maximums on total benefits paid and longer waiting periods for eligibility. Indirect cost shifting has less opposition than direct cost shifting, because it affects only those who need medical services.

Cost-Saving Measure	Implemented 1994–1997 (%)	Planned for 1998 (%)
Increase retiree contribution	21.3	10.2
Offer Medicare HMO option	17.1	7.9
Implement managed-care review procedures	17.0	3.5
Establish separate prescription drug plan	13.9	3.6
Increase deductible	11.3	3.0
Change eligibility requirements	11.0	4.4
Increase out-of-pocket maximum	10.9	2.2
Change plan integration with Medicare	9.5	2.2
Change to defined contribution or fixed-dollar plan	6.6	2.7
Decrease benefits	2.2	1.8
Switch to "Medigap" policy	2.1	2.2

EXHIBIT 6-5. Prevalence of organizations implementing retiree medical benefits cost-saving measure. (Source: Watson Wyatt Data Services, June 25, 1998.)

Plan Type	Employee-Only Coverage	Employee Plus One Coverage	Full-Family Coverage
HMO	$151	$300	$422
PPO	175	344	468
POS	161	334	454
Indemnity	177	345	484

EXHIBIT 6-6. Employer health care contributions (monthly), by plan and coverage type. (Source: *1998 Employee Survey on Managed Care,* Deloitte & Touche LLP, April 21, 1998.)

Another common way to shift costs to employees indirectly is to offer a lower level of benefits. This happens when you change health plans from a richer indemnity plan to a basic coverage HMO, or from a comprehensive coverage HMO to a restrictive PPO. Lower benefits mean lower costs to the employer but are likely to result in higher cost to employees when they require health care services. Exhibit 6-6 shows the different monthly costs for four basic plan types, with HMOs, the most restrictive model, being the least expensive. You need to carefully evaluate employee response to such changes and the financial impact to your organization if plan changes trigger wage demands, increase turnover, make employee recruitment difficult, or affect employee relations.

From Employer Plans to Other Programs

Typical cost shifts to other programs pass costs along to social programs such as Medicare and Medicaid and to other health plans from which the employee has coverage. The largest public health plan is Medicare, which pays for health claims of the elderly, the disabled, and those with end-stage renal disease.

Some employers adopt an attitude that Medicare provides adequate coverage for retirees, so they reduce or eliminate retiree benefits. You will want to have your staff aware of the timetable for disabled employees to enroll in Medicare, whether you provide retiree coverage or not, to encourage prompt use of the program. Chapter 10 on legislation describes Medicare notices and enrollment.

Other types of social or public programs include Medicaid, which provides coverage for some chronic conditions and for the poor; Child Health Plus, a national program, which covers children to age eighteen; state and local health service programs; and various non-profit services provided by local organizations and some hospitals and health centers.

For example, some of the benefits and services provided by the federal Children's Health Insurance Program (CHIP) initiated January 1, 1998, are hospital services, doctor visits, emergency and preventive services such as immunizations, dental care, speech and hearing services, vision care, mental health and substance abuse care, durable medical equipment, and wheelchairs. Funding for this program comes from federal taxes and provides $24 billion nationally for eligible children. Each state is responsible for developing its own program; New York State spends $256 million of federal funds, matched by an additional 15 percent from state tax dollars, to provide services tailored to meet the needs of the state's underinsured children. Your employees, especially if they are lower paid, may be eligible for free medical care for children or to have coverage for children under age 18 for a minimal contribution. It's expected that by the year 2001 families with incomes of about $41,000 will be able to purchase this coverage for children under age 18 years for $15 per month, with a maximum payment of $45 per month per family. There may be variations from state to state under the program.

Other programs can supplement your health plan for employees and may be of special value if you employ lower-paid workers. It is often desirable to use local public or non-profit programs for lower-cost health services, including flu shots, psychiatric counseling, well-child care, elder care, child care, diagnosis of learning disabilities or physical and mental handicaps, rehabilitation, and physical examinations. Your county health department can provide you with a listing of such services and where to access them. Your employees will appreciate the effort when you alert them to low-cost local services that are convenient and offer high quality.

Another large public program is Workers Compensation, required by state law and provided by insurance carriers, various pools, and directly by employers who self-fund. The purpose of Workers Compensation is to pay for work-related injury—both wage replacement and medical services. Its goal is to encourage a return to work; often rehabilitation and work-hardening services that help the injured worker with physical conditioning, training, and counseling support are part of treatment. Some coordination between Workers Compensation and your health plan is appropriate, especially since medical services for work-related injury are paid at a lower cost on a restricted sliding, established-fee schedule. You want to be sure your health plan is not billed for Workers Compensation medical services.

Cost shifting to other plans occurs when you decide to cover only the retiree and not any family members. Exhibit 6-7 shows the relative cost of individual and family coverage for all types of plans and by size of company for 1996. It is interesting to note that there is no monthly cost given for retiree family coverage. In a survey of the fifty largest U.S. companies in 1994, the Wyatt Company found that more than half restricted retiree coverage by establishing restrictions based on age, service, and date of hire or retirement. Forty-seven of these companies required retiree contributions to the health plan. Changes reported by these companies from the preceding year included higher retiree contribution rates, higher deductibles, higher coinsurance amounts, and other limiting plan design changes.

An earlier study on retirees by KPMG Peat Marwick, reported in the May 1993 issue of *Healthcare Trends Report,* noted the greatest decline in retiree benefits occurred in companies with between 200 and 999 employees. Only 37 percent of such companies offered retiree benefits in 1992, compared to 44 percent the year before. Only 52 percent of employers with 1,000 to 4,999 employees offered retiree benefits, down from 56 percent a year earlier. During 1992 only 49 percent of workers were promised retiree benefits, compared to 66 percent of workers a decade earlier.

This trend is likely to continue for several reasons. One major impact on retiree benefits was the 1990 Federal Accounting Standards Board Statement No. 106. This regulation dramatically changed the way most private companies account for their retiree health benefits. It requires that retiree benefits be recognized explicitly on balance sheets as a liability, which directly affects the bottom line of the financial statement and can affect the company's ability to borrow, as well as the financial picture of the organization.

Some companies dropped retiree health benefits in response to this regulation; others drastically cut back on the benefits provided or changed to a defined contribution plan, in which they pay a specified monthly amount regardless of the cost of coverage (many employers cut back to reimbursing the Medicare Part B premium).

	500 or Fewer	501– 1,000	1,001– 5,000	5,001– 10,000	10,001 or More
Medical Funding					
Self-insured and self-administered	3%	8%	8%	8%	13%
Self-insured and third party administered	32%	50%	57%	72%	61%
Minimum premium	8%	8%	6%	—	3%
Fully insured	52%	30%	22%	11%	12%
Combination	5%	6%	10%	9%	11%
Medical (prevalent plan)					
Employee coverage	$184.12	$175.59	$174.92	$171.69	$165.17
Family coverage	$491.01	$470.88	$478.89	$480.91	$446.86
Fee-for-service					
Employee coverage	$199.99	$197.42	$196.39	$171.00	$169.51
Family coverage	$897.35	$522.55	$549.65	$503.31	$448.06
PPO					
Employee coverage	$189.04	$181.74	$181.02	$177.73	$165.68
Family coverage	$491.09	$484.14	$499.97	$484.85	$461.79
HMO					
Employee coverage	$161.28	$165.97	$156.02	$160.10	$187.26
Family coverage	$441.82	$444.25	$438.13	$443.39	$438.95
POS					
Employee coverage	$189.17	$161.60	$176.80	$161.61	$177.00
Family coverage	$520.01	$483.77	$435.41	$486.50	$488.09
Retiree Medical (Age 65 or Over)					
Employee coverage	$197.56	$134.00	$145.01	$121.78	$159.02

EXHIBIT 6-7. Medical plan funding prevalence and average premium cost, by size of company. (Source: *Hay/Huggins Benefits Report,* 1998.)

Other factors in declining retiree family coverage include the increase of women in the workforce. In 1960 only 30.5 percent of married women worked; by 1993 that number jumped to 59.4 percent, according to the Employee Benefit Research Institute. Today, in most families, both spouses work and have independent health coverage. Hence, when one spouse retires, the other may have family coverage as an active employee that provides the retiree with medical coverage before Medicare benefits apply.

There are also fewer family households today—71 percent in 1993 compared to 85 percent in 1960—and so, arguably, there is less need for retiree family coverage with the growth of single-member households.

One way to transfer cost to some retirees more than others is to institute a tier system of retiree benefits. Your program might be based on a combination of length of service and wages, weighted to benefit those who work longer at lower salaries, for example. Exhibit 6-8 shows you an example of a tiered contribution for retirees. It includes a formula to balance the retiree costs for older workers who retire sooner, with a point system that considers age, service, and wages.

When you review your retiree health plan policy, consider the average age of your employees, and evaluate demographic data to help you objectively assess your alternatives.

(a) Employees who retire shall have the option to elect contributory health insurance coverage based on the following schedule:

Service Credit Years	Share of Coverage Individual	Dependent
10–14 years	50%	35%
15–19 years	60%	45%
20–24 years	70%	55%
25 years or more	80%	65%

(b) Surviving spouses receiving health insurance coverage through a retired Employee as described above shall have the option to continue either individual or dependent health insurance coverage on a contributory basis. The company will pay 50% toward the cost of individual coverage. The surviving spouse shall pay the balance of the individual coverage premium cost. In the event the surviving spouse elects dependent coverage, the surviving spouse shall be responsible for the total cost of dependent coverage.

EXHIBIT 6-8. Sample tiered retiree benefit schedule. (Source: Halo Associates.)

Do you have a large number of employees in a specific age cohort—age 30 to 40, age 40 to 50, or above age 55? Consider the average income, employment status, and longevity of your employees, and the impact on these of their ethnicity, educational level, and citizenship. Think about the percentage of your employees who will retire in the coming decades. The accounting regulation that requires you to include the liability of retiree health premiums and other benefits on your balance sheet may also have an impact on your decision. You will want to check with your tax adviser to project the impact of retiree coverage on your organization.

A major employee relations concern is how your health plan treatment of retirees will affect the morale of active employees, especially those facing retirement in ten or twenty years, or sooner.

■ ADMINISTRATIVE CHARGES

If yours is a very small organization (two to fifty employees), the administrative fees for your health insurance are built into your premium and are also included if you purchase coverage from a pool or association plan. You can identify the amount of and the basis for administrative charges by asking for a premium illustration and by requesting a breakdown of costs from the plan, pool, or association administrator. Reports on pool or association administrative costs and plan premiums and costs for the past three years should be readily available for your review before you decide on a health plan.

If you are a larger employer, chart the cost of your claims for the past three years, if the data are available to you, and list the administrative fees and charges. The ratio of claims paid to administrative costs should remain fairly constant, no matter how your administrative charges are developed. A rule of thumb is to keep total plan administrative expenses to a range of 4 to 6 percent of claims cost. Negotiate a base annual fee to give the administrator a guarantee and to ensure specific, more limited services that are most essential. This arrangement for administrative fees may result in a lower payment than other methods.

There are several common methods of charging for administrative services. Claims cost, administrative charges, and other fees are projected separately by claims administrators. If your organization has between fifty and 5,000 employees, you will have a greater opportunity to consider options for your fee basis. Charges usually take the form of one of these:

- Per-member-per-month charges (capitation)
- A percentage of claims
- A base administrative annual fee with contractual additions for optional services
- Performance-based fees
- Pooled or group purchase fees

Fees per Member per Month

This type of fee depends on the number of members in the plan. Such fees can vary widely. An annual edition of *Business Insurance* magazine reports and updates the services, and fees charged by third party administrators (TPAs) who in 1998 were reported to typically charge between five dollars and fifteen dollars per member per month (PMPM) or per employee per month (PEPM). Fees might range up to thirty-five dollars, PMPM, depending on the services provided, the size of the employer group, and the location of the administrator.

Smaller plans are likely to have higher fees per member, and larger plans will have lower fees, simply because of the economy of scale that occurs when an administrator can spread certain overhead costs across a larger group. For a comprehensive health plan, these fees might be broken down for specific coverages or services. For example, the administrative fee for dental benefits, for the drug plan, for discounted network access, for COBRA administration, and for the major medical/hospitalization coverage might be separately quoted for each plan member per month.

Be sure to review the carrier's breakdown of fees and charges and to retain your right to accept any part or all of a submitted service proposal. You can require multiyear fee guarantees with the right to contract annually. This puts you in the driver's seat and keeps the administration firm on their toes.

Percentage of Claims

Administrative fees based on volume of claims are related to the total dollar amount of claims paid. This arrangement can have the advantage of keeping administrative costs low, if claims cost is low for the year. The theory is that if fewer and lower-cost claims are filed by your employees (e.g., if you have a younger, healthier workforce), the administrative charges ought to reflect the low volume and reduced workload.

On the other hand, there is little incentive for the administrator to help keep costs down when the fee is based on claim dollars spent. The method of determining the cost of claims, including the time period to be covered, should be established in a clear contract. You should negotiate a flat percentage to be paid monthly throughout the year, subject to a maximum dollar amount.

For plans in which you assume risk, such as self-funded, ASO, or minimum premium, you will want to establish a capped maximum administrative fee. It is calculated when the plan year is over based on claims that are outstanding. You will also benefit if you establish a cut-off date by which claims should be paid and after which you will not be liable for additional administrative fees. A multiyear agreement might be easier to budget and enable you to negotiate a lower percentage fee.

You should also negotiate a reduction in the administrative fee for high-cost claims. Claims adjudication for claims over $5,000 should be paid at a lower rate than lower-cost claims. Not only is there proportionately less work for one claim of $5,000 than for ten claims of $500, but the higher cost claim may be assigned for negotiation and monitoring by a case management firm. You should require that the administrator conduct concurrent review on such claims, and you should consider a periodic retrospective audit of these claims and their associated administrative fees.

If you seek these safeguards in a percentage-based arrangement, the administrator will realize that it is a two-way street, that you are entitled to pay less when services are provided at a lower level or contracted to a case management firm. With regard to the audit, the administrator should welcome the opportunity to demonstrate valuable services rendered and to have an independent validation of administrative fees.

Base Annual Fee With Additions

Your premium or administrative fee may be a lump sum payment for a specific set of services for one year, regardless of fluctuations in your plan enrollment. If you add or delete few members, the administrative burden of tracking changes in enrollment may be more costly than it is worth. This may be an option if you have little turnover and no planned growth or downsizing during the year. The administrator has a guarantee for certain income for the year in exchange for explicit services. From your point of view, it is easy to budget and eliminates cost fluctuations.

Optional services will be spelled out for you so that you are able to select those you feel are needed and eliminate those that you feel won't add value to your health plan. You may find that optional services are not essential to your plan's operation.

Performance-Based Fees

Administrators are increasingly expected to reduce claims cost and to improve the plan's efficiency. Performance-based fees may provide a minimum level of monthly fee for administrative services, with an incentive for better-than-average performance, compared to that in previous years. The advantage of this type of arrangement for the administrator is that it ensures a stable fee, with the possibility of bonuses if there is demonstrable efficiency or cost-effectiveness.

Performance Standards and Cost

Health plan premiums for similar companies can vary up to 20 percent, and lower costs are usually connected to effective negotiation. One of the ways to be sure you receive quality plan management and administration services, regardless of the method used to pay premiums, is to incorporate performance standards in your health plan contracts. Exhibit 6-9 presents the most commonly used performance standards. According to a recent Deloitte & Touche LLP report, fewer than half (41.9 percent) of employers currently use performance standards in their contracts with health plans, and fewer than 18 percent include performance guarantees. This report casts a dismal

	Percent with Performance Standard	Percent Putting Fees/Premiums at Risk
Claim turnaround time	83.5	46.9
Claim financial accuracy	68.8	45.1
Phone response and abandonment rates	59.7	34.9
Claim coding accuracy	50.6	33.1
ID card distribution	36.9	15.4
Access to care	33.5	7.4
Network access	30.7	7.4
Provision of cost and utilization reports	30.7	11.4
Grievance resolution	29.5	5.1
Timeliness of written responses	24.4	8.6
Plan information/certificate distribution	22.2	5.7
HEDIS quality of care	16.5	2.3
Provider credentialing	11.9	2.3
Provider turnover rate	10.2	4.0
Other	10.2	9.1

EXHIBIT 6-9. Prevalence of use of performance standards. (Source: *1998 Employee Survey on Managed Care,* Deloitte & Touche LLP, April 21, 1998.)

picture on the proficiency of health plan purchasers. Why not require that your plan administrator meet industry standards?

Easier said than done. The mystery of health plan management seems to elude most decision makers, who focus on cost, access to care, satisfaction, and degree of choice as their primary concerns. The nuts and bolts of administration include how claims are paid, whether reports are useful, and whether providers are happy with the plan. These bottom-line issues are often left out of the monitoring process. Indeed, the report found that fewer than half the employers covered by the report monitored quality of care.

Let's take the mystery out of it. Simply put, you are entitled to prompt, accurate claims services and satisfactory telephone service and printed materials, including reports. You should receive assurances of network access, quality of care, and consistency of services. These are typical performance standards that can make your health plan meet the needs of your employees. Absent these standards, or absent your discussion of these standards with health plan administrators, you will find yourself fixing problems throughout the year that should be addressed when you negotiate fees at contract time.

Your contract can require, for instance, a turnaround time of ten working days or less on 75 percent of claims or more. If you add such a clause, you will need to have the measurement process and methodology in place and agreed to by your plan administrator. For instance, you might specify quarterly audits by an objective third party. You can require an error rate, subject to periodic audit, of 1 percent or less on claims adjudication. Or you can require network access to a specified number of specialists and primary care physicians or access to certain hospitals and facilities. The details of the performance standard are based upon negotiation with your plan administrator and relate to the services and plan provisions most important to your organization.

Financial incentives can take the form of withholds pending audit results, reimbursements, reduced per capita administrative fees, or retrospective rebates.

Performance-Based Incentives

If you want a new program or expanded services for your plan, you should explore a contract that links performance to fees. You can try new things, such as health decision support, disease management, or a provider discount program with a performance-based fee arrangement, which requires that your plan adviser or administrator be willing to risk added effort in exchange for the possibility of additional fees. This is often useful when the new service or specific goal is not a standard in the industry. As an unproved commodity, it is hard to know its value to your plan.

You should cap the performance-based fee, within reason, so that you don't find yourself responsible for an exorbitant fee that is hard to justify.

As with any contract issues, you should consult with your health plan adviser and legal counsel. Discuss the need for performance standards in your contract with these professionals to learn about acceptable industry standards and the legalities involved.

Pooled and Group Purchasing

Smaller and mid-sized employers who cannot self-fund health benefits without serious risk to their organizations might take advantage of pools and group purchased plans. In a pool, membership is determined through the underwriting process. If your organization is a good risk, with losses lower than premiums, you will be a welcome addition. The rules and administration of a pool are often liberal and consumer oriented, with many pools established to keep administrative cost low and quality of services and benefits high. The advantage to your organization is clear; the disadvantage is your reliance on the pool to operate fairly, cost-effectively, and reliably.

Group purchasing plans may be industry association plans open to your organization or regional plans that allow you to take advantage of negotiated discounts with administrators.

Both of these types of administrative plans allow your organization to take advantage of the Law of Large Numbers, no matter how small you are. The lower cost enjoyed by joining with a larger group can be an important factor in the health plan you provide.

You can start with this checklist of pooling issues to consider:

- How long the pool or group purchasing plan has been in existence?
- What premiums and expenses has the plan had over the past three years?
- Do published financial reports show stability, growth, or membership fluctuations?
- Have there been documented problems with benefits or services?
- Are there different rates for pool or group members, and, if so, on what basis?
- Are advance discounts or retrospective credits available, and how are they earned?
- Is there a lower-cost administrative option?

You should check references from other organizations that are part of the pooled or association plan. The best references are those from organizations about the same size as yours, perhaps in the same geographic region and in a similar industry. Find out how long the reference has been a member of the health plan, and how it became a member.

■ SELF-FUNDED AND ASO PLANS

Administrative fees paid to a third party administrator or carrier, if your organization is large enough to self-fund, are highly negotiable. There are some fees and charges for services that would be included in a general premium if you were insured. The amount of administrative cost is greatly reduced if you are self-funded or if you purchase administrative services only from a carrier. To be able to do so, you are likely to be a larger employer with stable financial resources. Financing your plan, if you are self-insured, is covered in greater detail in Chapter 12.

In the ASO or Administrative Services Only contract, offered by an insurance carrier, the risk is held by the employer and the carrier is paid only to administer the plan. Both of these types of plans require closer monitoring of plan costs by your organization. An example of a comparison of office visit charges, monitored by a self-funded employer, is shown in Exhibit 6-10.

Re: Office Visit Charges vs UCR payments

I thought it would be helpful regarding our work on the referenced matter, as delegated to us during negotiations, to have the following cost comparison information:

Office Visit CPT Code	Average Charge	Empire Allowance	Medicare Allowance	Area HMO
99201	$ 75.00	$ 35.00	$ 33.05	*
99202	85.00	45.00	51.17	55.00
99203	110.00	57.00	69.60	65.00
99204	150.00	62.00	103.78	85.00
99205	200.00	70.00	129.03	130.00
99211	$ 55.00	27.00	15.99	35.00
99212	70.00	33.00	27.87	45.00
99213	85.00	39.00	39.29	55.00
99214	100.00	46.00	59.92	65.00
99215	150.00	54.00	94.72	*

This provides a comparison for a range of office visit codes that are included under your provision for office visit charges. The codes may vary when billed by a doctor within these categories, depending on the level of service rendered. The average charge is based upon Mid Hudson Valley average of UCR, and the area HMO rate average.

The above may also be useful for a comparison of our POS payments compared to the Empire allowance and HMO payment schedules. Please give me a call with any question you may have on this matter.

EXHIBIT 6-10. Comparison of local office visit charges to UCR. (Source: Halo Associates.)

Stop-Loss Coverage

Stop-loss coverage is referred to by some insurance professionals as "sleep insurance," because you can sleep easier when you have it. In essence, it comes in two varieties—aggregate and specific. Aggregate stop-loss simply means that your entire health plan would have to exceed a certain dollar amount for the year, usually 125 percent of the expected costs, in order for you to collect. Then, you might collect up to a specified amount, or excess layer. Your premium-equivalent would be based on the expected claims or losses for the year, which is then apportioned for individual and family enrollments in your plan on a monthly basis. Aggregate stop-loss would pay once you exceeded, as a plan, the amount projected for annual losses plus 25 percent. If your plan was budgeted for $5 million in losses, aggregate stop-loss would begin to pay once claims rose above $6 million. Normally, it would cover only claims from $6 million to a set amount—perhaps $7.5 million. The more coverage you wanted, the higher your stop-loss premium would be.

Specific stop-loss coverage pertains to the individual members' claims. If you set a dollar amount of $50,000 specific stop-loss, for instance, you would collect each time a member's costs exceeded $50,000, up to a maximum (e.g., $100,000). The $50,000 is called your attachment point; the lower it is, the higher your premium will be. That's logical, because the lower your attachment point, the more likely you will collect.

My opinion of stop-loss coverage is pretty definite. Unless you believe your employees as a whole will be subjected to a major health risk, aggregate stop-loss is a useless expense. When you do collect, the stop-loss carrier raises your premium so you can't afford to continue to purchase it.

As far as specific stop-loss goes, it can be useful for the employer with fewer than 5,000 employees. If your employees have had good claims experience and are not at high risk due to age, gender, or other factors, you will be able to purchase specific stop-loss at a reasonable attachment point and at reasonable cost. It is more likely that you will collect from this type of insurance and that it will serve the purpose of safeguarding your organization from catastrophic loss due to several high-cost claims. Typical claims of concern are transplant claims, some cancer treatments, high cost multiple surgery, complex chronic conditions, and the birth of premature infants. You probably recognize some of the health risks and conditions mentioned. They are more and more common as diagnosis and treatment become more sophisticated.

High-cost claim reports and actively-at-work provisions come into play with stop-loss insurance. The stop-loss carrier requires that it review any claims over a certain dollar amount, usually $5,000 to $10,000. To reduce its losses, the carrier might intervene to negotiate lower cost services or to provide case management to lower costs for those claims. Its motive is to reduce the total cost of such claims and, thereby, its expense. Actively-at-work provisions ensure that the stop-loss carrier isn't covering a plan member who may be out of work due to a catastrophic or chronic condition when coverage begins.

Some words of warning about this type of coverage are in order, despite its purpose for self funded plans in smaller organizations. Commissions for stop-loss insurance are paid to your broker or agent, and are traditionally as high as 20 to 35 percent of the premium. Consequently, your insurance professional is well rewarded for writing this policy. In addition, when stop-loss coverage is bid on renewal, the underwriter takes into account any high-cost claims you have reported or experienced. It is not uncommon to have specific members who have high-cost conditions "carved out" from the bid. Finally, it is common for stop-loss to be quoted on a twelve-month/twelve-month basis. This means that you are covered for claims incurred and reported during a twelve-month period only. Some stop-loss carriers offer a twelve-month/fifteen-month policy where claims may be incurred during twelve months but reported or submitted for payment for up to fifteen months. You should realize that high-cost claims often take months to manifest themselves, as specialists are seen and diagnoses are confirmed. It can also take months to arrange for some surgeries and treatments. In the case of transplant patients, it may take years for surgery to occur. The twelve-month/twelve-month stop-loss policy and the industry standard of "carving out" means you will probably not collect on the highly complex catastrophic claims that take time to identify and treat.

You should remember, however, that stop-loss insurance is widely accepted, sold, and valued by many small and mid-sized organizations that are partially or fully self-funded. Larger organizations are more likely to develop a surplus or reserve from their self-funded plan that acts as a stop-loss fund for their occasional excess losses.

Where is stop-loss purchased? It is sold, subject to state law, by carriers who specialize in it. An analysis of your demographics, claims history, and organizational stability is conducted by the broker or carrier before you are provided with a bid for stop-loss insurance. The stop-loss carrier evaluates complex underwriting and actuarial projections of your anticipated losses before submitting a bid or agreeing to provide coverage. One of my insurance colleagues likened this aspect of the insurance business to a "crap shoot." It seems an apt comparison.

Self-funding is the assumption of risk. The degree to which you can assume risk, and the comfort level of your organization with risk, can be supplemented by the excess risk the stop-loss carrier assumes. The premiums are highly competitive, so you will need to get several bids from insurance brokers or agents who will shop the stop-loss market for you.

■ SUMMARY

At this point, you may have an idea, based on your size or organizational needs, about the health care financing choices that are best suited to you. Managing cost alone is not enough, however. Your health plan management includes cost, medical and member services, and employee satisfaction. The next two chapters discuss how you can improve employee satisfaction through communication and with work-site wellness and patient advocacy programs.

CHAPTER 7

Employee Communication and Cooperation

How should you communicate with employees about your health plan and answer their questions about it? What are you required by law to communicate? In what ways can you prepare for your communication needs? How can you best remind and encourage employees to use the health plan wisely? Is it possible, through employee communication, to measure how well the plan is used? Answers to these and other questions are important for effective management of your health plan.

The beginning, middle, and end of your health plan has to do with your employees, and possibly your retirees. Your organization's concern for employees and its commitment to their health and well-being should be clearly expressed in regular communications about the health plan. You should distribute consistent health plan information that is accurate. After all, employees rely upon you to advise them about the health plan and its procedures and services. This responsibility is a serious one that can directly affect how employees view the health plan and whether or not they value it.

Some communications about your health plan are not an option but are required by federal and state laws and often by employee contracts. Any violation of law or a contract is obviously not good business or good employee relations.

Most states regulate health plans that are also approved by them. These include fully insured plans that you purchase from a carrier or MCO. Any communication mandates by the state will have been met by the insurer prior to gaining state approval. State law doesn't regulate self-funded plans, which are subject to federal law. If your plan is self-funded, you will have to meet the ERISA (Employee Retirement Income Security Act) standards and other federal requirements for communication. During your selection of a plan administrator, you should confirm and state in your contract that the administrator is responsible for compliance with federal requirements. Exhibit 7-1 presents sample contract language on communications.

■ COMMUNICATIONS REQUIRED BY FEDERAL LAW

Federal law requires that employees receive specific information about their health plan. Several federal laws and their mandates are described here.

1. **ERISA.** The Employee Retirement Income Security Act of 1974 is landmark legislation that applies to employer-sponsored health plans. It established the current requirements that an employer disclose and report certain health plan information to employees.

Specifically, the Act spells out the following list of employee communications that employers must automatically provide:

The set of provisions presented here is typical of what is found in administrative contracts to ensure that specific communication needs are met.

Printed Materials and Identification Cards

1. Assist plan sponsor in design and print all necessary plan claim forms, enrollment forms, and other forms or documents related to plan claims administration, including benefit checks.
2. Provide plan sponsor with design and text for plan benefit booklets (SPDs), identification cards, summary of material modifications (SMMs) as needed throughout the plan year, summary annual reports (SARs), and other printed materials required by law or to meet industry standards for disclosure and reporting to plan members.
3. Provide plan participants with explanations of benefits (EOBs) with each claim payment made that explain clearly the amount paid, provider, service rendered, and date of service. Each EOB should include information on how to file an appeal or to contact the plan administrator with questions about the benefit payment.
4. Provide plan participants with claims appeal forms and notifications, and provide plan sponsor with reports on claims appeal activities and outcomes.

In addition to the specific type of provision included here, there are general statements that should be included to cover compliance with federal and state communication requirements:

Scope of Services

Plan Administrator agrees to perform consistent with reasonable standards of care, and in strict compliance with all applicable federal, state and local laws, regulations, and procedures that may from time to time be adopted or amended, and in a manner acceptable to (plan sponsor name), the following services:

[A list of each item of service to be included in your health plan administration contract should follow, in categories such as: Claims Processing and Adjudication, Claims Administrative Services, Plan Management, Printed Materials and Communications, Reports, and Member Services.]

This information is not intended to provide legal advice or language for legal documents; it is intended to serve as an explanation and supplement and to encourage you to develop a legal agreement concerning health plan communication. Your legal adviser and health plan adviser should determine the language and content of any agreement you enter with regard to plan administration or other services.

EXHIBIT 7-1. Contractual requirements for communication. (Source: Halo Associates.)

- *Summary plan description (SPD)*, which describes the plan's benefits and coverage provisions and eligibility and enrollment conditions and procedures, identifies the plan sponsor, claims administrator, and describes how to and where to file an appeal of claims denial. The SPD is commonly referred to as the plan booklet. This must be furnished to new employees within ninety days.
- *Summary of material modifications (SMM)*, which are the changes made to the plan in between editions of the SPD. These can be changes that affect plan coverage, administration, service, or employee cost. Any change to the health plan that has a measurable impact on employees is covered by this requirement, and the time frame to distribute it to employees has been shortened recently to sixty days from the date of the change. Exhibit 7-2 presents a sample SMM.
- *Summary Annual Report (SAR)*, which is a simplified and condensed version of the annual report furnished to the federal government under ERISA. The enrollment in the plan, expenditures on claims and administration and other costs, total costs, and employee contributions are also included. This can be provided to employees in a newsletter, or through an insert in payroll, a distributed or posted notice, or a year-end statement of benefits, if you provide one.

EXHIBIT 7-2. Sample material modifications to health plans. (Source: Halo Associates.)

- *Statement of Benefits on Termination*, which is a report to a terminated employee of benefits or coverage the employee is entitled to, such as COBRA or continuation of coverage rights.
- *Written Claim Denial*, which sets forth the reason for denying payment of a claim.

Other communications that need not be provided automatically but that must be available on request of employees are supporting plan documents, which include contracts with administrators, employees, and service firms associated with the plan; an annual financial form (federal form 5500); the IRS application for tax qualification for the plan; a personal benefit statement, if requested in writing (not more than once each plan year); and the plan termination report (IRS form 5310).

These materials have to be kept available at a distinct location and must be provided within ten days on request if you have fifty or more employees.

ERISA applies to organizations with fifteen or more employees and does not change the relationship with already retired workers. This law also doesn't apply to public entities such as government employers or school districts.

2. **COBRA.** This federal legislation calls for continued medical coverage, for a specific period of time, at the option of a terminated employee or a plan member who loses eligibility, subject to the person's making any required premium payments to the plan. Monthly COBRA premiums cannot exceed 102 percent of the health plan premium paid for active employees.

Certain notices are required for distribution to employees and plan members who lose coverage and are eligible for COBRA election. These include a form advising the employee of COBRA rights and offering an election for COBRA coverage. This must be provided within sixty days of a terminating event or loss of coverage. There are strict rules about maintaining COBRA files, notification procedures, and payment collection and reporting. For more details about these requirements, see Chapter 10 on legislation. An employee notification letter for COBRA is shown here as Exhibit 7-3.

3. **Medicare.** The law provides a health plan for aged and disabled persons and those with end-stage renal disease, though required coverage (Part A, hospitalization) and voluntary coverage (Part B, major medical). Changes to the law in 1997 allowed for optional purchase of Medicare coverage from managed-care plans and others that may provide additional benefits. Employers may reimburse retirees for Medicare Part B; if your organization does so, you will have an opportunity to communicate with retirees and Medicare enrollees with each reimbursement check, which is usually provided semiannually.

Since Medicare provides primary coverage for those aged and disabled persons who are not actively working and for employees age 70 and over, you will be required to provide notices to employees who become disabled and to alert those who are age 65 and older of their rights under Medicare. Your local Social Security Office is the service center for Medicare, and employees should be referred to this office for questions and enrollment forms.

4. **FMLA.** The Family Medical Leave Act requires that membership in the employee's health plan continue during a leave of up to twelve weeks taken for medical or family reasons, subject to justification and advance approvals. Exhibit 7-4 is a sample FMLA leave request and physician certification.

5. **HIPAA.** The Health Insurance Portability and Accountability Act protects employees by allowing them to change jobs without a break in health coverage and prohibits health plans from discriminating on the basis of an employee's health status. Special open-enrollment periods are mandated to allow employees who lose other coverage to enroll in the health plan on the job. There are also safeguards in the law to guarantee renewability of health insurance for small and large organizations.

Employee communications required by HIPAA include the certificate of coverage, which is largely the employer's responsibility, although it is issued by the health plan administrator. It must include the following:

- Date
- Name of group health plan
- Name and ID of the participant
- Names of covered dependents
- When the waiting or affiliation period began
- When coverage began and ended

These certificates of coverage are used to determine any preexisting condition exclusion that may still be allowed for a maximum period of twelve to eighteen months, under HIPAA, depending on whether the employee enrolls in the health plan during the initial enrollment period or later.

Impact of Legislation on Communication

ERISA is an example of how federal legislation can directly affect your organization, and specifically, your communication with employees about their health plan. As noted earlier, the law requires that you provide employees with a written description of the plan, written notice of changes to it, financial reports about it, instructions on how to appeal a claim denial, and descriptions of their rights to coverage if they stop working for you, whether because of retirement, death, disability, or termination.

This legislation is regarded as the most sweeping benefit legislation passed to date. It puts a burden on your organization to communicate regularly with plan members and to keep records accessible to plan members on request. Lots of paperwork, and lots of responsibility.

☐ Mailed

COBRA Continuation Coverage Election Form
(Termination or Reduction in Hours of Employment)

Date of Notice:

Qualified Beneficiary Information

Name: _____ SS#:

Address: _____ Date of Birth:

City, State, Zip: _____

Marital Status ☐ Single ☐ Married

No. of Dependent Children: N/A

Entitlement to COBRA Coverage

As explained in the notice of rights accompanying this form, you and your spouse and dependent child(ren), if any, could be entitled to continue health coverage under the   group health plan due to the following qualifying event, which is effective June 26, 1998.

☐ Termination of Employment   ☐ Reduction in hours of employment

This qualifying event will result in the loss of health coverage unless you elect continuation coverage. If you would like to elect continuation coverage, please read and sign this form and return it to the address below as soon as possible.

If this election form is not returned within sixty days of the date of this notice, you will lose your right to elect coverage, and your coverage under the company's group health plan will terminate effective July 31, 1998.

Continuation coverage under COBRA is provided subject to your eligibility. The Plan Administrator reserves the right to terminate your COBRA coverage retroactively if you are determined to be ineligible for coverage.

IF YOU DO NOT RETURN THIS ELECTION FORM WITHIN SIXTY DAYS
YOU WILL LOSE YOUR RIGHT TO ELECT CONTINUATION COVERAGE.

Length of COBRA Coverage

You and your spouse and dependent child(ren), if any, are eligible to receive up to eighteen MONTHS of continuation coverage from the date of termination or reduction of hours of employment. However, coverage may extend beyond that period or terminate early, as explained in your election notice.

COBRA Coverage Premiums

Within forty-five days after the date that you elect COBRA coverage, you must pay an initial premium, which includes:

Premium payments are generally due within thirty days after the first day of each month of coverage. Premium amounts change from time to time. You will be notified of any change in the premium amount.

EXHIBIT 7-3. COBRA notification. (Source: Rockland County, NY.)

You are eligible for (circle one) FAMILY SINGLE coverage. Unless you expressly elect otherwise, this coverage will be continued for you (and your spouse and your dependent child(ren), if any). The regular cost of coverage will be as follows:

Family Coverage	Single Coverage
$618.64 per month	$268.82 per month

Make checks payable to:

**IF PREMIUM PAYMENT IS NOT RECEIVED ON TIME,
COVERAGE WILL TERMINATE AND MAY NOT BE REINSTATED.**

COBRA Coverage Election Agreement

I have read this form and the notice of my election rights. I understand my rights to elect continuation coverage and would like to take action indicated below. I understand that if I elect continuation coverage and I fail to pay any premium payment on time, this coverage will terminate. I also agree to notify the _____ if I or any member of my family become(s) covered under another group health plan or entitled to Medicare.

Please check ONE only.

☐ I elect to continue family coverage under the plan. (To be checked only by those qualified beneficiaries who had family coverage before the qualifying event.)

List dependents to be covered:

Name	Relationship	Date of Birth

☐ I elect to continue single coverage under the plan.

☐ I have read this form and the notice of rights. I am waiving my right to continuation coverage under the plan.

Signature: _____ Date: _____

Name (Please Print): _____

Address: _____

_____

Telephone: _____

Send form to:

Inquiries should be directed to:

For Office Use Only:
    Received by Administrator _____   Date: _____

The intent of the law is to make benefit and plan information readily available. Remember, employee health benefits are tax deductible to the employer as an expense. The federal government wants to be sure the tax break is appropriately used to benefit all employees who will be eligible for your health plan.

The requirements of federal legislation apply only to employers with more than fifteen, twenty-five, or fifty employees, depending on the law. The federal government recognizes that smaller employers would face an unfair burden if these laws applied to them.

It is also understood that employers of this size are almost always fully insured and that the insurer must provide required communication under state law. If your organization is exempted from these laws, due to size, your communication job is limited to distribution of information provided by your insurer.

This summary has included federal legislation that introduced, expanded, or detailed health plan communication. There may be other requirements of state law and employee contracts to which you must adhere, such as those described next.

REQUEST FOR FAMILY AND MEDICAL LEAVE (FMLA)

EMPLOYEE REQUEST

Name _____ Date of Request _____
(please print or type)

Department _____ Title _____

Date FMLA leave to begin _____ Date FMLA leave to end _____

Duration and type of leave: ☐ Full Time Continuous   ☐ Intermittant
☐ LFT/PT   No. of work days

Are you requesting paid ☐ or unpaid ☐ FMLA leave?

If paid, what leave credits do you plan to use? _____

Reason for Leave: ☐ Employee Medical*
☐ Family Medical (Relationship to employee _____)*
☐ Birth of a child
☐ Care of a child
☐ Adoption/foster care

*Attach medical certification (form FMLA-2)

Please explain the type of care to be provided: _____
_____
_____

_____   _____
Employee Signature   Date

DEPARTMENTAL REVIEW

Name of Supervisor _____ Title _____

Describe the impact of employee's requested leave on the operation of your department
_____
_____

Was the employee paid for a minimum of 1,250 hours during the 52 weeks immediately preceding this request? ☐ Yes   ☐ No

_____   _____
Authorized Departmental Signature   Date

DEPARTMENT HEAD DETERMINATION

Have you approved the employee's leave request? ☐ Yes   ☐ No

If no, please explain: _____
_____
_____

_____   _____
Department Head Signature   Date

_____   _____
Signature   Date

EXHIBIT 7-4. FMLA request. (Source: Rockland County Department of Insurance.)

CERTIFICATION OF PHYSICIAN OR PRACTITIONER
Family and Medical Leave Act of 1993 (FMLA)

Employee Name _____

Patient's Name (if other than employee) ___(please print or type)_____

Relationship of patient to employee _____

Diagnosis:

Date condition commenced: _____   Probable duration of condition: _____

Regimen of treatment to be prescribed. (Indicate number of visits, general nature and duration of treatment, including referral to other provider of health services. Include schedule of visits or treatment if it is medically necessary for the employee to be off work or work less than the employee's natural schedule of hours per day or days per week.)

a) By physician or practitioner:

b) By another provider of health services (if referred by physician or practitioner):

IF PATIENT IS EMPLOYEE:	Yes	No	IF PATIENT IS EMPLOYEE'S SERIOUSLY ILL FAMILY MEMBER:	Yes	No
Is patient hospitalization required?	☐	☐	Is inpatient hospitalization required?	☐	☐
Is employee able to perform work of any kind?	☐	☐	Does (or will) the patient require assistance for basic medical care, nutritional needs, safety, or transportation, i.e., daily living needs?	☐	☐
Is employee able to perform the essential functions of his/her position? (Answer after reviewing employee's statement of essential functions of position or, if none provided, after discussion with employee.)	☐	☐	After review of the employee's signed statement (see below), is the employee's assistance necessary, i.e., would it be beneficial for the care of the patient? (This may include psychological comfort)	☐	☐
			Estimate the period of time care is needed or the employee's assistance would be beneficial: _____		

Physician or Practitioner _____ Date _____
(Signature)

Type of Practice (Field of Specialization, if any) _____

Employee Signature _____ Date _____

Other Legal Constraints

Because ERISA is federal law, it cannot be changed by state legislation, and some health plans are protected from state regulation because they are ERISA plans. However, states also enact laws that affect plan communications. Thirty-five states proposed or enacted regulations on health plan coverage or procedures in 1998. Some of these set forth specific requirements for notification regarding coverage, status changes, eligibility, and termination.

Other state regulations require that employees receive information on how to select and change a primary care physician; a provider listing by specialty; a description of how the health plan pays providers; a list of treatments requiring prior authorization; conditions for coverage of emergency care; and information on grievance or appeals procedures, how to obtain referrals to specialists, and claims processing procedures.

Employee contracts entered into through collective bargaining have included health benefits since 1947, as a right granted by a decision of the National Labor Relations Board. These employee agreements may require employer oversight, notification, reports, or other communication. Particularly in union welfare plans, the manner of making changes to coverage, administration, and services is addressed by the Taft-Hartley Act, which specifies that a committee composed equally of representatives of management and of employees should make decisions about coverage, administration, finances, communication, and all aspects of plan management.

Such contracts may specify a notification and approval procedure for any plan changes; they may also limit the nature and extent of changes that may be made without a complete renegotiation of the contract or make changes subject to membership approval. They usually set forth the grievance procedure, if a member believes the health plan is not living up to the terms of the negotiated contract. As with any collective bargaining process, the range of possible issues that can be included in a contract is limited only by the imagination of those who negotiate it.

The communication responsibilities connected to an employee contract usually rest with your organization. You will be expected to develop and communicate information about the plan, the contract provisions that affect health coverage or services, and any costs associated with the contract. Before sending anything out to employees, you should seek approval of the document from employee representatives, and from your legal and employee relations staff.

Another constraint on your health plan activities can be self-imposed. You should consider, if you have complex issues to resolve with your health plan, creation of committee of employees, including managers, who can meet to discuss alternatives. Your committee can issue recommendations as the result of consensus and can serve as advocates to all employees about your health plan. Once you have delegated responsibility to an employee committee, you should be guided by its suggestions and viewpoint. As a result, you should carefully identify the topics you want it to discuss and provide, in advance, an understanding of its role and limits. A health insurance or health plan advisory committee is an enlightened way to reach out to employees for their input on health plan review and decisions and to have continuous communication about such activities.

■ COMMUNICATION BY CHOICE

There may be times you choose to communicate with your employees about your health plan. Let's say you want to conduct a review or evaluate your health plan regarding:

- Improvements in service
- Plans costs and utilization
- Coverage and benefits provided
- Employee satisfaction surveys and their results
- Preventive health and wellness initiatives
- Reminders about new services
- Wise use of health care services

- Comparison of your health plan with others
- High cost claims and their management

Some basic guidelines can be followed, keeping in mind that health insurance is important to employees and communication about it can have an emotional response.

Content

This covers what you have to say and how you say it, including any quotations, statistical data, financial projections, or testimonials. You should strive for plain language and useful illustrations of how information can be used by employees or applies to them. Develop key messages that include information on:

- The current environment
- Any changes to be made
- Why they are being made
- Whom they affect
- How and where to get information
- When further information can be expected

Be sure any benefit issues are drafted or reviewed by your health plan adviser, plan administrator, or appropriate legal or insurance specialist.

Timing

Surprises are not a good idea when it comes to health plans. Advance notice and timely announcements are most likely to engender confidence. The timing and frequency of communications and the methods used to communicate reflect the way your organization is structured, your philosophy, the importance of the communication, and your management capabilities.

The degree of urgency determines the frequency and influences the timing of communications. For routine information, such as open enrollment periods or reminders on standard procedures, your regular employee publication, memorandum, or announcement circular is appropriate. Prompt and clear communications are a necessity when changes to your health plan are planned or implemented. Most people need to hear or read something several times before they fully understand it; according to the advertising industry, which is expert in communicating a message, a message needs to be heard, seen, or presented seven times to be understood. Without being repetitive or boring, try following the seven-times rule for communication.

If you aren't able to give advance warning, for example, because of unexpected decisions or contract negotiations, limited staff, or an influx of new employees, be sure to have a system in place to post changes required by law. Simple preparations will save you untold expense and aggravation.

■ CHANNELS OF COMMUNICATION

How do you usually talk to employees? Do you send written notices that are posted, circulated, or addressed individually? Do you have supervisors, shop stewards, managers, or departments who usually distribute work notices and information? Examples of communication tools you may have at hand are payroll stuffers, letters and memorandums to employees, posters, bulletins, instruction sheets, newsletter articles, union notices, department head memorandums, health plan booklets and inserts, surveys, questionnaires, reports, group meetings, general employee meetings, and management meetings.

To effectively communicate with employees, you need a game plan that considers your organizational abilities and limits. Make a list of the channels of communication you already use to communicate with employees, and prioritize those that are best for health plan communications. Now you are ready to use your existing resources and procedures and to identify any gaps in your communication system.

Make an outline of your organizational structure. Include an evaluation of the strengths of your locations, departments, supervisors, or staff. Identify the need for approvals of health plan information and a procedure to obtain them in a timely fashion. Assess your organization's internal communication system, whether it's a message center, employee bulletin board, daily or weekly staff meetings, written memorandums, or informal briefings each morning.

If you have a small organization, chances are there is one person who usually makes announcements or you have a set pattern for sending circulars or memorandums on employment issues. In a mid-sized organization, you may have designated staff or a benefits office to handle health plan issues. If you are unionized, you may have requirements that certain information be distributed by the union and their representatives or shop stewards. You may be required to include them in the approval process.

Identify the priority level of the information. Determine whether it is more or less important as it relates to your employees and to your organization. If the information will have a major impact on employee relations or describes a change in costs, services, or procedures, you will want someone of stature to announce it and to answer questions. Employees will want to have answers and to be reassured that the information or change is based on careful planning and execution. The spokesperson for the change should be on good terms with employees, have their respect and confidence, and be knowledgeable about the health plan.

Take into account the complexity of the information. If it is confusing or complicated, it may be appropriate to have your benefit consultant, agent, broker, or insurance representative present. Even if someone from your organization is appropriate to open the discussion with employees, you might leave it to the benefits professionals to answer specific questions and describe the impact to individual employees.

Employee Meetings

Whether you are a small or mid-sized organization, it may be a good idea to discuss your health plan at an employee meeting. Here are some things you can do to make your meeting more successful:

- Arrange a comfortable setting for everyone.
- If you have a small workforce, arrange for coverage at work stations and a time that is quiet—perhaps before or after a workday begins.
- Be sure to have adequate handouts and seating.
- Depending on the length of the meeting, serve a beverage or refreshments.
- If there are visuals, have your employees seated so that all can see clearly and hear easily.
- Provide your employees with the agenda for the meeting and who will be speaking.
- Give a minimum of a week's notice and preferably two weeks to convey a sense of well-planned, well-executed change.

This sounds as if it is common sense. It is. Amazingly, few employers who plan a staff meeting on the health plan give it careful thought before sending out meeting announcements.

Time and again, small and mid-sized organizations face the frustration of getting employees together, only to have some people leave for ongoing work responsibilities, while others become disgruntled because the seating is inadequate or the benefit handouts run out. Your selection of a suitable space and setting and your preparations for the meeting send a message to your employees about the importance of the meeting and its agenda. It is also viewed by employees as a statement of how much you value them and whether you have a sincere commitment to their health and well-being.

Individual or Small-Group Meetings

If you are a small or mid-sized organization, you may want to try holding individual or private meetings on your health plan. Often, more personal communications are appropriate for your managers, supervisors, employee representatives, labor-management committees, and key employees. Typically, they are informed about health plan issues earlier than rank-and-file employees. The purpose of this advance notice is to enlist their support and to give them an opportunity to fully understand what you are doing. A meeting of supervisors or managers, to explain the change, its intent, and impact on employees, can help you reach all employees. Hearing from the boss with timely and clear communication on a health plan sends a message about its importance and its seriousness to everyone. Also, the supervisors and department heads are covered by the plan and will be affected by the change, and so may appreciate a separate meeting to answer their concerns.

Written Notices

Ensure that all employees have access to notices at work. Bulletin boards, posting centers near coffee or water supplies, circular distributions, e-mail, voice mail, and individual interoffice mail are all ways to reach employees with written materials and announcements. In small organizations it may be easier to guarantee that all employees read and receive benefit information. Don't forget part-timers who are affected, night or evening workers, and those who work on the road, such as salespeople.

Keep mailing labels to send notices to employees' homes when urgent situations arise, as an alternative to office-based communications, so that all employees receive information consistently. This will permit you to keep employees routinely informed without expecting them to attend meetings or read postings.

Small organizations traditionally rely more on word of mouth, which is not reliable when it comes to timing or content of the message. If you are a small employer, offset the possibility of misinformation by keeping a bulletin board on which you display all required employee notices. Or enclose a short notice in a pay envelope as a routine. Even a handwritten note will clarify health plan activities and keep your employees accurately and promptly informed.

Mid-sized organizations usually have established channels of communication, but these communication safeguards can be useful to them, too.

■ ONGOING COMMUNICATIONS

In the normal routine of your organization, there are hundreds of opportunities to communicate with employees. The art of communications is to skillfully weave important health plan information into the fiber of your organization so that it is seamlessly absorbed by your employees. Weekly staff meetings, monthly sales reports, management meetings, and quarterly in-service training sessions are typical opportunities to include health plan information and announcements as part of your established routines. Consider whether this will work for your organization. Make health plan information an important subject that your organization communicates with employees. Designate an agenda item or a short time period at the beginning or end of regular meetings to introduce benefit information or to answer questions about your health plan. When you routinely take the time to answer questions or invite comments, it will be easier to nip problems in the bud.

Institute a suggestion box or interoffice channel for benefit concerns, payment or claims issues, and requests for assistance. To make this concept work, you will have to adequately inform employees about its use and purpose and assign someone to respond.

If you are a small organization, you might ask your insurance professional or adviser to visit on a regular basis to answer questions that you gather between visits. If you are mid-sized, you might schedule quarterly, biannual, or annual meetings for plan members to get answers to their questions. Open enrollment periods, when plan members can opt to make changes, is always a good time for individual or group sessions with plan representatives.

Establish a benefit question time during the workweek for plan members to contact your benefit staff by telephone. If you designate such a time period, be sure that qualified staff is on hand to respond verbally and with written follow-up. Copies of pages of your benefit booklet, claim forms, appeal information, or carrier 800-numbers should all be accessible.

Displays with claim forms, benefit booklets, updated plan change notices, legislative flyers that affect your plan, enrollment forms, change-of-status forms, and other plan materials should be placed at convenient locations. A benefit or personnel office is commonly the site for such a display. If you are a small organization, keep all of these materials in handy files, perhaps located on a counter or desktop where employees can see them. A mid-sized organization may need several sites, standard display racks, and a system for replenishing or replacing supplies.

Employee Newsletters

Employee newsletters or circulars are excellent means by which to communicate. They have several advantages over other communications. First, they become an accepted mode of communication, and information they contain has the appearance of orderly planning. Generally they are written in plain, easily understood terms. Their message is viewed as management policy, since they are sponsored by the organization.

By using a regular employee publication, it is easier to comply with the law related to notification. Of course, you need to have a distribution and posting system established to ensure that all of your employees get the newsletter or circular. The tone and content of such a publication can be created from its beginning to encourage feedback and to incorporate organizational concern for employee well-being. Then, when health plan news is announced, it can be in the context of positive employee relations. A step-by-step process can be followed with consecutive newsletters, describing stages of activity and detailed health plan information. Multiple messages are helpful to fully describe health plan issues, any solutions that are adopted, and the reasons for them.

There are, of course, some cautions about relying on employee newsletters. Some of the problems relate to the support it receives from your organization. Start a newsletter only under the following conditions:

- You have the staff and resources to write, edit, and produce it.
- You are fully supported by your organization in the mission and goals of the newsletter.
- You are able to distribute it to all employees, and possibly to retirees.
- You are capable of creating timely and interesting articles when needed.
- You are clear on the tone, content, editing, and approval process.
- You have a chain of command for changes and input to the newsletter.

It is easy to get into trouble when you do something new, but if you plan carefully, you can avoid most of the problems associated with newsletters. Be sure, for example, that you can keep deadlines and publish on schedule. You also want to limit the number of issues to a reasonable amount, given the number of other communications with employees.

My personal preference for the timing of an internal newsletter is quarterly, although many organizations prefer publishing a health and benefit newsletter two or three times a year or monthly. Many school districts publish three times a year, with their summer schedule in mind, for example. Seasonal organizations might find two issues are more than enough for their employees.

The quality of your publication may be an issue. If it is too attractive, and obviously expensive, employees may feel it is a waste of money. If it is not attractive enough, it will go into the round file without being read. Your goal should be to balance interesting information that is timely with enough personalized information about your organization so that your employees value the newsletter and look forward to receiving it.

To save wear and tear on your staff, especially if you are a small or mid-sized organization, consider outsourced newsletters. Be sure to ask about publication and delivery details when you compare outsourced newsletters. Many will personalize the front page, masthead, or entire publication for a reasonable fee. Ask to review future publication topics and past editions, including personalized versions.

Regardless of the size of your organization, outsourcing your newsletter can be a painless way to provide employees with health and benefit information, either distributed internally or by direct mail. Purchasing a newsletter from an outside source has the advantage of limiting your responsibility for the writing, editing, and production, while enabling you to keep deadlines and an information schedule. In addition, your commitment to an outsourced health and benefit newsletter conveys its importance to employees. Exhibit 7-5 is a sample of an outsourced, personalized newsletter.

RESPONSIBILITY FOR EMPLOYEE COMMUNICATION

Whether your organization is small or mid-sized, you will need to identify who is responsible for health plan communications. It is a mistake to assume that a communication can be written on one occasion by one manager and on another by a different staff member. Consistency and control of content will be lost if you don't have a clearly assigned person to write and communicate health plan information. That doesn't mean

Fall 1997 Vol. I No. 2   Orange County's Health & Wellness Newsletter

Monitoring the Pressure

High blood pressure has been called the silent killer because it presents no symptoms, and can go undetected for years. Left uncontrolled, hypertension, as it is medically known, can lead to heart disease and/or stroke.

Factors increasing risk of high blood pressure

When was the last time you had your blood pressure checked? Do you know what your normal blood pressure is? Do you have a family history of high blood pressure, heart disease or stroke? Do you smoke? Is your cholesterol level above 200? Are you a woman reaching menopause? All of these are factors which can increase your risk of developing high blood pressure, heart disease or stroke.

So, what can you do if you've answered yes to any of the risk factors for hypertension For one thing, OCCC employees can stop by the college health office. The nurses in Health Services will provide you with a free blood pressure screening. We can also provide you with health information on almost any topic including hypertension, diet, and cholesterol. We can monitor your blood pressure over a period of time, which can help your doctor make the decision to start, stop or change high blood pressure medication.

Help at OCCC

The OCCC Health Services Office, located in the Physical Education Building, Room 224, is open to all students, faculty, and staff. A registered nurse is on duty each day from 8:00 AM to 9:00 PM, Monday - Thursday, and 8:00 AM to 4:00 PM on Friday. No appointment is necessary. You can reach us by telephone at extension 4870 if you have questions, or just stop by any time. We look forward to seeing you, and to helping you stay well.

It's Still Option Transfer Month

Now is the time for you to consider a transfer to the Orange County Health Plan. October is open enrollment month for all employees covered by the county for health benefits. Some key features of the Orange County Health Plan include:

- ✔ **Freedom of choice for local or out of area physicians and specialists,— without referral**
- ✔ **Choice of local and out of area testing and laboratory facilities**
- ✔ **Choice of hospitals for inpatient stays**
- ✔ **Extensive prescription drug coverage and mail order services**

For a description of plan services and coverage, ask for a Summary Plan Description from the Division of Risk Management at 291-2131.

JUST A REMINDER

Pre-Admission Certification

Here to help

Please contact Kate Rogers, RN at SIEBA Ltd/EM Associates (800-252-4624) prior to ANY major treatment or medical equipment purchase. She is set up to provide the most comprehensive assistance to all of the participants in the Orange County Health Plan (OCHP). Kate is there to help you when you need it, so please call.

Plan coverage

As everyone is undoubtedly aware, Section 5 of the OCHP states:

"Payment of covered Hospital expenses incurred by Covered Persons who fail to obtain pre-admission certification will be reduced by 20% of the amount of the covered Hospital expense that the plan would otherwise pay. In order to avoid this 20% reduction, Covered Persons must notify the Plan's Case Management Consultant prior to non emergency Hospital admissions or within 48 hours after emergency Hospital admissions."

We do not want to apply this reduction to anyone's claim. So, just pick up the phone and call! We in Risk Management, at SIEBA and EM Associates are here to help.

Trekking & Hiking Tips

The close of summer doesn't mean it's time to hibernate. Take advantage of the cool, crisp air and the friendly crackle of leaves beneath your feet. Get in touch with nature – take a hike!

Be Prepared

▲ Wear hiking boots that provide the right traction and ankle support. Low boots for easier trails, and high boots for harder ones.
▲ Wear socks that fit and keep your feet dry. Bring extra socks.
▲ Assemble a fanny or back pack. Include a compass, flashlight, whistle, pocketknife, first-aid kit, and snacks. Make appropriate adjustments for little trekkers.
▲ Bring adequate water — one quart for every 2-3 hours of moderate hiking.

To Get Started & Keep Going:

▲ Maintain good posture. Don't lean forward or you're likely to get cramps.
▲ Avoid sunburn by wearing a hat and using sunscreen.
▲ Avoid ticks by skirting underbrush and tall grassy areas, and tucking pant legs into boots. Check for ticks once home.

Happier Holidays

Before your holiday ho ho's turn into ho hums:

Take time to reflect on the memories & traditions that mean the most to you.

Ask your family to share their thoughts and wishes for the holidays.

Do less. Spend less. Enjoy more.

Slow down and get organized, but don't procrastinate.

Perhaps the greatest gift you can give yourself and your family is permission to relax and enjoy the holidays.

EXHIBIT 7-5. Sample outsourced newsletter. (Source: *For Your Benefit*, vol. 1, no. 2, Fall 1997, p. 1; copyright © by the Wellness Institute Inc.)

everything about your health plan has to be created from scratch. In fact, most information and plan materials are provided by the plan carrier, HMO, plan administrator, or your health plan adviser.

Create a communications flow chart. Identify who should make health plan announcements and the order in which the information will be distributed or disseminated to all employees. You should have a contingency plan so that a backup person is in place if a particular individual isn't available when an announcement is needed. Also decide the setting and circumstances for announcing and distributing information.

The compilation of information, timing and method of distribution, and addition of your organization's message to standard brochures and notices is a vital function. Select someone on your staff, regardless of your organization's size, who is trustworthy, reliable, diligent, and organized. Be sure to provide this person with adequate resources of information, access to your insurance professionals, a distribution procedure, and funding and support for mailings, meetings, or other communication activities. It will do you no good to give someone the job of communicating if you overlook providing the resources for the job. You should require progress reports during the planning stage, and approvals before publication, to eliminate unforeseen problems.

When to Keep Mum

There are circumstances when you should make no announcement until after the fact. Some typical times for discretion include when the business is about to be sold or merged, when cutbacks and other changes are in negotiation with employee representatives, and when premature announcements might adversely affect sales or services.

A basic rule of thumb is to determine whether an announcement would impede your organization's goals and whether your plans might be affected, stopped, or altered by advance employee notice. It is a matter of timing only, since employees eventually have to be notified about any plan review or changes that affect them.

Weigh the pros and cons of employee awareness. Try to predict the impact of withholding information on future employee relations, as well as other factors such as wage requests, pensions, and turnover that are related to your health plan coverage and costs. Consider the volatility of your workforce and the existing state of employee relations. If your organization is going through other changes, such as relocation, expansion or constriction, management or structural change, building or facilities remodeling, unionization, or financing or investment review, to name a few, you will want to limit any further upheaval or postpone an announcement to a time when your employees have a more stabile environment.

If your employees have usually been unhappy with your health plan, you may wish to restrict advance notice to key employees, employee representatives, top management, or an established labor-management committee. Again, this is only a timing issue to enable you to consider and evaluate possible actions without undue employee pressure on your decision.

■ SPREADING THE WORD

Often, in small and mid-sized organizations, there are few secrets. Employees notice insurance professionals and salespeople coming in the door and note meetings that occur.

It can be wise, in this case, to have an open policy so that rumors and unrest don't exaggerate the situation.

Employee Surveys

Advance notice might take the form of an employee interest survey on health coverage. You can begin by asking your insurance professional whether a standard survey is available on benefit issues that you can use or modify. If not, you can create one by keeping a list of employee concerns and issues. These can be conveyed through a suggestion box, newsletter questionnaire, contact with your plan administrator, or your benefits staff. A more formal survey can be prepared and distributed to all employees under the aegis of your health plan committee. Exhibit 7-6 presents a sample employee survey on health benefits.

These guidelines for employee surveys can help you get a greater response and encourage more honest input.

- Be clear about your purpose.
- Invite comments in addition to responses to the survey questions.
- Allow anonymous responses.
- Provide all employees with a survey, and make it easy for them to return it to you.
- Write all survey questions in plain language.
- Cover all areas of benefits provided or planned for your health coverage.
- Make help with survey questions impartially available.
- Give a deadline for return.
- State what will be done with the results and how employees will be advised of any outcome.

Before you distribute and receive back the health plan survey, you will need to plan for its tally and evaluation. Your preparation of the survey should include decisions on how responses will be handled and used. A committee or a small group of management or labor-management representatives can evaluate survey responses that express employee concerns and determine whether the responses should be used to guide a review of the health plan. A tally of the responses can be used as a discussion basis for health plan review. Your insurance professional should be involved in this process to lend a hand in interpreting the outcome, including a forecast of the cost of suggestions.

When you use survey results to plan benefit changes, it is a positive statement, one in keeping with a trend toward employee empowerment. Although individual employees may not see enacted items that they have recommended, you can defend your actions more readily when a widely distributed, high-response survey can be cited as a planning tool.

Involvement of representatives from each area of your workforce—different locations, departments, disciplines, wage levels—can also help bring employees on board. Being given the opportunity for input is nearly as important as having that input used. Information about cost impact and implementation issues can be circulated among committee members more easily and with more trust once they have established a working relationship. Such information is more readily accepted than if it is announced by a management spokesperson. These committee members can also advise on the timing of employee notification and can be asked to participate in some of the presentations on the health plan.

HEALTH PLAN SURVEY

To All Employees:

The following survey is being conducted to evaluate your satisfaction with the health coverage provided. We are seeing the cost of the Plan rise for participants who need freedom of choice of providers when they are seriously ill, retired with limited Medicare benefits, or newly diagnosed with a major illness. We are also seeing some changes and recent developments in the healthcare system that affect HMO coverage.

We need to know your preference and opinion. We appreciate your time and effort to respond to the survey. Thank you.

Facts about you.

Please complete the following information:

Name of your Plan: _____   Years in this Plan: _____

Your age: ___ under 25 ___ 26–35 ___ 36–50 ___ 51–65 ___ Over 65

Sex: ___ M ___ F   # Covered Dependents, if any: ___

Your health status: Excellent ___ Good ___ Fair ___ Poor ___ Serious ___

Comments: Please include any comments related to the survey here, once you have completed the other side of this survey response.

_____

_____

_____

_____

(continues)

EXHIBIT 7-6. Employee satisfaction survey. (Source: Halo Associates.)

HEALTH PLAN SURVEY

Indicate your rating, for the type of health plan you have by noting a plus (+) for good or better, a minus (–) for poor or needs improvement, a zero (0) for no opinion, and a question mark (?) if you don't know.

Question or category	Employees Health Benefit Plan		MVP, CHP, Wellcare HMO
	Indemnity	POS option	
Doctors, Hospitals, Coverage			
Overall experience with your plan			
Your ability to choose any doctor			
The number and quality of doctors in your plan			
Your access to needed services or procedures			
Your ability to see nonnetwork doctors			
Ease of getting a referral for medical services			
Availability of chiropractic care			
Mental health coverage			
Pharmacy services and coverage			
Lab and radiology services			
Emergency Room services			
Use of nonlocal hospital services			
Immunization and well-child care			
Birth control prescriptions			
Physicals			
Mammography/breast cancer services			
At home services after hospitalization			
Physical therapy			
Telephone assistance with health care questions			
Claims, Enrollment, Billing			
Overall satisfaction with the plan's service			
Ease of paperwork for network claims			
Ease of paperwork for nonnetwork claims			
Dispute resolution for claims not paid			
Courtesy/manner of plan service reps			
Denials of service or coverage			
Complaint response			
	Yes	No	Not Sure
General			
Do you expect to re-enroll in your plan?			
Which type of plan is most important to offer—Indemnity/POS or HMO?			

Please return to address shown on reverse side

EXHIBIT 7-6. Continued

Health Plan Announcements

Information sessions with employee groups are a good idea to announce a major change or new services or procedures or to respond to questions about coverage. For more typical and everyday information, written channels of communication should be used. Basically, the more important the information, the more important it becomes to plan extensive information sessions. These meetings should be distinct from regular meetings such as those mentioned earlier in this chapter, although the same guidelines apply for scheduling, facilities, speakers, and so forth. It is almost essential at such sessions that your health insurance adviser be involved in the preparation and presentation of plan materials and descriptions.

Communication With Retirees

With regard to retirees who are covered by your health plan, keep in mind the degree to which they rely upon your organization for health plan information. If they are Medicare eligible, this changes somewhat. For those retirees over age 65 who are not covered elsewhere or for those active employees over age 70, your responsibility may be diminished, because Medicare is primary and often retiree benefits are eliminated or reduced. If you pay some part of Medicare costs or continue to provide retiree coverage, you should use ongoing communications with retirees to encourage their wise use of the health plan.

If your organization reimburses retirees for Medicare Part B, you should use your regular reimbursement mailing to include your newsletter, inserts on health care consumer issues, and reminders of any coverage limits. This, in addition to your telephone interaction with them, may be the only way you have to keep in touch. Many retirees relocate out of the area, so mailed and telephone communication are the only means possible. With the growth of Internet use, you should consider e-mail communications and possibly create a Web site for retiree and employee health plan and benefit inquiries.

When you communicate with retirees, consider these pointers:

- Keep message content direct, using larger-than-normal type when possible.
- Encourage retirees to find out what their out-of-pocket cost will be before receiving services.
- Give specific examples of how the retiree is affected.
- Work with retiree family members when the retiree is unable to communicate with you.
- Encourage use of case management services offered by your plan for those with catastrophic or chronic conditions.
- Explain cost-saving features, such as mail-order drugs.
- Provide telephone numbers, contact staff and resources, and addresses of interest.

Active employees will watch how an organization deals with retirees as an indicator of how they will be treated when they retire. If you provide retiree health benefits, it's good business to follow the same high standards for communication with retirees that you follow with those still actively at work.

Communication and Employee Problems

In every organization there are employees who have health plan problems. You may have an employee whose attitude is negative and who feels that the plan is unfair anytime it denies a claim, regardless of reason. This employee can make your life miserable and be on the phone with your benefits staff whenever coverage is denied. Another employee may have a major illness and require high-cost treatment and services. The same communication needs exist for both situations, and these general rules apply:

- Always document an employee complaint or concern.
- Maintain a good speaking tone and exchange, regardless of the employee's attitude or responses.
- Act promptly to resolve those issues that are your responsibility, and document your actions.
- Communicate immediately and follow up in writing with others who have responsibility to handle the problem that has arisen. It may be best to have a fax or e-mail system in place for the eventuality of such problems.
- Alert your staff about any follow-up for which they are responsible, and notify them in case the employee calls when you are unavailable.
- If there is a complaint, review the employee's history so you can put it in perspective.
- Contact your insurance adviser to discuss provisions in your coverage related to the issue.
- Refer the employee, when appropriate, to health plan staff who work for the carrier, HMO, or plan administrator on your account.
- If you are asked a complex question that cannot be answered immediately, inform the employee that you will do some research and respond. Be sure to ask when is the best time to reach the employee.
- If the matter is urgent, treat it urgently.

These are a few principles that can help you respond when someone needs assistance with your health plan. Remember that you are not able to say yes to everyone, and your final response may have to be an explanation of why the service or claim is not covered. You may have to explain why and how a change was made that eliminated or reduced some coverage now relied upon by the employee. It may not be a pleasant experience. Be prepared to assist the employee with nonhealth plan alternatives, such as local nonprofit services and other free or low-cost choices. If you have case management in place for your plan, guidance may be given by health professionals, as described in Chapter 8.

Communicating Change

When you need to inform employees of changes to the health plan or its services, you should be prepared well in advance with information on how any change will affect them. Health plan change should occur in a flowing manner and not in peaks and valleys, with your employees clinging for dear life as if on a roller-coaster ride.

■ SUMMARY

In earlier discussions, we have explored organizational philosophy and goals as they relate to health plan change. If your organization needs to improve profit and lower overhead without reducing staff, one of the objectives of benefits change can be to reduce cost. If your organization needs to grow quickly and hire specialist employees for whom there is a lot of competition, your health plan goals may be to expand benefits and improve the cost-sharing formula to be more attractive to potential employees.

Your need to review or to make a change is an organizational one, entered into with forethought and good judgment. We are far removed from the days where the boss decided, in a vacuum, what the health plan ought to be and who should be covered. Paternalistic management still exists, but employees today are not drawn to work in such an environment.

By putting a high priority on health plan communications, you can encourage higher productivity and gain the support of your employees for your health plan review or for any changes that affect them. It's a good start to think of your organization's health plan as your employees' health plan. That message will be conveyed in every notice you write, every meeting you plan, and in the health plan's daily operation.

CHAPTER 8

Wellness and Case Management Services

My purpose in this chapter is to guide you toward services that help reduce health plan costs. Wellness and case management are two growing interest areas that have a direct impact on high cost claims and can reduce those costs. At the same time, they can provide services that employees value. When you initiate these services, you go to the essence of what good health plan management is about—reducing costs and encouraging appropriate use of your plan.

My role as a benefits consultant since 1981 has been to reduce costs. It has included structuring provider discounts and creating networks, helping design new plan types and delivery systems, negotiating with employees for higher contributions and copayments, and fine-tuning retiree and employee health coverage to eliminate waste. Throughout, I have had the conviction that the best way to reduce health plan costs over the long term is to utilize wellness initiatives that keep employees healthier longer and to put in place case management services to reduce the impact of catastrophic and chronic conditions. In this chapter I show you how it can be done cost-effectively and offer some substantive discussion about wellness and disease management.

Wellness initiatives and disease management share some interesting traits:

- Employees benefit directly.
- Employees choose their involvement.
- Reduced out-of-pocket cost often occurs for the employee.
- Better use of health care services results.
- Employers initiate and sponsor them.
- Services are related to employment status.
- Employers generate communication about them.
- Outside professionals are needed to deliver the services.
- Internal resources can be used in an integrated delivery system.
- They can be tailored to meet your organization's needs.

Despite their common traits, and what I see as their common purpose related to a health plan, they need to be described and presented separately.

■ WELLNESS FIRST

There is no doubt that wellness programs have come into their own, with more employers making them available at the work site. The Employee Benefit Research Institute *Brief No. 177* notes that 88 percent of U.S. employers offered work-site wellness and preventive health services in 1993. Legislation at the state and the federal level support work-site wellness programs and preventive health programs. Some state requirements for insured plans include annual mammograms for women over age 50, routine physical examinations, guidelines for prostate cancer screenings, immunizations, and more. The National Committee for Quality Assurance (NCQA) national nonprofit organization that certifies HMOs for quality assurance requires that HMOs document preventive services in a report each year. Exhibit 8-1 is a summary of the report's contents, with an extensive listing of well-care and preventive services included in the Effectiveness of Care section. This report, called HEIDIS, is a measurement and monitoring tool used as a report card by employers to track HMO service levels.

Employees like wellness programs, too; a study by the Conference Board, published in the September 27, 1997, issue of *What's New in Benefits & Compensation*, ranks wellness programs third on the benefits wish lists of childless employees, and a national survey found wellness programs among the top two priorities for recent college graduates. Nationally, more than 56 percent of all employees participate in preventive health or wellness programs each year.

A wide range of programs and services is offered to employees, including education, screening, self-care, and various classes and training. Exhibit 8-2 presents the results of one national study of the percentage of work sites offering different kinds of health promotion activities. It found that 81 percent of companies with fifty or more employees had at least one health promotion activity during 1992. The prevalence and range of programs continue to grow, and, as happens in other competitive fields, the number of providers for these services is growing, too.

The Payoff

Research studies, large-employer reports, and the popular media point to the same conclusions: wellness pays off for employers and employees. Return on investment for the plethora of programs out there is well publicized—from self-care manuals, which yield a 24 percent savings according to a study by the American Institute of Preventive Medicine in 1998; to work-site fitness programs reported in "Inside Preventive Health" to have a four-to-one return; to early detection of breast cancer reported recently by the Coors Company, which reduces cost from $157,000 to $12,000 per claim and saves lives in the bargain. Exhibit 8-3 is a compilation of selected cost impact studies for work-site wellness programs in the United States that have been publicly reported in recent years.

The experts understand that cost and preventable illness are connected. The annual *Health Insurance Association of America Source Book* attributes $188 billion of health expenditures in 1995 to risky behaviors, such as smoking, failure to use seat belts, and substance abuse. In *National Underwriter* (April 18, 1994), a report of claims reviewed by the William Mercer consulting firm in 1994 found that one-third of claims expenses were associated with preventable conditions; an analysis by the Health Project Consortium, published by Dr. James F. Fries and Dr. C. Everett Koop, concluded that preventable illness accounts for approximately 70 percent of illness and its associated costs. They note the extensive research conducted by *Healthy People 2000* and that group's conclusions that 980,000 preventable deaths occurred in 1992. They further note that an average return on investment from the more than 200 wellness and preventive health programs they reviewed was three to one.

Considering that about a third of a person's lifetime medical costs are incurred in the final year of life and that chronic and catastrophic conditions account for 75–80 percent

HEIDIS 3.0 REPORTING AND TESTING SET MEASURES

Effectiveness of Care

Reporting Set

Advising smokers to quit.
Beta blocker treatment after a heart attack.
Use of appropriate medications for people with asthma.
The health of seniors.
Eye exams for people with diabetes.
Flu shot for older adults.
Flu shots for high-risk adults.
Cervical cancer screening.
Breast cancer screening.
Childhood immunization status.
Adolescent immunization status.
Treating children's ear infections.
Prenatal care in the first trimester.
Low birth weight babies.
Check ups after delivery.

Testing Set

Number of people in the plan who smoke.
Smokers who quit.
Monitoring diabetes patients.
Chlamydia screening.
HIV patient management.
Cholesterol management of patients hospitalized for coronary artery disease.
Aspirin treatment after a heart attack.
Outpatient care of patients hospitalized for congestive heart failure.
Controlling high blood pressure.
Prevention of stroke in people with atrial fibrillation.
Colorectal cancer screening.
Follow-up after abnormal pap smear.
Follow-up after abnormal mammogram.
Stage at which breast cancer was detected.
Functional assessment of breast cancer therapy.
Continuity of care—substance abuse.
Substance abuse counseling for adolescents.
Availability of medication management—schizophrenia
Patient reported behavioral health measure.
Family visit for children 12 years of age or younger undergoing mental health treatment.
Treatment failure—substance abuse.
Chemical dependency screening.
Diagnosis supporting the use of psychotherapeutic drugs.
Rate of continuation treatment of depression.

Access to/Availability of Care

Reporting Set

Appointment access.
Telephone access.
Availability of primary care providers.

Children's access to primary care providers.
Availability of mental health/chemical dependency providers.
Annual dental visit.
Availability of dentists.
Adults' access to preventive/ambulatory health services.
Initiation of prenatal care.
Availability of obstetrical/prenatal care providers.
Low birth weight deliveries at facilities for high-risk deliveries and neonates.
Availability of language interpretation services.

Testing Set

Problems with obtaining care.

Satisfaction with the Experience of Care

Reporting Set

The annual member health survey.
Survey descriptive information.

Testing Set

Member disenrollment survey.
Satisfaction with breast cancer treatment.

Health Plan Stability

Reporting Set

Member disenrollment.
Physician turnover.
Narrative information on rate trends, financial stability, and insolvency protection.
Performance indicators.
Years in business/total membership.

Use of Services

Reporting Set

Well-child visits in the first 15 months of life.
Well-child visits in the third, fourth, fifth, and sixth year of life.
Adolescent well-care visit.
Frequency of selected procedures.
Inpatient utilization—non-acute care.
Inpatient utilization general hospital/acute care.
Ambulatory care.
C-section and vaginal birth after C-section rate.
Discharge and average length of stay for females in maternity care.
Births and average lengths of stay, newborns.
Frequency of ongoing prenatal care.
Mental health utilization—percentage of members receiving inpatient day/night and ambulatory services.
Readmission for specified mental health disorders.

Chemical dependency utilization—inpatient discharges and average length of stay.
Chemical dependency utilization—percentage of members receiving inpatient, day/night care and ambulatory services.
Mental health utilization—inpatient discharges and average length of stay.
Readmission for chemical dependency.
Outpatient drug utilization.

Testing Set

Use of behavioral health services.

Cost of Care

Reporting Set

High-occurrence/high cost DRGs.
Rate trends.

Testing Set

Health plan costs per member per month.

Informed Health Care Choices

Reporting Set

Language translation services.
New member orientation/education.

Testing Set

Counseling women about hormone replacement therapy.

Health Plan Descriptive Information

Reporting Set

Board certification/residency completion.
Provider compensation.
Physicians under capitation.
Recredentialing of physicians.
Pediatric mental health network.
Chemical dependency services.
Arrangements with public health, educational and social service entities.
Weeks of pregnancy at time of enrollment.
Family planning.
Preventive care and health promotion.
Quality assessment and improvement.
Case management.
Utilization management.
Risk management.
Cultural diversity of Medicaid membership.
Unduplicated count of Medicaid members.
Enrollment by payer (member years/months).
Total enrollment.

EXHIBIT 8-1. Summary of HEIDIS report content. (Source: Inside Preventive Care, Arlington, VA, 1998.)

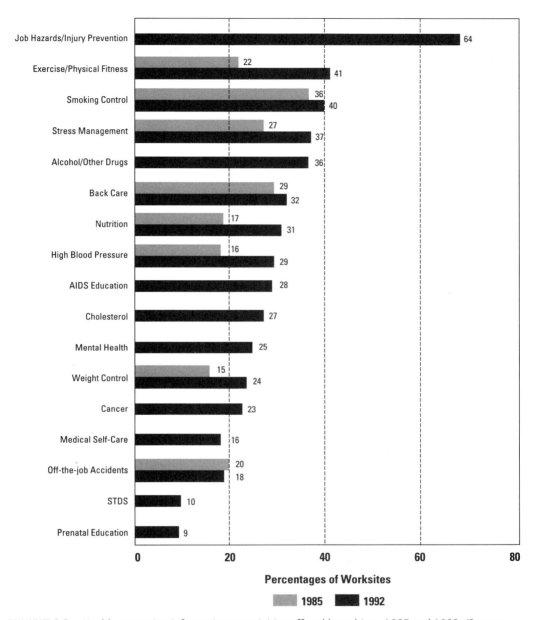

EXHIBIT 8-2. Health promotion information or activities offered by subject, 1985 and 1992. (Source: ODPHP National Survey of Worksite Health Promotion Activities, 1992.)

of health plan claims each year, it's simple good management of your health plan to control those costs as much as possible. What kind of costs, by condition, are common?

The Cost of Some Preventable Conditions

Consider the implications of smoking as a health habit. More than 30 percent of cancer deaths in 1997 were due to tobacco use. Smokers cost about one-third more in health claims each year than nonsmokers; their likelihood of premature death is 60 percent higher than that of nonsmokers; the American Cancer Society data book for 1997 attributes

General Studies Reported Source	Type of Work Site or Program	Findings and Cost Impact
American Medical Association	Four manufacturing companies	Active intervention with hypertension reduced medical claims by 24%–75%
Blue Cross/Blue Shield of VA	Plan members	Low birth weight babies and prenatal claims were reduced on an average from $9,815 to $6,581 with education and early prenatal treatment
American Journal of Health Promotion	Reported study of multiple employer groups	Health claims for obese employees as compared to lean employees showed increased absentee costs of $512/year for obese employees
Centers for Disease Control	National study	50% of all health care costs related to preventable disease
Reuters News Service	National poll	75% of all Americans have a strong interest in learning about health and health care; 70% of adult men, 80% of adult women
New England Journal of Medicine	Regional study	Intervention and education saved on cost of care for diabetics by $2,319 annually
Heart Lung & Blood Institute	National study	Smokers cost $221/year to every American
Specific Studies and Reports Rand Corporation	Smokers vs. nonsmokers	Total additional cost of smokers is $1,900 a year, including medical claims, absenteeism, support and productivity costs.
Mesa Petroleum	Sedentary workers study	$217 additional cost for sedentary employees
Tenneco	Fitness evaluation and sedentary workers	$442/year additional cost for lowest fitness level employees
General Electric Co.	Fitness impact on health costs	$184/year for sedentary employees
Steel Case Mfg.	Fitness impact on health claims	55% more health care cost for workers who are sedentary or lowest fitness level
Rockland County, NY w/Columbia University	Intervention program at work 4,000 employees, 200 studied Hypertension Control Program	50% reduction in health claims of those in worksite hypertension treatment program
HealthExaminetics, Inc.	Return on Investment for worksite physical exam and followup	ROI at employer of 450 employees increased $3.17 first year to $5.33 fourth year for every dollar spent
Wellness Institute, Inc.	Impact of call center services on group of 5,500 employees	$90.65 saved per caller for first six months of services, including avoidance of unnecessary MD and ER visits, counseling
American Institute of Preventive Medicine	700 employer study of self care impact with call center services	24% reduction in cost when integrated call center service included self care materials
Children's Hospital in San Diego	Cost impact of back care	$200,000 saved first year, back stress claims down by 400%
Pacific Bell	30,000 employees in wellness program—outcomes	83% improvement in hypertensives, 65% smokers quit, 20% improvement in obesity
Johnson & Johnson Corp.	Employee Wellness Program Live for Life	$378/year reduced health claims and lower absenteeism in programs with checkups, nutrition and fitness components
Helen Hayes Hospital in West Haverstraw, NY	Osteoporosis Intervention	195 employees, 61% shown to make lifestyle changes that reduce osteoporortic fracture by 50% through early diagnosis/intervention

Note: This is a sampling of thousands of studies reported in medical journals, trade publications, at conferences, and in newspapers. The range of savings reported depends on the individual characteristics of the program and work site.

EXHIBIT 8-3. Wellness programs cost impact. (Source: Wellness Institute Inc.; © 1998.)

174,000 deaths from cancer to tobacco use and says they could have been prevented. The health care costs directly connected to smoking totaled $50 billion in 1996, according to the Centers for Disease Control and Prevention. The case against tobacco is strong enough to suggest that it's prudent for you, as the employer, to encourage and provide smoking cessation programs as another way to reduce the cost of your health plan.

Heart disease is the leading cause of death in the United States, costing $274.2 billion annually and causing about 960,000 deaths each year, according to the American Heart Association's 1998 annual report. The cost of coronary artery bypass surgery is about $45,000, and 573,000 procedures were performed in 1997; of these, 44 percent were performed on patients under age 65. Compare this cost to an average drug therapy cost of $2,000–$3,000 per year to lower cholesterol, in conjunction with lifestyle changes needed to provide longer-term good health to the patient.

Stroke is the third leading cause of death. Prevention and control of high blood pressure, which causes stroke and heart disease, is lifestyle-focused, according to the *Guide to Clinical Preventive Services,* produced by the Department of Health and Human Service, which calls for dietary and exercise interventions for mild hypertension, adding appropriate medications for more severe hypertension. It is estimated that 21 percent of hypertension can be controlled through early diagnosis of high blood pressure and appropriate intervention. The cost of stroke is $43.3 billion annually, more than $5.3 billion of which is for rehabilitation and related medical services. As a result of prevention programs during the past twenty-five years, the death toll from heart attacks has been cut by one-third and from strokes by half. Treatment of key risk factors is credited for these gains.

Diabetes is now the fifth leading cause of death in women and the seventh leading cause in men. African Americans, Hispanics, and Asians are particularly at risk. The incidence of diabetes has doubled during the past two decades, and the disease now affects 8.7 million Americans, 95 percent of whom have the milder, noninsulin-dependent Type II. Although age increases diabetes risk, it is also related to obesity, smoking, lack of exercise, and unhealthy diet. Complications of diabetes include loss of vision, amputations (more than 50,000 in 1998), and kidney failure and heart disease. The American Heart Association reports that 80 percent of all diabetics die from some form of heart disease. Not a pretty picture, and one that can be improved if the disease is diagnosed early. The risk for cardiovascular disease among diabetics rises to 60–70 percent depending on the presence of preventable risk factors such as high blood pressure, obesity, high cholesterol, and current smoking. The cost of this chronic condition is high; more than 493,000 diabetics were hospitalized for treatment in 1995. The average diabetic costs a health plan about $6,000 a year.

Chronic disease and high cost go together (see Exhibit 8-4a, b). Breast cancer, skin cancer, prostate cancer, problem pregnancies, osteoporosis, asthma—all benefit from early detection, as do rarer diseases such as multiple sclerosis, Crohn's disease, and cerebral palsy. Because of available services and technology, some diseases are easier to treat in work-site-based programs. You should prioritize your choices for wellness services and base them on the demographics of the workforce, the interests of your employees, the cost and availability of meaningful programs, and your ability to implement them.

Employee Needs Assessment

Before you start to analyze your workforce, it's important to survey your employees to find out about their interests. A review of your demographics is in order before you prepare a survey that will alert employees to potential new services at work. You need to determine

	% of All Enrollees	% Who Are High Cost	% of High-Cost Enrollees	% of Total Costs	Ratio (% total costs to % enrollees)
All Enrollees (n = 722)	100	15	100	100	1.0
Pregnant	1.7	66.7	7.3	4.5	2.65
Treated Chronic Disease					
Cancer	2.4	47.1	7.3	16.7	6.96
Diabetes	2.8	65.0	11.9	12.3	4.39
Heart disease	5.3	47.4	16.5	13.0	2.45
COPD/asthma[a]	3.6	30.8	7.3	8.0	2.22
Hypertension	8.2	27.1	14.7	17.4	2.12
Arthritis	7.3	22.6	11.0	9.0	1.23
Treated Chronic Symptom					
Abdominal pain	6.4	30.4	12.8	14.7	2.30
Headache	4.2	33.3	9.2	9.4	2.24
Fatigue	3.9	25.0	6.4	6.1	1.56
Back pain	8.3	21.7	11.9	11.9	1.43
Psychological Illness					
Depression	3.6	38.5	9.2	9.1	2.53
Anxiety	2.8	40.0	7.3	4.0	1.43

Note: When stratified into low, medium, and high cost enrollees, the estimated mean cost of care was about $200 for low-cost enrollees, $800 for medium-cost enrollees, and $4,400 for high-cost enrollees. Costs were estimated by actuarial methods reflecting both the direct and indirect costs of care.
[a]Chronic obstructive pulmonary disease.

EXHIBIT 8-4a. Characteristics of high-cost patients and the percentage they consume of all costs for selected chronic conditions. (Source: Michael Von Korff and Jean Marshall, *HMO Practice*, vol. 6, no. 1, 1992; copyright © 1992 HMO Practice.)

the prevalence of men, women, certain age groups, ethnicities or races, and educational levels. Special needs of handicapped and hearing- or vision-impaired employees and those whose first language is not English should be noted. You can avoid problems with employee access to programs and enthusiasm by identifying these needs in the planning process.

	Direct Costs	Total Costs
33% higher than average body mass	$122	$ 448
100 more minutes of exercise per week	50	362
One cigarette pack per week (vs. no packs)	287	1,902
100% vs. 50% seat belt use	34	772
More than two drinks per day (vs. two or fewer)	104	814
Total annual cost savings	598	4,298

EXHIBIT 8-4b. Summary of habits, health, and annual costs in a group of retirees. (Source: J. Paul Leigh and James F. Fries, *Inquiry*, Spring 1992.)

As life expectancy continues to rise, the issues of how to reduce health care costs and provide useful wellness programs for your aging work force is of particular concern. Retirees also have some specific wellness issues resulting from their absence from the work site and their relocation to distant areas. Despite the barriers to communication, the need to provide services related to chronic conditions increases with workers' ages. As Exhibit 8-4b shows, there is a relationship between health habits and subsequent medical costs among retirees. It is clear that lifestyle change can affect many of the costs shown.

The need of older plan members is for longer-term, high-cost treatments for preventable disease. With this sort of plan member there is a logical need for wellness and disease management programs that target chronic disease and improve the coordination of services and early treatment for it.

An important reason to examine your demographics is to select programs that target conditions likely to be prevalent among your employees. The Wellness Councils of America have developed guidelines on risk factors found in the average group of 100 employees (see Exhibit 8-5). It's useful to know that your workforce is above or below an average for established risk factors—it indicates the presence or absence of healthy behaviors.

Work-site schedules, facilities, implementation problems, and locations have to be considered, too. For instance, if you have several smaller work sites and one central site, you should be aware of the problems of offering programs at the main site only or of bringing services to a nominal number of employees at an outlying site. A work site assessment should be conducted. Using the assessment in Exhibit 8-6 as a model, you can create your own survey topics that will help you plan wellness services better.

A wellness survey of employees should follow the communications procedures, timetable, preparation, distribution, publicity, tallying, and reporting stages described in Chapter 7 for the survey on benefits. It is important to have the support, in advance, of top management and to involve employees and other managers in the development, distribution, tallying, and analysis of survey results.

You can opt to have a section on lifestyle risks to gather information about potential health issues, or you can rely upon demographic data to project the incidence of certain conditions and focus your survey on programs and services, as in Exhibit 8-7. In either case, you will want to ensure anonymity, ease of completion, opportunity for comments and suggestions, and ease of return. You can add, delete, or amend sections and individual questions to suit your needs.

Once the results are in—from your survey of interest, your analysis of demographic data, and your work-site assessment—you should review claims data. Your plan administrator can furnish you with reports that identify higher-than-average costs for chronic conditions. This type of report is shown in Exhibit 8-8. You can track the impact of certain conditions on health plan costs, and, if this report is monitored every three months, you can monitor the effect of targeted wellness programs.

Types of Wellness Services

There are general categories of wellness services, and your creation of a unique program for your work site will be like selecting the proverbial "one from Column A, two from Column B." Among the options are these:

■ *On-site medical diagnosis and intervention.* This includes screening and clinical services for chronic conditions like hypertension, diabetes, heart health, breast cancer, osteoporosis, prostate cancer, asthma, and skin cancer. Diagnosis and intervention can

STATISTICALLY, IF THERE ARE 100 PEOPLE IN YOUR COMPANY OR DEPARTMENT...

Wellness Councils of America has taken these numbers from various sources and uses them here simply as illustration; they should not be considered research data. Sources included the American Heart Association, Centers for Disease Control and Prevention, National Center for Health Statistics, StayWell Health Management Systems, and the National Highway Traffic Safety Administration.

EXHIBIT 8-5. Incidence of health risk factors. (Source: Wellness Councils of America.)

be combined in a targeted medical visit or over a period of time with on-site visits and telephone or mailed contact.

- *Educational and counseling services.* These vary from health newsletters and bulletins, to targeted mailings, nurse call centers for triage and disease management, self-care guides and manuals, outbound calls by health professionals to manage and counsel patients with chronic or acute conditions, traditional employee assistance programs, and several types of on-site events and presentations.

(text continues on page 154)

Date _____ Location _____

Work Activity at site _____

Demographics of Work Force:
Employees _____ # Males _____ # Females _____
Retirees _____ # Males _____ # Females _____
Employees/Retirees 18–35 yrs. _____ 35–50 yrs. _____ 50–65 yrs. _____ >65 yrs. _____
Employment Status: blue collar ___ clerical/admin ___ managers ___ professionals ___

Check the conditions that apply to this work site:
__ non-English speaking employees   __ deaf or mute employees
__ disabled employees/mobility issues   __ other special needs _____
__ work shifts from ___ to ___   __ isolated facility, rural or remote
__ limited or no available space   __ lack of management interest/support
__ restricted or no communications   __ need to delay for further approval
__ small number of employees   __ reluctance to schedule now
__ facility unsuitable   __ work duty restricts employee availability
__ union issues need resolution   __ no breaks or lunch time

Assess the work site for:
Assign a number from 1=low to 5=high
__ stress level   __ physical demands on employees
__ presence of obesity   __ presence of smokers
__ sedentary lifestyle   __ safety/injury issues
__ mental health needs   __ substance abuse
__ employees are older   __ employees are young

ORGANIZATIONAL HISTORY:

Founded or organized in _____   Number of work site locations _____
Nature of business _____
Key Manager/Contact at site _____ Title _____
Telephone _____ Fax _____
Address _____

Check those that apply:
__ Health coverage provided to most employees   __ Health coverage provided to retirees
__ Recent change(s) in health plan   __ Management supports employee health
__ Growth in organization, last 5 years   __ Funding exists to support wellness
__ Cutbacks in organization, last 5 years   __ Employee income is relatively high
__ Growth expected in next 5 years   __ Wellness programs already exist
__ Decline expected in next 5 years   __ Current wellness efforts are successful
__ Employee relations positive   __ Wellness efforts are unsuccessful
__ Employee relations not positive   __ Peer activity/exchange is encouraged
__ Turnover is a concern   __ Absenteeism is high
__ Training/new skills common requirement   __ Recruitment is difficult

Notes on findings: _____
_____
_____
_____
_____

EXHIBIT 8-6. Work-site assessment. (Source: Wellness Institute Inc., copyright © 1997.)

CATEGORY I. INFORMATION AND NOTIFICATION SERVICES

How important are ongoing efforts to provide information and notification services to you? Please rate each item based on value to both you and your coworkers.
Please circle rating number to indicate a response: 5 = highest, 1 = lowest

	Level of Importance				
How do you rate the importance of any of the following suggested programs?	Very	High	Moderate	Somewhat	No
Discounts at fitness facilities and sporting goods stores	5	4	3	2	1
800# for your health and wellness questions for individual counseling with a nurse	5	4	3	2	1
Focus groups or forums on wellness issues so you can give input on program planning	5	4	3	2	1
Surveys on your opinion, such as this, or shorter ones on specific topics	5	4	3	2	1

Please list your suggestions for improving the information, notices and services now provided, or additional ways to communicate with you about programs and wellness issues:

_____

_____

_____

CATEGORY II. WORKSITE ASSESSMENT AND FOLLOW UP SERVICES

How important is it to provide these worksite screening and assessment programs? Please indicate the importance to your coworkers as well as to yourself in your rating.
Please circle rating number to indicate a response: 5 = highest, 1 = lowest

	Level of Importance				
	Very	High	Moderate	Somewhat	No
General rating for all such programs	5	4	3	2	1
Health risk appraisal, computerized measure of your health risks, or written questionnaire	5	4	3	2	1
Heart health testing for cholesterol and risk factors, and intervention	5	4	3	2	1
Breast cancer, mammography screening	5	4	3	2	1
Skin cancer assessment & intervention	5	4	3	2	1
Prostate cancer screening & awareness	5	4	3	2	1
Osteoporosis assessment & intervention	5	4	3	2	1
Depression & anxiety, confidential and individual assessment, by telephone	5	4	3	2	1
Hypertension, blood pressure screening and referral or intervention	5	4	3	2	1
Physical fitness testing for strength, endurance, and flexibility	5	4	3	2	1
Diabetes assessment, evaluation, and intervention services with ophthalmologist, podiatrist, and registered dietician	5	4	3	2	1
Eye health screening & intervention	5	4	3	2	1
Nutrition assessment, individual session	5	4	3	2	1

Please describe any other screening or assessment programs that you suggest:

_____

_____

_____

_____

CATEGORY III. SKILLS TRAINING EVENTS, PRESENTATIONS, CLASSES

Rate the benefit of the following programs to you and your coworkers. Please rate their importance whether or not you have participated in them at any time.
Please circle rating number to indicate a response: 5 = highest, 1 = lowest

	Level of Importance				
	Very	High	Moderate	Somewhat	No
General rating for all such programs	5	4	3	2	1
Yoga Demonstrations (posture, breathing)	5	4	3	2	1
Body Mechanics, training on lifting, sitting, standing, posture, presentation at breaks	5	4	3	2	1
Meditation Training, startup skills to begin to meditate	5	4	3	2	1
Sports Stretches, presentation on before and after stretches to reduce injury	5	4	3	2	1
Nutrition Seminars	5	4	3	2	1

Check your top priority topics
   Eating Out
   Vitamins & Supplements
   Healthy Holiday Eating
   High Fiber Made Easy
   Diabetes Control
   Heart-Healthy Snacks
   Lower Salt Meals
   Low Fat Foods

EXHIBIT 8-7. Employee survey on suggested wellness programs. (Source: Wellness Institute Inc., copyright © 1996.)

			Level of Importance		
	Very	High	Moderate	Somewhat	No
Skin Care: Preventing Sun Damage	5	4	3	2	1
Women & Aging in Good Health	5	4	3	2	1
Eye Care & Eye Health at All Ages	5	4	3	2	1
Finding Home Remedies That Work	5	4	3	2	1
Osteoporosis Prevention: Calcium Tips	5	4	3	2	1
Menopause—Before, During, and After	5	4	3	2	1
Sleep Deprivation	5	4	3	2	1
Alternative Medicine Primer	5	4	3	2	1
Dealing with Family Illness	5	4	3	2	1
How to Channel Anger	5	4	3	2	1
Visualization and Relaxation Techniques	5	4	3	2	1
Smoking—New Ways to Quit	5	4	3	2	1
Smoking—Create a Smokefree Environment	5	4	3	2	1
Child Safety at Home	5	4	3	2	1
Children: School Lunch Success	5	4	3	2	1
Events:					
Good Nutrition Snack Day at Work	5	4	3	2	1
Great American Smokeout	5	4	3	2	1

Please add any topics, wellness activities, or suggestions you may have:

_____
_____
_____

CATEGORY IV. BEHAVIOR MODIFICATION CLASSES AND ACTIVITIES

How important are the following programs to your health and to the health and well-being of your coworkers and their families? Please rate each item whether or not you would participate.

Please circle rating number to indicate a response: 5 = highest, 1 = lowest

			Level of Importance		
	Very	High	Moderate	Somewhat	No
General rating of this type of programs	5	4	3	2	1
Cooking Demonstrations:	5	4	3	2	1

Check those of interest:

  Low-Fat Cooking
  Summertime Healthy Grilling
  Vegetarian Delights
  Sugar Control for Desserts
  Tasty Less-Salt Meals
  Holiday Carving & Cooking
  Heart Healthy Italian
  Heart Healthy Chinese
  Quick 'n' Healthy Dinners

Classes:

	Very	High	Moderate	Somewhat	No
Weight Management Group, or Individual	5	4	3	2	1
Diabetic Control Counseling	5	4	3	2	1
CPR Training & Certification	5	4	3	2	1
Cycling Safety & Training	5	4	3	2	1
Light Weights for Bone Health	5	4	3	2	1
Stretchercise or Aerobics	5	4	3	2	1
T'ai Chi or Yoga Instruction	5	4	3	2	1
Healthy Back	5	4	3	2	1
Worksite Walking Program	5	4	3	2	1
Stress Reduction Skills	5	4	3	2	1
Self-Defense Training	5	4	3	2	1

Please note any additional classes, activities or programs that are of interest to you:

_____
_____
_____

If you need additional space, please use the back of this sheet.

Your response and interest are appreciated.
Thank You!

Unit	Employee/Total Paid		Diagnosis
17-002	Employee	$31,087.82	Cardiac inpatient treatment
17-002	Spouse	$30,007.73	Postpolio treatment
17-011	Dependent	$64,068.64	Respiratory disease lung removal
17-011	Self	$42,976,10	Gallbladder surgery complications
17-011	Self	$42,105.53	Lung cancer
17-011	Dependent	$33,364.78	Inpatient psych care
17-011	Dependent	$35,538.25	Inpatient psych care
17-011	Self	$39,454.36	Cardiac bypass surgery
17-011	Self	$28,650.65	Cardiac inpatient treatment

EXHIBIT 8-8. High-cost claims for chronic conditions. (Source: Halo Associates.)

- *Behavioral change and maintenance.* Classes, seminars, and combinations of these should have printed and telephonic support and follow-up for health risks. Multiple sessions and peer support have been successful in altering lifestyle behaviors that carry risks, such as lack of exercise, smoking, excessive stress, poor nutrition, and substance abuse. Work-site walking programs, meditation classes, aerobics classes, and weight control and smoking cessation programs are all examples.
- *Life skills training.* These programs are shorter term than behavioral change programs. They are often intervention programs for motivated employees who wish to learn new skills that can help them make desired lifestyle changes. Cooking classes featuring low-fat meals, training in self-defense, classes on dealing with anger, parenting or elder-care workshops, safe driving programs, and weight training are examples. Behavioral and life skills activities can be tailored to meet your needs, mixed and matched, or integrated with other services provided in-house or through your health plan.

Selecting Wellness Services

Now you are ready to select services that address employee needs and concerns and that can have an impact on your health plan costs. Which programs are most important? Which are easier to implement and most likely to be successful? How do you find appropriate outside resources, and when should you use your staff? What questions do you ask vendors, and what are standard issues to resolve before hiring someone?

If you followed the template provided here, you covered a lot of bases when you prepared your wellness survey. You should now have input from advisers, employees, and managers. Even with this comprehensive information about what employees want and need, you shouldn't expect to kick off a massive wellness program all at once. As with other initiatives at your organization, new programs take time.

Exhibit 8-9 gives you some idea of the range of programs provided at worksites. Some employers offer only one program each year, while others have a schedule of programs that take place monthly or quarterly. Once your wellness program begins, you'll have more than enough ideas to keep your program fresh. You can expect vendors, wellness committee members, and others in your organization to make suggestions about additional services.

Which programs are most important? That depends on the tally of your wellness

Levels of Intervention	Preventive Health	Nutrition and Weight Control	Fitness	Stress Management	Smoking Cessation
Communication and Awareness Programs	▪ Newsletter articles ▪ Health fair ▪ Check stuffers ▪ E-mail ▪ Posters ▪ Fliers	▪ Nutrition games ▪ National nutrition month events ▪ Newsletter articles ▪ Table tents	▪ Fitness events ▪ Newsletter articles ▪ Posters ▪ Fliers	▪ Newsletter articles ▪ Posters ▪ Fliers	▪ Newsletter articles ▪ Posters ▪ Fliers
Screening and Assessment Programs	▪ Blood pressure screening ▪ Health risk profile ▪ Cholesterol testing ▪ Health physical ▪ Cancer screening	▪ Nutrition assessment ▪ Computerized diet analysis ▪ Body-fat testing	▪ Cardiovascular risk appraisal ▪ Fitness testing ▪ Body-fat testing ▪ Blood pressure screening	▪ Biofeedback ▪ Blood pressure testing ▪ Psychoanalysis ▪ Stress questionnaires	▪ Smoking risk assessment ▪ Carbon monoxide testing ▪ Pulmonary testing
Education and Lifestyle Programs	▪ Seminars ▪ AIDS education ▪ CPR classes ▪ Physician referral system ▪ Community referral system ▪ Self-help kits	▪ Seminars ▪ Weight loss contests ▪ Weight loss courses ▪ Cooking classes ▪ Nutrition counseling ▪ Cholesterol programs	▪ Seminars ▪ Exercise ▪ Healthy back classes ▪ Personal training ▪ Aerobics classes ▪ Walking club ▪ Fitness contest	▪ Seminars ▪ Stress management workshop ▪ Time management workshop ▪ Lifestyle course ▪ Massage therapy ▪ Psychotherapy	▪ Seminars ▪ Support group ▪ Behavior modification courses ▪ Hypnosis ▪ Acupuncture
Behavior Change Support Systems	▪ Incentive system ▪ Goal setting ▪ Resource center ▪ Buddy system	▪ Cafeteria programs ▪ Healthy vending machines	▪ On-site fitness center ▪ Exercise equipment ▪ Exercise trails ▪ Corporate sports teams	▪ "Quiet" room ▪ Career development counseling ▪ Job satisfaction strategies ▪ Employee assistance programs	▪ Nicotine gum ▪ Smoking policy ▪ No-smoking areas ▪ Smoke-free worksite

EXHIBIT 8-9. Wellness and lifestyle modification programs. (Source: Reprinted by permission from Association for Fitness, 1992, *Guidelines for Employee Health Promotion Programs* [Champaign, IL: Human Kinetics], p. 25.)

survey and on your analysis of demographics. First, you should rank your employee responses numerically and prioritize them accordingly. Next, you should evaluate whether their choices are compatible with your demographic data. Exhibit 8-10 presents risk factors for which you might wish to screen and the impact of age, gender, and ethnicity on disease incidence.

By now you should have some idea of the behaviors and conditions that have the highest costs and those where early detection makes a major difference in cost. Exhibit 8-11 presents selected high-cost conditions and their reduced cost if detected early.

My preference is to start with on-site medical programs. There is nothing more moti-

(text continues on page 158)

GENDER, AGE & ETHNIC IMPACT ON CERTAIN CONDITIONS

Cancers:	Male	Female	Age	Ethnicity
Breast Cancer	5%	1:26	>40 yr	Caucasian
		1:14	>50 yr	
		1:8	>60 yr	
Prostate Cancer	20%	—	>40	African American
Skin Cancer	15%	11%	—	Caucasian

Diabetes:	Whites	Blacks	Age	Ethnicity
	11.3%	5.6%	>45	African American
	17.4%	9.5%	>65	Hispanic
	14.1%	10.2%	>75	Asian

Stroke:	Females	Males	Age	Ethnicity
	0.5%	1.6%	>40	African American
	1.2%	3.3%	>50	Hispanic
	3.3%	3.2%	>60	
	7.8%	9.3%	>70	
	12.8%	12.8%	>80	

Coronary Heart Disease:	Females	Males	Age	Ethnicity
	5.3%	6.8%	>40	Caucasian
	7.9%	12.7%	>50	
	11.0%	16.0%	>60	
	13.6%	22.0%	>70	
	18.2%	25.6%	>80	

RISK FACTORS AND THEIR RELATIONSHIP TO CHRONIC CONDITIONS

Obesity:	Age	Gender	Ethnicity	Conditions
25> BMI	>40	Females	African American	Cardiac Disease
			Asian	Diabetes
			Hispanics	Hypertension
		Males	African American	Some Cancers
			Hispanics	

Smoking:	Age	%	Gender	Ethnicity	Conditions
	>18	28.0	Males	Caucasian	Cardiac Disease
		24.7	Females	Caucasian	Hypertension
					Diabetes
					Cancer, especially Lung, Throat/ Pharynx, Breast, Prostate

Elevated Cholesterol:	>200 mg/dL	>240 mg/dL	Gender	Ethnicity	Conditions
	52%	17.3%	Males	Caucasian	Cardiac Disease
	51%	20.2%	Females	Caucasian	Diabetes
	46%	15.7%	Males	African American	Hypertension
	46%	19.8%	Females	African American	
	47%	17.8%	Males	Mexican-American	
	43%	17.5%	Females	Mexican-American	

Percentage of Americans by gender and ethnicity with elevated cholesterol. Above 240 mg/dL doubles cardiac risk.

EXHIBIT 8-10. Predisposing factors and risk factors for disease. (Source: Wellness Institute Inc., based on information from the American Heart Association's and the American Cancer Society's 1998 annual reports.)

Condition	Incidence	Intervention/Cost	Prevention/Cost	Potential Cost Savings
Breast Cancer	12% of women over 65 180,200 cases yr. and 43,900 deaths yr.	Surgery, radiation, chemotherapy, based on early or late diagnosis. Cost: $125,000–$160,000 for first year for late diagnosis	Mammogram & physical exam. Cost: $150–$250 yrly Early detection of breast cancer cost is $25,000–$50,000	$100,000–$110,000 for each breast cancer case detected early
Stroke	600,000 strokes yr. 158,000 deaths yr.	Inpatient hospital stay, Hemiplegia treatment & rehabilitation. Cost: $30,000 first yr.	Identify and monitor hypertension, alter diet & exercise, medication Cost: $350–$500/yr.	$25,000/yr. or more for each stroke avoided.
Osteoporosis Fracture (hip)	50% white women over 50 yrs, 25% women of color, 20% older men	Hospitalization, surgery, & rehabilitation, plus medication. 20% die prematurely, 10% return to active life Cost: $45,000 first yr.	Bone density test w/ dietary & exercise changes, medications and supplements. Cost: $200–$350/yr.	$44,000/yr. or more for each fracture avoided. 50% are avoided through early detection and treatment.
Heart Disease Coronary	50% of men and women over 55 yrs, 330,000 premature deaths yr, total deaths are 960,590 hr	Hospitalization, bypass surgery, rehabilitation, medications. Cost: $60,000 first yr.	Early detection w/ cholesterol test, dietary & exercise changes & medications. Cost: $1,500–2,500 yr.	$57,500–$58,500 yr for each patient with high cholesterol and weight under control
Prostate Cancer	41,800 deaths yr. 20% of men	Surgery, radiation, chemotherapy, medications, loss of function. Cost: $20,000–$40,000 first yr.	Early detection with PSA test, digital rectal exam, medication, lower cost options for better outcomes. Cost: $2,000–$2,500 yr.	$17,500–37,500 first yr. for each patient diagnosed with early stage controllable by monitoring, lifestyle change, medications
Diabetes	Occurs in 9.5–17.3% after age 65, and 5.6–11.3% ages 45–64 60,000 yr. premature deaths	Insulin dependency, complications with heart, kidney, blindness & amputation Cost: $6,000 yr. avg	Early detection w/ blood glucose test, dietary & lifestyle change, medication Preventive eye, foot, and cardiology visits. Cost: $1,500–$2,500 yr.	$3,500–$4,500 yr. w/ no complications to cause inpatient hospital stays and treatments for diabetics diagnosed early and who receive preventive services.
Skin Cancer	12.2% men & women, all ages, higher for fair skinned w/ burn history Survival rate early diagnosis is 95%, late diagnosis is 16%.	Surgery, radiation, chemotherapy. $2,500–$10,000 first yr.	Early detection w/ physical exam, change in exposure to sun & use of sunscreen. Cost: $300 yr.	$2,200–$9,300 yr. for early diagnosis at preventable stage
Low Birth Weight Babies	260,000 LBWB yr. 23,000 deaths yr.	Neonatal intensive care and follow-up Cost: Avg $100,000 yr.	Prenatal counseling, lifestyle change & regular prenatal visits Cost: $4,500.	$95,500 for neonatal intensive care avoided by better prenatal care and higher-weight baby

Note: Injuries, HIV infection, alcoholism, drug abuse, inadequate immunization, and influenza are all preventable with interventions that are costly. They, like the conditions shown, have lower cost when treated early through work-site wellness programs that inform, teach life skills, provide early-intervention services, and promote positive behavioral change.

EXHIBIT 8-11. Cost of treatment for certain preventable conditions. (Source: Wellness Institute Inc.)

vating to employees than to learn they are at risk for a chronic disease that has not yet fully manifested itself. When an employee is told that he has high blood pressure and is in danger of a stroke, he is more likely to seek appropriate medical treatment. The same is true if an employee is diagnosed with an early stage of breast cancer, skin cancer, or diabetes. Most chronic diseases can take years to show symptoms, and by the time the patient has symptoms, treatment options are more costly and often less successful at controlling the disease and avoiding premature death.

I don't advocate diagnosis programs that have no intervention component. In other words, if your wellness vendor provides a screening without follow-up, find another vendor. It does minimal good to inform an employee about a diagnosis without encouraging and finding out whether treatment is sought. Often employees don't understand the report or finding or are not sure of the diagnosis, what is recommended, how or where to seek medical treatment, and what they can do to help themselves. On-site written or telephonic follow-up by your wellness vendor ensures that employees will have a better understanding of and be more likely to comply with treatment recommendations.

I think employees feel better about a program that shows some concern for their individual situations, too. You can measure outcomes more accurately when follow-up is built into your program. When your wellness vendor reports on whether or not an employee sought treatment and is following recommendations and whether the condition has improved or is under control, the results have cost implications for your health plan. You will be able to justify expenses for wellness, and compare the year-to-year data when you can document outcomes consistently. Exhibit 8-12 presents a typical management report on utilization and outcomes of a work-site diagnosis and intervention program for osteoporosis.

It's important to integrate health education when you offer on-site medical services. Some vendors offer risk assessments and seminars by disease, appropriate to the on-site screening. You should take advantage of this related service so that employees who are not at risk do not waste health plan or wellness resources, and those who are at risk will be more aware of symptoms, risk factors, and treatments, whether or not they opt to participate in a screening. If you have health personnel, volunteers, or advisers who are competent to provide educational seminars, you may want to involve them. A risk assessment can be similar to a patient history, identifying risk factors, or it can be a questionnaire. Exhibit 8-13 presents a nutrition risk assessment used in a heart health program. These assessments should be provided by your wellness vendor as part of program materials.

Turnkey programs, where the outside vendor provides all written materials, presentations, and medical services, are the easiest for you to implement. You will need to check references and provide on-site support staff to facilitate scheduling and coordination, and you will be responsible for receiving, evaluating, and using any reports that are furnished.

Success will vary from program to program. You are bound to have some programs that are more popular than others. This is normal. When you offer wellness programs, issues of confidentiality, cost, scheduling, or convenience may arise. It's easier, when you outsource such services, to ensure confidentiality. You need to remind employees of the commitment to confidentiality at each stage of publicizing, enrolling, and providing wellness programs. The more you can delegate to the wellness vendor, the more employees will realize your involvement is removed, and the more relaxed they will be about confidentiality issues.

If you have planned carefully, in accordance with your site assessment, employee survey responses, and input from a wellness committee, you will have a better chance to

December 22, 1998

RE Report on Osteoporosis Program Screening:

Dear

    We are pleased to enclose an aggregate data report to you in connection with the recently conducted osteoporosis services we provided at   for your employees.

    The outcome of the 33 patients scanned is:

Normal bone: 14	Abnormal bone: 19
Osteoporotic: 5	Low bone mass: 14

    The relative lifetime fracture probability for those screened shows:

Normal fracture probability: 11
Higher than normal: 22

    The doctor's recommendations for the 33 patients screened include:

Dietary changes (increase calcium) 20	Increase exercise 15
See Primary Care Physician 10	See Specialist 5
Repeat scan in 1–3 years 13	Repeat scan later 17

    We are also enclosing a copy of the summary sheet from individual evaluations handed in at the results seminar by participants. We are pleased to note the very positive reaction to the program. Your employees also seem interested in other programs, suitable at the worksite. Our descriptions for some available programs are enclosed for your review.

    Thank you for the opportunity to be of service. Please give us a call with any questions, or if you wish to discuss further programs for your employees.

Very truly yours,

EXHIBIT 8-12. Sample letter. (Source: Wellness Institute Inc.)

minimize problems with cost, scheduling, and convenience. You should know all of the terms and conditions, in advance, for any program you schedule.

    Your biggest hurdle is to get employees to participate. Attractive advance program announcements, repeated notices and postings, and clear-cut program information from the wellness vendor, distributed by your staff and wellness committee, are essential to your success. Be sure your staff is aware of the schedule, program description, and any requirements for participation or enrollment. Enlist the help of wellness committee members, employee representatives, and management to encourage employee participation.

	never	sometimes	often	always
I eat most of my food daily after 5 PM	—	—	—	—
I eat meals alone	—	—	—	—
I eat fewer than 2 meals per day	—	—	—	—
I take 3 or more different drugs per day	—	—	—	—
I have tooth/mouth problems	—	—	—	—
I eat less than 5 fruits/veggies per day	—	—	—	—
I eat mostly meat and protein	—	—	—	—
I eat less than 1 dairy product daily	—	—	—	—
I snack on high fat or sweet foods	—	—	—	—
I eat less than 6 starches daily	—	—	—	—
I usually eat processed foods	—	—	—	—

What Counts As A Serving?

Bread: 1 slice, 1/2 cup cooked rice/pasta, 1/2 cup cooked cereal or 1 ounce ready-to-eat cereal, 3 or 4 small crackers, 1/2 bagel or roll.

Vegetables: 1 cup raw, leafy veggies, 1/2 cup others, cooked, chopped or raw. 1/2 cup veggie juice.

Fruits: 1 medium piece of fruit, 3/4 cup fruit juice, 1/2 cup canned fruit, 1/4 cup dried fruit.

Dairy: 1 cup milk or yogurt, 2 ounces processed cheese or 1 1/2 ounce natural cheese.

Meats: 2 1/2–3 ounces cooked, lean meat, poultry, or fish.
ount the following as 1 ounce lean meat: 1/2 cup cooked dry beans, 1 egg, 1/3 cup nuts, 2 T peanut butter.

Fats: 1 tsp oil, butter, mayonnaise, margarine or salad dressing

Fats, Oils, Sweets
Use Sparingly

Milk, Yogurt, Cheese
2–3 Servings Daily

Meat, Poultry, Fish, Dry Beans, Eggs, Nuts
2–3 Servings Daily

Vegetables
3–5 Servings Daily

Fruit
2–4 Servings Daily

Starches: Bread, Cereal, Rice, Pasta
6–11 Servings Daily

How Does Your Diet Measure Up?

	Recommended:	Your Total		Recommended:	Your Total:
Fats, oils, sweets	1–2/day	_____	Fruits	2–4/day	_____
Milk, yogurt, cheese	2–3/day	_____	Vegetables	3–5 day	_____
Meat, poultry, fish, eggs	2–3/day	_____	Bread, cereal, pasta	6–11/day	_____

To improve your diet, the following goals are recommended:

EXHIBIT 8-13. Nutrition assessment. (Source: Wellness Institute Inc., copyright © 1997.)

How do you measure success? Participation rates, number of diagnoses, employee satisfaction, outcomes—all are used to measure success. Longer-term success is measured in lower claims cost for chronic conditions, lowered absenteeism and turnover, and reduced incidence of chronic conditions. Exhibit 8-14 presents an employee evaluation of a work-site osteoporosis program. A tally of such evaluations should be provided as part of the wellness provider's service to you.

Participant Evaluation
Osteoporosis Intervention

Name: _____ Tel _____ Date _____

Employer: _____ Dept _____

Please complete the following questions about this worksite program.
Ratings for the program are: 1 = lowest, 5 = highest

Information services

How clear were the enrollment and advance materials	1	2	3	4	5
Was publicity for this program timely for your enrollment	1	2	3	4	5
How convenient was the scheduling for you	1	2	3	4	5
Was the worksite space acceptable and appropriate	1	2	3	4	5
How do you rate the prescreening seminar	1	2	3	4	5
How do you rate the postscreening seminar	1	2	3	4	5
What is your overall rating for information provided	1	2	3	4	5

Medical services

How helpful was the advance seminar to you	1	2	3	4	5
How helpful was the results seminar to you	1	2	3	4	5
Were the programs conducted at an appropriate pace	1	2	3	4	5
Were the displays and handouts clear and useful	1	2	3	4	5
Was nurse-counselor accessible and suitable	1	2	3	4	5
How do you rate the nurse-counselor session	1	2	3	4	5
How do you rate the radiology tech and your scan	1	2	3	4	5

Your knowledge

Rate your improvement in knowledge about osteoporosis from this program	1	2	3	4	5
Rate your ability to choose healthier eating habits to avoid osteoporosis from this program	1	2	3	4	5
Rate your understanding of the importance of exercise from this program	1	2	3	4	5

Comments: _____

_____

_____

Would you attend another WI worksite program   Yes __ Maybe __ No __

Please list other types of services you would find helpful if they were offered at your worksite:

__ Mammography/breast cancer	__ Prostate cancer
__ Hypertension	__ Diabetes
__ Cardiac/heart healthy	__ Skin Cancer
__ worksite walking program	__ worksite nutrition program(s)
__ worksite relaxation program	__ worksite flu shots

List additional subjects or interest areas that you or your coworkers might participate in:

_____

_____

EXHIBIT 8-14. Sample employee evaluation report. (Source: Wellness Institute Inc., copyright © 1997.)

Finding the Right Wellness Provider

Appropriate wellness services can be found through several sources:

- Your local hospital
- Nonprofit agencies such as the American Heart Association or American Cancer Society
- Wellness vendors found in the phone book
- Specialty hospitals that offer outreach programs
- Recommendation of other local employers
- Industry resources (see Appendix)

Be aware of what's out there. You can ask other organizations in your area, your local business association, your employees, and your health plan adviser about wellness services and programs. Your local newspaper might feature a program of interest or a provider you can call.

Once you have identified wellness providers of interest, there are standard questions you should ask as part of a request for proposals or during an interview process. These include:

- How long have you been providing this service?
- What type of staff do you use, and what are their credentials?
- How does the program work, including any follow-up you provide?
- What reports, if any, do you furnish on the program?
- What are the costs for the program, and who pays them?
- Do you provide all printed materials and program materials?
- What is the time frame for implementation?

One issue to resolve is the terms and conditions of service, including any fee payments. You also need to check the vendor's references; review the services and staffing to be sure they are acceptable; complete your internal approval process before commiting to the program; and clear up any concern you have about the provider's flexibility and service philosophy.

Liability insurance is an important item. You should require a certificate of insurance from the wellness vendor, which protects and indemnifies you against any legal action in connection with the vendor's services. It is good business to transfer this risk to the vendor, and it is fairly common to require a $1 million liability policy of vendors with whom you contract. There is often no cost to the wellness vendor for an insurance certificate that names you as the additional insured for services rendered by agreement at your site.

Reaching Undecided Employees

What if your results show that employees aren't aware of their health risks or wellness needs and seem unsure of the value of wellness services? There are activities you can offer to motivate employees to think about health risks, including:

- A written questionnaire or health risk assessment. This is completed by the employee as a self-assessment and so may be less accurate than other health appraisals. There are computer versions and several outsourced versions that provide scoring and a mailing to employees. The cost of the printed and computerized versions, with scoring, ranges from $1.25 per employee to $3. You have the option of creating your own, from the template shown in Exhibit 8-15 and from input from volunteers committee members and your health plan adviser.

HEALTHSTYLE: A SELF-TEST

All of us want good health. But many of us do not know how to be as healthy as possible. Health experts now describe *lifestyle* as one of the most important factors affecting health. In fact, it is estimated that as many as seven of the ten leading causes of death could be reduced through common-sense changes in lifestyle. That's what this brief test, developed by the Public Health Service, is all about. Its purpose is simply to tell you how well you are doing to stay healthy. The behaviors covered in the test are recommended for most Americans. Some of them may not apply to persons with certain chronic diseases or handicaps, or to pregnant women. Such persons may require special instructions from their physicians.

Cigarette Smoking

If you *never smoke,* enter a score of 10 for this section and go to the next section on *Alcohol and Drugs.*

	Almost Always	Sometimes	Almost Never
1. I avoid smoking cigarettes.	2	1	0
2. I smoke only low tar and nicotine cigarettes *or* I smoke a pipe or cigars.	2	1	0

Smoking Score: _____

Alcohol and Drugs

	Almost Always	Sometimes	Almost Never
1. I avoid drinking alcoholic beverages *or* I drink no more than 1 or 2 drinks a day.	4	1	0
2. I avoid using alcohol or other drugs (especially illegal drugs) as a way of handling stressful situations or the problems in my life.	2	1	0
3. I am careful not to drink alcohol when taking certain medicines (for example, medicine for sleeping, pain, colds, and allergies), or when pregnant.	2	1	0
4. I read and follow the label directions when using prescribed and over-the-counter drugs	2	1	0

Alcohol and Drugs Score: _____

Eating Habits

	Almost Always	Sometimes	Almost Never
1. I eat a variety of foods each day, such as fruits and vegetables, whole grain breads, and cereals, lean meats, dairy products, dry peas and beans, and nuts and seeds.	4	1	0
2. I limit the amount of fat, saturated fat, and cholesterol I eat (including fat on meats, eggs, butter, cream, shortenings, and organ meats such as liver).	2	1	0
3. I limit the amount of salt I eat by cooking with only small amounts, not adding salt at the table, and avoiding salty snacks.	2	1	0
4. I avoid eating too much sugar (especially frequent snacks of sticky candy or soft drinks).	2	1	0

Eating Habits Score: _____

Exercise/Fitness

	Almost Always	Sometimes	Almost Never
1. I maintain a desired weight, avoiding overweight and underweight.	3	1	0
2. I do vigorous exercises for 15–30 minutes at least 3 times a week (examples include running, swimming, brisk walking).	3	1	0
3. I do exercises that enhance my muscle tone for 15–30 minutes at least 3 times a week (examples include yoga and calisthenics).	2	1	0
4. I use part of my leisure time participating in individual, family, or team activities that increase my level of fitness (such as gardening, bowling, golf, and baseball).	2	1	0

Exercise/Fitness Score: _____

Stress Control

	Almost Always	Sometimes	Almost Never
1. I have a job or do other work that I enjoy.	2	1	0
2. I find it easy to relax and express my feelings freely.	2	1	0
3. I recognize early, and prepare for, events or situations likely to be stressful for me.	2	1	0
4. I have close friends, relatives, or others whom I can talk to about personal matters and call on for help when needed.	2	1	0
5. I participate in group activities (such as church and community organizations) or hobbies that I enjoy.	2	1	0

Stress Control Score: _____

Safety

	Almost Always	Sometimes	Almost Never
1. I wear a seat belt while riding in a car.	2	1	0
2. I avoid driving while under the influence of alcohol and other drugs.	2	1	0
3. I obey traffic rules and the speed limit when driving.	2	1	0
4. I am careful when using potentially harmful products or substances (such as household cleaners, poisons, and electrical devices).	2	1	0
5. I avoid smoking in bed.	2	1	0

Safety Score: _____

EXHIBIT 8-15. Sample self-assessment questionnaire. (Source: From *Healthstyle: A Self-Test*, National Health Information Clearinghouse, Washington, D.C., 1995.)

- On-site risk appraisals, including a physical examination. You can outsource the risk appraisal and examination by using a wellness vendor, or you can have on-site exams by a staff physician or nurse provided by your local hospital. You may have a medical provider who conducts physicals for hiring or in workers compensation cases. Usually, your health plan, if the physical exam is conducted by a physician, will cover the cost for eligible employees.
- A hybrid program, which requires some payment by your organization, combines an exam by a nurse or registered dietitian counselor with a patient history and risk assessment. This can be useful to motivate employees and can guide them about their health risks.

Whichever method you use to provide a general health and risk assessment for employees, be sure to have aggregate data reports provided to you. This can guide and justify your wellness program choices, which can be based on actual risk levels as reported.

Planning Your Program

There is no single right program to start with. But you should begin with a plan that covers the first year of operation, with specific services in mind for the first six months and a general idea about the second six months. You should be sure to evaluate each program as it is conducted and concluded. Exhibit 8-16 presents a survey of wellness committee members that asks for their input on potential upcoming programs. You should measure interest, reactions, and support of programs whenever possible; it will help keep you objective when selecting and scheduling programs.

Funding Your Program

Funding for your wellness program can come from a single source or many. Possible sources include:

- A line item in your insurance or benefit budget. Typically, 1–3 percent of your health plan costs are allocated for private-sector wellness expenses. This can be $15–$30 per employee for the year, depending on the cost of your health plan.
- A grant from your administrator, carrier, MCO, or other service provider to the plan.
- Grants from outside sources, both public and private. Contact your county health department to inquire about state, federal, and local programs.
- Pooled resources with other small and mid-sized organizations to create a wellness fund to bring services to all member work sites, coordinated by a joint wellness committee.
- Free services from nonprofit agencies, such as the American Heart Association or American Cancer Society, using materials and volunteers they can provide.
- Internal resources of your employees, health professionals on staff, retiree volunteers, or wellness committee members who have some training and credentials.
- Support services from departments or individuals for printing, distribution, posting, telephone contact, and clerical assistance.
- Contributions from participants to defray the cost. This will depend on your philosophy about cost sharing and to what degree you can support wellness services with organizational and other funds. Conditions can vary from nothing to 100 percent.
- Medical services, billed to the participants health plan.

PROPOSED WELLNESS ACTIVITIES

A variety of assessments, skills training, and behavior modification programs are available to employees from our wellness program. To help identify those that might be most needed and useful to employees, please prioritize your top six choices in each of the following categories (1 is the highest priority and 6 the lowest). You are also asked to list additional topics, suggested programs, and interest areas that you may wish to have explored.

Category I. Worksite Screenings and Assessments.

Select the top six and assign a priority number to each. Leave others blank.

Depression _____
Diabetes/Cholesterol _____
Employee Needs Assessment Survey _____
Health Risk Appraisal _____
Hypertension _____
Mammography _____
Physical Fitness Evaluation _____
Prostate Cancer _____
Skin Cancer _____
Other: _____

Category II. Skills Training Programs/Events.

Fitness:
Select the top six including your suggestions for "other".

Line Dancing	_____	Walk & Win	_____
Juggling	_____	Yoga	_____
T'ai Chi	_____	Meditation	_____
Step Aerobics	_____	Biking/Hiking	_____
Light Weights	_____	Healthy Back	_____
Stretchersize	_____	Body Mechanics	_____

Other: _____

Nutrition:
Select the top six, including your suggestions for "other".

Diet Support Group	_____	Recipe Book	_____
Seminars Low Fat	_____	Low Salt	_____
Low Sugar	_____	High Fiber	_____
Vitamins	_____	Snacking	_____
Eating Out	_____	Diabetes Control	_____
Holidays	_____	Heart Healthy	_____

Cooking Demos: Available on wide range of topics, can be related to seminars above. Indicate which you think are the most interesting from the above list, from your own interests. If you're not sure of topic(s) indicate general priority number.

General _____
Specific Topic(s) _____
List topics: _____

Other: _____

General:
List top six priorities, including your suggestions.

Menopause Seminar	_____	Osteoporosis	_____
Holistic Medicine	_____	Women and Aging	_____
Male Cander Seminar	_____	Home Remedies	_____
Sleep Deprivation	_____	Eye Care	_____
Dermatology Issues	_____	Arthritis Management	_____
Sport-specific toning	_____	Drug therapies*	_____

*Can be specific to diagnosis; i.e., hypertension, cardiovascular, diabetes, CPD, MS, lyme disease, etc.
Other: _____

Please complete your response and return to _____

EXHIBIT 8-16. Survey of Wellness Committee. (Source: Wellness Institute Inc.)

What about potential sponsors for wellness programs and contributors? Plan administrators are a potential source for wellness grants, as are local hospitals where you have a negotiated discount and perhaps can purchase wellness services.

Carriers and MCOs sometimes provide grants for specific programs on a case-by-case basis. Open-enrollment marketing activities of some MCOs, for example, may include work-site mammography or other free screenings. I am not a fan of this type of approach. It seems frivolous to rely upon the goodwill of a carrier for a serious medical service that should be provided with continuity and follow-up. Marketing-related services may be here today and gone tomorrow.

There's a simple reason for the lukewarm attempts at wellness activities among carriers and MCOs. They are in the one-year renewal business, with a short-term focus on the health and well-being of plan members. This is directly opposite to your approach to employees—you hope to retain your employees for the long term and have a commitment to their health and well being over time.

The Interplay With Prevention

What goes with your wellness program is prevention. For example, if you offer an osteoporosis program at the work site, the information and other services are made available to everyone, not just those at high risk. Much of your effort reaches lower-risk employees—those who are healthy. The message is shared with their families and coworkers and becomes part of a healthy attitude and environment at work. Thousands of studies have shown that you can encourage employees to eliminate and reduce risky behaviors when you provide them with information and programs at work.

Many wellness programs begin at the back end, as far as I am concerned. They start by trying to change high-risk behaviors, instead of with early diagnosis or individual assessment, which can motivate an employee to recognize the need for changed behavior. In the five stages of change developed by wellness researchers—precontemplative, awareness and contemplative, decision to try to change, taking the steps to change, and maintenance of the change—it's clear that only a percentage of your employees are prepared to jump right into a program when you offer it. The others just aren't ready. So, even with a wonderful program that meets a need, you will find it much harder to get participation if you fail to motivate employees in advance at various stages of change through individual assessment, information, or diagnosis.

Here's an example of how change occurs in stages, from real life. In 1982 I was consulting for a large county in the suburbs of New York City. There were eleven employees in my client's office. All but two were women, and nine smoked cigarettes. Although no one was obese, the afternoon and morning coffee breaks included homemade cakes and cookies, or occasional purchased donuts. The average age of the employees was thirty-five years.

The first year I promoted the Great American Smokeout at this work site, in conjunction with the local American Cancer Society, we made healthy snacks part of the enticement to quit smoking for the day. After two years, three of the smokers had quit, and morning and afternoon snacks now consisted of fresh fruits and bite-size veggies, bought by a pool of the employees. By the eighth year, the last of the nine smokers had finally quit. To this day, the afternoon and morning snacks are fruits and veggies. On top of that, eleven of the now thirteen employees in this office compete in a work-site walking program, so break times are spent trekking the parameter of the parking lot instead of snacking or smoking.

After some shifts in employees, the average age of this group is now in the mid-fifties. In this group, so far there is no hypertension, no diabetes, no cardiac condition, and no cancer. Luck of the draw, perhaps? It's not a scientific study, by far, but I think that awareness, annual mammograms and other screenings, sensible eating and exercise, supportive environments to control stress—all of these have helped create a healthy group. At this work site, health has been a focus for the past seventeen years, causing major behavioral change through peer pressure at the work site and removing barriers to information and programs that support change.

Okay, so this group might be unusual, right? I think not. Everyone wants to live longer and to avoid illness. Given appropriate information, encouragement, motivation, and support, the average employee is very likely to change behavior toward a healthier lifestyle—especially if peer pressure at the work site and a supportive organizational culture are enlisted in the effort.

Summary

Work-site wellness is based on a few principles that reflect our changing world, where more people are at work longer. Here are some basic rules to follow for a successful program that meets your goals and your employees' needs:

- Remove barriers to care of access to services, affordable cost, and quality providers.
- Provide appropriate and appealing activities to improve or maintain health.
- Offer adequate, accurate, and useful information on health topics.
- Support positive change from high-risk behavior to healthier lifestyles.
- Recognize the importance of the health and well-being of employees.
- Measure the results of your wellness efforts.

Wellness is a concept that works, but, despite technological advances that bring more mobile services to work sites, it still takes time to develop a work-site culture to promote good health and discourage high-risk behavior. My experience is that it takes a consistent effort over three to five years to yield results. If you expect to see measurable results of wellness programs before that, you will be disappointed.

■ THE DISEASE MANAGEMENT LINK

My linking wellness programs and disease management stems from the similarities I noted at the beginning of this chapter and the way chronic and catastrophic conditions relate to them both. I have made the assumption that the primary purpose of your wellness program is to focus on these conditions, since they provide the best opportunity for you to control and reduce health plan costs.

It's clear that you need to diagnose a catastrophic or chronic condition before you can manage it, and the earlier you diagnose it, the better opportunity for meaningful patient advocacy and coordination of services. If you can identify high-cost disease before it is symptomatic, before intensive treatment is needed, when it can be controlled by lifestyle changes and medications, then you will see a reduction in cost and a lengthening of productive life among your employees. The connection of early diagnosis and productive disease management is the message of this chapter.

Elements of Disease Management

Programs for intervention in the disease process vary in intensity and specific protocols, but most have common characteristics, including

- Written and telephonic support of patients with chronic or catastrophic disease
- Services provided by nurses, doctors, and other health professionals
- Case management protocols for assessing a patient's condition and environment
- Coordination of care between various caregivers, including multiple physicians, at-home care, diagnostic and laboratory services, family members, and nonprofit agencies
- Patient education and counseling about treatment options and self-care
- Identification of local resources, sometimes free or low cost, to meet patient needs
- Help with sorting out medications and treatments prescribed by various providers
- Ongoing support and assistance to the patient and family

Most disease management programs provide these services—and they do it with an attitude of concern and caring that promotes positive response from your employees and their families when illness strikes. Help with a chronic or catastrophic disease is welcomed by employees and can help reduce your cost and the cost to the patient.

Self-Care

Among disease management services, it is useful to discuss those that are newer, and perhaps less understood. One of these is self-care, by which we mean being empowered with information to decide whether or not a doctor or medical visit is needed and knowing how to ease discomfort or treat a condition appropriately at home. We are more aware as a society of the importance of self-care. Of those employees who contact a call center with symptoms, an estimated 20 percent to 30 percent are able to do self-care at home, according to Kristin Crosby of IntraCorp, as reported in the March 2, 1997, issue of *National Underwriter*.

Various studies show that self-care has made great strides toward reducing the number of unnecessary emergency room and doctor visits and that employees feel good about taking charge of their health. Confidence and consumer awareness are developed by the use of self-care manuals that walk you through symptoms and actions step by step (see Exhibit 8-17). One approach taken by work-site wellness programs is to provide self-care manuals to all employees at information sessions on their appropriate use. Exhibit 8-18 presents a recent report on the cost reductions achieved by such programs.

Other self-care support is given through telephone counseling by case management and specialist nurses, who may call from your health plan administrator, your disease management program, or a wellness provider. Some larger organizations have in-house staff make case management calls and assign a trained health professional to that task. This may raise issues of confidentiality and so should be carefully evaluated. Ultimately, with self-care materials and counseling, employees will make better health decisions based on greater knowledge of their choices and the consequences of each.

The savings reported from the use of self-care manuals were generated as a result of additional activities, such as a nurse advice line, and on-site training seminars in the use of the manual. This program was implemented by the American Institute of Preventive Medicine in conjunction with an insurance carrier and a group of large employers.

Earaches

Earaches can be mild or very painful. The most common cause of an earache is plugged eustachian tubes. These tubes go from the back of the throat to your middle ear. When the eustachian tube gets blocked, fluid gathers, causing pain. Things that make this happen include an infection of the middle ear, colds, sinus infections, and allergies. Other things that can cause ear pain include changes in air pressure in a plane, something stuck in the ear, too much earwax, tooth problems, and ear injuries.

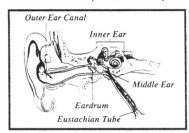

Very bad ear pain should be treated by a health care provider. Treatment will depend on its cause. Most often this includes pain relievers, an antibiotic for infection and methods to dry up or clear the blocked ear canal. You can, however, use Self-Care Tips if ear pain is mild and produces no other symptoms. One example is with a mild case of "swimmer's ear", which affects the outer ear. (See "To Treat a Mild Case of Swimmer's Ear" on page 52.)

Prevention

Much can be done to prevent earaches. Heed the old saying, "Never put anything smaller than your elbow into your ear." This includes cotton-tipped swabs, bobby pins, your fingers, etc. Doing so could damage your eardrum. When you blow your nose, do so gently, one nostril at a time. Don't smoke. Smoking and secondhand smoke can increase the risk of blocking the eustachian tube.

Questions to Ask

Did the pain start after a blow to the ear or recent head trauma? **YES** Get Emergency Care

NO

With the earache do you also have these symptoms?
• Stiff neck
• Fever
• Drowsiness
• Nausea, vomiting

YES Get Emergency Care

NO

In a child:
Does a child not respond to any sound, even a whistle or a loud clap? **YES** See Provider

NO

Are there any of the following signs of infection?
• Fever (especially 102°F or higher)
• Sticky, green, or bloody discharge
• Severe ear pain and/or increased pain when wiggling the ear lobe

YES See Provider

NO

EXHIBIT 8-17. Sample self-care guide. (Source: *Health At Home™, Your Complete Guide to Symptoms, Solutions & Self-Care* [Farmington Hills, MI: American Institute for Preventive Medicine Press, 1997], p. 56; copyright © 1997 by the American Institute for Preventive Medicine.)

Organization	Year	N	No. of Months	Savings/Person in Dollars			
				Dr. Visit	ER Visit	Total	ROI
Lewis-Gale Clinic	1997	327	12	$57.79	$14.44	$72.23	14:1
Health Net	1996	165	6	17.88	16.97	34.85	14:1
Western Southern Life	1996	197	6	17.00	40.61	57.61	26:1
Lewis-Gale Clinic	1996	79	5	25.97	12.19	38.16	15:1
Capital Blue Cross	1995	371	12	26.01	13.05	39.06	5:1
Capital Blue Cross	1995	938	12	16.45	5.22	21.67	7:1
Indian Industries	1995	197	6	8.88	66.45	75.33	30:1
Florida Hospital	1994	365	5	18.99	65.82	84.81	42:1
Florida Hospital	1994	436	5	17.53	49.80	67.33	34:1
Bell South	1994	229	3	18.56	21.63	40.18	16:1
EDS	1994	65	6	15.24	35.38	50.62	20:1
Florida Hospital-Children's	1995	183	5	11.72	78.26	89.98	45:1
York Health System-Seniors	1996	107	12	21.26	36.23	57.49	17:1

EXHIBIT 8-18. Savings and return on investment (ROI) for use of self-care guides. (Source: American Institute for Preventive Medicine, Farmington Hills, MI, 1998.)

■ WHY DISEASE MANAGEMENT?

Patient advocacy is the term used to describe the counseling, patient education, research on questions, interaction with various medical professionals, identification of needed services, and overall support given to patients by disease management staff. With the current spate of lawsuits and complaints about the limitations on services available from managed-care health plans and the growth in the number of their enrollees, it is more important than ever to have a patient advocate who will seek appropriate services for your employees from an insured plan. It is equally important to advise employees about the need to prove medical necessity and available options before they schedule services.

In 1987, 22 million Americans were identified as having chronic conditions. By 1993, that number had increased by more than 20 percent to 27 million, according to the February 1, 1997, issue of *Insurance Advocate*, and only one-quarter of them were elderly. There were 41 million people in 1995 with conditions that were disabling, of whom fewer than one-third were elderly; and of the 9 million people homebound with disabilities, only 40 percent were elderly. Younger people, who will require longer-term medical services, are suffering from chronic disease and disabling conditions in greater numbers. One of the proven ways to enhance services, coordinate care, and reduce the cost for the chronically ill and disabled plan member is through disease management services.

Chronic care consumes the largest share of U.S. health care expenditures, with $425 billion spent on direct medical costs for these needs in 1990 and lost productivity estimated at another $234 billion. It is good business to address the needs of chronic conditions and to work at controlling their cost.

Prescription drugs are another area for disease management attention. More than 40 percent of hospital admissions for those over age 65 are for reactions to contraindicated prescriptions. The cost of prescription drugs is rising more rapidly than other medical costs and was expected to rise between 11 and 14 percent in 1998. Coordination of care and patient assessment by trained disease management staff can reduce excessive and contraindicated medications and can increase the patient's understanding about generic drugs and lower-cost alternatives. Prescription drugs account for 15 to 25 percent of health plan costs and often provide an option that replaces surgery or other invasive treatments.

Disparity in the cost of care suggests the need for disease management. Health expenditures per capita vary widely from state to state and from rural to urban settings. One report, "The Dartmouth Atlas of Health Care" distributed by the American Hospital Association, suggests that per capita expenses are twice as high in Boston as in New Haven and another reports that expenses are twice as high in Miami as in Lincoln, Nebraska. Other high-priced regions included New Orleans, Pittsburgh, Nashville, and Baltimore, with less expensive regions identified as Buffalo and Albany, New York, and Arlington, Virginia.

Frequency of procedures accounts for major cost differences between locales. For instance, in an analysis of national Medicare data from 1993, the Dartmouth Medical School reported that in certain parts of the country, radical mastectomies were performed thirty-three times as often as breast-saving lumpectomies for women with breast cancer. Cesarean section rates vary from 9.6 percent to 31.8 percent of all births, depending on region of the country, and in some communities of Maine more than 50 percent of men undergo prostatectomy, compared with only 15 percent in nearby communities.

It is increasingly obvious that more invasive and therefore more costly procedures do not automatically result in better outcomes. It is also documented that patients who are given information and alternatives tend to select less invasive and less expensive procedures. Disease management has a role to play here. With patient counseling and intervention before invasive procedures are scheduled or undertaken, there can be a reduction of 7 percent to 17 percent in the rates of use of services, according to the Health Project Consortium article published by Dr. James F. Fries, Dr. C. Everett Koop, and their colleagues. Regional differences in the incidence of specific disease and in customary treatments can be individually addressed with disease management services.

Another good reason to have disease management services in place for your organization's health plan is the overlap of services among those who require medical care and who are also disabled or on workers compensation. Integration of medical plans with disability management is a buzz phrase that many benefits managers hear today. A recent Towers Perrin study found that 90 percent of employers felt their medical and disability programs should be combined, and the researchers identified these goals for effective management:

- Simplified employee access to benefit information
- Reduction in the impact of employee absenteeism on productivity
- Reductions in overall medical and disability costs

All of these goals can be addressed with effective disease management, in tandem with early identification of and intervention with chronic conditions.

Disease Manager Selection and Fees

Once you have concluded that you want to include disease management services as part of your health plan, these services may be yours for the asking, available at no cost from your plan administrator or already included in your insurance premium. If you are self-funded or are a larger employer and the services are not automatically included by your plan administrator, you should consider hiring a disease management company. Begin by identifying companies in your area, and invite those of interest to submit a proposal or to make a presentation. Resources for locating such companies appear in Appendix A. Then you should evaluate the philosophy and attitude of each bidder before making a selection, remembering that this company will work with your employees when they are under stress and often with diminished capacity.

Exhibit 8-19 provides sample specifications for these services. The specifications cover experience, staff and credentialing, range of services and facilities, stability, and track record. They all need to be evaluated during your selection of a disease management company. You should follow the same distribution and review steps for this specification and bid process as you followed for selecting your health plan administrator as described in Chapter 4.

You should discuss the cost basis with each bidder. There are three basic methods used by disease management firms:

- *Hourly or per case charges.* This method is the most common. The hourly rate can vary in regions of the country from $65 an hour to $250 an hour and can be reduced for lower-level interventions. For instance, if you accept a practical nurse or registered nurse for some levels of service and have limited need for a case management, utilization review, or specialist nurses such as diabetes management nurses, you can reduce your costs. The hourly fee reflects the use of lower-level staff.

(text continues on page 174)

Managed Care Specifications
DRAFT
Revised 6/12/9X

1. Experience
   a. How long has your firm been in business?
   b. Do you have other municipal clients and/or business related to the public sector? Please describe.
   c. Please discuss your client base, including information such as range of size, length of relationship, and type(s) of service provided. Include TPA, carrier and/or HMO accounts as appropriate.
   d. Is your firm specialized in managed care services for health plans, or diversified in additional health-related services, or in unrelated fields? Please explain the objectives of your organization with regard to any diversification.
   e. What proportion of your managed care business is devoted to health benefits services; and what is the proportion devoted, if any, to such services for workers' comp and/or DBL?
   f. Please discuss your relationship with medical providers, including doctors and hospitals, etc.
   g. Please list those area hospitals (Mid-Hudson and greater New York areas) with whom you have an ongoing relationship.
   h. Please indicate whether you have had experience with a DRG payment methodology, two-party check methodology, and a transition from DRG to non-DRG in the past. Explain.
   i. Discuss your relationship and service philosophy with plan participants and/or covered patients. Include your standard procedures to develop cooperation with plan participants. When do you discontinue services for non-cooperation from participant?
   j. In what way do you measure participant/patient satisfaction with your services, and how is this reported to the plan sponsor?
   k. Describe your relationship(s) with third-party administrators for health plans for which you provide managed care services. Specify the typical procedures with regard to preadmission certification, concurrent review and discharge planning.
   l. Indicate your experience with managed care services for PPO/POS networks of providers.
   m. Provide a description of your hospital billing audit services, including your use of discount programs.

2. Facilities and Services
   a. Detail the geographic region(s) in which you offer service to employees/retirees.
   b. Explain the methods of automation (reporting/processing ability) you have in place.
   c. Please list your standard reports and enclose samples.
   d. Please describe your capabilities to provide special reports.
   e. Are your record keeping and billing procedures industry acceptable? Please describe.
   f. What are your dispute resolution procedures and methods? Please describe your capacity for prompt resolution of same.
   g. Do you currently provide services for a claims review or appeal process for use by plan participants? Please describe. If not, have you had experience in providing same?
   h. Expand on your ability to provide out-of-state services. Indicate by location(s).
   i. Indicate your routine contact by telephone, or other means with plan participants and/or their families. Identify the various purposes of the contact as it relates to your managed-care services.
   j. Describe your standard procedures for at-home or in-hospital visits to plan participants/patients.

EXHIBIT 8-19. Sample specifications for case management. (Source: Halo Associates.)

k. Describe your retrospective review procedures and capability.

l. What training do you provide to the plan sponsor and/or administrative staff in connection with managed care? Include any written guidelines routinely used.

m. Describe your relationship with and use of other community agencies, nonprofit organizations, and local volunteer services.

3. Staff
   a. Please discuss the following:
      1. Retrospective review staff and resources, including hospital audit personnel.
      2. Case management staff, including recruitment, training, oversight, and credentials.
      3. Medical/professional consultation or peer review panel. Procedures for referral and selection.
      4. Credentials criteria and procedures for selection for all professional staff.
      5. Telephone and/or initial contact staff.
      6. Service representatives to the plan sponsor.
      7. Please discuss any additional special or general staff provided by your organization to deliver managed care services.
   b. Do you provide patient information and specialty services for those who are permanently disabled (i.e., Medicare/SSI)?
   c. Describe the interrelationship of your staff.
   d. What complaint or reassignment procedures do you have in place when a participant/patient is dissatisfied with your staff person(s)?

4. General
   a. Please provide references from existing clients.
   b. Expand on your flexibility for the County's needs.
   c. If available, provide reference(s) from third-party administration firms, or carriers/HMOs, and area hospitals.
   d. Discuss your typical interaction(s) with County staff.
   e. Do you provide information about your services for distribution to County plan participants, and can that information be customized for County use?
   f. Attach information about your credit rating and/or financial standing.

5. Scope of Services and Cost
   a. Describe the basis for your fees (i.e., flat fee, per capita, percentage, etc.). These should be indicated for each type of service provided, as appropriate.
   b. On what basis are additional charges assessed and how are increases determined?
   c. Explain your capability to negotiate discounts for both inpatient and outpatient services.
   d. How do you bill for retrospective review services?
   e. Describe your reporting capability with regard to the following:
      1. Initial assessment
      2. Status reports
      3. Field visits
      4. Billing audits, inpatient and outpatient
      5. Monthly, quarterly, or periodic summary reports
      6. Specialized reports by diagnosis, service, or cost

Enclose copies of each type above, as available.

- *Per case rates.* This can be a flat $150–$475 depending on location, complexity of the case mix, and the range of services you require. The disease management company should specify its ability to meet your needs, explain its procedures and protocols, and provide examples of its reports.

- *Per member per month.* This method is a flat fee based on the number of employees in your health plan. These fees range from $.50 per member per month to $7 per member per month, depending on the service you require and the size of your plan. Services include preadmission certification, utilization review, case management, a nurse advice line, network referral, and pharmacy management. Fees may be guaranteed for a period of one or two years. This arrangement ensures that the disease management company will receive a steady cash flow and is based upon the anticipated incidence of high-cost claims and the time required to handle them.

For each of these methods, you can build in performance or incentive agreements that are tied to reduced cost for chronic and catastrophic conditions. You may provide a percentage of the savings as a bonus or retrospective incentive. If you enter into this sort of agreement, you will need to carefully outline the measurements to be used for establishing base costs and for determining any increase or decrease. The terms of payment for such incentives or bonuses also need to be clearly stated.

Reports on Cost Impact and Interventions

Disease management companies issue a variety of reports, depending on the range of services provided. If, for example, a nurse triage or counseling line is part of the service, the company will report on the extent and nature of inbound calls. Exhibit 8-20 shows such a report. You can identify your employees' concerns from this report and pick up early indications of potential high-cost illness. Since these reports are not patient specific but contain aggregate data, employee confidentiality is ensured.

Typical case management and disease management reports that are patient-specific do the following:

- Indicate an assessment of the patient's condition
- Provide a summary of interventions and their outcomes
- Update the patient file on treatments and providers
- Include a recommendation for follow-up activity
- Document any printed materials or other support staff provided
- Estimate the additional time and activity needed

Exhibit 8-21 presents a standard narrative report. This is used by the disease management company to maintain updated patient files and to help it provide needed services. From your point of view, it is a backup to a cost savings report that the company will also furnish. Exhibit 8-22 is such a report and identifies the areas of savings that can be documented.

Other disease management reports include patient satisfaction surveys, utilization review reports on audited hospital or doctor bills, annual and monthly reports on interventions and outcomes, savings reports by diagnosis, and projections of intervention with complex cases. These topics are discussed in Chapter 9.

Monitoring the Disease Management Process

You should monitor reports of cost impact and interventions and disease management services, whether they are provided by your plan administrator or contracted directly.

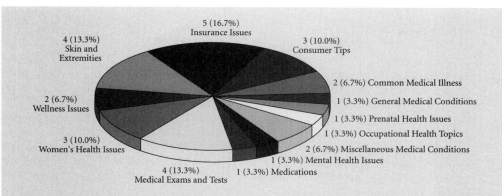

QUARTERLY UTILIZATION ANALYSIS

Top Categories of Calls—# of callers, # of increments:

Code	Description	#	Increments
277	Insurance Terms/Coverage	12	18
246	Doctors & their specialties	10	19
260	Questions about medications	6	12
256	Routine Lab/Diag Tests	3	12
048	Diarrhea	3	14
400	Neurological	2	10
040	Shingles (also 151)	3	9

Chronic and Catastrophic Codes:

16 callers with 60 increments of calls in various disease categories. Average length of call 25 minutes.

Various Specific Illness Codes:

30 callers with 99 increments of calls for issues on treatment, symptoms, options. Average length of call 20 minutes.

Doctor Visit Questions and Preparation Codes:

14 callers with 30 increments of calls for various doctor visit-related issues. Average length of call 15 minutes.

Insurance-related Codes:

12 callers with 18 increments of calls for insurance questions and referral guidance. Average length of call 9 minutes.

Medication-related Codes:

8 callers with 17 increments of calls for issues on dosage, usage, contra-indications. Average length of call 13 minutes.

Miscellaneous calls were received for wellness, preventive, referral to non covered services, and general health information.

EXHIBIT 8-20. Calls by condition group, with quarterly utilization analysis. (Source: Health Qs 800, Wellness Institute Inc.)

Benchmarks to use to measure quality include your subjective evaluation of the reports you receive. For instance, you can check when the case was referred and how long it took for the service organization to contact the patient. Check the time intervals between contacts when there are several. Review random patient assessments to see what they reveal. Read narrative reports to determine if recommendations are comprehensive and if outcomes seem reasonable.

This case manager was contacted by the hospital discharge planner to provide home care for this claimant with recurrent cervical cancer. This case manager visited this claimant once at her home and later at the Fishkill Care Center. This case manager provided and negotiated costs on home care, injectable medications and provided referrals to the claimant and her family for other cancer care alternatives. This case manager maintained contact with the home care providers and physician who had some difficulties with a very independent and proud claimant who resisted services, even though badly required. Contact was maintained and this case manager assisted the claimant and her brother as the claimant's condition became terminal and treatment discontinued. The physician and caregivers were encouraged to respect the claimant's wish for continued dignity and maintenance of comfort.

This claimant underwent spinal fusion of the lumbar spine resulting from spinal cord injury sustained as a child. This case manager was requested to evaluate the claimant's need for admission to a rehab facility. This case manager visited the claimant and was able to determine the claimant was not recovering full function after surgery as well as was hoped prior to surgery. A sub acute unit or continued home therapy was recommended but not available near the claimant's home. The claimant was admitted to Burke Rehab. The claimant continued, in fact, to lose function of the right leg. At this time it is suspected the claimant has neurological deficits from an auto immune disease, such as multiple sclerosis. A definitive diagnosis has not been made, but, Multiple Sclerosis can be triggered by trauma such as surgery. This case manager negotiated costs and encouraged a timely discharge from Burke. Physical therapy costs and medically necessary, equipment expenses were also negotiated.

EXHIBIT 8-21. Typical narrative case management reports. (Sources: Wellness Institute Inc. and United Review Services, Inc.)

Legal issues are part of disease management, and some attention to them is appropriate. As a plan sponsor you have a fiduciary liability for utilization review and case management decisions and should therefore have legal counsel review the features of your disease management program.

Legal Issues to Consider

- Who provides the review, and what are their credentials? Are they physicians who are available for consultation, or nurses with special training?
- Who makes the ultimate decision about care?
- Is there an appropriate appeals procedure?
- Are standards for disease management, utilization review, and case management made clear in all plan booklets and printed materials?
- Are these standards applied in a uniform manner to all employees?
- Is there a mechanism to provide timely services and decisions?
- Does the disease management organization have appropriate insurance to cover errors and omissions, malpractice and negligence?

It is always better to be safe rather than sorry. Most of the time, however, as a small or mid-sized organization, you will rely upon your plan administrator to monitor cases. If you hire the disease management firm directly, your plan administrator or benefits adviser will help with this evaluation.

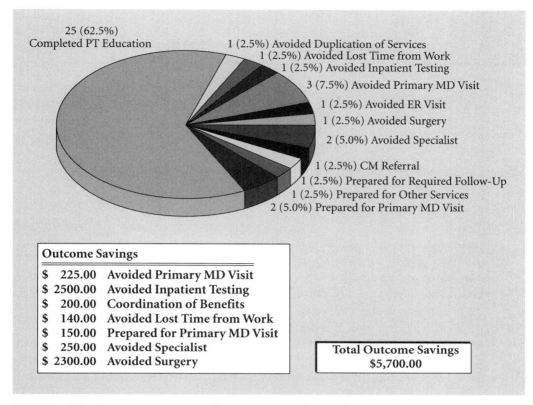

EXHIBIT 8-22. Outcomes and savings. (Source: Health Qs 800, Wellness Institute Inc.)

Summary

There are many goals for disease management, but the bottom line is the same: it represents improved services to your employees and their families when chronic or catastrophic disease strikes. Your purpose in providing a health plan is to protect employees and their families from financial disaster. There is no better way than to provide meaningful services when they are needed, and to do so with an eye on your health plan budget as well as on employee relations.

I make a connection between identification of serious conditions through well-designed wellness programs and follow-up services that include disease management. This continuum of service will improve your health plan's cost effectiveness and result in better treatment for those who have chronic or catastrophic conditions. There are many qualified companies that can bring these services to you with a minimum of effort on your part and at minimal cost to your organization.

CHAPTER 9

Monitoring Your Health Plan

Some years ago I walked into the office of a risk manager who had hired me to help evaluate an employee health plan, and I noticed a stack of unread computer reports, nearly three feet high, in the corner of his office. One of my goals with that client was to reduce the information provided to a manageable amount and to make it relevant to his needs. Two years later, he received one manila envelope each month with the right data to help him manage his plan efficiently and to track its performance.

Your health plan, if it reflects the national average, accounts for 10 percent of your payroll expense and costs between $2,000 and $4,000 a year for each employee. For the small and mid-sized organization, the opportunity to manage your health plan wisely is an opportunity to control these costs and to improve services to your employees at the same time. To accomplish these goals, you need good information that is useful.

This chapter focuses on minimizing the information glut that can so easily be generated by the information systems for employee health plans. It also discusses how reports and feedback are used to monitor health plan operations, to measure and justify the expense of resources, and to plan for the future. Boiled down to its essence, I'd apply one rule to all reporting and monitoring activities: *simplify*, *eliminate*, and *customize*.

■ DESIGN YOUR INFORMATION REPORTING SYSTEM

There are practical steps you can take to design an effective information reporting system. The first is to design reports you need and to identify other information procedures that work for your organization.

Choosing Your Reports

There are three basic purposes for reports—to identify short term, long term, and special needs. Short-term reports help you operate your plan throughout the year. Long-term reports provide a basis for planning, change, and decision making. Special needs reports address one particular area of interest or study.

There are some constants that apply to all types of reports. For example, you should assign the reporting function. Select someone to gather the data and generate the report. For one type of report it may be someone who works in your benefits office and answers the phone; for another type of report, it may be a specialized benefit consultant or the plan administrator. Or you may opt for a composite effort, where two or three standard reports from your plan administrator are consolidated by staff for your review.

Decide on the contents of reports you need. Prioritize reports on finance, participation or enrollment, utilization, network activity, and benefit studies. Eliminate reports that are not of interest to you. If you want to have a report that is broken into categories (e.g., by employee group, facility, job function, or status [active or retired]), you should know why the breakdown is useful to you. When two reports seem to convey the same information or related information, ask that they be consolidated or eliminate one. If you don't need the information in some reports, discontinue them. You are the best judge of which information is useful at any point in time. Remember that your needs will probably change over time as you address different issues. Be flexible, but be firm about the particular information you want to receive regularly.

Determine the frequency of reports. If you want a particular report monthly, be sure to specify its expected delivery. If another report is needed only quarterly or sporadically, say so. Identify the reporting responsibilities of plan vendors. If your drug plan administrator, for instance, is to furnish you with quarterly reports on utilization and costs, make the requirement part of your contract, or confirm it in writing. Then diary your calendar to follow up if it isn't received in a timely fashion. When a plan administrator is required to furnish weekly, monthly, quarterly, and annual reports, hold it accountable for timely delivery.

Ask for report formats that are best for you. If you prefer a graph or chart, as easier to use in your organization, ask that the data be provided in that format. Sometimes it is most convenient to have your staff adapt and reformat data from standard reports received from your plan administrator. Exhibit 9-1a, b shows the source of data and the summary reformatted report prepared by staff. If you need columns with totals in place of detailed narrative, for instance, request the simplified version. If narrative summaries of data are useful, specify them. Your requests for personalized formats and reports should be purposeful. You should ask what the report is used for and understand how it fits into your plan management needs before you agree to have it provided to you.

Reports should be provided to you with a presentation or explanation when needed. If you have staff, an outside expert, your plan adviser, administrator, or health insurance professional provide you with a report, you should be able to ask questions and be sure of the information you have received. When there are routine or regular reports, it is often easier to discuss questions over the telephone. When you need to present a report to a committee or to management, be sure to ask for a briefing in advance. This will give you an opportunity to digest the information, understand it more fully, and amend it to suit your needs. Clarify your expectation for on-site presentations, especially for new reports, annual reports, and special-needs reports. These are most likely to cause confusion and to be unfamiliar.

Keep your emphasis not on more but on better.

■ SHORT-TERM REPORTS AND FEEDBACK

Short-term reports, which focus on operations, should be summarized and are often provided in comparison form to enable you to tell at a glance how your health plan is performing, compared to the previous month, previous year, or other time period. Typical short-term reports include:

- Weekly and monthly claims registers that list every payment made to plan members during the reporting period. These can be used to notify you to replenish a fund balance

Client Activity Report
Financial Summary
Dispense Dates Between 01/01/9X and 06/30/9X

199X Service Dates

	1st Qtr.	2nd Qtr.	3rd Qtr.	4th Qtr.	YTD
# of Claims	2,728	2,616	0	0	5,344
Total Cost	72,694	72,495	0	0	145,189
Less Copay	11,975	11,605	0	0	23,580
Amount Paid	60,719	60,890	0	0	121,610
Average Total Cost	26.65	27.71	0.00	0.00	27.17
Single Source Brand	39.53	41.97	0.00	0.00	40.73
Multisource Brand	22.65	22.25	0.00	0.00	22.46
MAC	7.12	6.93	0.00	0.00	7.02
Other Generic	7.70	7.57	0.00	0.00	7.64
% MAC	25.4%	26.5%	0.0%	0.0%	25.9%
% Other Generic	15.9%	13.9%	0.0%	0.0%	14.9%
% Multisource Brand	16.6%	16.9%	0.0%	0.0%	16.7%
% Single Source Brand	42.0%	42.8%	0.0%	0.0%	42.4%
Amt. Paid as % of Total Cost	83.5%	84.0%	0.0%	0.0%	83.8%

Top 20 Drugs—by Ingredient Cost
April–June 199X
--- Client =   :   ---

Rank	Drug Name	Total Rxs	Quantity	Average Quantity/Rx	Ingredient Cost	Average Cost/Rx	% of Ingred. Cost	Amount Paid
1	Prilosec	55	1,273	23.15	$4,165.39	$75.73	6.5%	$4,081.14
2	Zithromax	27	475	17.59	$2,464.71	$91.29	3.8%	$2,426.71
3	Suprax	11	370	33.64	$2,155.64	$195.97	3.4%	$2,141.89
4	Prozac	29	905	31.21	$1,895.52	$65.36	2.9%	$1,836.77
5	Biaxin	22	511	23.23	$1,468.52	$66.75	2.3%	$1,440.53
6	Ceftin	8	260	32.50	$1,267.53	$158.44	2.0%	$1,257.53
7	Zocor	23	466	20.26	$1,130.50	$49.15	1.8%	$1,101.75
8	Zantac	19	758	39.89	$1,122.36	$59.07	1.7%	$1,083.61
9	Cipro	19	371	19.53	$1,092.92	$57.52	1.7%	$1,064.67
10	Atrovent	20	974	48.70	$867.88	$43.39	1.3%	$839.13
11	Cefaclor	17	957	56.29	$863.71	$50.81	1.3%	$872.71
12	Procardia XL	20	427	21.35	$772.38	$38.62	1.2%	$731.38
13	Vasotec	32	771	24.09	$708.74	$22.15	1.1%	$631.24
14	Mevacor	15	357	23.80	$688.61	$45.91	1.1%	$639.36
15	Augmentin 500	7	247	35.29	$640.67	$91.52	1.0%	$631.92
16	Sporanox	3	126	42.00	$635.49	$211.83	1.0%	$631.74
17	Flonase	17	272	16.00	$619.97	$36.47	1.0%	$598.47
18	Dovonex	9	540	60.00	$605.16	$67.24	0.9%	$593.91
19	Pepcid	12	399	33.25	$601.85	$50.15	0.9%	$586.85
20	Timoptic	14	190	13.57	$579.20	$41.37	0.9%	$520.95

EXHIBIT 9-1a. Initial data reports. (Source: Halo Associates.)

Drug Costs and Utilization

The 199X Report of Utilization and Costs has been received and reviewed for the self funded plan's card service. The following points are of interest.

1. The largest category of prescriptions filled is for the most expensive, the single source brand drug. It is 41.9% of the total for 199X.

2. The MAC generic drugs are the next largest category for 199X at 27.8% and reflect the effort to control cost through dispensing of these reduced cost drugs.

3. Refills and utilization data indicate that many of the most ordered drugs may be multiple short-term prescriptions. This is not in keeping with the intent of the plan which is to encourage mail order prescriptions once the drug is ordered for any duration. For example, of the top fifty drugs shown, many are for chronic conditions.

4. Volume of prescriptions ordered exceeds the short term 21-day supply or less for prescriptions covered under the card service.

5. Our top fifty drugs have changed in order somewhat and indicate the nature of illness treated and drugs provided under this coverage. More chronic and ongoing medications for lifestyle related illness and catastrophic illness are shown. There is an increase in arthritis medications, and stress-related GI disorders, for example.

EXHIBIT 9-1b. Reformatted synopsis. (Source: Halo Associates.)

when your health plan is self-funded, receives administrative services only, or is retrospectively rated.

- Monthly or quarterly plan costs, by benefit categories.
- Reports on utilization of plan benefits, including number of services, total costs, and providers used.
- Summaries on network use, including number of services, cost, any discounts applied.
- Comparative cost reports indicating short-term, year-to-date expense by month and including the previous year, month by month.

I prefer for the information to be included in one or two comprehensive reports, rather than provided piecemeal. Short-term reports are used to monitor efficiency, cost savings, and utilization. They are also used to identify short-term problems that require management intervention. You need to read and interpret the information a short-term report contains so that you can use it wisely.

Exhibit 9-2 is a good example of a comprehensive monthly health plan report. It provides a wealth of information that includes the increase or decrease in expenses month to month for the current plan year to date, with the previous plan years shown for comparison. Not only can you note changes in benefit categories of major medical, hospitalization, and drugs, but you can see whether the plan is on budget for the year. This type of report is most commonly used by self-funded plans, although administrative-services-only plans, partially self-funded plans, and some fully insured plans should track this information, too.

If you track the monthly, quarterly, or annual expenses of your health plan with this information, you should be able to measure whether you are paying too much or too little and to determine whether there is an area of utilization that is a problem. For instance, major swings in your hospitalization can be the result of a few catastrophic claims. You should inquire whether or not case management is in place and if advance

1998	Jan	Feb	Mar	Apr	May	Jun	Jul	Aug	Sep	Oct	Nov	Dec	YTD	Budget (45/55)	Balance	% Spent YTD
Basic Benefits	229,079.63	212,224.43	250,968.60	280,606.79	243,180.32	193,144.75	438,686.08	295,367.81					2,143,258.41	3,285,000.00	1,141,741.59	65.24%
Major Medical Benefits	355,115.35	242,780.48	226,726.03	372,869.86	282,602.20	286,017.78	358,967.33	351,047.08					2,476,126.11	4,015,000.00	1,538,873.89	61.67%
Total Medical	584,194.98	455,004.91	477,694.63	653,476.65	525,782.52	479,162.53	797,653.41	646,414.89	0.00	0.00	0.00	0.00	4,619,384.52	7,300,000.00	2,680,615.48	63.28%
Percent of Budget Expensed	7.80%	6.07%	6.38%	8.72%	7.02%	6.40%	10.65%	8.63%	0.00%	0.00%	0.00%	0.00%	63.28%			

	Jan	Feb	Mar	Apr	May	Jun	Jul	Aug	Sep	Oct	Nov	Dec	YTD	Budget (80/20)	Balance	% Spent YTD
Prescriptions (card)	94,241.02	74,069.50	84,568.82	97,001.23	84,516.21	82,327.10	143,814.22	89,608.69					750,146.79	1,448,000.00	697,853.21	51.81%
Prescriptions (mail)	0.00	85,738.44	0.00	0.00	69,615.52	3,321.88	23,079.67	27,088.48					208,843.99	362,000.00	153,156.01	57.69%
Total Prescriptions	94,241.02	159,807.94	84,568.82	97,001.23	154,131.73	85,648.98	166,893.89	116,697.17	0.00	0.00	0.00	0.00	958,990.78	1,810,000.00	851,009.22	52.98%
Percent of Budget Expensed	6.23%	10.57%	5.59%	6.42%	10.19%	5.66%	11.04%	7.72%	0.00%	0.00%	0.00%	0.00%	52.98%			
1998 Claim Totals	678,436.00	614,812.85	562,263.45	750,477.88	679,914.25	564,811.51	964,547.30	763,112.06	0.00	0.00	0.00	0.00	5,578,375.30	9,110,000.00	3,531,624.70	61.23%
Percent of Budget Expensed	7.53%	6.83%	6.24%	8.33%	7.55%	6.27%	10.71%	8.48%	0.00%	0.00%	0.00%	0.00%	61.23%			
		14.36%	20.61%	28.94%	36.49%	42.77%	53.48%	61.95%	61.95%	61.95%	61.95%	61.95%	6,073,333.33	9,110,000.00	3,036,666.67	66.67%

12 Month Straight Line

YTD Straight Line - YTD Actual   494,958.03

Summary of Years: (cumulative)	Jan	Feb	Mar	Apr	May	Jun	Jul	Aug	Sep	Oct	Nov	Dec	YTD
1996	727,203.70	1,123,150	1,550,731	2,084,110	3,499,434	4,316,238	4,789,058	5,460,062	6,009,905	6,860,531	7,499,648	7,886,375	
	9.46%												
1997	700,713.27	1,320,420	1,863,021	2,608,033	3,234,569	3,872,290	4,821,981	5,529,994	6,381,215	7,187,856	7,899,814	8,620,529	
	7.78%												
1998	678,436.00	1,293,249	1,855,512	2,605,990	3,285,904	3,850,716	4,815,263	5,578,375	5,578,375	5,578,375	5,578,375	5,578,375	
	7.53%												

EXHIBIT 9-2. Comprehensive monthly health plan report. (Source: Halo Associates.)

discounts were negotiated. Or you might notice a sizable decrease in plan drug costs if you have just instituted a generic drug substitution policy or established a mail-order discount service, or eliminated drug coverage for retirees. You can monitor the year-to-year fluctuation in physician costs, as they relate to your plan's physician network expansion or reduction. There should be a direct correlation in your monthly reports with changes made to the plan's benefits, administration, eligibility, or enrollment procedures. You can identify the impact of programs that reduce the cost of catastrophic and chronic conditions.

Another use of short-term reports is to ascertain the actual administrative and service costs you are paying and to give you the opportunity to negotiate for lower costs in the future. You will be able to monitor the cost-effectiveness of network membership by seeing the discounts provided relative to the administrative fee charged.

Monthly reports, which can be quarterly for the smaller employer, are a useful way to maintain accountability, flag problem areas, and monitor the year-to-date costs of your health plan. They are essential if you are self-funded, because they enable you to ensure that adequate funds are transferred to pay claims, and they are meaningful for all plans to measure costs and utilization of benefits. These reviews encourage your administrator to stay on top of high-cost claims and help you manage plan activity and services better.

Exhibit 9-3 is an example of a report for an administrative-services-only plan that compares the monthly cost of claim and administrative expenses to premiums paid. This type of monitoring is provided whether the plan is on a retrospective, pay-up-later, or pay-in-advance basis, with the carrier providing the administrative services.

Quarterly reports cover issues that you need to be aware of but over which you have little immediate control. Generally, these report health plan data that can help you project future costs and utilization patterns. Some examples of this type of report are:

Client	Claims	Admin. Fees	Hosp. Cost	Retention	Total Cost
County-active	$500,533.	$32,534.	$238.974.	$143,338.	$ 786,380.
County-retired	$164,777.	$10,710.	$119,724.	$ 7,183.	$ 302,396.
City, active	$176,318.	$11,460.	$217,247.	$ 13,034.	$ 418,061.
City, retired	$ 62,492.	$ 4,062.	$ 29,043.	$ 1,742.	$ 97,340.
Town, A	$ 2,875.	$ 186.	$ 686.	$ 41.	$ 3,790.
Town, B	$ 29,622.	$ 1,925.	$ 7,504.	$ 450.	$ 39,501.
Village, A	$ 13,829.	$ 898.	$ 8,407.	$ 504.	$ 23,640.
Totals	$950,446.	$61,775.	$621,635.	$166,292.	$1,671,108.
Percentage of total.	55.88%	3.6%	36.2%	8.95%	

Note: The purpose of this report is for the members of this pooled plan (i.e., county, towns, villages, etc.) to determine their relative cost for medical claims, administrative fees, hospital claims, and retention. A combination of retention and administrative fees are what the carrier charges the plan, with retention the amount held by the carrier against higher-than-anticipated losses, which will become profit to the carrier if not used.

In this report, the medical claims and hospital claims are accounted for separately. This is due to the arrangement of the plan with the carrier at one level of administrative fees for hospital charges and another for medical claims. It is also of interest in a plan where hospital costs are of special concern due to a new hospital network, for instance, or if a new regulation is expected to influence hospital costs.

EXHIBIT 9-3. Sample year-to-date cost report for an administrative-services-only plan, January–March. (Source: Halo Associates.)

Employee Name	Claim#	SS Number	Dept.	Total Claim Amount	Diagnosis
				Claims Paid in Excess of $25,000 for 01/01/98 – 6/30/98	
C	050300	—	01910	$ 57,792.07	Cardiac
D	050084	—	04310	$ 36,681.13	Cancer
K	050059	—	06010	$ 83,264.45	Cystic fibrosis
N	050277	—	04310	$ 41,564.25	Cancer
R	050093	—	01002	$ 73,286.37	CPD/Asthma with diabetes
T	050025	—	01910	$ 69,779.00	Cardiac
V	050071	—	06010	$100,000.00	Mental health/psych.
Y	050091	—	06010	$111,852.78	Premature infant
			Total Claims:	$635,739.53	

Prognosis is listed by claim on a separate, narrative report.

EXHIBIT 9-4. A high-cost claim report. (Source: Halo Associates.)

- Specific benefit reports, such as those for your dental plan, drug coverage, or other plan area that you need to specifically monitor.
- High-cost claims reports to provide you with a summary, on a quarterly basis, of the members who have catastrophic claims, total dollars expended, diagnosis, and prognosis.
- Utilization and claims reports, issued annually, biannually, or quarterly, that list members by social security number and total dollar amount paid by plan year on their behalf

If you have stop-loss insurance because you are self-funded, you will receive:

- Aggregate deductible reports, which provide cumulative and monthly tallies of your claims, year-to-date and loss ratios for the plan as a whole
- Specific deductible reports, which list all employees whose claims have exceeded a designated percentage of the stop-loss attachment point and whose claims are therefore sent for review to the stop-loss carrier

The high-cost claim report shown in Exhibit 9-4 provides data on types of claims that can drive your plan costs up and require other plan services. The report can help you to identify the need for case management services, monitor whether they are provided, and project the cost impact of such claims for the plan year.

If you have auditing services in place, you should receive reports on negotiated savings that result from retrospective audits of hospital bills (see Exhibit 9-5). These are reductions of cost to your plan, resulting from a careful review of medical charges and their accuracy. A summary is helpful to put the audit report in perspective for your organization. Although you have limited control over these outcomes, they benefit your plan and should be monitored quarterly and documented for a year-end cost-saving report.

Inpatient hospital stays are covered in another short-term report, which should be cumulative, reporting the year to date (see Exhibit 9-6). This report tells you which hospitals are used by your plan members, by diagnosis. This can help you monitor inpatient costs, negotiate increased hospital discounts, and identify hospitals where a discount arrangement could result in savings to your plan. You can manage costs by requesting that

7/1/9X Through 7/31/9X

	This Period	*199X to Date*	*Total to Date*
Audits Completed	15	133	375
Total Amount Billed	$42,986.52	$503,478.99	$2,387,161.15
Total Savings	$4,278.39	$38,913.85	$165,902.69
Total Costs	$1,051.43	$9,391.30	$20,659.56
Percent Saved	9.95%	7.73%	6.95%
R.O.I.	$4.07	$4.14	$8.03

EXHIBIT 9-5. Sample of an auditing results summary. (Source: United Review Services, Inc.)

Provider Utilization Report
For the Quarter Ending September 30, 199X

Company Name:
Administered By:

Provider Last Name: Provider City, State: New York, NY

RELATION TO EMPLOYEE	NOTIFIED DATE	TYPE OF PROCEDURE	PRIMARY DIAGNOSIS	PLACE OF TREATMENT
DEPENDENT	09/15/9X	EMERGENCY	Kearn's-Sayre Syndrome	PRESBYTERIAN HOSPITAL

Cases Reviewed for the Provider: 1

Provider Last Name: Provider City, State: Tenafly, NJ

RELATION TO EMPLOYEE	NOTIFIED DATE	TYPE OF PROCEDURE	PRIMARY DIAGNOSIS	PLACE OF TREATMENT
DEPENDENT	08/02/9X	ELECTIVE	Deviated Septum	Englewood Hospital Assn

Cases Reviewed for the Provider: 1

Provider Last Name: Provider City, State: New York, NY

RELATION TO EMPLOYEE	NOTIFIED DATE	TYPE OF PROCEDURE	PRIMARY DIAGNOSIS	PLACE OF TREATMENT
SELF	07/13/9X	URGENT	Spontaneous Abortion	New York Hospital

Cases Reviewed for the Provider: 1

Provider Last Name: Provider City, State: West New York, NY

RELATION TO EMPLOYEE	NOTIFIED DATE	TYPE OF PROCEDURE	PRIMARY DIAGNOSIS	PLACE OF TREATMENT
SELF	07/07/9X	EMERGENCY	Full Term Pregnancy	PALISADES GENERAL HOSPITAL

Cases Reviewed for the Provider: 1

EXHIBIT 9-6. Report on inpatient hospital stays. (Source: Halo Associates.)

Year	Month	Total Dental Paid
1998	July	7,774.15
1998	June	15,109.10
1998	May	14,350.85
1998	April	13,375.71
1998	March	12,832.10
1998	February	10,591.65
1998	January	15,181.95
1997	December	11,737.65
1997	November	10,231.40
1997	October	16,192.80
1997	September	4,837.40
1997	August	6,767.40
	Totals:	$138,982.16

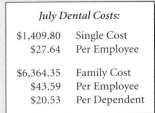

July Dental Costs:

$1,409.80	Single Cost
$27.64	Per Employee
$6,364.35	Family Cost
$43.59	Per Employee
$20.53	Per Dependent

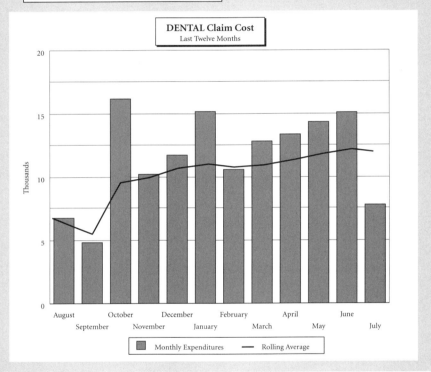

EXHIBIT 9-7. Dental claims cost analysis. (Source: North American Administrators.)

a hospital be added to a network or by directing your case management company to negotiate in advance with the hospital. You can negotiate a better discount at the hospitals most often used by your employees and use these reports to document use.

A report used to monitor cash flow for a dental plan, with twelve months of activity, is shown in Exhibit 9-7. This report is presented in graph form so that it is easy to note fluctuations in claims cost month to month.

Summaries from monthly claim registers prove useful. Exhibit 9-8 presents a claims register with basic information; Exhibit 9-9 is the summary report drawn from it. Some organizations refer the claims register to their accounting department but use the summary for plan management.

Employer: 00 0 –

Location 0001—Nonbargaining Group

For the period of: July 1, 199X thru July 31, 199X

Incurred Date	Check Date	Claim Number	Employee Soc. Sec. #	Employee Name	Patient Name	Amount of Service	Covered Expense	Due from Employee	Pat. Id.	Paid by Plan	Pd to	Check Number
2/16/98	7/02/98	80701	—	Diane	Louis	400.00	400.00	200.00	01	200.00	P	00000002325
2/13/98	7/16/98	80715	—	Diane	Louis	135.00	135.00	.00	01	47.00	P	00000002352
1/13/98	7/02/98	80701	—	Diane	Michael	150.00	150.00	75.00	02	75.00	P	00000002324
1/26/98	7/16/98	80715	—	Diane	Justin	88.00	88.00	26.40	04	61.60	P	00000002351
7/03/98	7/16/98	80715	—	Margaret	Margaret	209.00	109.00	132.70	00	76.30	P	00000002355
7/21/98	7/30/98	80729	—	Margaret	Jessica	100.00	100.00	50.00	02	50.00	P	00000002380
7/20/98	7/30/98	80729	—	Anthony	Anthony	95.00	95.00	.00	00	95.00	P	00000002378
7/01/98	7/16/98	80715	—	Wanda	Lawrence	90.00	90.00	.00	01	90.00	P	00000002356
1/31/98	7/16/98	80715	—	Maureen	Maureen	115.00	.00	115.00	00	.00	P	NO CHECK
7/01/98	7/16/98	80715	—	Priscilla	Michael	98.00	98.00	.00	01	98.00	P	00000002353
6/23/98	7/02/98	80701	—	Miriam	Miriam	84.00	.00	84.00	00	.00	P	NO CHECK
6/24/98	7/02/98	80701	—	Miriam	Miriam	84.00	.00	84.00	00	.00	P	NO CHECK
5/30/98	7/02/98	80701	—	Miriam	Jerrold	185.00	160.00	25.00	01	133.00	P	00000002319
5/08/98	7/02/98	80701	—	Miriam	Jerrold	688.00	688.00	169.65	01	223.35	P	00000002320
7/09/98	7/23/98	80722	—	Donald	Donald	95.00	92.00	3.00	00	92.00	P	00000002365
7/09/98	7/23/98	80722	—	Donald	Donald	215.00	196.00	19.00	00	196.00	P	00000002366
6/29/98	7/08/98	80707	—	Theodore	Theodore	55.00	55.00	.00	00	55.00	P	00000002343
7/21/98	7/30/98	80729	—	Susan	Jessica	205.00	105.00	131.50	01	73.50	P	00000002374
7/21/98	7/30/98	80729	—	Susan	John	205.00	105.00	131.50	02	73.50	P	00000002375

*Totals for Division 0001   Number of Claims 39   8,041.00   6,324.00   3,240.45   4,225.95

**Totals for Division for Claim Year 1   .00   for Claim Year 2   4,225.95

Total Dental Claims   39   for the Amount of   4,225.95

EXHIBIT 9-8. Claims register. (Source: North American Administrators.)

| Year | Month | Dental Preventive | | Dental Basic Services | | Dental Major Services | | Dental Orthodontia | | Other Miscellaneous | | Total Dental |
		Items	Total Paid	Items	Total Paid	Items	Total Paid	Items	Total Paid	Items	Total Paid	Paid
1998	Jul	96	2,654.10	52	3,796.70	5	1,085.85	4	237.50	0	0.00	7,774.15
1998	Jun	74	1,935.54	56	7,267.66	18	5,363.40	9	542.50	0	0.00	15,109.10
1998	May	140	3,788.70	63	7,063.65	9	3,311.00	3	187.50	0	0.00	14,350.85
1998	Apr	142	3,762.90	50	6,028.68	10	2,506.62	12	1,077.51	0	0.00	13,375.71
1998	Mar	79	2,047.70	43	6,377.40	13	3,557.00	5	950.00	0	0.00	12,832.10
1998	Feb	68	1,931.00	62	6,062.65	7	1,863.00	5	735.00	0	0.00	10,591.65
1998	Jan	113	2,947.62	65	8,613.83	12	2,895.50	5	725.00	0	0.00	15,181.95
1997	Dec	118	2,984.70	73	6,142.90	8	1,770.00	8	840.05	0	0.00	11,737.65
1997	Nov	77	2,060.40	35	5,249.50	10	2,771.50	3	150.00	0	0.00	10,231.40
1997	Oct	154	4,085.31	80	7,988.50	17	3,968.99	3	150.00	0	0.00	16,192.80
1997	Sep	62	1,583.00	9	1,569.40	5	1,685.00	0	0.00	0	0.00	4,837.40
1997	Aug	71	2,053.24	30	3,169.16	4	1,325.00	4	220.00	0	0.00	6,767.40
Totals		1,194	$31,834.21	618	$69,330.03	118	$32,102.86	61	$5,715.06	0	$0.00	$138,982.16

EXHIBIT 9-9. Summary of claims activity. (Source: North American Administrators.)

A monthly summary of health plan costs is shown in Exhibit 9-10. It includes some interpretation of claims and administrative data provided by the plan's consultant. When a narrative is included with monthly expense, utilization, and comparative data, it should be brief and useful.

The financial information below compares November 1998 with the cost information for November 1997 and the 1997 year-end monthly averages.

	Average 1997	November 1997	November 1998
Hospital	$102,920	$ 66,638	$120,136
Major Medical	70,139	52,068	58,307
Drugs	46,792	49,756	86,104
PCS	17,900	17,089	20,785
Mail	28,891	32,667	65,318
Totals	$219,851	$168,462	$264,547

A comparison of November 1998 with November 1997 and the 1997 monthly average shows a dramatic increase in all costs (totally +57%), and a solid increase over the 1997 average (+20.3%) but a reduction from the 1998 YTD of –2.5%. This indicates that although November this year was a higher-cost month compared to last year, costs are settling down.

The year-to-date costs from budget are at 107.51% of budget for eleven months of claims. A projection of year-end costs indicates between $450,000–475,000 over budget for 1998.

Costs for 1998 seem to be leveling off, even with additional chronic/catastrophic claims that have occurred. The administrative and case management services for the plan continue to work with claimants who have chronic and catastrophic illness to coordinate care and to encourage efficient use of plan resources. This will be enhanced by plan changes in 1999 that will introduce managed care services earlier at the precertification stage.

EXHIBIT 9-10. Monthly cost summary. (Source: Halo Associates.)

Additional Short-Term Feedback

There are additional ways to monitor your health plan in the short term besides reports. You should also establish procedures and systems within your organization for feedback on your health plan. These should include suggestions, comments, and complaints from employees, employee representatives, your plan adviser or insurance professional, the plan administrator, and your staff.

There are many ways to get feedback from your employees. Which methods you use to measure how well your employees accept and value your health plan depends on the size and culture of your organization. Whether your organization is small or mid-sized, you should determine whether employees feel your health plan accomplishes its goals for service and cost. You will want to have several vehicles for employees to convey their concerns and experiences with the health plan. Be prepared that all responses may not be what you want to hear.

First, you need to establish two-way communication with your employees and to develop specific reports and reporting avenues to reach them. Some ways to do this are the following:

- Start a newsletter, or write a column in an existing employee newsletter, devoted to health plan information, news, and articles. If you are receiving monthly reports and updates, there will be plenty of information to share with employees about your health plan. Exhibit 9-11 presents an example of a newsletter article on health plan information. Be sure to invite employee comments, calls, and suggestions.

- Conduct a benefit question hour periodically with your staff, and encourage or require other department heads to do the same. Provide benefits staff to assist them, if needed.

- Send out interoffice or homebound mailings on benefit issues, plan changes, and important plan information. Include a response opportunity with each mailing. These

---

Changes—For the Better

The Orange County Health Plan is pleased to announce the following changes for 1998 effective January 1:

Oral contraceptives are covered under the prescription plan. A plan participant can obtain a month's supply with a prescription and a $5.00 co-pay.

Emergency Room coverage has been simplified by a $25.00 co-payment per visit, which now includes ancillary and affiliated services (ER doctors, diagnostic tests, interpretations, etc.) up to reasonable and customary charges.

This improvement replaces the old $15.00 co-pay which covered hospital emergency room fees only, and made it necessary to pay for other, additional services out of pocket and then submit for reimbursement through the provisions of the Major Medical benefit.

The Emergency Care Benefit is for the timely treatment of conditions caused by accident, or for acute, severe illness. Co-payment is waived if an inpatient admission results directly from emergency room care.

As always, non-acute care performed in a hospital emergency room remains covered under Major Medical, not the Emergency Care Benefit, and is subject to deductible and co-payment

---

EXHIBIT 9-11. Sample of a newsletter article on health plan information. (Source: *For Your Benefit*, vol. 2, no. 1, Spring 1998, p. 1; copyright © by the Wellness Institute Inc.)

COPAYMENT FOR HOSPITAL OUTPATIENT SERVICES:

You must pay a $15 copayment for each visit where you receive one or more of the following covered hospital outpatient services. (Hospitals may require payment of this charge at the time of service.)

→ Emergency care within 72 hours of an accidental injury of within 12 hours of the sudden onset of an illness

→ Surgery

→ Diagnostic X-rays

→ Diagnostic laboratory tests

→ Preadmission testing

→ Administration of Desferal for treatment of Cooley's Anemia

You will not have to pay this hospital outpatient copayment if you are treated in the outpatient department of a hospital and it becomes necessary for the hospital to admit you at that time as an inpatient.

The copayment does not apply to outpatient services for:

* Chemotherapy
* Physical therapy
* Radiation therapy
* Kidney dialysis

COPAYMENT FOR ALCOHOL OR SUBSTANCE ABUSE TREATMENT

You must pay an $8 copayment for each visit to an approved facility for the diagnosis and treatment of alcohol or substance abuse even if the services are rendered on the same day and at the same facility as any of the services listed above. This copayment will not be waived even if you are admitted as an inpatient at that time.

EMERGENCY ROOM CLAIMS

Benefits related to the emergency room in connection with a condition not considered life-threatening may be benefited under the Major Medical Plan, subject to the annual deductible and coinsurance payments.

EXHIBIT 9-12. Notice of benefits changes. (Source: Halo Associates.)

should also be prominently posted where employees gather. Exhibit 9-12 is a typical notice of benefit changes.

■ Offer electronic access to health plan information and to enable employees to check on the status of their own benefits and/or claims. Include a response function.

■ Provide a telephone call center, appropriately staffed, for calls on benefit and coverage issues and on health topics. This can be contracted with outside providers. Exhibit 9-13 presents a satisfaction report on call center services and employee responses.

■ Evaluate employee attitudes periodically, through short satisfaction surveys, possibly completed at open enrollment; exit interviews; and recruitment interviews.

Once you establish ongoing employee input, you'll need to monitor the responses and reactions. Some procedures you should follow are these:

■ Keep a log of calls, electronic feedback, and written responses. Be sure they are reviewed regularly and that a monthly summary is prepared for your file and for

HealthQs 800 Customer Evaluations
July 1–December 31, 1998

Total Calls by Quarter:	**60 Third Q**	**83 Fourth Q**
Felt that they received helpful advice	59	80
Information was easy to understand	52	71
Felt better prepared after HealthQs	53	68
Report that HealthQs was useful for taking care of self/family	57	70

Note: Customer satisfaction is measured through the use of exit questions at the end of each call to ensure that the HealthQs staff monitors caller satisfaction on a daily basis. There is an opportunity for negative feedback given to each caller. No negative feedback responses were received this quarter, although the responses noted above include where the caller did not complete answers to all exit questions.

EXHIBIT 9-13. Satisfaction report. (Source: Health Qs 800, Halo Associates.)

management review. Exhibit 9-14 shows a telephone log used to record feedback and complaints.

- Log written comments or responses. Keep a tickler file of those which require follow-up or action. Compile a monthly summary of written issues, complaints, and suggestions.
- Hold meetings with employee representatives, the benefits committee, and the benefits staff on a regular basis to review any employee concerns or problems. Some or all of the issues summarized in monthly log reports can be discussed. The monthly meetings can review financial issues, assess future needs, and discuss ways to improve communications.
- Ask your carrier, MCO, or administrator to provide you with a report on employee calls and letters, and on complaints and appeal requests they receive. You should request a quarterly report on complaints and appeals, and track the number and outcome of employee appeals of claim payments.
- In addition to scheduled meetings, be sure to keep in touch with employee representatives and key supervisors during the year to hear first-hand whether or not any problems have flared up.

You should follow up and take action on the input you receive. As with any management issue, you should ascertain what the problem seems to be, determine how to address it, and then take action with your staff, health plan adviser, or plan administrator to correct it.

Whenever you learn of health plan problems, you should document what you have done to resolve them, and then monitor whether the problem persists, subsides, or increases. You should seek advice and guidance from your health insurance professional or plan adviser on complex complaints and issues, and resolve problems related to the plan's terms and conditions with the carrier, HMO, or administrator. Your insurance professional should work with you to be sure you receive services according to industry standard and that problems with your plan members are resolved promptly.

Name	Tel #/Address	Date/Time	Issue	Action

Instructions: If the caller is anonymous, note gender and other available information. For the Issue section, describe whether the call is in the nature of a comment, complaint, problem, or general question; then describe it briefly but completely (i.e., eligibility and coverage for newborn child in hospital premature care). Include the date of action taken or follow-up required in the Action box (i.e., advised regarding newborn, sent copy of benefit booklet, alerted managed care to follow up).

Note: No benefit information or information specific to an employee, retiree, or dependent should be given over the telephone without verification of the caller's identification. Ask for the social security number of the covered member, and department of the employee, to verify identification (i.e., for a spouse calling: name, social security number, and name and department/position of your employee member).

EXHIBIT 9-14. Sample telephone log. (Source: Halo Associates, copyright © 1994.)

Short-term reports and monitoring are used to nip problems in the bud, to allocate resources needed, and to exert operational control over your health plan. Following these reports closely makes sense, since short-term issues often become longer-term problems if left alone.

■ LONG-TERM REPORTS AND INFORMATION

Unlike operational reports and feedback, your long-term reports can have various purposes. They may be used to comply with regulations for annual reporting and filing or to inform employees of plan procedures, changes, and options. They also serve two important management purposes:

- To give you a basis from which to measure and justify plan costs
- To help you plan for the future

Most long-term reports summarize the value of services or benefits received. There are several types of these reports, including:

- Reports to employees, such as annual explanations of benefits, updates on plan choices, comparisons of plan costs and coverage, required reports on finances, and notices of benefit changes. Exhibit 9-15 presents a sample employer-generated report to employees that provides year-end statement of benefits received.

- Summary reports to management, including:
  - ☐ Annual reports
  - ☐ Cost summaries in general or by employee category

```
              199X - BENEFIT PLAN
------------------------------------------------------------
THIS STATEMENT HAS BEEN PREPARED ESPECIALLY FOR:


SOCIAL SEC. NO.                              DEPT...........
DATE OF HIRE...

**********************************************************
        - - - - - BENEFIT  STATEMENT - - - - -
**********************************************************

HEALTH:              INDEPENDENT HEALTH  -  FAMILY COVERAGE
----------
         ANNUAL PREMIUM.......     $5,089.20
         YOUR CONTRIBUTION.....  –     $.00**
                                 ----------
                  CONTRIBUTION ..............   $5,089.20

DENTAL:              CSEA/EBF  -  INDIVIDUAL COVERAGE
----------
         ANNUAL PREMIUM.......      $128.28
         YOUR CONTRIBUTION.....  –     $.00**
                                 ----------
                  CONTRIBUTION ..............    $128.28

VISION:              TRAVELERS  -  INDIVIDUAL COVERAGE
---------
         ANNUAL PREMIUM.......       $49.32
         YOUR CONTRIBUTION.....  –     $.00**
                                 ----------
                  CONTRIBUTION ..............     $49.32


IN ADDITION TO YOUR ANNUAL SALARY OF -----------------

CONTRIBUTES $5,266.80 TOWARD YOUR HEALTH, DENTAL AND VISION COVERAGE.
            ---------

**YOUR ANNUALIZED CONTRIBUTION OF    $.00    IS BASED ON CURRENT
                                 -------------
PAYROLL DEDUCTION TIMES 26 PAYROLLS.
```

EXHIBIT 9-15. Employer's report to employees. (Source: Halo Associates.)

□ Annual reports of savings by benefits category or plan vendor activity, such as case management, consultant, discount network, and plan administrator.
□ Fiscal and utilization reports on plan design issues
■ Internal reports used in plan management, and those required by government, including the annual 5500 (a summary annual report filed with the federal government, which covers plan enrollment, administrative, and claims costs, and reports the financial activity of the plan; see Exhibit 9-16) and the annual 1099 report, which lists all providers paid by your health plan administrator and the amount of total payments.

(text continues on page 199)

INSURANCE INFORMATION FOR COMPLETION OF PART III
SCHEDULE A, FORM 5500

Name of Carrier:

8. Group Contract: Data for Period:

9. (a) Premiums:
        Total Premium .... $
        Pooled Premium ....
        Net Premium .... $

  (b) Benefit Charges:
        Claims Paid .... $
        Pooled Claims ....
        Changes in Claim Reserves ....
        Incurred Claims Charges .... $

  (c) Remainder of Premium:

    1. Retention Charges:
        a. Renewal Commissions .... $
        b. Administrative Service or Other Fees ....
        c. Acquisition Expense ....
        d. Expenses ....
        e. Taxes ....
        f. Risk or Contingencies ....
        g. Interest Adjustment ....
        h. Total Retention .... $
        Conversion Charge .... $

    2. Dividends or Retroactive Rate Refund (Deficit) .... $
        Prior Deficit .... $
        Contract Premium Due .... $
        Stabilization Reserve Transfer .... $
        Transfer To/From Other Policies .... $
        Net Balance .... $

  (d) Status of Claim Reserves At End of Year .... $

EXHIBIT 9-16. Samples from IRS Form 5500 showing the kind of information needed to complete the form.

Form **5500**	**Annual Return/Report of Employee Benefit Plan**	OMB Nos. 1210-0016

Form **5500**

Department of the Treasury
Internal Revenue Service

Department of Labor
Pension and Welfare Benefits
Administration

Pension Benefit Guaranty Corporation

Annual Return/Report of Employee Benefit Plan
(With 100 or more participants)

This form is required to be filed under sections 104 and 4065 of the Employee Retirement Income Security Act of 1974 and sections 6039D, 6047(e), 6057(b), and 6058(a) of the Internal Revenue Code, referred to as the Code.
▶ See separate instructions.

OMB Nos. 1210-0016
1210-0089

19**98**

This Form Is Open to Public Inspection.

For the calendar plan year 1998 or fiscal plan year beginning , 1998, and ending , 19

If A(1) through A(4), B, C, and/or D, do not apply to this year's return/report, leave the boxes unmarked.

For IRS Use Only

EP–ID

A This return/report is:
- (1) ☐ the first return/report filed for the plan;
- (2) ☐ an amended return/report;
- (3) ☐ the final return/report filed for the plan; or
- (4) ☐ a short plan year return/report (less than 12 months).

B Check here if any information reported in 1a, 2a, 2b, or 5a changed since the last return/report for this plan . . . . ▶ ☐

C If your plan year changed since the last return/report, check here . . . . ▶ ☐

D If you filed for an extension of time to file this return/report, check here and attach a copy of the extension . . . . ▶ ☐

1a Name and address of plan sponsor (employer, if for a single-employer plan) (Address should include room or suite no.)

1b Employer identification number (EIN)

1c Sponsor's telephone number

1d Business code (see instructions, page 20)

1e CUSIP issuer number

2a Name and address of plan administrator (if same as plan sponsor, enter "Same")

2b Administrator's EIN

2c Administrator's telephone number

3 If the name, address, and EIN of the plan sponsor or plan administrator has changed since the last return/report filed for this plan, enter the information from the last return/report in line 3a and/or line 3b and complete line 3c.

a Sponsor... EIN .... Plan number ....

b Administrator.. EIN ....

c If line 3a indicates a change in the sponsor's name, address, and EIN, is this a change in sponsorship only? (See line 3c on page 8 of the instructions for the definition of sponsorship.) Enter "Yes" or "No." ▶

4 **ENTITY CODE.** (If not shown, enter the applicable code from page 8 of the instructions.) ▶

5a Name of plan ▶

5b Effective date of plan (mo., day, yr.)

5c Three-digit plan number ▶

All filers must complete 6a through 6d, as applicable.

6a ☐ Welfare benefit plan **6b** ☐ Pension benefit plan
(Enter the applicable codes from page 8 of the instructions in the boxes.)

6c Pension plan features. (Enter the applicable pension plan feature codes from page 8 of the instructions in the boxes.)

6d ☐ Fringe benefit plan. Attach Schedule F (Form 5500). See instructions.

Caution: *A penalty for the late or incomplete filing of this return/report will be assessed unless reasonable cause is established.*

Under penalties of perjury and other penalties set forth in the instructions, I declare that I have examined this return/report, including accompanying schedules and statements, and to the best of my knowledge and belief, it is true, correct, and complete.

Signature of employer/plan sponsor ▶ .... Date ▶ ....

Type or print name of individual signing above ....

Signature of plan administrator ▶ ....

Type or print name of individual signing above .... Date ▶ ....

For Paperwork Reduction Act Notice, see the instructions for Form 5500. Cat. No. 13500F Form **5500** (1998)

(continues)

6e Check all applicable investment arrangements below (see instructions on page 9):

    (1) ☐ Master trust   *(2)* ☐ 103-12 investment entity

    (3) ☐ Common/collective trust   *(4)* ☐ Pooled separate account

----

----

  f Single-employer plans enter the tax year end of the employer in which this plan year ends ▶ Month .... Day .... Year ....

  g Is any part of this plan funded by an insurance contract described in Code section 412(i)? . . . . ☐ Yes ☐ No

  h If line **6g** is "Yes," was the part subject to the minimum funding standards for either of the prior 2 plan years? . . . ☐ Yes ☐ No

7 Number of participants as of the end of the plan year (welfare plans complete only lines 7a(4), 7b, 7c, and 7d):

a Active participants:	*(1)* Number fully vested	**a(1)**	
	(2) Number partially vested	**a(2)**	
	(3) Number nonvested.	**a(3)**	
	(4) Total	**a(4)**	
b Retired or separated participants receiving benefits	**b**	
c Retired or separated participants entitled to future benefits	**c**	
d Subtotal. Add lines **7a(4), 7b,** and **7c**	**d**	
e Deceased participants whose beneficiaries are receiving or are entitled to receive benefits	**e**	
f Total. Add lines **7d** and **7e**	**f**	
g Number of participants with account balances. (Defined benefit plans do not complete this line item.) . . .	**g**	
h Number of participants that terminated employment during the plan year with accrued benefits that were less than 100% vested	**h**	

		Yes	No
i *(1)* Was any participant(s) separated from service with a deferred vested benefit for which a Schedule SSA (Form 5500) is required to be attached? (See instructions.)	**i(1)**		
(2) If "Yes," enter the number of separated participants required to be reported ▶			

		Yes	No
8a Was this plan ever amended since its effective date? If "Yes," complete line **8b** . . .	**8a**		
If the amendment was adopted in this plan year, complete lines **8c** through **8e.**			
b If line **8a** is "Yes," enter the date the most recent amendment was adopted ▶ Month .... Day .... Year			
c Did any amendment during the current plan year result in the retroactive reduction of accrued benefits for any participants?	**c**		
d During this plan year did any amendment change the information contained in the latest summary plan descriptions or summary description of modifications available at the time of amendment?.	**d**		
e If line **8d** is "Yes," has a summary plan description or summary description of modifications that reflects the plan amendments referred to on line **8d** been furnished to participants? (see instructions)	**e**		

		Yes	No
9a Was this plan terminated during this plan year or any prior plan year? If "Yes," enter the year ▶	**9a**		
b Were all the plan assets either distributed to participants or beneficiaries, transferred to another plan, or brought under the control of PBGC? (see instructions.)	**b**		
c Was a resolution to terminate this plan adopted during this plan year or any prior plan year?	**c**		
d If line **9a** or line **9c** is "Yes," have you received a favorable determination letter from the IRS for the termination? . .	**d**		
e If line **9d** is "No," has a determination letter been requested from the IRS?	**e**		
f If line **9a** or line **9c** is "Yes," have participants and beneficiaries been notified of the termination or the proposed termination?	**f**		
g If line **9a** is "Yes" and the plan is covered by PBGC, is the plan continuing to file a PBGC Form 1 and pay premiums until the end of the plan year in which assets are distributed or brought under the control of PBGC? . . .	**g**		
h During this plan year, did any trust assets revert to the employer for which the Code section 4980 excise tax is due?	**h**		
i If line **9h** is "Yes," enter the amount of tax paid with Form 5330 ▶ $			

10a In this plan year, was this plan merged or consolidated into another plan(s), or were assets or liabilities transferred to another plan(s)? If "Yes," complete lines **10b** through **10e** . . . . ▶ ☐ Yes ☐ No			
If "Yes," identify the other plan(s)	**c** Employer identification number(s)	**d** Plan number(s)	
b Name of plan(s) ▶	....	....	
e If required, has a Form 5310-A been filed? . . . . ▶ ☐ Yes ☐ No			

11 Enter the plan funding arrangement code from page 10 of the instructions . . . . ▶	**12** Enter the plan benefit arrangement code from page 10 of the instructions ▶

		Yes	No
13a Is this a plan established or maintained pursuant to one or more collective bargaining agreements?	**13a**		
b If line **13a** is "Yes," enter the appropriate six-digit LM number(s) of the sponsoring labor organization(s) (see instructions):			
(1) *(2)* *(3)*			
14 If any benefits are provided by an insurance company, insurance service, or similar organization, enter the number of **Schedules A (Form 5500),** Insurance Information, attached. If none, enter "-0-." ▶			

EXHIBIT 9-16. Continued

FORM 5500 SUPPLEMENT

Data for use in preparing Schedule A for Form 5500
as required under ERISA—Public Law—93-406

PART III (Item 8)			
GROUP CONTRACT NUMBER	TYPE OF BENEFIT	GROSS PREMIUM FOR EACH CONTRACT	PREMIUM RATE* ☐ M ☐ Q ☐ SA ☐ A
174832	Hospitalization	$1,458,591.05	Ind. – $28.20
			Fam. – $70.55
			M.S.C. – $28.20
174833	Hospitalization	$ 14,505.36	Ind. – $28.20
			Fam. – $70.55
			M.S.C. – $28.20
174834	Hospitalization	$ 215,117.53	Ind. – $28.20
			Fam. – $70.55
			M.S.C. – $28.20
174835	Hospitalization	$ 2,172.53	Ind. – $28.20
			Fam. – $70.55
			M.S.C. – $28.20
174833	Basic Medical	$ 14,795.36	Ind. – $28.75
			Fam. – $71.97
			M.S.C. – $28.75
174835	Basic Medical	$ 2,215.84	Ind. – $28.75
			Fam. – $71.97
			M.S.C. – $28.75
174832	Major Medical	$1,192,818.45	Ind. – $23.05
			Fam. – $57.70
			M.S.C. – $23.05

*PREMIUM RATE CODE:
M = MONTHLY
Q = QUARTERLY
SA = SEMI-ANNUAL
A = ANNUAL

TYPE OF CONTRACT:
IND. = INDIVIDUAL
FAM. = FAMILY
COMP. = COMPOSITE
H & W = HUSBAND & WIFE
P & C = PARENT & CHILD
MSC = MEDICARE SUPPLEMENTARY COVERAGE

INSURED HOSPITAL CONTRACT
CURRENT COST DATA

	1998
PREMIUM	$4,818,369
CLAIMS PAID	3,171,755
ADMINISTRATION CHARGES	289,102
ACCUMULATIVE RESERVE FOR CLAIMS PAYMENT	1,357,512

INSURED HOSPITAL CONTRACT
PROJECTED COST DATA 199X

PREMIUM	$4,284,618
CLAIMS PAID	4,092,038
*ADMINISTRATION CHARGES	192,580
ACCUMULATIVE RESERVE FOR CLAIMS PAYMENT	-0-

*Per agreement, combined hospital retention and ASO administrative charges cannot exceed $425,000.

EXHIBIT 9-17. Summary of claims and administrative costs. (Source: Halo Associates.)

Township of _____

Utilization Management Results

November, 199X

Employee ID	Service	Urgency	Req'd Days	Actual Days	Days Saved	Stay Reduction Savings	Room Rate Savings	Additional Savings	Total Savings
10814	Same day	Elective	1	1	0	$0.00	$0.00	$0.00	$0.00
10890	Same day	Elective	1	1	0	$0.00	$0.00	$0.00	$0.00
10904	Same day	Elective	1	1	0	$0.00	$0.00	$118.49	$118.49
10905	Inpatient	Urgent	2	2	0	$0.00	$0.00	$0.00	$0.00
10913	Inpatient	Emergency	17	16	1	$750.00	$0.00	$0.00	$750.00
10917	Inpatient	Emergency	2	2	0	$0.00	$0.00	$0.00	$0.00
10918	Inpatient	Urgent	6	4	2	$1870.00	$0.00	$0.00	$1,870.00
10928	Same day	Elective	1	1	0	$0.00	$0.00	$0.00	$0.00
10937	Inpatient	Emergency	14	14	0	$0.00	$0.00	$0.00	$0.00
10941	Same day	Urgent	1	1	0	$0.00	$0.00	$0.00	$0.00
10960	Inpatient	Elective	28	28	0	$0.00	$0.00	$452.59	$452.59
Total:			74	71	3	$2620.00	$0.00	$571.08	$3,191.08
Count:	11								

EXHIBIT 9-18. Report on utilization savings. (Source: Halo Associates.)

Claim Number	Check Number	Hospital	Per Diem Cost	Drug Cost	120% of Drug	Discounts	Type Discount	Amount Paid
50136	23793	Presbyterian	75,106.70	Exempt		32,478.73	Rubin	42,627.97
50731	24160	Sloan Kettering	35,729.44			6,425.60	Rubin	29,303.84
50425	24793	Charles River Hosp	35,987.72	Exempt		4,926.56	negotiate	27,917.15
50750	25497	Fairwinds Hosp	27,122.78	Exempt		10,170.98	Rubin	16,951.80
50105	25622	Craig Hosp	4,597.50			919.50	Rubin	3,678.00
50105	26081	Craig Hosp	14,939.00			2,987.80	Rubin	11,951.20
50059	21476	Westchester	12,500.00	14,182.37	17,018.85	164.37	Rubin	12,335.63
50084	22847	Hosp Spec Surg	37,459.56	42,953.56	51,544.28	1,479.27	Rubin	35,980.71
50059	23686	Westchester	17,018.85	14,182.37	15,884.25	3,545.59	Rubin	12,338.66
50059	23329	Westchester	10,000.00	14,182.37	17,018.85	7,016.85	Rubin	10,000.00
50084	22849	Burke Rehab	22,280.94	19,637.10	23,564.52			19,637.10
50084	23977	Burke Rehab	2,468.39	1,309.14	1,570.97			1,309.14
		Total	295,210.88			70,117.25		224,031.20

EXHIBIT 9-19. Report on inpatient hospital stay activity and discounts. (Source: Halo Associates.)

Reports used annually for planning and evaluation are:

- The year-end summary of claims and administrative costs and a projection of these costs for the coming year (Exhibit 9-17)
- Various summaries, by vendors, of case management, precertification, and discounted savings (Exhibit 9-18)
- Inpatient hospital stay activity and discounts (Exhibit 9-19)
- Annual network utilization and costs (Exhibit 9-20)

Network Analysis		
Hospital	Amount Paid	Percentage
Nonnetwork	$ 1,016,618	27%
Network	$ 2,477,794	73%
Subtotal	$ 3,761,412	100%
Major Medical		
Nonnetwork	$ 3,718,584	55%
Network	$ 3,009,742	45%
Subtotal	$ 6,728,326	100%
Total		
Nonnetwork	$ 4,735,202	45%
Network	$ 5,754,536	55%
Total	$10,489,738	100%
PPO Fee Reductions	$ 656,483	
Total Percentage Discount Paid		

EXHIBIT 9-20. Network utilization and costs. (Source: Halo Associates.)

Employer:_____ Worksite(s):_____

Program: _____ Date(s): _____

Presenter(s): _____

Program Administration

Enrollment & Advance Materials. Ratings: _____ Other: _____

Publicity. Rating:_____ Other: _____

Cost. Rating: _____ Other: _____

Convenient Schedule. Rating: _____ Other: _____

Worksite Location. Rating: _____ Other: _____

Facilities. Rating: _____ Other: _____

Staff & Presenters

Handouts. Rating: _____ Other: _____

Program Pace. Rating: _____ Other: _____

Displays & Demonstrations. Rating: _____ Other: _____

WI Staff. Rating: _____ Other: _____

Presenter(s). Rating: _____ Other: _____

Information & Needs. Rating: _____ Other: _____

Content & Substance. Rating: _____ Other: _____

General

Attend Another WI program?   Yes _____ No _____ Maybe _____

Attend on same topic?   Yes _____ No _____ Maybe _____

Other topics noted:

Best time. Before Work _____ After work _____   Lunch Hour _____

Summary of Program Comments.

_____

_____

Summary of Suggestions.

_____

_____

Observations of onsite WI Representative.

_____

_____

Prepared by: _____ Date Submitted: _____

Submitted to: _____

EXHIBIT 9-21. Wellness program summary. (Source: Wellness Institite, copyright © 1995, all rights reserved.)

- Wellness program summary (Exhibit 9-21) and cost impact. The summary is used to evaluate employee response to a particular program.

  The number of reports you receive will be determined by the size of your organization and the type of plan you have. For instance, an HMO can furnish you with its federal HEIDIS report, or a summary of it. Your carrier can furnish you with cost, utilization, and network data. Exhibit 9-22 presents an HMO utilization annual summary provided to an employer.

MEMBER MONTHS	199X YTD
Coplan A	0
Coplan 3	0
Coplan 5	0
Coplan 5+	0
Coplan 10	2154
Coplan 10+	0
Coplan 15	0
Coplan 15+	0
TOTAL	2154

GROUP UTILIZATION REPORT
XYZ Health Plan, Inc.

Report Date:

	199X	ACTUAL	Y-T-D	199X	ACTUAL
	FREQ PMPY	AVG COST	199X CAP	Total Freq.	TOTAL Cost
I. INPATIENT HOSPITAL					
A. In Area	0.074	2279.91	14.10	13	29,639
B. Out-of-Area	0.000	0.00	0.00	0	0
C. Newborn	0.017	1040.41	1.48	3	3,121
D. Preadmission Testing	0.000	0.00	0.00	0	0
E. PAT Lab			0.00		
F. I/P Drug Riders			0.17		
II. OUTPATIENT SURGERY					
A. Surgery	0.229	142.20	2.71	40	5,688
B. O/P Surgery Lab			0.33		
III. EMERGENCY ROOM					
A. Emergency Room	0.983	62.10	5.09	165	10,247
B. ER Lab			0.19		
IV. HOME HEALTH	0.006	5406.30	2.57	1	5,406
V. AMBULANCE	0.000	0.00	0.00	0	0
VI. DURABLE MED. EQUIP.					
A. Equipment	0.023	74.75	0.14	4	299
B. DME Capitation			0.21		
TOTAL HMO			27.00	226	54,401
Less Copayment			(1.89)		
Less COB			0.00		
NET HMO					
VII. PHYSICIAN					
A. Office Visits	4.143	50.42	17.41	737	37,161
B. Inpatient Visits	0.445	39.97	1.48	77	3,078
C. Inpatient Visits—Newborn	0.064	47.48	0.25	11	522
D. Home Visits	0.000	0.00	0.00	0	0
E. Consultations	0.121	121.50	1.23	21	2,551
F. Psych	0.052	97.78	0.42	9	880
G. Emergency Room Visits	0.012	69.50	0.07	2	139
VIII. SURGERY/OB					
A. 1. General Surgery	0.526	230.73	10.11	91	20,996
2. Anesthesia	0.127	287.00	3.04	22	6,314
B. 1. Obstetrics—Delivery	0.023	1767.55	3.40	4	7,070
2. Anesthesia	0.000	0.00	0.00	0	0
TOTAL PHYSICIAN			37.42	974	78,712
Less Copayments			(3.95)		
Less COB			0.00		
NET PHYSICIAN			33.47		

EXHIBIT 9-22. HMO utilization summary. (Source: Halo Associates.)

With the current trend toward employee choice, it's not unusual for a small or mid-sized organization to have four or five health plan vendors. Some plans routinely provide helpful reports, and others don't have the capability. At a minimum, you should receive comprehensive annual reports from carriers and MCOs in time to monitor whether you receive full value for your premiums and to review your options.

If you are self-funded, your plan adviser will work closely with you on specific and general reports you will need, both short term and long term. Self-funded plans are less bound by regulations, because they are regulated primarily by ERISA and not by state insurance departments. On the other hand, reporting is more important for them because they are not insured, so plan use and cost have a direct and immediate effect. Reports are customized, and specific, to the needs of self-funded plans. Poor performance by a plan administrator reflects on the health plan manager, who is responsible for the plan. It is through reports that you can monitor the effectiveness of claims processing and other administrative services, which are usually contracted to outside professionals.

The Annual Report

Reporting to others in your organization should be a scheduled activity. Whether your organization is small or mid-sized, an annual report, including cost savings, should be provided to top managers and, possibly, to employee representatives, within three months after the end of the plan year. This report is your chance to convey bottom-line information and should cover the financial activity of your health plan, some background about it, and specific cost and utilization information. You should also include a narrative section that describes what has occurred during the past year and sets forth your plans for the coming year.

Among the items that should be incorporated into your annual report are these:

- Introduction and history of plan
  - Premium history for past three years
  - Cost of claims by category (i.e., major medical, hospitalization, drugs)
- Cost comparison with other plans
  - Indemnity plan(s) offered to employees or under consideration
  - Average regional increases for specific carriers in area
  - HMO increases as quoted
- Administrative cost savings
  - Utilization review and case management
  - Drug plan, including utilization review and formularies
  - Hospital discounts
  - Administrative review and negotiated payments
  - Subrogation and coordination of benefits
- Point of service and out-of-network options
  - Description of network(s) provided
  - Identification of savings to plan and to participants with POS or PPO use
  - Marketing and informational materials for POS or PPO
- Description of procedural and administrative improvements with cost impact
  - Managed care for chronic and catastrophic claims
  - Hospital audit results
  - Drug utilization review and drug utilization management, including formularies

- Benefit design activities, such as mental health, chiropractic, copays, etc.
- Wellness programs and screenings or early intervention activities
- New plan documents, including booklets, claims forms, etc.
- Reenrollment process for the year and its outcome
- Future plans
  - Benefit issues (e.g., retiree cost shifting, transplant coverage)
  - Communications (e.g., marketing of dental benefit and wellness programs)
  - Electronic reporting and information services for employees
  - Third-party administration services, bidding, and selection
  - Review of mail-order drug services
  - Response to federal and state regulations affecting hospital payments
  - Establishment of plan reserves account for excess claims cost

You should also include subreports in the annual report, including:

- An enrollment study that identifies the number of participants in each health plan offered and notes the increase or decrease for the year (see Exhibit 9-23).
- A synopsis of any changes in the plan's design.
- A cost savings report that identifies the discounts and negotiated or network savings your health plan has enjoyed during the year. This report shows your efforts to control health plan cost. It identifies savings such as coordination of benefits, subrogation, and the impact of plan design changes and employee cost sharing (see Exhibit 9-24).

Specific reports should be appended if they were the focus of plan management during the year. For example, you might need to report the year's activity for a wellness program or for case management services (see Exhibits 9-25 and 9-26).

When you summarize the health plan's year in the annual report, your conclusions should be based on the facts, as shown in your data or appended reports. If you have gathered employee feedback or surveys, you can refer to them. You probably provided management with a summary of employee responses when they were received, unless they were scheduled for return when the annual report was developed, in which event you can include a summary of the results. When you describe your plans for the upcoming year, include their impact on cost, benefits, administration, and employee relations.

Year	Indemnity Plan	HMO #1	HMO #2	HMO #3	HMO #4	Total
93	744	605	603	8	115	2075
94	677 (−9%)	832	719	9		2237 (+7.8%)
95	647 (−4%)	924	673	6	76	2326 (+3.9%)
96	585 (−9.6%)	969	646	5 WC	66	2271 (−2.4%)
97	592 (+1.2%)	919	547	23 WC	25	2106 (−7.3%)
Total +/−[a]	−20.4%	+51.9%	−9.2%	—	−78.2%	+1.5%

[a]Percentages increase or decrease cumulatively.

EXHIBIT 9-23. Enrollment study. (Source: Halo Associates.)

Table of Savings
Annual Report 1998

Employees Health Benefit Plan

Description of Savings	Amount Saved	Cost 1997 to 1998
Hospitalization:		−11.2%
Two-Party Check Method of Payment (represents 26% savings on hosp expenses)	$ 73,680	
Additional negotiated discounts (Rubin discounts, prompt payment and other)	18,550	
Major Medical:		−45.77%
Point of Service Network savings (includes plan and participant savings)	92,647	
Other Provider discounts (at home, durable medical, labs, x-ray)	1,580	
Drugs:		+5.1%
Administrative Savings (card service review and price reductions)	20,750	
Mail Order Savings (negotiated reduced dispensing fee)	13,108*	
Total Savings:	$220,315	

It should be noted that total costs for 1997 were less than for 1998, as follows:

1998	$2,904,634
1997	2,201,620
Difference:	$ −703,014 (−24.2%)

As a result of lower costs, in part due to the above savings, plan premium equivalents (monthly cost for individual or family participation) were reduced by 6.5%.

EXHIBIT 9-24. Annual cost savings report. (Source: Halo Associates.)

Depending on the interest of top management, you can include other specific reports, such as those described in the next section.

Special-Needs Reports

There are times during your management of the health plan when you need to measure use or plan activity, or when problems arise because of unusual use of benefits, a new administrative procedure, or the health care environment. Examples of the sort of reports generated in such cases are these:

- An analysis of inpatient stays at area and out-of-area hospitals, including available discounts, length of stay, and diagnosis. This report may be required to help determine

Activity	Jan	Feb	Mar	Apr	May	Jun	July	Aug	Sept	Oct	Nov	Dec
Newsletter		10		5			14		8	20		15
Wellness Mtgs		1		5			12			25		
Satellite Mtg		6										
Screenings												
Hypertension					24	1						
Health Risk		20										
Skin Cancer												
Prostate C.								x	x			
Breast C.									x	x		
Nutrition Mo		x	x	x								
Seminars			29	4, 12								
Recipe Book			x									
Weight Mgmt	26	23	23	20	18	15						
Focus Grps						x	x					
Fitness												
Walk & Win	x	x	31	1	x	x	x	x	x	x	x	
Line Dancing	23	x	x	24	x	19						
Yoga					30	x	11					
T'ai Chi												
Juggling					30	x	11					
Stress Wkshp				8								
Stop Smoking										x	16	
Knitting Class												
Gender Semnr										x	x	

EXHIBIT 9-25. Sample wellness activities chart showing dates of activities (1996). (Source: Halo Associates.)

whether to join a particular hospital network, contract with a network provider for specialty care, or limit or expand the precertification requirement of your plan for certain services. (See Exhibit 9-27.)

- An evaluation of the cost-effectiveness of network and nonnetwork providers, including the number of services, their cost per service, and frequency of use. This report might be needed to determine whether a network was adequately used, whether network providers were comparable to nonnetwork providers in cost and services, and whether a network delivered discounted services for the fee charged. (See Exhibit 9-28.)

- An analysis of prenatal costs before and after counseling and early-intervention programs to reduce problem pregnancies, encourage vaginal deliveries, and decrease the number of low birthweight babies. Comparison is made on incidence, costs, and changes due to this health plan effort.

File	Date Billed	File Number	Amount Billed	Amount Saved
2343	4/3/95	235800876	$453.76	
2349	4/5/95	141267476	$445.56	$0.00
2146	4/7/95	206262806	$517.12	$18.98
2352	4/20/95	140203979	$340.63	$76440.00
2155	5/1/95	148220428	$577.99	$712.00
2348	5/2/95	139343040	$243.65	$350.40
2299	5/3/95	138449828	$588.20	
2146	5/5/95	206262806	$599.02	$53.83
2379	5/9/95	237882831	$143.80	
2349	5/18/95	141267476	$126.10	
2155	5/25/95	148220428	$639.33	$2238.72
2348	5/29/95	139343040	$206.44	$360.00
2146	5/31/95	206262806	$593.56	$11974.88
2379		237882831	$465.07	$9840.00
2299	6/1/95	138449828	$332.00	
2395	6/14/95	157643840	$299.04	
2155	6/19/95	148220428	$513.36	$640.00
2395	6/22/95	157643840	$481.24	$5033.00
2146		206262806	$442.68	$1763.65
2348	6/26/95	139343040	$440.00	$360.00
2379	6/27/95	237882831	$239.28	
2299	7/3/95	138449828	$407.12	
2146	7/13/95	206262806	$802.86	$933.00
2155	7/14/95	148220428	$589.25	$1660.00
2348	7/21/95	139343040	$479.30	$471.10
2299	7/26/95	138449828	$254.52	$2736.00
2379	7/27/95	237882831	$400.46	$13800.00
2431	12/27/95	153266341	$294.74	$0.00
2436		151440951	$284.14	$40783.14
Total:			$36658.34	$330622.75

EXHIBIT 9-26. Sample case management savings and invoice report (1/1/9X through 12/31/9X). (Source: Halo Associates.)

Quarterly Utilization Report
For the Quarter Ending September 30, 199X

Company Name:
Administered By:

URS FILE NUMBER	RELATION TO EMPLOYEE	NOTIFIED DATE	TYPE OF PROCEDURE	PROCEDURE DATE	PRIMARY DIAGNOSIS
10565	SELF	07/07/9X	EMERGENCY	07/07/9X	Full-Term Pregnancy
10611	SELF	07/19/9X	ELECTIVE	07/24/9X	Cyst Rt Eyelid
10674	DEPENDENT	08/02/9X	ELECTIVE	08/14/9X	Deviated Septum
10747	SELF	08/10/9X	ELECTIVE	09/20/9X	Term Pregnancy
10597	SELF	07/13/9X	URGENT	07/14/9X	Spontaneous Abortion
10793	DEPENDENT	09/15/9X	EMERGENCY	09/13/9X	Kearn's-Sayre Syndrome

Summary Analysis:
  Cases Reviewed: 6
  Covered Employees: 63
  Savings Derived from Intervention: $850.00
  Savings per Employee: $13.49

EXHIBIT 9-27. Utilization report. (Source: United Review Services, Inc.)

	IN PLAN			OUT-OF-PLAN EXPERIENCE					
HEALTH SERVICE CATEGORY	REQUEST $	PAID $	REQUESTED %	MAX ALLOWED $	DED. & COIN $	NOT COVERED $	PAID $	$	%
Inpat Hospital—Facl	31,555	10,197	7.4	9,889	11,174	1,099	0	10,075	7.3
Hosp Visits—Physician	150	80	0.1	744	0	0	744	0	0.0
Emergency Room—Facl	1,057	507	0.4	145	0	0	145	0	0.0
Emergency Room—Phys	2,744	2,331	1.7	322	0	0	322	0	0.0
Ambulance Runs	0	0	0.0	240	240	0	0	240	0.2
Inpatient Proc—Phys	10,328	3,462	2.5	5,885	2,620	680	945	1,940	1.4
Hosp Outpat Proc—Facl	1,320	1,320	1.0	4,107	4,107	905	0	3,202	2.3
Hosp Outpat Proc—Phys	6,100	3,769	2.7	5,685	3,550	710	2,135	2,840	2.1
Office Proc—Phys	5,445	2,428	1.8	5,926	2,628	1,195	3,034	1,433	1.0
Anesthesia	3,926	3,588	2.6	1,050	0	0	1,050	0	0.0
Psych Inpatient	0	0	0.0	0	0	0	0	0	0.0
Psych Outpat—Phys	3,128	1,460	1.1	13,632	12,179	7,206	1,280	4,973	3.6
Chem Dep Inpat	0	0	0.0	0	0	0	0	0	0.0
Chem Dep Outpat	0	0	0.0	0	0	0	0	0	0.0
Detox Inpat	0	0	0.0	0	0	0	0	0	0.0
Extended Care—Facl	0	0	0.0	0	0	0	0	0	0.0
Extended Care—Phys	0	0	0.0	0	0	0	0	0	0.0
Injection & Immunizatio	829	603	0.4	120	35	7	80	28	0.0
Office Visits	28,617	21,545	15.6	6,431	6,000	4,185	185	1,815	1.3
Periodic Examinations	750	578	0.4	178	0	0	178	0	0.0
Well-Baby Care	2,361	1,683	1.2	75	0	0	75	0	0.0
Pediatrics	60	46	0.0	55	0	0	55	0	0.0
Consultations	705	615	0.4	1,142	994	866	90	128	0.1
Obstetrics	0	0	0.0	0	0	0	0	0	0.0
Allergy Services	1,278	892	0.6	0	0	0	0	0	0.0
Cardiac Testing	1,686	1,242	0.9	3,794	534	454	3,260	80	0.1
X-Ray/Diagnostics	13,380	7,944	5.7	3,677	2,177	996	1,123	1,180	0.9
Laboratory	2,906	1,605	1.2	2,237	1,886	1,133	163	753	0.5
Laboratory Capitation	0	2,368	1.7	0	0	0	0	0	0.0
Physical Therapy	0	0	0.0	3,946	2,937	1,523	724	1,413	1.0
Home Health	0	0	0.0	40	40	40	0	0	0.0
Adult & Ped Dental	642	584	0.4	44,421	35,090	14,734	5,461	20,357	14.7
Vision	4,750	2,223	1.6	20	0	0	20	0	0.0
Miscellaneous	6,536	0	0.0	3,714	0	0	3,714	0	0.0
Pharmaceutical Prescrip	16,914	16,914	12.2	0	0	0	0	0	0.0
TOTALS	147,167	87,984	63.6	117,475	86,191	35,733	24,783	50,457	36.4

CONSOLIDATED FOR:
GROUP UTILIZATION SUMMARY
FOR STARTING DATE OF 01-01-98 TO ENDING DATE OF 09-30-98

EXHIBIT 9-28. Network and nonnetwork costs. (Source: Halo Associates.)

■ A study of retiree costs and projected costs, including the impact of Medicare coverage, spousal coverage, and administrative expense. This report might be a prelude to a review of retiree coverage or used to determine whether such coverage should be curtailed, maintained, or adjusted in some way. (See Exhibit 9-29.)

A special-needs report can study almost any aspect of your health plan. One may be needed to justify or examine the impact of benefit design changes, administrative or procedural changes, or changes in health plan options. It may be used to justify keeping things as they are. The reports can be commissioned from your benefits consultant, plan administrator, specialty adviser, or in-house expert staff.

Reports to Justify Expenses

A major reason to prepare a report is to show whether money was spent wisely or staff was used efficiently. As it relates to a health plan, this might mean combining several reports to justify expense. Examples of such reports include:

```
                        RETIREES
                HOSPITAL RATE CALCULATION

1.  Paid Claims (1/1/97–12/31/97)                    $415,522
2.  Incurred Claims                                   430,297
3.  Trended Incurred Claims (1/1/97–3/31/98)          512,437
    (15%/year for 15 months)
4.  Retention (7% of Premium)                          40,762
5.  Margin (5% of Premium)                             29,116
6.  Required Premium (1/1/98–12/31/98)               $582,315

    Required Premium Rates (Monthly) as of 4/1/98:
        Individual        $68.29
        Family            142.03
```

EXHIBIT 9-29. Hospital costs for retiree benefits based on projections. (Source: Halo Associates.)

■ A year-end summary of costs compared to those for the previous year, including administrative fees and charges, can be combined with an enrollment report to indicate whether the plan is rising in cost and whether employees who contribute are choosing other options.

■ A cost-savings report at year-end can be used to justify the use of case management or consulting expertise or the implementation of a new, reduced-cost feature, such as mail-order drugs or a discount network.

■ The responses to an employee satisfaction survey can indicate whether plan changes in benefits and/or administration are well received and whether employees feel their cost sharing is appropriate. If large number of employees respond, it justifies the cost of the survey and provides a valuable guide for future activities.

Special-needs reports can be designed to give you specific data about changes. For instance, you should track any increase in dental visits, services, and costs if you have amended your dental plan. Such a report can provide a comparison with the two previous years to measure the cost and service impact. If you have altered the amount of copayment, deductible, or other out-of-pocket expense for your plan members, and if enrollment is optional, you should monitor participation in your plan. You should note any change in dependent enrollment and any shift to other plan options, especially those that changed less in design, or required lower out-of-pocket contribution.

What you track and monitor, in other words, will be directly related to your plan needs. It's best to arrange for reports ahead of time so that comparison data can be gathered throughout the year. If you wait to develop reports or to start gathering data, you will have incomplete information that is less accurate when you need it.

For the self-funded health plan, there are specific reports to justify cost and to identify cost savings. Some of these are the same as the reports included here, although when a plan is self-funded the reports can be and are highly personalized. They reflect the membership in the plan and the needs of the plan manager to monitor costs and utilization more closely. Additional reports for self-funded plans are included in Chapter 12.

Reports to Plan for the Future

You should request an analysis of all reports, and recommendations based on them, from health insurance professionals, plan administrators, and your plan adviser to help you plan for the future. Plan recommendations should cover the coming year and three to five years into the future. They should cover the possibilities of no change, closer monitoring, minimal adjustments, a trial or temporary solution to problems, and further study. You should seek recommendations on:

- *Your plan and its benefits.* Are they appropriate, based on your employees' utilization of the health care services provided? Does your employee satisfaction survey show a high rating for plan benefits? In what specific areas do employees want improvement? Is the use of your plan commensurate with its expense to your organization? How can it be tailored to meet employee needs and to meet your budget? Your health plan adviser will make recommendations on plan design and procedures to reduce cost in the context of the health care industry. Exhibit 9-30 is an example of recommendations made by a plan administrator.

- *Your plan services.* Is your network cost-effective and valued by your employees? Does your administrator provide responsive and cost-effective services? Is your plan adviser or health insurance professional helpful and proficient? Are ancillary specialists meeting your needs for legal and actuarial services? Do your reports show that the plan is efficient, budgeted properly, and operating smoothly? You can see from a review of regular and annual reports whether the plan is functioning as it should and whether your plan

---

PROPOSED BENEFIT MODIFICATIONS

MEDICAL SAVINGS

I. $8 Copay	1.1%
II. Prescription Drugs	
with $8 copay	12%
with $10 copay	16%
with 80/20 Coinsurance	12%
III. Durable Medical Equipment under Major Medical	0.1%
IV. Ambulance under Major Medical	0.2%
V. $200 Deductible, $5,000 Maximum Out of Pocket	2.1%
VI. Eliminate Medicare Balance Billing	2.0%

HOSPITAL SAVINGS

I. 120-Day Plan, 80% for Non-Par Hospitals (Includes Alcohol & Substance Abuse)	2.5%

SAVINGS/COST*

Managed Care Savings (Hospital & Medical)	2.7%
Managed Care Cost	
	$1.30/contract/month

*% of Total Budget. Includes Second Surgical Opinion, Pre-Cert, Concurrent Review & Case Management.

EXHIBIT 9-30. Administrator's recommendations. (Source: Halo Associates.)

services are acceptable. For example, a report might show a comparison of plan costs versus actuarial projection which indicates the actuary was on target with the assumptions made and costs projected.

- *In-house resources.* Is your benefits staff tuned in to employee needs, and do they understand their role as service providers? Do you have sufficient support staff and resources to keep employees informed about your health plan? Are you able to project costs, budget properly, and track expenses with the staff and facilities at your disposal? You should ask your staff for suggestions to remedy problems, to improve efficiency, to reduce paperwork, and to fine-tune plan procedures.

- *Funding.* Does your health plan operate within the cash flow needs of your organization? Does your organization have adequate funds and the stability needed to maintain your health plan commitments to employees and retirees? Are your budgeting and cost projection on target? How well do your cost-sharing philosophy and your health plan match? You should consult with top management, finance staff, and your plan adviser when you consider these issues and develop alternatives based on their input and advice.

It has long been said that information is power—and nowhere is it more true than in the management of a health plan. Learn to use the information you are given, to limit reports to those you need, and to understand when special reports or analyses should be requested. Remember the basic rule when it comes to reports—*simplify, eliminate, customize.*

■ SUMMARY

Management responsibilities of planning, implementing, monitoring, and revising are essential with an employee health plan. When you are fully insured with a carrier or MCO, you are responsible for eligibility, enrollment, change-of-status matters, employee communication, funding, and for resolving claim problems. For this type of plan, your reports should focus on these areas and on recommendations to improve efficiency or service. Once an insured plan has been selected, you are removed from other direct plan activities. When you are self-funded, you manage claims processing, administrative costs and services, networks, and all aspects of the plan's operation.

Employees will hold you responsible, regardless of which avenue you have taken, and they will react strongly if the plan lets them down when they need it. Since you are accountable and will be asked to remedy any problems, it makes good sense for you to keep a close eye on your plan throughout the year. Careful monitoring is especially needed during times of change, when more things can go wrong. The good news is that when you receive reports, feedback, and the advice needed to efficiently manage your health plan, you will have ample notice of problems and a better opportunity to keep things running smoothly.

CHAPTER 10

Legislation and Your Health Plan

If you are a small organization and buy your health insurance from an insurer or MCO, why should you care about legislation? Doesn't the carrier take care of that for you? What provisions can affect your cost or cause you to be fined or penalized? If you are self-funded, is there an easy way for you to comply with state and federal law that governs health plans? What are you required to do? If you grow in size, will new laws or regulations affect you?

When it comes to compliance, I believe it's better to be safe than sorry. Make sure you meet the state and federal laws that place requirements on you, when you provide an employer sponsored health plan. Tax writeoffs are allowed for employer-sponsored plans, which are considered a business expense under current tax law. This is the primary reason the federal government has the authority to control how these plans function. At the same time, the states have guarded their right to control business and commerce within state boundaries, and the insurance industry falls within that scope of authority. As a result, both the federal and the state governments end up having an influence on your organization's health plan.

The tension between the states and the federal government has resulted in a health care system that differs from state to state. Rules and requirements can vary widely by state, and so can the degree of regulation. Consequently, it's crucial for you to check the requirements in each location that you do business. A health plan adviser or plan administrator should know of any adjustments or restrictions that exist in your state that affect your health plan, and your employees.

■ CURRENT LEGISLATIVE TRENDS

For many years, the federal government concerned itself with limited issues related to health care. These included discrimination, reporting and disclosure, fiduciary and tax requirements, and the maintenance of a minimum standard of supervision of health plans. It was federal legislation that allowed unions to establish trust funds that sponsored health coverage for union members. It was social security law that began to cover the elderly and the disabled. It was Medicare that established a broader health care plan for the elderly; Medicaid did the same for the poor. All of these were federal initiatives. They are broad based and affect everyone in the United States, regardless of locale.

State law is more regulatory and specific. The states regulate insurance companies, which, in turn, affects what the companies offer you. State regulations might cover the way services are to be provided, complaint procedures, premiums or fees charged, and the plan's relationship with providers. Federal and state requirements affect your notification and enrollment procedures for employees.

In recent years both federal and state law have shifted focus. You have undoubtedly read about state-mandated coverage for certain procedures. States vary widely in their regulation of managed care in an array of areas, including company liability for health care decisions made by doctors in the plan; specific coverage levels, such as hospital stays after childbirth; and access to providers, such as availability of specialist services without a referral. (See Exhibit 10-1.) This type of legislation has a direct impact on insurance plans, often raising their costs and affecting patient care and satisfaction.

Recent actions by federal government have required continued coverage after an employee's job is terminated, and for an increased time, and have shifted cost to employer health plans for older employees and family members. President Clinton has proposed and Congress has passed laws that echo and amplify state legislation on coverage, access, and patient rights. Advocates of smaller government view this as meddling, and consumer

Type of Law	States Enacting
Comprehensive (patient protection)	Ariz., Ark., Colo., Conn., Fla., Idaho, Kan., La., Minn., Mo., Mont., Neb., Nev., N.H., N.J., N.M., Okla., Ore., Texas
Access to specialists	Ark., Fla., Ga., Idaho, Kan., Minn., Mont., N.J., N.M., Okla., Texas
Appeals/grievances	Ariz., Ark., Colo., Conn., Fla., Ga., Idaho, Ind., Kan., La., Md., Minn., Mo., Nev., N.H., N.J., N.M., Okla., Ore., Texas, Va.
Disclosure of rules	Ariz., Ark., Colo., Conn., Fla., Idaho, Ind., Kan., La., Maine, Md., Minn., Mo., Mont., Nev., N.H., N.M., Okla., Ore., R.I., S.C., Texas, Va.
Disclosure of financial incentives	Minn., Neb., Nev., N.J., Ore.
Emergency care coverage	Ariz., Conn., Ga., Kan., Minn., Mo., Mont., Nev., N.H., N.J., N.M., Texas, Va.
Gag clause ban	Ariz., Ark., Colo., Conn., Fla., Ga., Idaho, Kan., Minn., Mo., Mont., Neb., Nev., N.J., N.M., N.D., Okla., Ore., Texas, Utah, Wyo.
Mastectomy hospital-stay coverage (48 hr.)	Ark., Conn., Fla., Ill., Mont., R.I., Texas
Maternity hospital-stay coverage (48 hr.)	Ariz., Ark., Idaho, Mont., R.I., Texas
Mental health (typically parity)	Mo., N.J., N.D., Texas, Vt.
Network mandates (access)	Ariz., Ark., Colo., Fla., Hi., Idaho, Iowa, Kan., Maine, Md., Minn., Mont., Neb., N.J., N.M., Okla., Ore., S.C., S.D., Tenn., Texas, Utah, Va., Wash., Wyo.
Point-of-service option mandate	Iowa, Mo., Mont.
Utilization review procedures	Ariz., Ark., Colo., Conn., Fla., Idaho, Iowa, La., Minn., Mont., Nev., N.H., N.J., N.M., Okla., Ore., Texas, W.V.

EXHIBIT 10-1. State legislation summary. (Source: The Health Policy Tracking Service of the National Conference of State Legislatures, 1997.)

rights supporters see it as necessary control over an essential public need—affordable health care.

These current trends of government involvement in plan design, provider access, eligibility and enrollment practices, and reporting and communications on plan activities all add cost to the employer health plan. Compliance costs money, and noncompliance carries heavy fines and penalties. It makes for more complex administration when government passes new requirements, and that can add more cost. Administrators, plan advisers, and insurance companies add to their fees when administration is more difficult or more time-consuming. Your staff will need more time, too, if a new law requires them to prepare a report, file a form, send out a notice, or track information.

■ FEDERAL BENEFITS LEGISLATION

There are a number of federal laws that are of interest. I will limit the discussion to those that have a direct impact on your organization and that you should understand to better manage your health plan. These include ERISA, Medicare and Medicaid, COBRA, Social Security Law, TEFRA, DEFRA, FMLA, ADA, and HIPAA. Don't be concerned about the alphabet soup of these laws—they are described in plain language as they relate to your health plan. They span the decades from the Social Security Act of 1935 to the Portability Act (HIPAA) of 1996, and a review of them should help you understand how they can influence your health plan, your employees, and your organization, and the climate for health plans that exists today.

ERISA (Employee Retirement Income Security Act, 1974)

This landmark legislation created employer responsibility and accountability for the funding and operation of employee health plans. It established two major areas of regulation that affect your health plan: Reporting and Disclosure and Fiduciary Responsibilities. If you have an insured plan, you will be most concerned with reporting and disclosure. Employers who have plans in which premiums and other expenses are deducted from their business or organizational tax return must comply by furnishing employees with specific reports and information about the health plan. A typical listing of information required by ERISA is shown in Exhibit 10-2.

ERISA is specific about the manner of communication and details of publications about health plans, such as the size of the type, plain language, and help for those who don't speak English. It also requires that records and information be kept available on request for employees who are plan members. Information that must be included in your benefits booklet is spelled out in the law, and in some cases the location of such information in your booklet is mandated. You are required within specific time limits to publish new booklets, changes, or amendments to your plan, as well as other notifications. Exhibit 10-3 lists ERISA requirements for a summary plan description.

Communication costs money and may require staff and other resources. What happens if you don't follow the letter of the law? ERISA provides for serious penalties, including substantial fines and imprisonment, with some violations tried in criminal court and some in civil court. This is a law with teeth. The Department of Labor, one of the enforcement agencies for ERISA, has initiated more than 340 civil and 65 criminal investigations since 1980, according to the Pellerino Consulting Services Newsletter for September 1998.

ERISA describes who is a fiduciary and the responsibilities of a person or firm designated as a fiduciary to a health plan. In essence, it governs the potential conflicts of interest and

To Whom:	What:
To Government each year:	Summary Plan Description (SPD)
	Summary of Material Modifications (SMM)
	Annual financial report, Form 5500
To plan members each year:	Summary Plan Description (SPD)
	Summary of Material Modifications (SMM)
	Summary Annual Report (SAR)
	Written claim denial, if appropriate
	Statement of benefits on termination, if appropriate
To employees on request:*	Supporting plan documents including contracts and agreements
	IRS applications for tax qualified plan
	Documents establishing the plan
	Documents terminating the plan (IRS form 5310)
	Personal benefit statement, including payments made, status, etc.
	(requested in writing, must be provided once each 12 months)
	Complete annual financial report

*These items must be in a distinct physical location where there are 50+ employees. They must be provided within 10 days of receipt of the employee request. If there are multiple locations, copies must be readily available.

Updated Information:

There are changes to ERISA reporting and disclosure requirements in new federal legislation, HIPAA, effective June 30, 1997. These are:

1. The SMM, which announces plan changes to employees, used to be required within seven months or 210 days after the end of the plan year in which the change was made. Now, the change must be reported to plan members within 60 days of its adoption. However, it can be announced in an employee newsletter, instead of with individual notice, if the newsletter is published at least quarterly. Individual notices still must be sent to those off-site, such as retirees, employees on leave, or those who might not receive the newsletter.

Examples of benefit reductions to be reported are those that: eliminate covered benefits, reduce the amount paid by the plan directly, or by changing formulas or payment methods by which the plan determines benefit payments, increases to deductible or copayments, or other out of pocket expenses, reduce the service area of the plan, establish new conditions or requirements such as pre-authorization or discharge planning, for services or benefits to be covered.

2. The guideline for what is substantial or material is what the average employee would consider important.

3. The employer or plan sponsor is responsible to report plan changes made by insurers and MCOs to plan members. This includes changes in reimbursement or payment methodology. Plan sponsors should ask insurers to provide this information so that that can meet the law's 60-day time frame.

EXHIBIT 10-2. ERISA requirements for reporting and disclosure. (Source: Halo Associates.)

sets forth stiff penalties, including fines and imprisonment if someone responsible for health plan decisions and policy is in violation of the law. Fiduciaries of a health plan include administrators, advisers, board or committee members who make policy decisions, management and owners who sponsor and oversee plans, lawyers and actuaries who provide interpretative advice on policy issues, and consultants who provide reports and recommendations. Most plan management activities are provided by fiduciaries. The exception is for those who provide "ministerial duties" only, such as clerks and staff who handle the paperwork for enrollment, eligibility, plan communications, or claims processing but do not have any policy-making authority or duties.

The Summary Plan Document is the benefits booklet that informs and guides employees and plan members with regard to what is covered, how eligibility and enrollment work, and where to get needed information about the health plan, including rights to appeal, file claims, and request further information. It is regulated by ERISA and HIPAA, both federal laws.

When is it provided?

The SPD must be provided to new employees and to beneficiaries of the plan within ninety days of their first eligibility as a plan member.

For a current plan member, the SPD must be provided within ten days on written request of a plan member or employee.

For a new plan, the SPD must be provided within 120 days to plan members and filed with the Department of Labor at the same time.

New SPDs must be prepared, distributed and filed no less than every ten years. If there are material changes, the SPD must be prepared, distributed and filed every five years.

What must be included?

Name and address for each board member who is a fiduciary to the plan.

Name and address with instruction on who receives legal process for the plan.

Name and address of the plan sponsor.

Name and address of the plan administrator, including the process for filing claims.

Name and address of the insurer or HMO that provide financing or administration for the plan, including the role that they play in the plan.

A statement of ERISA rights, including the address of the Department of Labor in Washington, DC, which enforces plan member rights under ERISA reporting and disclosure.

A description of terms and conditions of coverage, including enrollment and eligibility, under the plan for employees, retirees, and their dependents.

A description of the coverage provided under the plan with definitions of terms or phrases that are used to make the description clear to the average person.

A description of the claims appeal process for the plan, including the name and address of where to file an appeal, and any requirements and instructions needed to do so. This must include deadlines by which a decision will be reported to the plan member.

What style and language is required?

Clear and understandable language must be used, readily understood by the average person. The type face must be easy to read and large enough to be comfortably read.

The language and content must be accurate and comprehensive.

If there are a number of employees and/or plan members who do not speak English, and that is the language that the SPD is prepared in, there must be a notice posted and distributed in the native language of those employees and plan members. This notice must advise them that help is available to read and explain the health plan to them in their own language.

SPDs are reviewed when filed, to ensure that they are on paper, using ink and type that is acceptable, so that they are easy to read and to understand. They are the primary communication about the health plan with employees.

EXHIBIT 10-3. ERISA requirements for summary plan documents (SPDs). (Source: Halo Associates.)

Being a plan fiduciary is a heavy responsibility and carries a requirement that the fiduciary act in the "sole and exclusive interest of " plan members when making all decisions related to the health plan. Conflict of interest penalties are severe.

The federal government regulates self-funded plans under ERISA, and this includes union pension funds that provide health benefits and multiemployer trusts that pool to provide health benefits. ERISA does not regulate benefits; the law concentrates on keeping employees informed of their rights to benefits and to information about the health plan, including financial information, and to plan management that keeps the plan solvent. State governments have little control over ERISA plans, and state mandates for coverage or other services do not apply to such plans. However, state regulations that affect hospital or provider costs, such as surcharges applied to outpatient or inpatient services that must be paid by the plans using the services, have an impact on ERISA plans.

Because of the preemption of ERISA plans from state regulations, employers who are self-funded can achieve more uniformity in their health plan if they have employees in several states. They can avoid the variations required by one state or another. This ability of self-funded plans to sidestep state regulation is often attacked by consumer rights groups and state regulators who believe that more regulation will improve ERISA plans. Plan sponsors, on the other hand, argue that their innovative and cost-effective programs wouldn't be possible if they were subject to state regulation. According to the U.S. General Accounting Office, close to 50 million individuals were in self-funded or ERISA plans in 1998. Recent changes to ERISA regulations were made by the Health Insurance Portability and Accountability Act of 1996; more detailed information needs to appear in your summary plan description (SPD), and you need to report plan changes more quickly to employees. A listing of these changes is provided under the HIPAA discussion in this chapter.

As an employer, if you are self-funded, you need to be sure your plan administrator and plan adviser keep you in compliance with ERISA at all times. Here are some particular things to do:

- Check your benefit booklet, the SPD, to see if it meets ERISA requirements shown in Exhibit 10-2.
- When you receive copies of year-end 5500 reports from your plan administrator, review them to see that they accurately reflect the enrollment and financial activity of your plan.
- Be sure that employees receive the minimal reporting required and that plan documents are readily available at convenient locations within your organization in case they should be requested by employees. Follow the listing in Exhibit 10-2. This is a case where preparation and advance planning can save money and avoid problems.

ERISA regulates self-funded and fully insured plans. The U.S. Supreme Court has ruled that both types of plans are subject to direct regulation at the federal level, while only insured plans are subject, indirectly, to state control. Congress reaffirmed its jurisdiction over all health plans in legislation, passed in 1996, providing for portability and increased reporting standards. Public-sector or government plans are not subject to ERISA, because one level of government can't regulate another in this manner; however, most public sector plans are negotiated through collective bargaining and require accountability and reporting as part of the relationship. Usually, it's easier to comply with ERISA as an acceptable standard for communication, benefit development, and fiscal management than to devise your own standard.

Medicare and Medicaid (1965)

Medicare initially provided health coverage to Americans age 65 and older. It was amended in 1972 to provide coverage for the severely disabled and those with end-stage renal disease. It was further amended in 1997 to increase the choices of Medicare participants to include various managed-care options for coverage. It's estimated that we will see an increase in those enrolled in Medicare from 13.6 percent of the population in 1995 to 24.7 percent of the population by 2070. Exhibit 10-4 shows Medicare's impact on health care spending and projections for increases in Medicare spending and enrollee contributions through 2070.

These two federal programs had a combined cost of $354.0 billion in 1996, according to the Health Care Financing Administration. The cost of the Medicare program is closely tied to the age of the population, since nonworking people become eligible at 65 years. Medicare and Medicaid costs have increased dramatically since 1980, as shown by Exhibit 10-5. These costs are expected to continue to rise as the baby boomers age. Experts predict that these two federal programs will continue to pay for an increasing share of the nation's health care costs.

Calendar Year	Enrollment as a Percentage of Population	Spending as a Percentage of GDP	Premiums as a Percentage of GDP	Net Spending as a Percentage of GDP	Premiums as a Percentage of	
					Medicare Spending	Enrollee Income
1995	13.6	2.6	0.3	2.3	10.7	3.2
2010	15.2	3.7	0.9	2.7	25.7	10.0
2030	22.0	6.3	1.7	4.6	26.4	12.2
2050	23.1	7.0	1.7	5.3	24.5	12.0
2070	24.7	7.8	1.9	5.8	24.6	12.5

EXHIBIT 10-4. Medicare enrollment and spending projected to 2070. These figures assume that collections from enrollees are increased to cover 50 percent of supplemental insurance costs starting in 2000. (Source: *Long-term Budgetary Pressures and Policy Options*, Congressional Budget Office, May 10, 1996.)

Fiscal Year	Total	Medicare[a]	Medicaid[b]
		(in billions)	
1980	$57.9	$33.9	$24.0
1990	175.9	107.2	68.7
1995	326.7	176.9	149.8
1996[c]	354.0	193.9	160.1

[a]Medicare amounts are gross outlays for benefits and administration.
[b]Medicaid amounts include both the Federal and State share of benefit payments and administrative costs.
[c]Estimated.

EXHIBIT 10-5. Program outlays/trends. (Source: Health Care Financing Administration, Office Financial and Human Resources; data from the Division of Budget, April 1998.)

Eligibility for Medicare

Medicare eligibility for the aged, the disabled, and those with end-stage renal disease is determined by the local Social Security Administration Office, or you can call 1-800-772-1213 for information.

Generally, an employee may be eligible at age 65 , or when his or her spouse reaches age 65; at age 55 or older if a widow or widower of a spouse who was eligible; under age 65 if the employee has been entitled to Social Security disability for twenty-four months; or at any age, subject to Medicare requirements for disability and for end-stage renal disease.

You should have employees who are still actively working but eligible for Medicare enroll promptly to avoid any penalties for late enrollment.

Medicare has three parts:

- Part A, which is basic hospitalization coverage for inpatient services
- Part B, which is major medical coverage for physician and other services
- Part C, which offers a choice to the Medicare enrollee of several managed-care plans to cover their health care needs

Part A of Medicare is mandatory, and enrollees pay no premium. The money for services comes from the general fund of the government and is accumulated from payroll taxes paid by the employee and the employer and other sources. Much has been written about whether this fund is sufficient to cover anticipated costs as our population ages. It offers limited long-term care provisions and limited skilled nursing home and custodial care coverage primarily designed to cover major hospital stays for serious illness. Exhibit 10-6 shows the hospital and skilled nursing home deductible and coinsurance in effect for 1998, and the Part B premium, deductible, and coinsurance.

Medicare Part A—Hospital Insurance
(Amounts apply to each benefit period)

Hospital   **Skilled Nursing Facility**
Inpatient Deductible $764.00
Coinsurance Days: Coinsurance Days:
61 through 90 $191.00*   21 through 100 $95.50*
91 through 150 $382.00*

*Amount charged per day

Medicare Part B—Medical Insurance
Part B Premium: $43.80 per mo. (No increase from 1997)
Annual Deductible: $100.00

Coinsurance:
Medical Services   20% of approved charges*
Outpatient Hospital 20% of billed charges*

*There is no coinsurance for certain Part B services, such as diagnostic laboratory tests and flu and pneumonia vaccine shots.

EXHIBIT 10-6. 1998 Medicare deductible and coinsurance amounts. (Source: Office for the Aging, Rockland County, January 1998.)

Part B of Medicare, referred to as Supplementary Medical Insurance, has increased in expenditures by more than 48 percent from 1990–1995, according to the Health Care Financing Administration. This coverage pays for physicians, at-home health care, durable medical equipment, labs and testing, and outpatient services. There is no coverage for prescription drugs under Part B. Part B is voluntary and must be chosen by the Medicare enrollee, who is expected to pay a monthly premium for the coverage ($43.80 in 1998).

Some employers choose to pay the Medicare premium for Part B as their only retiree coverage. They either pay the premium directly or reimburse the Medicare enrollee on a quarterly basis. If an eligible person doesn't enroll for Medicare when first eligible, the person will be penalized by paying 10 percent more in premiums for each twelve-month period enrollment is delayed. As an employer, you should urge employees who approach age 65 to enroll as a matter of course, whether or not Medicare will be the primary plan.

What if the retiree is Medicare-eligible and suddenly the employer opts to stop reimbursing for Medicare Part B to save money? What effect will this have on costs and on coverage for the retiree?

First, let's accept the thought that Medicare is a good buy. It has been shown over the years that Medicare collects premiums for only 25 percent of its total costs, and in the Budget Reconciliation Act of 1998 Congress has said it will keep the premium at 25 percent. In other words, Medicare premiums cover only one-fourth of the actual claims paid by the plan, with the general fund of the United States government picking up the balance of 75 percent of the cost. Even for those employers who offer retiree coverage for benefits Medicare doesn't cover, Part B is a good buy. Retirees will seek services earlier and control chronic and catastrophic disease better. Use of the Medicare program is a cost-shifting away from the employer health plan and toward government. Medicare Part A and Part B can help meet an employer commitment to provide retirees with a health plan and the economic security it can mean.

Currently, the trend is to enroll Medicare recipients in managed-care programs under Part C, although with the recent decline in HMO profits, several large HMOs and insurers have stopped offering Medicare plans. MCOs are in the Medicare business nationally, and it is increasingly common for employers to provide for Medicare only and to encourage retirees to enroll in managed-care options. Exhibit 10-7 shows the Health Care Finance Administration's projections for the number of Medicare enrollees in HMOs through 2007.

The Budget Reconciliation Act of 1998 encourages such shifting and recognizes that many managed-care plans offer additional benefits over what is provided by the original Medicare program. It's possible for a retiree on Medicare to enroll in a managed-care plan that provides wellness services, flu shots, and prescription drugs, for instance.

The overall medical expenses of the Medicare program are shown in Exhibit 10-8 for three years, projected to 1997 for both Parts A (hospital insurance) and B (medical insurance).

In 1997 32 million aged and 4 million disabled persons chose to enroll in the Part B program. Total expenses for the year reached $72.8 billion, and the average benefit per enrollee increased 5 percent, to $1,999. Payments went to physicians (61 percent), facilities (24 percent), and managed-care plans (15 percent).

Other Coverage Under Medicare

In 1998 it was estimated that about 170,000 people with end-stage renal disease received Medicare coverage, with 80,000 of those also disabled. Exhibit 10-9 shows the historical

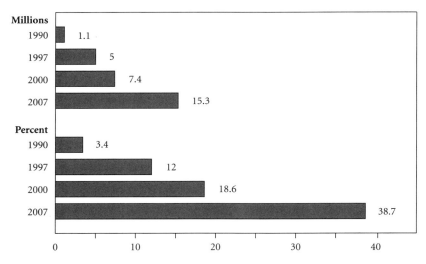

EXHIBIT 10-7. Projected Medicare enrollment in HMOs. (Source: Health Care Financing Administration, Congressional Research Service. From *Source Book of Health Insurance Data: 1997–1998*, Washington, D.C.: Health Insurance Association of America, 1998, p. 73; copyright © 1998 by the Health Insurance Association of America.)

and projected enrollment in Medicare by those with ESRD and its historical and projected cost. It's estimated that 200,000 Americans were on dialysis in 1998 and that the U.S. morbidity rate for dialysis patients was 23 percent, twice as high as that of Japan. Medicare provides a capitated rate to the provider for this service. There are 54,500 dialysis patients currently waiting for a kidney transplant. This serious health issue affects us all because of its cost

	1995 (millions)	1996 (millions)	1997[a] (millions)
Total Hospital Insurance	$113,403	$124,841	$136,799
Inpatient hospital	87,512	94,397	101,976
Skilled nursing facility	9,142	10,823	12,251
Home health agency	14,895	17,174	19,567
Hospice	1,854	2,447	3,035
Total Supplementary Medical Insurance	$ 63,482	$ 69,055	$ 76,287
Physician/other providers	40,376	42,166	45,063
Outpatient	14,576	16,581	18,979
Home health agency	133	239	285
Group practice prepayment	6,297	7,791	9,384
Independent laboratory	2,067	2,278	2,576

[a]Estimated.

EXHIBIT 10-8. Medicare payments, by type of benefit, 1995–1997. (Source: Health Care Financing Administration, Data Compendium, 1996. From *Source Book of Health Insurance Data: 1997–1998*, Washington, D.C.: Health Insurance Association of America, 1998, p. 79; copyright © 1998 by the Health Insurance Association of America.)

Year Ending June 30	Average Enrollment (thousands)		Reimbursement (millions)	
	Disabled ESRD	ESRD Only	Disabled ESRD	ESRD Only
Historical Data:				
1975	7	11	$ 84	$ 131
1980	19	22	235	299
1985	30	37	430	522
1986	32	40	455	562
1987	34	43	480	592
1988	36	46	546	673
1989	38	51	601	787
1990	40	56	640	908
1991	43	62	742	1,028
1992	46	68	857	1,077
1993	55	69	949	1,153
1994	61	73	1,106	1,222
1995	66	76	1,283	1,338
1996	70	79	1,414	1,444
Projections:				
1997	75	84	1,537	1,567
1998	80	90	1,659	1,687
1999	85	95	1,779	1,804
2000	90	100	1,906	1,930
2001	95	106	2,054	2,081
2002	100	112	2,233	2,264
2003	106	117	2,431	2,468
2004	111	123	2,645	2,695
2005	117	129	2,887	2,929
2006	123	133	3,156	3,157
2007	129	138	3,451	3,401

EXHIBIT 10-9. Medicare enrollment and incurred reimbursement for end-stage renal disease. (Source: Health Care Financing Administration, Office of the Actuary.)

If you have employees with end-stage renal disease, you need to advise them about Medicare coverage for health care services they will need and to encourage them to pursue enrollment in Medicare at the earliest opportunity.

The Medicare program recovers billions of dollars that are available from other sources for services it covers. For instance, it receives revenue from Workers Compensation and disability coverage, from automobile insurance, from the working aged and from those covered elsewhere for end-stage renal disease. Exhibit 10-10 shows millions of dollars saved to the Medicare system attributable to secondary payors.

Who Pays First—Your Health Plan or Medicare?

There are straightforward rules that govern which plan is primary for Medicare-eligible retirees or employees and their family. It depends on the size of your organization and whether the employee is working or retired.

	Workers Comp.	Working Aged	ESRD	Auto	Disability	Total
1993	111.7	1,465.3	166.4	268.5	850.1	2,862.0
1994	109.5	1,499.2	162.0	288.6	894.1	2,963.4
1995	117.5	1,428.3	181.0	335.7	944.4	3,006.9

EXHIBIT 10-10. Savings from secondary payors; fiscal year data, in millions of dollars. (Source: Health Care Financing Administration, Bureau of Program Operations; data from the Office of Benefits Integrity.)

Your health plan will pay first as long as any of the following are true:

- The employee is age 65 or older and your organization has twenty or more employees.
- The employee is Medicare-eligible due to disability and both of the following apply:
  1. The individual has "current employment status" with your organization.
  2. Your health plan has 100 or more employees.
- The employee has end-stage renal disease. However, your health plan is responsible only for the first thirty months after Medicare eligibility for this reason.

Again, it's important to have your employee with end-stage renal disease enroll for Medicare as soon as possible. This will help to reduce your cost and provide needed coverage to your employee.

Medicare will pay first if:

- The individual is Medicare-eligible because he or she is at least 65 years old, and your organization has fewer than twenty employees.
- The individual is retired.
- The individual is disabled and the above conditions aren't met.
- The individual has end-stage renal disease and is entitled to Medicare, but only after the first eighteen months of eligibility during which Medicare does not pay first.

The Medicaid Program

Most Medicaid enrollees (71.5 percent) are aged or disabled, including the blind. Dependent children and adults with dependent children receive 26.1 percent of Medicaid funds.

To receive Medicaid coverage, applicants must meet income eligibility guidelines implemented by the Departments of Social Service in states and counties. The poverty level of children and adults in the 1990s has been reported by the U.S. Census Bureau to be 20.6 percent to 22.7 percent of those under age 18, 11.4 percent to 12.4 percent of those ages 18–64 and 11.7 percent to 12.9 percent for those 65 years and older.

Medicare and Medicaid Regional Differences

Medicare and Medicaid expenses vary widely across the nation. The number of enrollees and the cost of their care varies from region to region in the United States. Exhibit 10-11 shows the amounts, in millions, paid in major regions of the country for Medicare and Medicaid for fiscal 1995. There are also variations in the amount of money paid monthly to HMOs by Medicare under Part C, for example, $367.35 paid in Staten Island, New York, and $321.06 paid in Marion County, Oregon.

Medicare and Medicaid are important because of the sheer number of people they cover and, more important, as ways to meet the increasing need for such coverage as our

		Medicaid	
	Medicare[a]	Computable[b]	Net Adjusted[c]
		(in millions)	
All Regions	$176,884	$151,812	$86,468
Boston	10,440	10,683	5,566
New York	20,382	29,756	14,920
Philadelphia	19,460	14,232	7,760
Atlanta	36,370	24,300	15,754
Chicago	29,318	24,614	13,978
Dallas	19,479	15,863	10,731

[a]Distribution by region is estimated.
[b]Total medical assistance payments computable for federal funding.
[c]Net adjusted federal share. Does not include administrative expenditures.

EXHIBIT 10-11. Medical payments by region; data as of fiscal year 1995. (Sources: Health Care Financing Administration, Bureau of Data Management and Strategy, data from the division of Health Care Information Services; Office of Financial and Human Resources, data from the Division of Budget; and the Medicaid Bureau, data from the Division of Financial Management.)

workforce ages. As the number of elderly Americans increases, the burden of these social programs falls on all Americans and is of special importance to employers, who have traditionally provided health coverage. Your organization should stay abreast of changes, and threatened changes, to these programs.

The shift of retirees to managed Medicare programs, where additional benefits may be available, is one answer for organizations that cannot afford to continue supplemental or expanded coverage for retirees. The need to provide retiree benefits continues to be evaluated by many companies.

Financial Accounting Standards No. 106

The new focus on reduction of retiree benefits stems from the passage of the Federal Accounting Standards Board Rule 106, enacted in December 1990. This rule applies to postretirement benefits other than pensions and so covers health plans provided to retirees. The rule requires that organizations list employee and retiree benefit costs as a liability on their balance sheet. The projection of how long they would pay for retiree benefits was not something most organizations carefully measured or included in liabilities, until it was required by this provision. Once required, these projected benefits were seen to represent a sizable liability, in part because of longer life spans and earlier retirements.

Case law suggests that retiree benefits are not automatic rights, regardless of past practices. Exhibit 10-12 presents a summary of some applicable case laws. Your organization may have a long-standing policy, and employee morale may be linked with retiree benefits, making reduction or elimination of them unfeasible. You should, at the very least, consider the long-term impact of reducing retiree benefits.

1986. *Hansen v. White Farm Equipment* Sixth Circuit Court of Appeals. Ruling that welfare benefits do not automatically become permanent at retirement. SPD and plan documents clearly stated that the employer retained the right to terminate benefits.

1987 and 1988. *Anderson v. John Morell & Co.* and *Moore v. Metropolitan Life Insurance Co.* Eighth and Second Circuit Courts. Rulings that vesting and participation laws for pension plans do not apply to health plans, that the employer's obligation is exclusively governed by the plan documents and the SPD. Employers can modify or terminate retiree medical benefits if the right to do so was either expressly reserved or not clearly given up in the plan documents, even if informal communications implied the opposite, as long as no fraud was involved.

1988. *Musto v. American General Corp.* Sixth Circuit Court. Ruling that nothing in federal law prohibits employers from reducing or modifying retiree benefits if plan documents expressly reserve the right to do so.

Since 1988, cases have focused on traditional contract law and interpretation. The courts have carefully reviewed what the parties represent in written documents, such as collective bargaining agreements, summary plan descriptions, and written plan documents, including trust agreements and administrative contracts.

Case law suggests the following actions by employers:

- Employers need to carefully review what they have promised employees for retirements benefits and to examine all plan materials and documents to ensure that they accurately and specifically reflect these promises.

- Most important, employers need to expressly retain the right to amend or terminate these plans.

- Employers should educate and train employees who administer or communicate the provisions of retiree health plans, so that they make no statements implying that retirement health benefits are permanent or unchangeable.

- Manuals and answers to common questions should be prepared and reviewed for use by benefit staff.

EXHIBIT 10-12. Case law examples on providing retiree benefits. (Source: Halo Associates.)

And speaking of long-term impact, you might make information about long-term-care policies available to older workers and those about to retire. Exhibit 10-13 presents the types of benefits purchased under long-term-care policies, which are available from private carriers. A listing of carriers who are approved to offer long-term coverage is available from your state insurance department.

COBRA (Consolidated Omnibus Budget Reconciliation Act, 1985)

This legislation changed Medicare rules to shift responsibility for health care coverage to employers for older employees. Under COBRA, as long as an employee, or the employee's spouse, works and has a health plan from the employer, Medicare is the secondary payer. The employer health plan pays first, even for those over the Medicare age requirement.

Another important change enacted by COBRA was to require that employer plans offer and provide health coverage to those who are terminated. When an employee leaves, regardless of reason, the employer plan is expected to provide coverage, as long as the employee makes premium payments to the plan as the law provides. Exhibit 10-14 presents a listing of the conditions for COBRA eligibility for an employee and a covered spouse or dependent.

COBRA requires that the employer give you notice of your rights within thirty days and that the employee respond within sixty days after termination or another qualifying

Services	Nursing home care
	Home health care
	Alternate care
	Assisted living
	Hospice care
	Respite care
Other benefits/services	Care coordination/case management
	Homemaker/choice assistance
	Bed reservation
	Medical equipment coverage
	Spousal discount
Daily benefit	$40–250/day nursing home care
	$40–250/day home health care
Benefit eligibility	Medical necessity, or ADLs, or cognitive impairment
Maximum benefit period	Unlimited/lifetime
Deductible period	0–100 days
Pre-existing condition	6 months
	None if disclosed during application
Renewability	Guaranteed
Alzheimer's disease coverage	Yes
Age limits for purchasing	18 to 99 years
Waiver of premium	Yes
Free-look period	30 days
Inflation protection	Yes
Nonforfeiture benefit	Shortened benefit period, return of premium, or "reduced paid up"
Marketing	Company and independent agents

EXHIBIT 10-13. Typical coverage offered by leading sellers of long-term care insurance, 1995. (Source: Health Insurance Association of America, Long-Term Care Market Survey, 1996. From *Source Book of Health Insurance Data: 1997–1998*, Washington, D.C.: Health Insurance Association of America, 1998, p. 30; copyright © 1998 by the Health Insurance Association of America.)

event. As the employer, you can charge the employee up to 102 percent of your monthly premium for COBRA coverage, and you need provide it only for the eighteen-, twenty-four-, twenty-nine-, or thirty-six-month limit, depending on the cause of termination (see Exhibit 10-15).

Plan administrators offer COBRA administration for a fee, or you can have your staff follow the COBRA regulations for notification, record keeping, and premium collections. I recommend you purchase a COBRA guide, such as the one noted in the appendix; it will give you a comprehensive resource on the law and what you must do to meet its requirements.

COBRA was amended by the Health Insurance Portability and Accountability Act of 1996 (HIPAA), which allows those eligible for COBRA to declare a disability at any time during the sixty-day period for COBRA election, instead of requiring that the disability be declared at the time of the COBRA qualifying event. This extends the time a COBRA-eligible employee has to determine and declare a disability under the Social Security Act.

For the employee:

You have a right to choose continuation coverage if you lose group health coverage because of a reduction in your working hours or termination of employment (except for termination due to gross misconduct on your part).

For the spouse of an employee:

If you lost group coverage for one of the following four reasons, you have a right to choose continuation coverage: death of your spouse, termination of spouse's employment as above, divorce/legal separation from spouse, spouse's eligibility for Medicare.

For the dependent child of an employee:

If you lose group coverage for one of the following five reasons, you have a right to choose continuation coverage:

- Death of parent (covered employee)
- Termination of parent's employment as above
- Parent's divorce or legal separation
- Parent eligibility for Medicare
- Your cessation of dependent status under coverage rules

How to enroll for continuation coverage:

Your responsibility includes notifying the employer within sixty days of divorce/legal separation or a child losing dependent status of the event.

You will be notified by your employer that you have the right to choose continuation coverage as a result of the event. You will have sixty days from the date you would lose coverage to inform your employer that you want continuation coverage. If you do not choose continuation coverage, your group health coverage will end.

EXHIBIT 10-14. Extended coverage under COBRA. (Source: Halo Associates.)

Preexisting conditions under COBRA coverage were also affected by HIPAA, which restricts your right to terminate coverage when the employee becomes covered under another plan. A recent U.S. Supreme Court decision, *Geissal v. Moore Medical Corp.* (June 8, 1998), ruled that former employees may take COBRA, even if they have other coverage.

What is the impact of this federal requirement on your organization's health plan? First, it adds an administrative burden and is an added cost. In Issue Brief No. 194, the Employee Benefits Research Institute, in February 1998, reported that COBRA's cost exceeds the premiums collected by employers for the coverage and to that is added administrative costs that by some estimates range as high as 10 percent of the premium collected, instead of the 2 percent allowed. A survey reported in this Issue Brief, from Charles D. Spencer & Associates, concludes that of the 10.2 percent of employees eligible for COBRA, 28 percent elect it. They also found that employer costs for COBRA beneficiaries, who tend to be older than the average plan member, are $5,591 per year, compared to $3,332 for active employees in plans that were surveyed.

To reduce their COBRA costs, employers tend to look at alternatives that will affect all employees. Your organization might consider changing eligibility status for your health plan, to discourage those who tend to leave employment earlier and to reward those who are longer-term employees. You might consider other ways to reduce COBRA costs, such as shifting costs to active employees; reducing health plan benefits and therefore costs for COBRA and active employee plan members; and passing costs along to your clients or customers.

The coverage being continued will be the same as the coverage provided to similarly situated individuals to whom a Qualifying Event has not occurred.

Coverage will continue until the earliest of the following dates:

- Eighteen months from the date the Qualified Beneficiary's health coverage would have stopped due to a Qualifying Event based on employment stopping or work hours being reduced.
- If a Qualified Beneficiary is determined to be disabled under the Social Security Act at any time during the first sixty days of continued coverage due to the employee's employment stopping or work hours being reduced, that Qualified Beneficiary may elect an additional eleven months of coverage, subject to the following conditions:
  - The Qualified Beneficiary must provide the Employer with the Social Security Administration's determination of disability within sixty days of the time the determination is made and within the initial eighteen-month continuation period.
  - The Qualified Beneficiary must agree to pay any increase in the required payment necessary to continue the coverage for the additional eleven months.
  - If the Qualified Beneficiary entitled to the additional eleven months of coverage has nondisabled family members who are entitled to continuation coverage, those nondisabled family members are also entitled to the additional eleven months of continuation coverage.
- Thirty-six months from the date the health coverage would have stopped due to the Qualifying Event other than those described above.
- The date this Plan stops being in force.
- The date the Qualified Beneficiary fails to make the required payment for the coverage.
- The date the Qualified Beneficiary becomes entitled to benefits under Medicare.

EXHIBIT 10-15. Length of extended coverage under COBRA. (Source: Halo Associates.)

I don't recommend that you throw the baby out with the bath water, which is how I view an overreaction to COBRA costs. These costs are one more good reason to carefully design eligibility and enrollment requirements for your organization's health plan. COBRA shouldn't be handled in a vacuum. You need to assure employees of a meaningful health plan and to reconcile your organization to the expense of turnover, which includes COBRA costs.

Social Security Law (1935)

This is older legislation, familiar to most of us. The benefit provision of the law has to do with those who are disabled and your responsibility for them under your health plan. I advocate that you keep Social Security forms, the local office telephone and address, and the notification form in your personnel office. Your staff should be aware of the basics for disability claims filing with Social Security to advise employees who become disabled. There are strict rules about when an employee becomes covered after the Social Security Administration has determined they are disabled and when you can stop paying for employees' health care costs under your plan.

If, for instance, your employee is disabled and takes a leave of absence, your health plan may continue to cover the employee until Social Security kicks in—that is, for 39 months. If your employee doesn't enroll in a timely manner, there may be a period of time when the person is without coverage. Depending on your rules for disability leave, your disabled employee may be eligible for, and opt for, COBRA coverage under your plan, driving your utilization and costs up.

OBRA (Omnibus Budget Reconciliation Acts of 1986 and 1989)

In 1986, budget legislation required that physicians who do not accept either Medicare assignment or the allowable Medicare fee as payment in full file an elective surgery notification. It also set emergency medical condition standards for which notification might not be required, although requirements of patient notification and record keeping are stringent. The bill caps charges to Medicare patients at 115 percent of the allowable charge.

In 1989, OBRA shifted the cost of end-stage renal disease or kidney failure treatments more to employer-sponsored health plans. It expanded the requirement of the 1981 Budget Act that made Medicare secondary for the first twelve months. The 1989 law expanded the employer's health plan liability to eighteen months. As a result, employer health plans are carrying more of the burden of a treatment that is costly and has an average length of three years—of which employers now pay about half.

TEFRA (Tax Equity and Fiscal Responsibility Act, 1983)

This law changed Medicare responsibility for the aged. Employers are required to cover active employees age 65 and older and their dependents. With the aging of the workforce, this has had a long-term impact on employer health plan costs.

DEFRA (Deficit Reduction Act, 1985)

This act made the employer health plan primary for dependents of active employees ages 65–69, even if the active employee is under age 65 and therefore not Medicare-eligible. Two other provisions shifted cost to employer health plans and away from Medicare. First, as of May 1, 1986, the employer health plan became primary for those age 70 and over, and as of January 1, 1987, the employer health plan became primary for those employees and dependents who are Medicare-eligible due to disability but who are under age 65.

FMLA (Family Medical Leave Act, 1993)

This federal legislation took effect in 1994 and provides for the continuance of health coverage and employment status while an employee is on requested leave to care for an ill spouse, child, or parent or if the employee is unable to work due to a health condition.

The law requires that up to twelve weeks' unpaid leave in a twelve-month period be granted, usually on thirty days' notice, for any of the following reasons:

- To care for the employee's child after birth or for placement of an adoptive or foster care child
- To care for the employee's spouse, son or daughter, or parent who has a serious health condition
- For a serious health condition that makes the employee unable to work

The employee is required to provide advance notice and medical certification, within thirty days if the required leave is foreseeable. You can require medical certification, including second and third opinions at your expense, and a fitness-for-duty report before the employee returns to work.

As an employer, under FMLA, you are required to:

- Maintain the employee's health coverage under your group health plan, which includes all coverages, such as health, dental, vision.

- Restore the employee to his or her original or equivalent position with equivalent pay, benefits, and other employment terms.
- Refrain from using the FMLA leave to eliminate or lessen any employment benefit for the employee that accrued prior to the leave.

There are rules for spouses who work for the same employer and for situations where intermittent leave, taken in blocks of time, is allowed (see Exhibit 10-16). You may want to establish your right to collect premiums for health coverage from employees who don't return after an FMLA leave.

This legislation is enforced by the U.S. Department of Labor. Like other legislation, it does not supersede any employee agreement that provides greater family or medical leave rights to your employees.

FMLA Ripple Effect

Some states, following the federal law that provides for unpaid time off, have enacted legislation that allows more time off than FMLA allows. For instance, in Massachusetts, your organization must offer an eligible employee twenty-four hours of leave in any twelve-month period to participate in certain school activities on behalf of a child, to take a child

---

Intermittent Leave

Under some circumstances, an Employee may take a FMLA leave intermittently, which means taking a leave in blocks of time, or by reducing his or her normal weekly or daily work schedule.

- Where a FMLA leave is for birth or placement for adoption or foster care, use of intermittent leave is subject to the Employer's approval.
- A FMLA leave may be taken intermittently whenever it is Medically Necessary to care for a seriously ill family member, or because the Employee is seriously ill and unable to work.

Substitution of Paid Leave

Subject to certain conditions, Employees or Employers may choose to use accrued paid leave (such as sick or vacation leave) to cover some or all of the FMLA leave. The Employer is responsible for designating if paid leave used by the Employee counts as a FMLA leave, based on information provided by the Employee. In no case can an Employee's paid leave be credited as a FMLA leave after the leave has been completed.

Spouses Who Work for the Same Employer

Spouses employed by the same Employer are jointly entitled to a combined total of 12 work weeks of family leave for the birth of a child or placement of a child for adoption or foster care, and to care for such child or to care for a parent who has a serious health condition.

Reenrollment after a FMLA Leave

If any or all of an Employee's coverages end while the Employee is on a FMLA leave, those coverages will be reinstated on the later of:

- The date the Employee returns to work from a FMLA leave.
- The date the Employee reenrolls by filing a written request with the Employer to deduct the required contributions from his or her pay.

The Employee will not have to provide proof of insurability and any preexisting condition limitation, waiting period or non-confinement provision will be applied as if there had been no break in coverage provided the Employee reenrolls within one month from the date he or she returns to work.

EXHIBIT 10-16. Special FMLA situations. (Source: Halo Associates.)

or elder relative to routine medical or dental appointments, or to take an elderly relative for appointments such as nursing home interviews. In this case, however, the law allows the employer to require that the employee first use any accrued paid time off.

ADA (Americans with Disabilities Act, 1990)

Heralded as the most far-reaching civil rights legislation since the 1960s, this federal law applies to employers of fifteen employees or more, and forbids discrimination on the basis of disability with respect to hiring, compensation, advancement, training, and other terms and conditions of employment. When it was passed, there was much discussion about whether it would apply to an employer-sponsored health plan in the areas of pre-existing conditions exclusions, limitations on treatment or procedures, and capping or excluding of benefits for particular disabilities.

Current industry practice, now affected by HIPAA regulations about portability (discussed later in this chapter), has allowed preexisting condition exclusions in group health plans. The ADA does not change this but should make an employer more cautious in administering a preexisting condition clause. It cannot be a subterfuge to evade the purposes of the law. You need to apply preexisting conditions restrictions uniformly and consistently in order to be in compliance with the law.

There is increased litigation in this area, due to the increasing number of disabled workers entering the workforce and the prevalence of AIDS, which is considered a disability. The U.S. Supreme Court, in *Bragdon v. Abbott* (1998), held that HIV is a disability, even before the emergence of full-blown AIDS, so that a dentist, who was defined as operating a place of public accommodation, could not discriminate against a patient with the condition, unless it could be proved that the patient posed a direct threat to the safety of the dentist, his staff, or his other patients. This determination has far-reaching implications.

One of the possible outcomes of the court's finding is that health plan members may use it to argue for expanded benefits for fertility, for example, on the ground that their inability to reproduce is a disability. Other examples of disabilities can include schizophrenia or other mental illness and conditions related to diabetes and epilepsy.

The line between chronic conditions and disabilities seems blurred, and this court decision may mean more lawsuits for health plans that traditionally have been allowed to set limits on coverage. Your health plan is allowed to set limits if it can show, based on actuarial evaluation, that the benefit is too expensive or, under the Equal Employment Opportunity Commission's guidelines, that the treatment is needed by both disabled and nondisabled people, such as vision care and mental health coverage. Your plan is also allowed under EEOC rules to limit reimbursements for certain types of drugs or procedures, such as x-rays or experimental drugs.

Employers have capped benefits for certain conditions, such as AIDS. In *McGann v. H&H Music Company*, the U.S. Supreme Court allowed the employer to place a $5,000 cap on AIDS benefits. (Under ERISA, the plan sponsor can terminate or amend the plan or terminate any benefit at any time.)

The ADA, despite its far-reaching impact in the workplace and in society, has had little impact in employee health plans as long as the terms, conditions, and coverage apply uniformly and fairly to all employees. Your rights, as an employer, to limit plan coverage remain unchanged, including the right to limit or eliminate coverage for specific disabilities.

Employers look at disability costs and find that their costs for short-term disability, the period before their insured long-term disability plan begins to pay, are higher than their disability premiums. Furthermore, the Financial Accounting Standards Board's rule 112 now requires employers to establish a reserve at the time a disability occurs or to report the projected cost of the disability and other benefits that are provided after employment but before retirement. In response to this examination of such costs, employers should consider revising the definition of disability to encourage return to part-time work or limit coverage for certain disabling conditions by imposing lifetime maximums.

What can you do to help keep your disability costs at a minimum? Larger employers should evaluate whether to self-fund their long-term disability costs, and small or mid-sized organizations should frequently go to bid on the coverage to take advantage of a competitive marketplace.

Information and publications about ADA requirements are available from an automated telephone line, operated by the U.S. Department of Justice, available twenty-four hours a day, with specialists available to answer calls during business hours (see the Appendix).

HIPAA (Health Insurance Portability and Accountability Act of 1996)

Federal health care reform has been a focus of the federal government since the early 1990s. HIPAA legislation addresses the concerns about access and portability of health insurance and makes some changes in ERISA reporting and disclosure standards and in the availability of medical savings accounts for smaller organizations and the self-employed. The law applies to small organizations, those with from two to fifty employees, and larger organizations, too.

Under the law, employers and insurers are responsible for issuing certificates of coverage when an employee changes jobs. It ensures that employees and their dependents are not discriminated against because of health status and grants them the right to enroll in the employer-sponsored health plan following the loss of other coverage or because they have added a dependent. Insurers need to add HIPAA products for those individuals who lose group health plan coverage.

Nondiscrimination under HIPAA prohibits you, as an employer, from singling out individuals in a group based on health status by declaring them ineligible for your health plan or charging them a higher premium. This doesn't stop you from eliminating certain benefits from your plan as long as the change applies equally to all plan members.

HIPAA mandates a thirty-day enrollment period during which employees or dependents who lose other coverage can enroll in your health plan.

If an employee gets married or has a child, there is a thirty-day period during which the employee and dependents can enroll without being considered late enrollees.

An employee with eighteen months of creditable coverage has the right to purchase individual coverage. Creditable coverage includes group insurance through an employer-sponsored health plan, COBRA, Medicare, Medicaid, and individual coverage.

Each state is allowed to create an individual insurance market mechanism, or the way in which individuals will purchase approved products from insurers within the state.

HIPAA guarantees renewability for an individual who has eighteen months of creditable coverage, even when a person becomes eligible for Medicare.

Insurers are required to sell HIPAA individuals either:

- One of its two most popular policies, or
- Two policies that represent an average benefit of all policies the insurer sells, or two policies that represent the average of all policies sold the previous year

Access for employers is addressed by HIPAA, too. Renewability is guaranteed for small and large employers, and coverage is guaranteed for small employers. Insurers are not allowed to deny access to your organization because you had high losses and were a bad risk in the past. An insurer can refuse to provide coverage to a small employer if there is no minimum participation (i.e., too few employees are in the plan). Coverage can also be denied if the organization is located outside the insurer's service area or if the organization isn't able to pay the contributions required. There is no guarantee of the cost of the coverage, nor is there a requirement that employers must offer coverage to employees.

The law will have an impact in several areas:

- Premiums may increase as higher-risk groups are accepted for coverage.
- Insurers and MCOs will change the way they underwrite and rate groups, taking the impact of those high-risk groups they are now required to cover into account.
- Preexisting conditions exclusions are limited to the days a member did not have prior coverage. The preexisting condition can be excluded for twelve months for enrollees, or up to eighteen months for those enrolling late. It cannot apply to pregnancy, newborns, or adopted children, who are to be added within thirty days.
- A certificate, provided by the previous employer or insurer, will be issued to show previous coverage. This certificate can be requested by the terminated employee, a spouse, or other dependent up to twenty-four months after prior coverage ceases, causing an administrative burden on your health plan. Each certificate must include the date, name of group health plan, name and ID of the participant, names of covered dependents, when the waiting or affiliation period began, and when coverage began and ended.
- Under HIPAA, a delay in coverage is allowed for:
  □ An employer waiting period required of all plan members
  □ An HMO affiliation or waiting period of sixty days, or ninety days for late enrollees

Employers and insurers have several other new responsibilities under HIPAA:

- Employers must notify employees within sixty days of changes to a health plan, instead of the 210 days formerly allowed under ERISA. Your organization may also notify employees of substantial plan changes at least every ninety days by an employee newsletter or other publication.
- Employers were required to send out notices, by November 1, 1996, informing employees of the provisions of HIPAA and summarizing the new portability rules.
- Strict rules about portability notices to employees must be observed, including employees and dependents who lost coverage as far back as July 1, 1996. Your health plan administrator or insurer is responsible for issuing these certificates, and you should contact them if any employee or dependent requests one from you.
- Insurers must provide small employers with information outlining their rating practices.
- Insurers must disclose their right to change the following:
  □ Premium rates and factors that affect rates
  □ Employer's right to renewability of coverage
  □ How preexisting conditions will be handled and how creditable coverage will be counted
- Administrative simplification is required by HIPAA that will affect all who sponsor health plans, submit claims, pay premiums, coordinate benefits, query insur-

ance eligibility or claims status, or submit referral or enrollment information. The Secretary of Health and Human Services will establish a national standard for the transmission of health care transactions, to include identifiers for providers, employers, and individuals and to ensure security and privacy.

Penalties for violating HIPAA will include an excise tax levied by the Internal Revenue Service on employers who do not comply, while insurers are accountable to state insurance departments or the Department of Health and Human Services. Local and state government plans must comply under the Public Health Service Act, which includes civil penalties for noncompliance, although they are given the right to opt out of HIPAA.

Because of HIPAA, all employers and insurers will be required to accept health plan members at high risk. This major change in how the health insurance marketplace operates will affect the overall costs of health plans that are insured and self-insured, and it will guarantee coverage to those who previously could not purchase it. Going back to the Law of Large Numbers discussed in Chapter 2, it will spread the risk of high-cost claims across a broader base of those with health coverage.

Flex 125, and MSAs (Medical Savings Accounts)

Empowerment of employees, a trend that has expanded over the past decade and one that helped bring about the FMLA, has had other impacts. The Internal Revenue Service's rule 125 spawned a generation of programs that allowed employees to offset out-of-pocket costs for medical services and other family needs, tax-free. Referred to as Flex 125 plans, these require that an employee forecast a dollar amount for the year to be spent on medical and other allowed expenses. This forecast needs to be fairly accurate, up to a maximum set by the plan sponsor (i.e., the employer), because a use-it-or-lose-it rule is in effect such that an employee loses any funds set aside with pretax dollars that are not spent by year-end. Unused funds are divided at year-end among the Flex 125 accounts in the plan. Administration is usually provided by outside firms, with the employer forwarding payroll deductions.

Flex 125 plans were the forerunner of the Medical Savings Accounts, or MSAs, now available to small and mid-sized employers and to the self-employed, through HIPAA. The general idea of this provision is that funds are set aside, earmarked for medical and family expenses that can be projected or assumed.

The advantages of using the employee's pretax dollars to pay for anticipated medical and family costs are obvious. An employee is happy to plan ahead for likely expenses such as child care, a health plan deductible, and other out-of-pocket expenses. There has been a controversy regarding MSAs as to whether they should be required to be teamed with a high-deductible health plan. The law requires the following:

To qualify, an MSA plan must have a high annual deductible (minimum $1,500, maximum $2,250 for individual coverage, $3,000 minimum and $4,500 maximum for family coverage). Out-of-pocket expenses for covered benefits cannot exceed $3,000 for individual coverage and $5,500 for family coverage.

Insurers who offer high-deductible health plans that are qualified under HIPAA, are listed with the state insurance department.

In other developments, there is no out-of-pocket to the employer for making certain benefits available, at increased convenience and often at lower cost, for the employee. Examples of this trend include offering life insurance, automobile insurance, long-term-care insurance, legal benefits, education credits and courses, and elder care and day care at the work site. In some of these cases, the employer allows representatives of different companies and services to have access to employees and assists by implementing payroll deductions once the employee enrolls for a program or service. There may be lower cost passed along to the employee, as a result of a lower advertising and marketing cost.

Mental Health Parity and Maternity Coverages

Federal legislation that took effect January 1, 1998, requires that organizations with fifty or more employees offer a health plan that has the same requirement for lifetime maximum and annual coverage limits for mental health that it has for physical conditions. If your plan has no such limits for physical conditions, it can't impose them on mental health conditions under this legislation. The parity provision doesn't apply to substance abuse or chemical dependency, according to experts, and will not be enforced if it increases health plan costs by more than 1 percent. It's unclear whether a health plan would have to show an increase before being exempt. This does not prohibit an employer or health plan from imposing service limits (e.g., outpatient mental-health visits limited to thirty per year and sixty for lifetime).

Maternity coverage was also required to include a forty-eight-hour stay for routine deliveries and ninety-six hours for caesarean sections, without preauthorization. These time limits can be shortened if the treating physician and patient agree to earlier discharge. Penalties and incentives cannot be used to encourage earlier discharges.

Summary of Federal Initiatives

The federal government seems to be taking two directions when it comes to legislating health coverage. One is to focus on specific types of coverage, such as mental health and maternity. The other is to look more broadly at the system and to look at issues of access, affordability, and consumer rights, including the right to privacy.

The federal attention to specific health care issues and to medical services that seem to be limited by health plans is shown in an initiative related for breast cancer and mastectomy patients. It will require minimum lengths of stay and reconstruction options without preapproval.

In a different direction, federal legislation and hotly debated initiatives include those that will:

- Ensure that patients have more access to specialists, without authorizations.
- Guarantee access to emergency room care, within some limits.
- Require plain language for health plan information.
- Broaden rights of plan members to appeal claims and service denials.

Other features of such reform legislation includes a requirement that the insurer or plan provide information about its physicians, such as their experience with certain procedures, malpractice lawsuits and outcomes, and how they are paid. Other proposals look at the issue of liability—allowing plan members to sue an insurer, MCO, or other plan sponsor when care is denied that is harmful to the patient's health.

■ BENEFITS LEGISLATION BY STATES

Each state regulates the insurance industry within its boundaries, primarily through its insurance department. State government, for example, determines:

- The types of plans to be offered
- Which carriers and MCOs are authorized to operate within the state on a county-by-county basis
- Who has rate-setting authority and approval responsibilities (usually the insurance department)
- Regulations governing hospitals and doctors (usually done by the health department)
- Requirements for Medicare and Medicaid, often interfaced with a state Department of Social Services

State Limitations and Scope

State government is charged with the responsibility for implementing federal law locally and may pass legislation that will affect the health care system and providers within its state. State agencies that implement health plan legislation can include the Department of Labor and the Department of Taxation, as well as those for insurance, health, and social services. Some states have regulatory agencies devoted to MCOs, to health initiatives, and to pooling health plan. States often designate committees, task forces, or agencies to study regional or local health care needs and services.

States regulate fully insured plans offered by carriers and MCOs and approved at a state level. Mandates for specific coverage are often passed by state governments and enforced by state agencies. Each state may adopt surcharges or special taxes on premiums and medical service users, and they are responsible for the allocation of charity care dollars and graduate medical education budgets that are passed through them from the federal government. States license and regulate providers, including hospitals, doctors, outpatient facilities, nurses, and other health professionals.

Hot Topics at the State Level

Recent state legislation has concentrated on several areas: patient access, liability of insurers and MCOs for medical decisions, affordability of health coverage, and guarantees of certain coverage. If this sounds familiar, it is because the states and federal government have been working on the same issues for some time. Often a state law becomes a model to test a concept so that it can be fine-tuned before becoming federal law. Using state initiatives can make passing a federal law easier, because its impact is measured on a smaller scale. This doesn't always work, however, because broader, national needs may not be met by specific state innovations.

A downside to state legislation is its impact on multistate organizations. The differences among states' laws can drive a benefits manager to distraction. It is also disconcerting to employees who leave one state to work in another where the rules and the mandated coverage are totally different. Providers who straddle state boundaries often need to be credentialed in both states and aware of the differences in regulations and responsibilities. Patients who travel from one state to another for services are often caught in a maze of paperwork and approvals when they file claims for the services received.

Typical differences in the cost of medical procedures from state to state are shown in Exhibit 10-17. There are major differences in services available, demographics of the population, and number of residents covered by public or private plans on a state-by-state basis. What may be a problem in California—paying for the cost of nonresident aliens, for example—is not a problem in Iowa. And what may be a problem in North Dakota—developing resources to meet the rural population's needs—is not a problem in Boston.

	Electrocardiogram CPT 93005	Colonoscopy CPT 45378	Amniocentesis CPT 88235	Angiography (heart) CPT 93454	Bone Marrow (biopsy) CPT 85102
New York	$57	$872	$268	$414	$240
Chicago	57	795	241	609	214
District of Columbia	64	784	219	393	235
Los Angeles	74	905	180	372	210
Denver	83	612	203	375	166
Houston	54	684	205	446	172
Miami	62	803	268	447	156
Philadelphia	82	836	167	383	204
Boston	59	752	249	479	232
New Orleans	49	750	200	480	161
Minneapolis	49	635	186	457	191

EXHIBIT 10-17. Costs of frequently performed medical tests, selected cities, 1996. (Source: Health Insurance Association of America, Prevailing Healthcare Charges System, 1996. From *Source Book of Health Insurance Data: 1997–1998*, Washington, D.C.: Health Insurance Association of America, 1998, p. 111; copyright © 1998 by the Health Insurance Association of America.)

Individual and unique factors such as these cause state government to tailor legislation efforts to meet residents' needs. It's what our system of federal and state governments was designed to do, but it can be frustrating for employers who sponsor health plans at locations in several states.

States' Roles With Providers

States license providers. Each state monitors provider activities, including the complaints received from patients, utilization patterns, outcomes, and competency. Some providers, such as hospitals and ancillary facilities, have on-site inspections regularly from state officials to review and monitor their operation. Hospitals usually have a state review before they are allowed to expand or branch out with new services to ensure that duplication of services within a geographic area are not wasteful. Equipment, especially radiology equipment, is tested by state or county officials to ensure that it meets safety and accuracy standards.

States' Roles With Carriers and MCOs

Rate setting, approval of health plan products, and monitoring of financial and operational stability are part of the state's relationship with carriers and MCOs. States review rate requests from carriers and MCOs and hold hearings to determine if the request is reasonable. It is common for a state insurance department to approve a reduced rate increase on a review of the facts, including profitability, growth, and operating expense of the carrier or MCO. Each health plan offered to consumers in the state must be submitted to the state insurance department and approved by it.

States offer an appeal process for complaints and claims denials, handle requests from employers who are plan sponsors, and set requirements that reports and filings be made to the state on a regular basis. Financial stability is reviewed by the insurance department, and any questions of solvency or ability to pay claims are handled promptly. The state may levy penalties if a carrier or MCO deliberately holds up on paying claims. If there are operational problems, such as claims processing holdups due to lack of electronic capability, the state will make demands that the situation be remedied within a time limit, subject to financial penalties and possible loss of approval to do business in the state.

States' Roles With Smaller Employers

Some states offer pools that small employers can join to purchase health insurance and other worker coverages at lower-than-market rates. Other states have community rating laws, which set the maximum amount a carrier or MCO can charge in a given area to small employers and the self-employed who wish to purchase a health plan.

Some states, using a federally sponsored program, offer health plan subsidies to small businesses. You can contact your state insurance department to see if funding is available to help you establish an employee health plan. Generally, these have requirements that you have not offered an employee health plan to date or within a certain time frame and that you be below a specific income level set by the state if you are an owner or major stockholder.

State tax law varies with regard to deductions for employee health plans and their cost. You should have your plan adviser determine state requirements and the cost of premium taxes and other state surcharges or fees for an insured plan before establishing the plan. The same is true for a self-insured option, which may not be subject to state law but is regulated by ERISA, and may be liable for surcharges and fees required by the state.

Summary of State Legislative Initiatives

State laws and innovations are adopted more easily than federal legislation, because of the differences in size and complexity from the smaller to the larger government. The two types of government sometimes intertwine, for instance, federal mandates and programs make it difficult for the states with the financial burden they cause. In our system of government, states are essential to regulate, monitor, and manage health plans in their geographic area. The federal government, on the other hand, is essential to provide standards and broad-reaching programs, such as Medicare and Medicaid, that affect millions of Americans.

■ FUTURE LEGISLATION

My prediction for this regulatory maze is that it will not get easier—not for the patient, the employer who sponsors a health plan, the insurers and MCOs, the networks, the providers, and the professional advisers and companies who work in the field. To the contrary, the newer moves toward patient rights, electronic reporting, and mandates for specific benefits, in my view, are reactions, rather than initiatives. Some are reactions to the perceived excesses of a managed-care system that went too far to limit care; some are reactions to newer technology; and some are well-meant reactions to patient complaints and needs.

What will happen over the next ten years to health plan legislation? It will continue to create a patchwork of requirements for doctors, hospitals, insurers, and health plans that add administrative cost and burden. As new interest areas related to alternative therapies, disease management, wellness, and mobile services begin to bubble to the top, these will be regulated, too.

My belief that lawmakers will continue to legislate is based on the years I spent as a member of my county legislature—legislation is what government does. Legislative oversight is spurred, too, by the scope of the issues involved. The health care system in the United States is not broken, but it's expensive, and it's big business. The insurance industry alone accounts for more than 2.8 million jobs in the United States, nearly 860,000 of them in life and health insurance. Add to that another 680,000 physicians, each with an office staff, and, in addition, the roughly 5,200 hospitals nationwide. Big business is putting it mildly when we see that $988.5 billion was spent on health care in 1995. Government will continue to regulate and monitor this field—closely.

CHAPTER 11

Getting the Most From Your Consultant, Agent, or Broker

What does a health plan adviser do? How can you select the best adviser for your organization? Do you need more than one? What do advisers charge, and how can you measure their performance? Where can you find the right adviser for your health plan needs? You need to ask yourself all of these questions before you sign on the dotted line with a benefits consultant, broker, agent, or other health plan specialist.

When you conduct a health plan review or consider health plan changes, it's easy to get lost in the details. Sometimes it seems as if it won't matter which one you select, from the scores of vendors each anxious for your business, because they are all the same. This isn't true, in my experience. The most important selection you can make is an adviser whom you trust, whom you can communicate with openly and easily, and who understands, almost intuitively, about your concerns and organizational issues. You need, first and foremost, to have a comfort level with the individual you hire to help with health plan decisions.

■ ADVISER CAPABILITIES

The work of your health plan adviser will fall into several categories, regardless of the specific services you require. Your adviser should be able to do the following:

- Give you a broad overview of the insurance marketplace.
- Understand and convey information about specialty services you may need.
- Explain the economic conditions that affect your health plan choices.
- Provide information on trends in the health benefits market, from an employer and an employee perspective.
- Provide insight and judgment, based on experience, about plan types and plan performance.
- Guide your plan communications, employee relations, and the development and distribution of plan documents.
- Interpret and prepare reports and financial analysis of your plan activity.
- Help you monitor and adjust your plan.
- Ensure access and an understanding of health insurance markets and services.
- Supply flexible and relevant advisory services on day-to-day issues.
- Contribute an objective opinion and guidance for plan problems or issues that arise.

Sounds like a lot to expect, doesn't it? It may be, but your health plan is vital to the smooth operation of your organization. It demands professional and effective management and advisory services.

■ THE NEED FOR A HEALTH PLAN ADVISER

If you are responsible for the day-to-day operation of your health plan, you know that situations routinely arise that may require objective and expert advice and guidance. Some include:

- New legislation or regulations that affect your plan's operation or cost
- Employee complaints about fuzzy language in plan materials
- Claim services that are slow or unresponsive, or questions about eligibility and cost sharing
- Increasing plan costs
- Consideration of new plan features

There are literally thousands of issues that can arise. Some of them will have a quick resolution. Perhaps you can provide new plan materials, or your plan adviser can arrange for additional claims services. Other problems and issues will be the subject of more intensive analysis, review, and recommendations.

Key Advisory Services

You will need outside input and expertise when you conduct a plan review, or when you consider a health plan change, or during the implementation of these activities. It's easy to be overwhelmed by the technical questions presented. In these situations, your health plan adviser should assist you in several key areas.

Compliance in its various forms is a primary service provided by health plan advisers. You may need to comply with legislation, regulations, employee agreements, and industry standards, each of which affects coverage, eligibility and enrollment, communications, and service to employees and to your organization. Your plan adviser should provide you with suggestions, implementation assistance, guidance in day-to-day operations, written materials, and meetings to plan and monitor your compliance effort.

Your plan adviser should also provide services to help you prepare, print, review, edit, and distribute a variety of needed plan materials. Plan communications must meet legal and contractual requirements. They should be updated, explain existing plan provisions, and contain useful plan information. You need to tell employees about the impact of changes in coverage, procedures, and cost as they relate to plan members and their families.

An objective, expert adviser is essential when financial issues relate to plan review. Your adviser will analyze current costs, project future costs, and evaluate the impact on your organization and your employees. Broad, objective information gives you a basis for discussion and enables you to compare your plan's performance to a norm.

For comprehensive plan needs, you may require multiple advisers who function as a team. They can be contracted individually with you or provided by your primary adviser. A multispecialty team will provide you with input, reports, and projections from legal, actuarial, benefits, and employee relations specialists. Exhibit 11-1 presents a projection

Discussion:

Presently the employer pays 90 percent of the individual coverage and 75 percent of dependent coverage for retirees who retired before 1985 and 50 percent of individual and 35 percent of dependent coverage for retirees who retired after 1985. This disparity has created negotiations barriers during health plan negotiations and is an unfair burden on older workers who retired after 1985. The goal of this change is to create a cost saving to the employer and more equity in retiree coverage through a new contribution formula that takes into account the age and years of service of the retiree.

The change proposed, which adjusts the employer share by retiree age and years of service, would reduce the employer's contribution to the following, for the retirees currently covered:

Retire formula is:	Service years, plus age	Employer pays Individual	- Family
	0–65	50%	30%
	66–75	60%	40%
	76–100	80%	60%

Retired before 1985: I/Fam %		Retired after 1985: I/Fam %	
50/30%	3 retirees	60/40%	16 retirees
60/40%	31 retirees	70/50%	19 retirees
70/50%	42 retirees	80/60%	22 retirees
80/60%	158 retirees		

The fiscal impact of this change is favorable: **12 month savings projected to be $88,542.13** for the first year of implemented, based on currently projected premiums. Future savings would be affected by health insurance rate increases but would be favorable.

EXHIBIT 11-1. Impact of retiree contribution change. (Source: Halo Associates.)

of the cost impact of a new contribution formula, prepared by a benefits consultant in collaboration with an actuary and an employee relations lawyer.

Plan design is another area commonly reviewed and fine tuned by a plan adviser. You may need to examine how plan design affects your costs and performance, including the plan's value to employees. Your advisor can interpret fluctuations in utilization and compare other plans and their experience in your region or industry. If you decide to make any changes or adjustments, your adviser should assist you with implementation and monitoring of coverage and administrative procedures.

Employee relations are important to your health plan. With the help of your adviser, you can prepare surveys and questionnaires to gauge the satisfaction levels of your employees, retirees, and their families. These can be used to evaluate your plan's design or the benefits provided, procedures for eligibility, enrollment, and claims payment. Exhibit 11-2 shows a priority listing, based on an employee survey, to guide discussions on benefit design.

Do you need several advisers? This question has to be answered in the context of your organization and your plan. Are there complex legal or actuarial issues to consider? If so, you might want a general adviser to work with legal or actuarial specialists and to help interpret their findings for you.

SUMMARY
Hospital Portion
Employee Needs Assessment

From the tallies of employee response to the Hospital portion of the Employee Needs Assessment for both Inpatient and Outpatient hospital care, some observations are made to stimulate discussion:

- Utilization of inpatient hospitalization is limited, however the importance of such coverage is very high.
- Emergency room coverage rated the highest in importance by comparison with other coverages although utilization was fairly low.
- Adequacy of coverage received a high and medium rating, in part because of former Blue Cross coverage.
- Psychiatric inpatient coverage received a substantially low rating compared to other inpatient coverage.
- The concept of copayment for outpatient and inpatient hospital services had meaningful acceptance.
- Questions on home health care and managed care got responses that indicated a need for education.
- Discharge planning, an element of managed care, received a strong acceptance.
- HMO limits to access received a mixed rating.
- Outpatient utilization needs were for diagnostic and preadmission testing, same-day surgery, and emergency services, in that order.
- A copayment for outpatient services received a stronger acceptance level than a deductible for them.
- Reduced cost for outpatient surgical service at specific facilities received a strong acceptance rating.

In summary, the areas for further attention and discussion include reduced cost facilities, information on specific cost containment programs (i.e., managed care), psychiatric inpatient services, and copayment features for hospital services (i.e., emergency room/testing & diagnostic, etc.).

Our administrator has been asked to review this information, together with utilization data and submit recommendations at our next meeting.

EXHIBIT 11-2. Employee plan priorities. (Source: Halo Associates.)

■ TYPES OF ADVISERS

You should understand the difference between the types of advisers who work with employer-sponsored health plans:

Benefits Consultants

Benefits consultants usually have training and experience as health benefits consultants with employer groups of various sizes. Their experience and the scope of the services they offer can vary by region of the country and from rural to urban settings. There are some national standards as well as state requirements for benefits consultants. Certified Employee Benefit Specialists (CEBS) are academically trained and nationally accredited through a program run by the Wharton School of Business at the University of Pennsylvania.

To attain the CEBS certification, consultants need to pass ten courses of undergraduate- and graduate-level material, which totals about thirty-five college credits. The course work covers the gamut from employee relations to Social Security law and from health plan administration to legal benefits issues. Many CEBS graduates hold other degrees or credentials; they are frequently lawyers, accountants, human resources managers, risk managers, actuaries, and health plan administrators. The CEBS credential is considered tops in the health benefit consulting field.

Large and Small Consulting Firms

Larger consulting firms often assign specialists who are credentialed as benefit consultants, lawyers, actuaries, finance managers, or communications and computer experts as part of a team to meet your consulting needs. Smaller firms may follow this model but have fewer internal resources and so create a team of associates that provides the range of services you need. An individual consultant will have, for instance, an actuarial firm, a legal firm, financial and legislative experts, and communications advisers whose expertise will be brought to bear on a plan issue as needed. In such an arrangement, the smaller firm builds into a consulting contract the cost and scope of services to be provided, with ancillary services coordinated by the primary contractor.

Smaller firms tend to be regional in scope and provide personalized, in-depth, on-site services. They also tend to have fewer clients, so you may be a "large fish in a small pond" if you opt to hire such a firm. Services are usually provided at lower cost, since a small firm incurs lower overhead. The larger firms are probably better known, have a broader range of focus and experience, and usually are more expensive. Most large firms do not provide consulting services for organizations with fewer than three hundred or so employees. Smaller firms will work with employer groups of all sizes, although organizations of five thousand or more employees may be reluctant to rely on the smaller consulting organization.

Informally Trained Consultants

This category includes brokers and agents, third-party administrators, business managers, and representatives of carriers and MCOs, people who have had experience but limited training in setting up health plans. These consultants may have no formal training, and have acquired no standard body of knowledge. However, they usually provide advice based on years of experience with similar situations and with employer groups within your region or industry. They usually have knowledge about insurance and the marketplace. It's wise to keep their narrower perspective in mind when reviewing their recommendations.

Brokers

Brokers are, typically, plan advisers for the small and mid-sized organization, because the cost of their services is built into the premium. They earn a commission, which is paid by the carrier or MCO when the employer selects them. It therefore appears to the decision maker that no extra cost is incurred for services. The tradeoff, of course, is that advice given by those paid a commission is not always objective. The representation of the plan is normally the focus, not the particular needs you might have as an employer.

Brokers are trained in the legal and regulatory issues that affect insurance plans, whether a health insurance program such as an HMO, PPO, other MCO, indemnity coverage, stop-loss insurance, retiree Medigap coverage, or life insurance. Brokers have a vested interest in your well-being and have a fiduciary responsibility to you. They may, for instance, sell you several types of insurance, including property and casualty or liability insurance. As a result, they usually have a broad knowledge of your insurance needs as an organization. They work for smaller local or regional firms that provide on-site services throughout the year to your organization.

Agents

Agents are slightly different from brokers, although they also sell insurance of various types, and provide direct services to your organization. They work more directly on behalf of the insurance companies, MCOs, and vendors they represent. Agents have closer contractual ties with the insurance company, place more business with the company than brokers do, and often can deliver extensive services quickly and with fewer problems.

Agents are the intermediary between brokers, and insurance companies in many cases, and can ensure that you receive easier approvals for administrative services and more prompt attention from the company. They work directly with your organization, or indirectly through brokers, to expedite the resolution of problems and assist with implementation. They are paid part or all of a commission by the carrier or MCO, depending on whether a broker is involved.

Company Representatives

Carrier, network, and MCO representatives may offer you consulting and plan services. They are paid employees of the company and work for a salary and incentives or commissions. Consequently, their pay reflects the volume of sales they generate. They are the product of training provided by their company and often are exempt from state requirements for health insurance licensing. In this case, the carrier or MCO steeps the representative in procedures, benefit issues, and coverage terms and conditions that reflect products the company sells and services. Reps have obvious limitations. They have a limited knowledge of the insurance markets and of health care issues relevant to your needs, and they lack objectivity about which products and services are best suited to your organization.

The cost to the carrier or MCO for such representatives is lower than the commission paid to a broker or agent, although there is no reduced cost to you. In effect, the company makes more money on your account while providing the same or less service to you in exchange. Carrier or MCO representatives have much larger territory than your local broker or agent, and they sell no other insurance to you, so that you are less likely to be vital to their income.

If you deal with a company representative, it's a good idea to remember these cautions:

- Carrier and MCO representatives move from firm to firm.
- They have limited training in health benefits issues and are trained only in the types of plans and services offered by their employer and its immediate competitors.
- They have a limited and narrow focus.
- They have an insurance industry bias regarding product sales and restrictions.
- They provide minimal personalization and attention to individual client needs.
- They are not encouraged to develop original or creative approaches.

It is prudent for you to seek another, outside opinion when you are considering an insurance plan from a carrier or MCO representative. Health insurance is a very competitive business, and you won't receive exactly the same plan coverage and services from each carrier or MCO. You might gain needed services, at no additional cost, by shopping around.

Third-Party Administrators

Third-party administrators (TPAs) are hired to process claims and to administer self-funded health plans for mid-sized employers (see Chapter 12). They specialize in a range of services that may include communication, actuarial advice, reports on utilization, projected cost impact, and benefits design recommendations. They are generally not benefits specialists but rather a blending of insurance and operational managers who are widely experienced with health plan management. Some TPAs employ specialists, while others require that their managers and service staff undertake continuing education. There is little state regulation of this industry, since ERISA exempts self-funded plans, which they administer, from state authority; some TPAs belong to industry organizations.

Since TPAs have primary responsibility for processing claims and managing the flow of information to you and to your employees, I think it's unwise to vest them with responsibilities that may conflict with their purpose. In essence, you should not ask them to monitor and supervise their own activity. On the other hand, it can be useful to ask them for recommendations on how to improve plan function and operations and to improve plan efficiency. Exhibit 11-3 presents a TPA's recommendation for administrative improvements.

Specialist Advisers

From time to time you may consult an actuary, lawyer, certified public accountant, financial planner, certified life insurance underwriter, or health insurance salesman. Each of these offers a particular expertise and background, and you should be aware of their potential to help you.

Actuaries

Actuaries, who have special training, academic credentials, and membership in the American Society of Actuaries, interpret and project health plan costs and premiums, taking into account what are called actuarial assumptions, on which they base their projections and recommendations. You will need to consult an actuary to:

- Measure the cost impact of a particular group on your budget for health insurance. This can be a result of eligibility changes for plan membership, company growth or expansion, reduction in staff, or a changed demographic among your plan members.
- Project cost differentials among plan options for various benefit levels, administrative costs, other fees, self-funding, premium arrangements to improve cash flow, and changes in networks or provider access.
- Estimate participation and utilization when your plan is altered. For example, the actuary might be asked to project increases or decreases in membership resulting from changed cost-sharing among retirees or active employees or from a new benefit or elimination of a benefit.

Actuaries base their projections on a wide range of variables such as new technology, legislative or regulatory action, medical spending trends, demographic shifts, and regional influences. It is a complex activity, and different from a simple cost projection made by financial staff. If you need to carefully estimate the cost or other financial impact of a health plan, the actuary will be able to do it, given adequate information and data.

Actuarial projections are provided with what is called a confidence level. This simply assigns the probability of error to the actuary's findings or recommendations. Projections are guesses, so they are not completely reliable. A confidence level, for instance, of 95 percent asserts that the actuary believes there is a 95 percent chance that the projection is correct.

TO: Employee Health Plan Committee

FROM: Third-Party Administrator

DATE: May 7, 1998

RE: Plan Changes for the Upcoming Plan Year
           Beginning 1/1/99

The following recommendations are made for your consideration of plan design and administration, based on our review of the procedures, benefit levels, and utilization of your self-funded employee health plan during the past eighteen months.

1. **Hospital discounts**. Approval of contracts with two local hospitals negotiated by us with your benefit consultant will result in an estimated savings of $75,000 to $80,000 during the upcoming plan year. This is based on current utilization at these facilities and current plan enrollment.

2. **Eliminate Carry-Over Deductible**. If you successfully negotiate the elimination of a provision to allow the deductible to be applied for a 15-month period, your plan can realize about $30,000 to $34,000 in savings during the upcoming plan year. Deductibles would continue to be applied for services received during the 12-month plan year, but not for 15 months when the deductible is not met by year end.

3. **Institute Chiropractic Review Provisions**. Many other employers in your area and industry have established plan provisions to monitor chiropractic use, especially for out-of-state chiropractors. You should review utilization with your benefit consultant and advise us of your determination for the limit on visits before a review and the intervals at which a review is appropriate. This can be implemented within thirty days, at your written direction.

4. **Require a Discharge Planning Penalty**. Inappropriate and higher costs for services have been evidenced by plan members during the past 18 months when discharge from a hospital requires extensive at-home care and follow-up services. If discharge planning is required, subject to a penalty when it is not used, these unnecessary costs can be avoided. Existing case management services will be able to provide the discharge planning coordination and counseling, and we will coordinate with them. Savings would result from negotiated, discounted services for the at-home and follow-up care. A penalty of $500 is suggested.

5. **Emergency Room Limits**. Your benefit consultant has identified nearly $15,000 in nonurgent emergency room use during the past six months, and over $40,000 during the preceding plan year. We recommend that you limit emergency room use for services to those when an admission results and have your benefit consultant prepare specific language regarding non-life-threatening use of the emergency room. These services cost about eight times what a doctor office visit or other outpatient service costs. You might consider a penalty, or reduced coverage, or no coverage for frivolous use of emergency room services.

6. **Conduct a Reenrollment**. Records that are outdated and do not reflect other sources of coverage for dependents and spouses cost your health plan about $75,000 each year. Although it is an administrative burden on your staff, and a cost to us to update member records, it is a necessary expense. This reenrollment should be conducted at your option transfer period in October.

EXHIBIT 11-3. Sample TPA recommendations. (Source: Halo Associates.)

Benefits Lawyers

Lawyers can be key advisers to a health plan, especially when they are expert in benefits case law, legislation, and regulations. Often, benefits lawyers have experience with negotiations and employee relations. Related issues such as pension law, Social Security, and Medicare are usually part of the expertise of a benefits lawyer. The lawyer might provide services, such as drafting or preparing plan documents, summary plan descriptions

(SPDs), summaries of material modifications (SMMs), and any contracts with your employees or service vendors for your health plan.

Financial Planners

Because of their perspective on investments and remuneration, financial planners can help you understand the impact of health plan changes on pensions and other employee compensation. If you are self-funded and have plan assets to invest, the financial planner can also help you negotiate funding options with the carrier or MCO. If you have budgeting questions related to all benefits and compensation that need funding, the financial planner can help you project your short-term and long-term needs.

Certified Public Accountant

Specialists in business accounting and reporting systems, certified public accountants (CPAs), track, report, and project the expenses incurred by your health plan. Financial projections, budgeting needs, interest earnings, funding options, government and tax reporting and regulations, and impact of plan costs on the organization are all within the CPA's area of expertise.

Certified Life Underwriters

Certified life underwriters (CLUs) are more concerned about life insurance as a benefit than about your health insurance plan. In many rural communities the CLU designation is held by brokers and financial planners, who often wear several hats. These specialists provide access to markets and assistance with the purchase of insurance.

Licensed Health and Life Insurance Salespeople

Insurance departments in each state have licensing and continuing education requirements for salespeople. They must pass a standardized test, complete continuing education credits, and follow certain regulations and procedures for the sale of health insurance to groups and individuals. They provide services to individuals, brokers, and agents and are likely to provide you with guidance and informal, although knowledgeable, advisory services, limited to the companies with which they have experience.

Management consultants and data processing specialists may also be needed as health plan advisers, depending on your organization's goals to reorganize or develop more detailed information systems.

Existing Relationships

You may already have expertise in place for other business needs, and hire benefits professionals on an as-needed project basis. It's not likely that you have a complete listing of the specialists needed for a health plan. You should identify existing services and firms that can provide input and guidance on your health plan and be aware of others so that you can quickly identify appropriate specialists when you have to. There are several resources you can use to identify specialists. Professional organizations, such as the bar association in your area, can tell you which lawyers specialize in benefits or employee relations law. You should also depend upon your plan adviser, who may have a working relationship with several specialty firms and can recommend which might be best suited to you. You can seek recommendations from other vendors who work with your health plan, such as the plan administrator. Additional sources for specialty firms are listed in the Appendix and include adviser organizations.

■ HOW TO SELECT AN ADVISER

As with other health plan needs, you should follow a selection process that sets established specifications for services. Having a standard list of expected services will help you concretely and fairly evaluate advisers' proposals. Depending on your organization's size and complexity, you may opt for the longer or shorter of two versions, one shown as Exhibit 11-4 and the other given as the list of services offered by consultants given in the next section (Scope of Services). As with other templates in this book, these can be tailored to meet the needs of your organization.

SCOPE OF SERVICES:

1. Development and coordination of Health Insurance Advisory Committee, composed of employees from various bargaining units and management. To include attendance at monthly meetings, development of agenda, provision of information required, and follow-up work to assist their efforts.

2. Examine HMO participation, comparative costs, and delivery of service. To include discussions and preparation to have HMOs make presentations at a screening session.

3. Development and preparation of a needs assessment to be administered to employees and retirees to gauge their satisfaction and concerns with their health benefit plan. To include a review and discussion of the tally of same, and creation of a series of recommendations.

4. Monthly review of financial and utilization reports to track various trend factors for the plan. To include various reports furnished by the administrators on plan experience throughout 199 .

5. Development and implementation of monitoring and control procedures with regard to the administration firms who provide service to the program to maintain and improve service levels.

6. Examine benefit levels of the plan, and make recommendation regarding cost containment and procedures.

7. Provide actuarial services in connection with the plan for financial planning and cost projections for 199 .

8. Review of existing discount arrangements with area providers, to include rate and fee schedules and their implementation, in conjunction with the employer and the third party administrator. To include recommendations for changes in the discounted programs.

9. Provide a review and comparison of vendors for the prescription drug program, and its mail order components, to encourage cost containment.

10. Review and make recommendations on the managed care aspects of the plan from procedural and cost-effectiveness viewpoints.

11. Assist with the revision of plan documents, to include the development of a Summary Plan Description for distribution to plan participants.

12. Help develop and implement an ongoing communications program for employees and retirees on benefit issues.

13. Serve as a resource to provide input and documentation as requested with regard to benefit issues.

14. Provide reports, both written and verbal, periodically and on request to individuals or groups of employees. To include attendance at management meetings.

Travel and related expenses, as well as specialized services, in connection with the above are to be the responsibility of the consultant.

EXHIBIT 11-4. Sample short list of services. (Source: Halo Associates.)

A timetable for the selection process should be established so that you will have the services you need when you need them. The following timetable can provide a rough framework:

1. *Preparation and approval of specifications.* This stage will take about a month, even if you simply adopt and amend the brief version presented in Exhibit 11-4. You should be sure to get input from others in your organization—top management, employee representatives, and benefits staff.

2. *Identification of bidders and distributions of specifications.* This process should take two weeks once you have identified sources of bidders. You should alert your broker, agent, or representative and your plan administrator when you are beginning the process and seek their recommendations and suggestions about bidders. They may wish to bid and may make suggestions about other potential bidders. Appendix A includes sources for consulting services, including a reference to *Business Insurance*, a periodical that publishes updated listings annually of consultants, brokers, and other specialists. You should decide whether you prefer a larger or smaller consulting firm or service and whether you want a local or regional firm or whether a national firm can better service your organization. These parameters can guide your selection.

3. *Proposal Review.* This stage should take you another two weeks. A committee of top management, managers, your staff, or a health plan committee should be enlisted to shortlist the proposals received. You may wish to create a summary of each consultant's proposal on a comparison sheet like the one shown in Exhibit 11-5. This can enable others to easily identify their preferences and enable you to make an objective comparison of the value of each.

Firm Name and Cost	Experience	Services	Special Features
XYZ Firm $10,000 base fee $250/hour project basis Travel costs extra	20 years in business Client base of 10+ similar to our needs Clients 50–5,000 Ees Established references	Service rep on site Support services extensive Geographic suitability Legal/actuarial okay 800#, communications 1,500 employees	MIS excellent Known for reports and electronic capabilities
ABC Firm $12,500 base fee $200/hour project basis No travel costs	10 years in business Client base limited with similar clients, but well established Clients 150–10,000 Ees Good references	Service rep monthly Support services extensive Geographic moderate Legal/actuarial excellent 800#, communications 80 employees	MIS new, state of the art On-site support for use of electronic transmissions Service rep from area originally
Apple Firm $15,000 base fee All inclusive, no hourly charges for project No travel costs	15 years in business Client base identical with existing 8 clients Clients 500–25,000 Ees Outstanding references	Service rep on site Support services moderate Geographic excellent Legal/actuarial okay 800#, communications 12 employees	MIS excellent with custom reports and electronic capability at no charge Firm located nearby

Notes: Ees = client employees. 800# refers to capability for providing a toll-free telephone contact number. MIS refers to management information system or computer capabilities.

It's clear that the firms are different, although each seems to be competent and have a unique selling point. Here is where personality and rapport come into play. You need to identify the consultant who seems most tuned into your needs. As with most business decisions, it boils down to people. To prudently and carefully winnow the bidders down to three who seem competent, you need to address the issues described under experience, service capabilities, special features, and cost. Since most plan activities take time to develop and implement, it is likely that your plan adviser will be hired on a multiyear contract, often renewed annually. You should anticipate a long-term relationship.

EXHIBIT 11-5. Comparison of consultants' proposals. (Source: Halo Associates.)

4. *Presentations.* Short-listed firms can be invited to make a presentation or come to an interview. This is your opportunity to learn about any special services they provide. More important, you can gauge whether you have the necessary rapport and confidence needed to work successfully with a particular consultant or plan adviser. This process takes about two weeks to complete.

5. *Notification.* You should notify every firm that submitted, in writing, within a week of your decision. A phone call is in order, in advance, to the firm selected.

The entire selection process should take two to three months maximum.

■ SCOPE OF SERVICES

You can use the following list as a guideline when you discuss your needs with brokers, agents, specialists and consultants, regardless of the size of your organization. Each kind of consultant offers different services.

Services Offered by Consultants

1. Employee relations
   a. Guide and coordinate activities of the employee health plan committee. This includes but is not limited to preparation of agendas, attendance at committee meetings, research and evaluation of committee suggestions and concerns, and providing follow-up to committee decisions that require action.
   b. Create and develop reports and procedures for financial review and plan management, including monthly monitoring by the committee.
   c. Prepare and develop, with committee input, a series of employee communications, including but not limited to a satisfaction survey on various benefit plans offered. This should include an analysis of employee satisfaction, recommendations for plan design and administrative changes, and response to employee complaints or problems.
   d. Develop and implement or contribute to an employee benefit newsletter, and serve as a resource for newsletter topics, articles, and information to assist employer staff in its writing and review.
   e. Prepare and develop quarterly and annual reports to various bargaining units and management. These will reflect committee activity, including recommendations, new procedures, review of health plans and administrators, and financial monitoring of plan performance.
   f. Present information at annual employee meetings, held at various work sites for the purpose of answering questions, resolving problems, and announcing any pertinent information about health plans.
   g. Provide updated summary plan documents, summary of material modifications, annual financial statements, and other required written materials that will be distributed to plan members.
2. Support of internal staff
   a. Serve as a resource on benefit issues, regulations, employee contracts, health care trends, and financial issues to the director of personnel and other benefits staff.
   b. Provide reports to employer, on request, on issues that are relevant to plan management, design, financing, and communication.

   c. Assist with the specification and bidding process for any vendors or administrators required to implement and facilitate the employer's health plans.

   d. Conduct analyses and reviews of proposals submitted in connection with these processes.

   e. Assist with the selection and notification process for vendors and administrators.

   f. Provide training in plan procedures and forms to in-house staff when new regulations, changes to plan, or administrative procedures so require.

   g. Provide support services throughout the term of the agreement to in-house staff who are responsible for the day-to-day monitoring of the health plan.

3. Plan management

   a. Conduct audits of vendor and administrative services as directed by the employer, and publish reports annually or biannually, as needed.

   b. Recommend and furnish appropriate analysis and background materials for plan changes to improve utilization, such as institution of case management coordination for high-cost claims, and adjustments of the prescription drug coverage to reduce costs.

   c. Review and make recommendations with regard to reports on cost and utilization furnished by the various administrators and vendors throughout the term of the agreement.

   d. Create supervisory controls and a timetable for review of all firms that serve the health plans; meet with representatives and explore lower-cost alternatives.

   e. Review benefit areas for utilization and cost impact on plan, and alert employer of any necessary review or action to be taken.

   f. Provide cost projection and actuarial review of plan funds and financing procedures; make recommendations regarding future costs, cost savings, and methods to improve cash flow and to minimize expense.

   g. Establish a premium equivalent for the self-funded plan, and negotiate premium payments for the MCO plans selected.

   h. Create a provider network for major medical services, including an expanded specialist network in three geographic areas where employer has employees and facilities. This will include negotiating discounted fees, and establishing contractual agreements and credentialing of network members. This service is to be initiated in year one, implemented in year two, and expanded in year three of this agreement.

   i. Maintain positive relationship of health plan with area hospitals and other providers, by intervention when regulations, utilization, or costs so require.

   j. Track activity throughout each plan year, and report on the impact of network development to plan services, employee satisfaction, and costs.

4. Accountability to plan

   a. Maintain records of all plan management activities and furnish an annual report and periodic reports to be not more than quarterly on consulting activities and outcomes.

   b. Detail associate firms or providers who assist in the consulting function, including but not limited to actuaries, benefits specialists, attorneys, asset managers, and others who may be needed to provide a range of service covered by this agreement.

   c. Obtain advance approval for release of any information to outside firms, associate firms, or specialists who may be contracted by the consultant to assist with this scope of services.

d. Maintain fiduciary relationship with plan, plan sponsor, plan members, including observance of confidentiality, industry standards for reporting and review of plan documents, and regulatory compliance.

Designer vs. Ready-to-Wear

The difference between plan advisers and insurance salesmen is comparable to that between a fashion designer and a salesperson in a ready-to-wear department. There are needs for both services, and issues of cost and accessibility to consider.

Is there a cost difference between a benefits consultant or specialist adviser and insurance salespeople or carrier representatives? Can you negotiate performance standards into a contract and pay only when you save? Can fees be tied to time spent and activities accomplished?

When cost is discussed, you should remember that you get what you pay for with a health plan adviser, just as in other professional relationships. Your limits as a small or mid-sized organization need to be considered. What does it cost you for an informal adviser, or sales representative? The cost is built into your insurance premium and can vary, depending on the company and the type of health plan you purchase. Usually, a sales commission of 3 percent to 10 percent is included in your premium, although commissions on stop-loss insurance can range as high as 30 percent of the premium charged. Renewal commissions vary from plan to plan. If an average health insurance premium is $2,000 for your employees, you pay a commission of between $60 and $200 per year per employee. The commissions are shared between individual salespeople, brokers, and agents if they are involved.

I recommend that you ask your insurance professional for any free services available and expect to have their help. For the commissions earned, they should help with on-site issues during the year, open enrollment, and employee problems. You are paying for this help, whether or not you get advisory services.

What about benefits consultants and other specialty consultants? You contract for a separate fee and are fully aware of how much you are paying these experts and the services you expect them to provide. As with other plan services, you can negotiate performance standards as part of a consulting contract. You can require a certain number of visits, timeliness of response, a listed group of tasks included as an appendix to the contract, dedicated staff to be assigned to the project, and general services and guarantees to be provided to your plan and to your work site. Exhibit 11-6 includes sample contract language for performance guarantees. The most common performance contracts call for cash or deficit reductions and renewal rate reductions.

Consultant fees are highly negotiable and should be compared for all firms that submit proposals. This comparison is one good reason you should seek multiple bids for consulting services. If nothing else, such a process will help confirm that the fee you pay to your consultant is competitive for your geographic area. Fees for consultants can be hourly, daily, annual, or by the project. Fees can range from $100 an hour to $1,000 an hour, depending on the adviser. They can be quoted as a minimum, and with a maximum limit. Travel, ancillary services, and other expenses can be billed separately, or the contract can be all-inclusive. If your specifications call for additional specialty services, such as actuarial projections, legal review, or document preparation, it may be to your advantage to have the primary contractor coordinate the project, at no extra cost, and subcontract to associate firms for specialty services. This can relieve you of the burden of

Typical performance standard clauses include:

Time limit and financial penalties:

a. The Provider shall develop and assist with the preparation and distribution of an employee needs assessment, to survey employee and retiree attitudes and concerns about the health plan. The Provider shall ensure that said survey is distributed no later than _____, subject to a penalty of 10 percent of the agreed upon fee, contained in section _____ of this agreement, for each 30-day period that said survey is delayed, commencing with _____ .

b. The Provider shall participate and contribute to the review of responses to said survey, and evaluate same, to prepare a submission of findings. Said submission must be provided by written report of responses and proposed options for restructuring to the County Administrator by _____ , subject to a financial penalty of $1,000.00 which amount will be deducted from a final fee payment as set forth in section _____ of this agreement.

Renewal penalties and performance standards:

Term of Agreement

1. This Agreement shall become effective _____ and shall terminate on _____ . This agreement can be extended for another twelve months to _____ on written agreement by both parties, subject to the following conditions:

a. That the Provider under this agreement furnish written reports and claims records that document a reduction in cost of at least two percent (2 percent) of the current cost of claims experienced by the self-funded plan as shown in Appendix A.1 attached herewith;

b. And further, that the Provider agree to accept the annual fee set forth in section _____ as payment in full for the extended twelve months to be paid in accordance with the terms and conditions set forth, and to be limited thereto, notwithstanding the amount of the demonstrated reduction in the cost of claims during the term of this agreement.

Note: An agreement can set forth any terms that are negotiated, and should be drafted and revised until both parties are clear as to the intent and meaning stated.

EXHIBIT 11-6. Consultant performance standards. (Source: Halo Associates.)

selection and individual contracts, and give your primary adviser the opportunity to work closely with specialists with whom he or she is familiar.

Consultants as Money Savers

Consultants often claim that they save you money. They can document this if you track plan expenses. Exhibit 11-7 presents a cost-savings report for a self-funded plan that shows reduced cost from a network developed by a consultant for the plan. The return on investment for the consulting fee is six to one for the first year of operation. A pretty good return—and a reason that consultants are often used for such projects.

Since consulting contracts often have a specific time frame and are awarded on a project basis or annually, you want to project long- and short-term savings from the short-term expense of a consultant.

Some of the services for which you can hire a consultant to reduce plan costs are these:

- Development of flexible benefit choices to reduce plan costs and improve employee satisfaction at no increase in plan budget
- Establishment of a provider discount network with doctors and hospitals
- Negotiation with discount networks to integrate care and services for your plan

Claim Number	Check Number	Hospital	Claimant	Per Diem Cost	Drug Cost	113% of Drug	Discounts	Type Discount	Amount Paid	Date
				Negotiated Discounts						
50059	35810	Westchester	K	17,215.06	11,539.38	13,039.50	3,000.24	Rubin	10,039.26	01/95
50059	36255	Westchester	K	17,215.00	12,106.00	13,679.78	4,289.78	URS	9,390.00	02/95
50145	36297	Sloan Kettering	O	30,704.88	21,174.60	23,927.30	7,062.60	Rubin	16,864.70	02/95
50506	36573	Presbyterian Hosp.	B	36,027.76	14,101.11	15,934.13	3,243.13	Rubin	12,691.00	03/95
50663	36914	Westchester	S	20,600.00	4,030.15	4,554.07	1,047.84	Rubin	3,506.23	03/95
50506	37333	Burke Rehab.	B	29,730.55	32,136.30	36,314.02	2,575.15	URS	27,155.40	04/95
50059	37416	Westchester	K	19,800.00	12,285.61	13,882.76	3,194.36	Rubin	10,688.40	04/95
50022	37503	Hosp. Spec. Surgery	H	8,447.71	6,627.67	7,489.27	1,391.81	Rubin	6,097.46	04/95
50503	37576	Sloan Kettering	T	31,963.63	23,758.00	26,846.54	5,464.34	Rubin	21,382.20	04/95
50506	37225	Burke Rehab.	B	31,301.85			5,051.63	URS	26,250.22	05/95
50059	38050	Westchester	K	23,100.00	12,304.58	13,904.18	3,199.20	Rubin	10,704.98	05/95
50059	38782	Westchester	K	31,550.00	12,304.81	13,904.44	3,199.26	Rubin	10,705.18	07/95
50059	39351	Westchester	K	26,400.00	12,330.22	13,933.15	1,602.93	Rubin	10,727.29	08/95
50669	40275	New York Hosp.	J	19,792.19	22,049.94	24,916.44	989.61	Rubin	18,802.58	09/95
50089	40448	Sharon Hosp.	M	26,527.40			530.55	URS	25,996.85	09/95
50089	40449	Sharon Hosp.	M	12,495.55			249.91	URS	12,245.64	09/95
50059	40734	Westchester	K	18,150.00	12,185.82	13,769.98			18,150.00	10/95
50125	40763	Presbyterian Hosp.	R	45,766.82	30,631.21	34,613.27			45,766.82	10/95
50178	42197	Four Winds Hosp.	S	9,411.92					9,411.92	12/95
		Total		456,200.32			46,092.34		306,576.13	

EXHIBIT 11-7. Sample cost savings report. (Source: Halo Associates.)

- Redesign of your health plan to shift costs to retirees and/or to active employees
- Establishment of a self-funded health plan to reduce operating and administrative expenses, while maintaining benefits
- Negotiations with employee representatives to reduce plan costs
- Handling of the bid and specification process to select vendors for plan administration, case management, wellness, or selection of various health plans from among options

In addition to handling special projects, consultants are often hired to manage health plans efficiently. They fine-tune plan management, help accustom staff to new regulations and legislation, report on utilization and cost data, make periodic recommendations on cost-saving actions, and develop employee communications for your use. Just about any problem you have with a health plan can be turned over to a plan adviser for examination and attention.

The ultimate goals of a consulting service are to improve employee satisfaction, to develop efficient and cost-effective services for your health plan, and to keep costs within reason for your organizations. In accomplishing these, your consultant helps you comply with laws and regulations, meet contractual obligations, budget sensibly, maintain positive employee communications about your plan, and stay current about benefits trends and developments.

■ FINDING A CONSULTANT

There are as many ways to meet your consulting needs as there are to meet your other plan needs. My advice is that you stay updated on the top consulting firms in your area. You can find them in the yellow pages, by asking colleagues at business meetings, and by referring to national and regional listings that appear each year in trade publications. Your insurance professional may have suggestions for consulting services; other resources are included in the Appendix.

■ HOW TO PREPARE TO WORK WITH AN ADVISER

You need to prepare for the adviser's visit and for the work you expect the adviser to do. To do this, follow these steps:

- *Gather information.* If you plan to ask for a review of your plan, you will need to locate pertinent information. For example, have your employee demographics available, such as a listing of employees by gender, ages, health plan enrollment, and employment status. You may also need copies of previous reports, printouts of utilization, experience reports on plan costs and activity, previous benefits contracts, and historical or background information on your health plan. It may take time for you to locate and prepare these materials, but without them, you will be asking your adviser to do the impossible.
- *Prepare a checklist.* Use the first meeting with your adviser to prepare a list of what you need to gather and the purpose it will serve. Alternatively, review a checklist over the telephone in advance of your meeting, with adequate time to gather the materials. Transmit materials by mail or fax in advance, or have them ready when you meet.
- *State your purpose and goals.* Nothing is worse than to meet with your plan adviser and have no idea what it is you want or expect. When you prepared your specifications for the consulting contract, you identified the project or tasks you needed done. Rely upon the scope of services developed then. Your goal may be general—to review overall

costs and efficiency—or specific—to help select a new drug administrator. It can be accomplished in the short term, or the long term, or in stages.

- *Understand and identify the tasks to be assigned.* If your overall goal is to evaluate plan costs and efficiency, be aware of what the plan adviser needs to do, such as demonstrate the cost variations of the health plan by plan type, enrollment, for retirees and active employees, and over the past three to five years. Tasks can include that the adviser identify the cost-effectiveness of the benefits provided and review the administrative issues of eligibility, enrollment, and cost sharing; compare the cost and cost impact of various plans; compare costs and utilization within your region and among other employers in your industry; and prepare a report with findings and recommendations.

- *Redefine goals and purposes as needed.* You may develop specific goals with your adviser. In many cases, it's a good idea to ask your adviser for a draft of goals, based on your plan performance and general purpose. There may be a difference between your view and your adviser's view of the situation.

■ HOW TO WORK WITH YOUR ADVISER

You should expect to follow certain working routines with your plan adviser. These include:

- *Regular visits.* On-site work with your adviser serves two major purposes. First, it encourages you to meet deadlines for activities such as gathering data, assigning staff, or calling a meeting. Second, it creates a structure for you to exchange information that is necessary in order for your adviser to perform properly. It is wise to keep notes on your regular meetings with your adviser. You will have an ongoing record of accomplishment, and also a checklist of work tasks to which you can refer in between visits. (See Exhibit 11-8.)

- *Written communications.* You should have a routine in place, and train your staff to follow it, for providing your adviser with regular and urgent information or copies of material. It can be an in-box set aside for your plan adviser, augmented by fax or mail for standard, bulky transmissions or urgent communications. You should clearly indicate when you expect a written response or whether you expect a review and discussion. You might use stick-on notes to alert your adviser when a call needs to be made to the letter writer, or flag a written memorandum if it alters a deadline or other activity, or identify those items that require feedback or discussion.

- *Telephone communications.* It sounds simple, but if you don't get numbers and a schedule of availability, telephone tag becomes the routine of reality with a plan adviser. Avoid this at all costs. Your time is valuable, and so is that of your adviser. Be aware of your adviser's schedule and telephone availability. Have a preestablished alternative contact with whom you can discuss any urgent requests or follow-up. There is nothing more frustrating for you both than for you and your plan adviser to play telephone tag for a day or two when a few minutes on the telephone could have resolved an important matter. You should decide whether you want an adviser to contact you at home, and under what conditions, and ask if your adviser wants to provide a home number or car or cell phone number for use when travel or tight office schedule make telephone contact difficult.

- *Verbal and written reports.* The purpose and content of reports, to your office and to others, should be clarified and discussed when they are requested. The deadline for

9/15/98

Client: XYZ County

Contact: Maria X

1. Prepare reports for upcoming health plan committee meeting:
   Updated enrollment report with costs and variables including enrollment trends from 1990–98 for all plans offered.
   Inpatient hospital stay comparison. Review, analyze, and prepare presentation including activity, precertification savings, utilization review reports, and diagnoses, especially chronic or catastrophic conditions.

2. Review employee survey tally on new benefit changes. Provide priority listing of employee recommendations to consider with health plan committee.

3. Meet with actuary to review his opinion on premium equivalent for next plan year, and to prepare it for presentation at next health plan committee meeting.

4. Examine utilization and cost trends for 1997 and year to date to identify impact of plan changes in 1997, especially with regard to network providers.

5. Stop Loss. Review reserve fund for adequacy, and project impact on premium for upcoming plan year. Prepare summary of stop loss transfers due to high cost claims in current plan year.

6. Review prescription drug costs at out of state pharmacies, located in adjacent counties.

7. Prepare monthly financial report and third-quarter reports for October meeting. Follow up with plan vendors to obtain data needed.
   Next meeting date: 10/1/98
   Next committee meeting date: 10/15/98

EXHIBIT 11-8. Sample of meeting notes. (Source: Halo Associates.)

such reports, arrangements for approval in advance of submission, procedure for editing and revisions—all of these need to be agreed upon in advance. You don't need to know each and every item you will be requesting of your adviser, but the manner in which such requests will be made and then met should be understood. If there are to be additional charges, that should be clear at the onset. You should ask your adviser, during the selection process and at your first few meetings when tasks are assigned, what standard reports are recommended and furnished. You may not have the experience or background to suggest useful reports concerning your health plan and so will be pleasantly surprised at the user-friendly reports available. Things can be simple, when an outside professional is hired to make them so.

- *Assistance with implementation.* You should have a clear understanding of how involved or uninvolved your adviser will be when it comes time to implement recommendations. There should be no surprise responsibilities thrust at your plan adviser, nor should your staff pick up the slack for an outside expert. Your health plan adviser should be like the proverbial mother hen, watching over activities related to your plan and its implementation. At times, this will mean a heightened involvement. For instance, it may mean more intensive interaction with you and your staff during startup and then during initial monitoring of plan activities. It may be necessary for your adviser to be on hand for a few days in a row, instead of at regular meetings. You should be prepared and alert your staff, so that appropriate space and support are provided during these on-site hours. Exhibit 11-9 presents a typical implementation checklist for open enrollment meetings and describes the responsibilities of staff and of the outside adviser.

1. Internal Staff and Benefits Office

Benefits Manager and staff
a. Prepare meeting notices on plan changes for distribution to:
  - All employees in paycheck, week of September 28th
  - All department heads at department head meeting mid-September
  - Top management one week prior to department head meeting
  - Employee representatives, if appropriate
b. Arrange space and schedule for enrollment meetings, presentations, and counseling.
  - Confirm in writing and alert appropriate staff and plan representatives
  - Transmit directions to site(s) as needed
c. Assess on-hand materials needed for open enrollment and request additional supplies
  - From MCOs and carriers, request adequate plan booklets, claim forms, enrollment forms, status change forms, and marketing brochures
  - From staff, request plan comparisons, including difference in contributions, if applicable, and any handouts from benefits office, including descriptions of new procedures, plan changes, or other modifications
d. Request consulting review and input in advance for needed materials to be developed and produced in house for open enrollment packets
e. Order and approve identification cards, and any changes necessitated by plan review or modifications
f. Request support services and follow-up from the plan adviser or consultant

Finance and Legal Staff
a. Review contracts and funding availability for administrators, vendors, and plans for the plan year
b. Gather needed credentials, insurance certificates, and other supporting documents from administrators and vendors affected by open enrollment

2. Consultant
a. Notify administrators and vendors for the plan regarding open enrollment and follow up with their activities so that they provide new descriptive materials and support materials in advance
b. Review plan documents and notices before they are distributed, to give input on their accuracy, appropriateness, and language
c. Discuss enrollment activities and procedures with benefits manager and assist with staff training, if needed, on new procedures, plans, or benefit changes
d. Assist with the development of identification cards, and other plan materials which require modification due to plan design or administration changes
e. Provide on-site presentations, if needed, to employee representatives, management, and groups of employees or plan members
f. Track and monitor the enrollment activities to measure their impact on plan performance

Note: This checklist is a guide and will vary by site. It illustrates the range of activities and duties needed to conduct option transfer, or open enrollment activities. These are important when you offer new plans, change existing plans, or switch to new administrators or vendors and when there is employee concern about your health plan. Open communication, sufficient materials, and advance planning will make open enrollment positive for your organization.

EXHIBIT 11-9. Sample implementation checklist for an open enrollment meeting. (Source: Halo Associates.)

- *Periodic meetings.* You should establish a meeting schedule, purpose and goals for meetings, and a timetable for notifications and adjustments at the onset of your relationship with your adviser. You might need your adviser to meet with management, employees, bargaining units, health plan vendors or administrators, and others. You should make your priorities and time constraints known to your plan adviser and identify the demands of your organization as they relate to periodic meetings. For the best results, you should plan meetings well in advance, to promote a mutual respect and trust with your adviser and to emphasize that the adviser's time is valued. Your adviser can help with the preparation of agendas and of backup materials for discussions, reports, studies, evaluations, and other support materials. If you require presentations, your adviser should be given ample time to prepare and review them. It may take time to have presentation materials reproduced, collated, and distributed, whether it is your responsibility or the adviser's.

  The adviser might need to meet with a health plan committee, with top management, with employee representatives, with internal financial or legal staff. Preparation is the key to a well-run, useful meeting that accomplishes its purposes. Well-planned and well-executed meetings convey an image of professionalism, efficiency, expertise, and good management.

- *Urgent meetings.* Sometimes you will need immediate and interactive help with a health plan problem that cannot be handled over the telephone. Your plan adviser is accustomed to being asked to problem solve; it's what consultants do. You can help by doing the following:

  - Promptly ask your adviser for guidance on information and materials that are needed.
  - Be prepared to describe the facts of the situation accurately, with as much detail as possible.
  - Have a good understanding about what you are asked to do in response to the problem.
  - Identify what you are asking of the adviser. Do you need a revised cost projection, or immediate revised language, or an analysis of legislative impact during benefit negotiations? Depending on the answer, you may be asking your adviser to draft the statement or report, to do research on background for it, or to conduct a financial or legal study.

■ PERFORMANCE STANDARDS

How do you measure what sort of job your plan adviser is doing? What resources do you have to know if you are getting value from your adviser? How can you improve the adviser's performance? These are some management issues that you need to consider and that can help you justify the expense of a plan adviser to top management.

One of your responsibilities is to read previous contracts and consultant or adviser reports to help you measure outcomes achieved with previous advisers. When you remind yourself this way of past expectations, scope of services, and costs, it will refresh your thinking about how to work best with your current adviser. Make note of what worked and what didn't in the past. Try to understand why. Be honest with yourself. If the problem was too little focus or support on your end, try to correct the problems this time around. Whether the consulting effort was successful or unsuccessful, try to evaluate the role of timing, management support, staff issues, employee relations, funding, and other organizational influences.

■ SOME CAUTIONS

A few words of caution about advisers is in order. There is no one who will be able to solve every health plan problem or pull every chestnut out of the fire for you, no matter how good the firm or individual is. Be realistic about what you expect. Even when things don't go the way you want, remember that having an outside, objective, and expert adviser can improve your chances. It can be a haven in a storm to have a confident and trusted adviser with whom to discuss plan problems and organizational concerns. When top management and your employees question your ability, motives, and activities, it's comforting to point to a bona fide expert who structured, recommended, and monitored what was done.

There have been many times when a client hired a consultant to write a report, saying exactly what the client wanted to hear. That's not to say that the consultant wrote or submitted something incorrect or wrong for the organization, or wrote without conviction. It does reflect the conservative nature of some managers, who will not embark on a project even when they are convinced it is in the best interest of their organization, unless a consultant concurs on the record. Such managers are looking for a stamp of approval and may not act without it.

You should remember that, like all professionals, advisers have limits and restrictions on their time, responsiveness, and ability. These are limits to which you may gradually become accustomed. That's not to say that after you hire a benefits consultant or plan adviser you should expect substandard services. However, recognize that your adviser will not always be at your beck and call.

■ OBTAINING SOME FREE SERVICES

You may not know that useful information, materials, and services are often available to you through your broker, agent, health insurance salesperson, or company representative. Your broker or agent can provide you with plan documents, ID cards, explanatory materials, and, often, interpretations of legal and regulatory issues that require compliance from a carrier or MCO the broker or agent represents. These are usually not personalized for your use, but generic. Nor do they address any unique characteristics of your organization and your health plan. Some cost reports and data will be available from which your broker, agent, or company representative can help you draw conclusions.

In most cases, an informal adviser will not be able to provide you with detailed, objective, comparative data for several options or from other plans comparable to yours. To the contrary, the perspective of the informal adviser is usually one of a salesperson who is interested in selling you a particular product, for which the salesperson earns a commission.

When plan questions arise, you can ask your broker, agent, or plan representative to assist at open enrollment meetings, employee meetings, or committee and management meetings. This can be a useful service and can help to address any complaints or concerns. However, you need to keep in mind that these insurance professionals are trained in their products and will be intent on presenting their plan in the best light from a highly partial viewpoint. Most often, no decision maker from the health plan will be present who can affect any new services or respond definitively to actual problems.

Standard Free Services

There are some standard free services you can request from your agent or broker that you might have to pay for if you hired a benefits consultant. They include the following:

- *Communication materials.* Instead of inventing the wheel, you can use standard forms and written materials from the plan, including enrollment forms, claim forms, benefits booklets, retiree notices, student verification forms, COBRA notices, and notices of plan changes. These might be able to be personalized with the name of your organization and the name of a contact. The plan representative may offer to pay for such personalization to get your business.

- *Updates on new legislation and regulations.* Interpretations and discussions about new laws and requirements may be available. These will not have an analysis personalized for your organization, but they may inform you about the responsibilities of employers in general.

- *Trade publications and articles.* When you have a particular interest area, alert your plan representative to keep an eye out for articles and publications on that issue. Trends in the industry and standards for performance can be reviewed by noting these timely publications. You can inquire about current benefit issues during visits with your plan representative. Ask for documentation of information they provide. The Appendix also suggests reading resources.

- *Help with problem solving.* Although limited resources and a different focus make it hard for your plan representative to provide you with hands-on problem-solving advice, it is part of their job and why they get paid. If you are a large client, you will get more and better services when you have a problem. The advice and assistance you receive will not have the depth of expertise, objectivity, or commitment that you would get from a plan adviser who is a benefits consultant or specialist, and who will give undivided and specific attention to your problem or project.

Your need for attention will vary with the complexity of your health plans, issues specific to your organization and your workforce, and the internal resources you have to manage your health plan without outside assistance. Some of your need will be determined by the corporate philosophy, and its greater or lesser emphasis on employee health and well-being, and on how management perceives your health plan in relation to employee remuneration and organizational purpose.

■ WHEN TO USE INTERNAL RESOURCES

If you have an organization with expert staff, able to assist with health plan needs, you might question whether an insurance or benefits professional is useful. You need to decide if the resources at your disposal are adequate, based on the following criteria:

- Are your internal experts skilled in the issues?
- Do they have current, updated knowledge and experience?
- Can you rely on their objectivity?
- Are they trustworthy and cooperative?
- Do they have integrity and a commitment to their work?

Remember, your health plan covers your internal staff, and they are human. Their judgment about the plan can be swayed by factors that are personal or related to their management status. Their priorities may differ from yours, with a focus on employee relations, profitability, or limited resources that can affect their advice and viewpoint. You will probably need outside consulting expertise to stay abreast of the health care environment and technological advances as they affect your health plan and your employees,

You should consider a combination of in-house expertise and an external plan adviser. One way to achieve a combined effort is to create a health plan committee or task force, composed of staff and managers from your organization and assisted by your health plan adviser. A combined approach has several advantages. It allows for valued input and opinion from internal resources, through a recognized channel of communication. At the same time, you can benefit from the advice of an objective plan adviser, and ensure your control over decisions. An environment of discussion and consensus develops within the health plan committee. Of course, in this instance, your selection of an outside adviser should take into account the dynamics of the group.

■ SUMMARY

It's not an impossible task to find the right consultant, but it takes some doing. You may be the kind of manager who prefers going it alone, using this text and other support material as a guide. Or, you may see the value of an outside expert but have limited funds to engage one. Or, you may decide to hire a consultant for a specific job and leave the rest to your plan administrator and staff.

Whichever approach you take, and it may vary from time to time depending on your needs, you should strive to identify a consultant who can meet a range of health plan needs. It's better to have someone on deck than to have to scramble when a problem occurs. Once you have found a consultant who meets your criteria, it's important to keep in touch, even when you aren't actively working together. If a consultant works well with you, is responsive, gets results that can be measured, and keeps your health plan on target, you will be wise to forge a strong, long-term relationship.

CHAPTER 12

Self-Funding

Self-funding health benefits is a concept that has grown in popularity over the past thirty years, taking deeper root during the 1980s, when health care costs were rising by double-digit amounts each year. According to the February 16, 1998, issue of *Business Insurance*, the number of organizations with 500 or more employees that are self-funded ranges from 73 percent for PPO plans to 10 percent for HMO plans. Exhibit 12-1 presents the prevalence of self-funding by health plan types.

What exactly is self-funding? When it decides to self-fund, an organization pays directly for health plan claims, administration, and expenses, instead of purchasing a health plan from an insurance carrier or MCO. Organizations that provide benefits through self-funding select what they wish to offer from among standard benefit plans or design their own benefit plan. They are at risk for the health claims of plan members. In a self-funded plan, the organization hires or contracts with health insurance professionals and specialists to provide claims processing and other services to the plan that are provided by the insurance carrier or MCO in an insured plan. Exhibit 12-2 compares an insured plan with a self-insured plan in several basic areas.

■ HOW DOES SELF-FUNDING WORK?

Funding is the major difference between self-funded and insured plans. Benefits may stay the same or be slightly altered. Plan administration still includes claims processing, an appeal and peer review process, member services, employee communication, ID cards, claim forms, reports to the plan sponsor, and evaluation of cost-effectiveness and member satisfaction. As with other financial needs and budgeting issues, the most important thing to do is to plan ahead. The numerous advantages of self-funding are shown in Exhibit 12-3.

Type of Plan	1996	1997
Indemnity	70%	72%
PPO	72	73
Point-of-service	52	46
HMO	6	10

EXHIBIT 12-1. Percentage of employers (500+ employees) self-funding. (Source: William M. Mercer Incorporated, January 1998.)

SELF-INSURED	FULLY INSURED
	Administration
Third-Party Administrator	Insurance Company
Employee/retiree files claim directly to administrator, which processes it.	Employee/retiree files claim directly to insurance company, which processes it.
ID cards, claim forms, booklets, and other plan member needs are supplied to employer for employees and retirees by administrator.	ID cards, claim forms, booklets, and other plan member needs are supplied to employer for employees and retirees by insurance company.
Claims to be processed within 15 working days, unless held for specific follow-up.	Claims processed without time limit—as much as 90 days with past experience.
Reports on costs furnished to employer monthly and quarterly to assist with financial projections and planning/budgeting.	Regular reports on request.
	Funding
Employer budgets and funds cost of plan, including the expected cost of claims, cost of administration/plan management, and morbidity fluctuation.	Employer budgets and funds cost of plan with monthly payment of premium to insurance company for their projected cost of claims, retention, pooling charge, and administrative fees.
	Service
Contact with doctors and hospitals on behalf of employees/retirees is done by administrator. A network of providers is developed for plan. In some cases, discounts are arranged to help contain cost.	Contact with doctors and hospitals on behalf of employees and retirees is done by insurance company. Any discount increases their profit.
Turnaround time to be held to 15 working days by performance contract.	Turnaround time not controlled.
Drug card national and fully computerized.	Drug card national.

EXHIBIT 12-2. Comparison of fully insured and self-funded plans. (Source: Halo Associates.)

Self-Funded Plan Savings

Since the primary reason to self-fund is to reduce cost, an understanding of how self-funding cuts cost is essential to this discussion. Savings are experienced by the self-funded plan in three areas:

1. *Cash flow and interest earnings.* Claims are paid when they are incurred, so there is a delay of several months when a plan begins before claims are incurred, filed, and paid. This cash-flow advantage results because only nine to ten months of claims are paid out the first twelve months of self-funding, compared to twelve months of full premiums if the plan were insured.

There can be other short-term cash-flow advantages in subsequent years, when claims are lower than anticipated. It is normal for a self-funded plan to fluctuate month to month in its need for cash. In addition, there are interest earnings on the plan's fund, which accumulate throughout the year. In an insured plan, deposit premiums are often collected

Funding advantages of a self-funded plan stem:

Administration: Insurance companies charge 8–13 percent to process claims (based on dollar volume of claims paid, usually so there is no incentive for them to cut your costs). With self-funding, costs of administration, including all plan management needs, run 4–6 percent of the total plan cost.

Retention: Insurance companies charge "retention," which is analogous to "profit," of 10–20 percent each year for each account. In self-funding, there is no retention charged.

Pooling Charge: Insurance companies charge for the cost of anticipated excess claims (over projected amounts) or directly for the purchase of stop-loss insurance to cover these extraordinary amounts. In self-funding, an amount for these fluctuations is budgeted and held by the plan sponsor and remains part of the plan assets for use when extraordinary costs are experienced.

Cash Flow: Insurance companies charge a monthly premium that is paid out by the employer, and, regardless of actual costs, is then income to the insurance company. In self-funding, the money needed to pay claims is funded from a budgeted fund as it is required. Interest earned on the fund balance is kept as part of the overall financial result of the plan.

Payment of Claims: Insurance companies have a payment philosophy of pay-and-then-pursue on claims that require follow-up, coordination of benefits, subrogation, etc. They have no incentive to contain costs, because they are paid on the basis of how much claims cost. In self-funding, the cost of claims has a direct, measurable impact on the fund balance and the ultimate cost of the plan. Through utilization reports and cost containment programs, plan cost is a major focus of the third-party administrator and plan sponsor.

EXHIBIT 12-3. Benefits of self-funding. (Source: Halo Associates.)

in lump sums of three or more months of premiums, and there is no relation to between when premiums are collected and when claims are paid.

2. *Lower administrative costs.* In a self-funded plan, administrative fees and expenses are typically 4–6 percent of total plan costs. In an insured plan, administration costs, retention, pooling charges, and premium taxes account for 15–20 percent of total plan costs. On top of actual lower costs, there is a synergy of administrative savings in a self-funded plan, due in part to the sentinel effect of self-funding—the plan sponsor is always watching. This often means stricter attention to high cost claims and how they are handled and can result in lower cost.

3. *Control of plan coverage and providers.* Savings can result when an organization controls benefit levels and provider relations for its health plan. One source of savings derives from a uniform set of benefits provided for locations in several states. In this case, self-funding allows the employer to avoid state mandates for coverage it chooses not to include in its plan. The freedom to avoid the cost and the complexity of complying with multiple state laws can be a good reason to self-fund.

Costs can also be reduced by self-funding in states where insured plans must be community-rated instead of experience-rated. If the organization chose to be fully insured, higher community-rating premiums would be required. If yours is an organization with younger, healthier employees, community rating means that your organization will subsidize the higher-cost groups in your geographic area.

Another area of increased control for self-funded companies is that networks of providers can be selected independently and not as part of an insured package. There are physicians and facilities who choose not to participate with insurance carriers and MCOs, because of their payment rates and their policies. By working directly with providers, a self-funded plan has more leverage, and more freedom of choice among providers. As a result, plan members may have better access to doctors, hospitals, and specialists.

Provider relations with a self-funded plan are enhanced when payments to providers are prompter and less complicated than they might be with an insured plan. The self-funded plan can ensure prompt payment by requiring contractually that the administrator pay claims within a turnaround time of ten days to two weeks. Most third-party administrators are mid-sized organizations that provide dedicated service staff who are familiar with plan provisions and provider arrangements, who can assist providers when they call with payment or service issues.

In a self-funded plan, your organization should ask for employee involvement in provider relations. You can ask for feedback through regular channels when a problem occurs with a provider, and you can encourage plan members to ask their physicians to join the self-funded network.

Employee Services

Plan members often receive improved services through self-funding. The employer has more control over services with an administrator that is directly contracted and that follows the plan's requirements for service to plan members. Self-funded plans usually have more communication with employees about the plan, as part of managing plan costs and encouraging appropriate use of benefits. Self-funded plans are more likely to offer wellness and preventive health programs to reduce the cost of catastrophic and chronic illness. They are also more inclined to provide case management and self-care services that can reduce cost and improve employee satisfaction with benefits at the same time.

■ SAFEGUARDS FOR SELF-FUNDING

What happens if the employer runs out of money? The employer is responsible for the claims incurred during the plan year, just as an insurance carrier is when a plan is insured. There are safeguards, including the purchase of stop-loss insurance, which insures the plan for claims that exceed plan funds. In addition to stop-loss coverage, many employers limit their self-funded exposure by insuring a part of their plan, often the most costly part, the hospitalization portion.

The premium equivalent, or the amount to be set aside for claims and other costs on a monthly basis for each plan member, is developed carefully to ensure that enough funds are available to meet expenses. Actuarial services are used for premium development to account for the complex variables of medical trends, enrollment changes, legislative impact, technological advances, and so forth. Some self-funded plans establish a reserve fund to cover excess costs when they occur.

Because losses are the responsibility of your organization, self-funded plans are closely monitored and evaluated throughout the year. No one wants the surprise of a huge outstanding debt at year end.

Plan Regulation

Federal and some state statutes regulate self-funded plans. There are, however, fewer overall regulations, because federal ERISA legislation takes precedence over state law and so is the primary regulation that governs self-funded plans. A self-funded health plan can be subject to employee contracts, multiemployer trust agreements, pooling contracts, labor law for union welfare plans, and some state regulations.

A self-funded plan deducts premium equivalents and plan cost as an operating expense on the same basis as an insured health plan. As such, the plan is subject to the Internal Revenue Service regulations for tax filing and reporting. Surcharges on medical services established by each state may apply to self-funded plans that pay for care provided in the state. Your plan administrator will be aware of these state laws and how they apply to your plan.

■ PLAN ADMINISTRATION

The sponsor for self-funded plans is usually the employer, who is responsible for administrative and other services for the plan. Many self-funded plans are sponsored by labor unions under the Taft-Hartley Act, which regulates their operation. When a pool, multiemployer trust, or union fund is involved, plan administration is the responsibility of the sponsoring entity, subject to a plan agreement with each employer or group. These plans are usually run by a board of trustees or directors, which reports to the membership.

The most common type of administration is a third-party administrator who specializes in claims processing, reporting, and plan services to self-funded health plans. These companies are usually regional and may provide claims processing and other services for health plans, dental plans, vision plans, and pharmacy benefits, as well as for related self-funded plans such as disability or workers compensation programs.

Some self-funded plans contract with insurance carriers under administrative-services-only (ASO) contracts to provide claims and other services to the plan. The advantage of using a carrier or MCO to administer your plan is the use of its provider networks and its recognition by employees and providers. When ASO plans are implemented, employees are often not aware that the plan has become self-funded because the administrator is an insurance organization. This can be a transitional form of administration when employees or management are uneasy with self-funding.

Other self-funded plans hire and train internal staff and self-administer their health plans. Generally, large employers and union welfare funds are most likely to self-administer health plans. It is complex to self-administer, because of legislation, regulations, the legal environment, and changes in the health care industry that require detailed knowledge and expertise. Administration of a self-funded health plan relies more and more on computerization and technically competent staff, making it expensive to self-administer.

■ SPECIAL NEEDS OF SELF-FUNDED PLANS

A self-funded plan has responsibilities that an insured plan doesn't. As a result, there are certain requirements that need to be met, such as setting up a procedure for claims appeal and claims review. When a plan member believes the administrator is wrong in processing or denying a claim, there are rules to follow in insured plans that are regulated by state insurance departments. The self-funded plan has to institute its own appeal process. Exhibit 12-4 is an example of a procedural guide used by a self-funded plan to govern its claims review process for plan members. Exhibit 12-5 is a description of the claims appeal process as it appears in an employee benefit booklet.

The Claims Administrator will provide a written explanation of benefits (EOB) showing the calculation of the total amount payable, charges not payable, and the reason therefor if the claim is denied in whole or in part.

A claimant, or his duly authorized representative, may appeal the denial of a claim by written request to the Claims Administrator within 60 days after the EOB has been received. This request should include any such additional information and comments supportive of the appeal. The Claims Administrator may request additional information from the claimant and physician and or a review by the Plan's Managed Care Agency for further consideration of the claim. The Claims Administrator shall respond in writing as to the results of this First-Level Appeal to the appellant within 60 days of receipt of the request for review. The response shall clearly identify the specific reason(s) for the decision with the appropriate reference(s) to the Plan Document. The appellant will be notified in writing of any delays in the appeals review processes, including the reason(s) for the delay.

Upon receipt of the decision from the First-Level Appeal, the claimant or his duly authorized representative may request a Second-Level Appeal by written request to the Plan Administrator (Risk Management Officer). The claim will be reviewed by an Appeals Subcommittee of the HBAC (Health Benefits Advisory Committee) within 30 days. The claimant or his duly authorized representative may appear before the Appeals Subcommittee to present the appeal. The appellant will be notified of the Appeals Subcommittee's decision within 30 days of its review. The appellant will be notified in writing of any delays in the appeals review processes, including the reason(s) for the delay. All decisions by the Appeals Subcommittee are final and binding.

If you are a member of a collective bargaining unit you may utilize any grievance process available to you in the unit after the completing of the Second-Level Appeal.

EXHIBIT 12-4. Sample claims appeal process. (Source: Halo Associates.)

Plan oversight or monitoring is another special need for the self-funded plan. This can be handled by a committee established to review health plan performance or by a management team and dedicated staff that work with the plan administrator and advisers.

Self-funded plans require plan advisers who are specialists. In some cases, these are provided by the carrier who administers the plan for the organization. Usually these services are contracted directly by the organization and include a benefits consultant, plan administrator, and legal and actuarial experts.

How to Appeal a Claim

In the event a claim has been denied, in whole or in part, you can request a review of your claim. This request for review should be sent to . . . within 60 days after you receive notice of denial of the claim. When requesting a review, please state the reason you believe the claim was improperly denied and submit any data, questions or comments you deem appropriate.

If the claim is denied by the process stated above, the appeal can be submitted to the . . . Insurance Appeal Committee within 30 days for a final determination.

Legal Actions

You may not sue on your health claim before 60 days after proof of loss has been given to the Plan. You may not sue after 3 years from the time proof of loss is required unless the law in the area where you live allows a longer period of time.

EXHIBIT 12-5. Sample description of claims appeal process from an employee handbook. (Source: Halo Associates.)

■ FACTORS IN DECIDING TO SELF-FUND

If you intend to self-fund your health plan, you will have to select specialists to assist with its implementation and operation and arrange for a team of staff and representatives from your organization who will help monitor plan activities. There are experienced companies and consultants who can assist you if you decide to self-fund. This type of health plan is definitely more work for your organization. The decision to self-fund should be carefully considered from many aspects before it is undertaken. Your motives, goals, and organizational characteristics should be examined as part of your decision.

For a long time, it was a prudent rule of thumb that self-funding for any organization under 1,000 employees was too risky. Gradually, increased experience with self-funding, and development of stop-loss insurance products has allowed smaller organizations to self-fund. Rapidly rising health insurance premiums have caused more organizations to consider taking a chance on self-funding. In addition, services and support professionals developed more fully and achieved a track record that is reassuring to the smaller organization. As a result, the threshold for self-funding has dropped to 500 employees and even lower. Today it's not uncommon for an employer with 100 employees to be partly or completely self-funded, with appropriate stop-loss coverage. It's not every employer, regardless of size or stop-loss coverage, who should self-fund. You should examine your organization critically for telling features and traits that affect the decision to self-fund.

Employer Motivation

The primary reason for self-funding is to reduce health plan cost; a secondary reason is to exert more control over the plan, its benefits, and administration. Historically, close to 30 percent of employers have chosen a health plan on the basis of cost; a 1998 survey by the Washington Business Group on Health confirms this. Other motivations include quality of care, employee satisfaction, access to health care services, and effective administration.

Employer Goals

You should set forth what you expect to accomplish, overall and year to year, with a self-funded plan. It may be apparent when you initiate a self-funded plan that you want to reduce cost, or improve service, or correct a plan design that isn't meeting your needs. But, as you proceed over the years, it is helpful to establish concrete goals for the plan that reflect its activity, the health care marketplace, and your organization's needs. Exhibit 12-6 is a sample statement of short-term and longer-term goals for a self-funded plan.

Size

Although the threshold for self-funding is lower today, around 100–500 employees, it is also dependent on the demographics of your employees. If your workforce is younger, it may be to your advantage to self-fund. If you have little or no chronic or catastrophic illness among your workforce, you also have an advantage. As your workforce ages, or has more long-term illness, you are at greater risk for higher losses in a self-funded plan, because it draws on a smaller pool of premium dollars than a fully insured plan. Your high-cost claims are absorbed by the larger pool of covered members in an insured plan, even though you may be assessed for some part of your excess losses through experience rating by the carrier.

EXHIBIT 12-6. Sample statement of plan goals. (Source: Halo Associates.)

Stability

Stability refers to your employee turnover rate and the financial stability of your organization. If your employees stay less than three years, you may find it hard to accurately project health plan expenses, and this can be a detriment to managing a self-funded plan. If your organization is not stable, with regular, dependable cash flow and capital, you will not be able to fund your plan reliably and to maintain the fund balance needed to ensure that claims will be paid. Your health plan is a long-term commitment, which requires stability throughout its operation.

Experience and Utilization of Benefits

You need to look at your health plan expenses for claims and other costs over the past three years before making any decision about self-funding your plan. You should not self-fund if:

- Your costs fluctuated wildly
- You had several high-cost claims

- Your costs were higher than average costs for any benefit category, such as hospitalization, major medical, or drugs, or for your total costs
- Your plan is a rich one with extravagant benefits that cannot be easily changed, or if you are not interested in changing them
- Your workforce is older, you cover a substantial number of retirees, or you have employees who have chronic or catastrophic conditions

When you self-fund, you want to be fairly certain that your costs will not exceed the amount you budget. Each of the red flags noted can indicate excessive costs, which are hard to project and are likely to exceed the cost of an insured plan.

As a case in point, your percentage of retirees may be an important factor. Typically, retirees under age 65 cost your plan between eight and twenty times the health claims costs of active employees, depending on their health status. This improves when they become eligible for Medicare but then gradually changes for the worse as they age further. To reduce the cost to a self-funded plan, you may opt to enact a transfer to managed care for your retirees, which can limit your cost and still allow you to provide them with coverage.

Location

If you have offices in multiple states, self-funding can simplify your plan and avoid state requirements, as described earlier. It is less costly to provide the same benefits to all employees than to offer several plans. Whether your organization is located in a rural, urban, or suburban setting or in a variety of these, you should evaluate the effect of geography and location on your health plan.

If you are in a rural location, you may be in a good geographic area for a self-funded plan, since rural areas have limited managed care plans and generally offer a lower level of benefits than more populated areas. Your employees will be less likely to expect enriched benefits, retiree coverage, and quality specialty services. You can negotiate with local providers more readily in a rural area, because you are a relatively large employer and there are fewer providers there.

An urban setting might also lend itself to self-funding. Self-funded plans are common among union welfare plans, which are often based in urban areas where there are adequate plan services available and existing networks accustomed to self-funded groups. If yours is a city-based organization, self-funding can make you more competitive with other employers because of good member services and an employee-oriented attitude.

Internal Staff and Employee Relations

You need to determine if you have adequate management and support staff to provide a self-funded plan to employees. You should list the additional work tasks, such as employee communication, monitoring and supervision of plan administrators and advisers, coordination with departments of personnel, finance, and legal, and planning activities. Then you should identify who will be responsible for these activities and determine whether you are comfortable with the resources available to you.

It is crucial to have the support of top management and of employee representatives when you initiate a self-funded plan. I have consulted with benefit managers and employers who explored self-funding only to find resistance from management or employees that slowed down or stopped the process. You can avoid this situation by including employees in the process at each step of the way and making sure top managers and decision makers are open-minded or favorable.

It's easier to get support when you are armed with information about costs and the advantages of self-funding to your organization. You should enlist health plan advisers, insurance professionals, and colleagues who understand self-funding during your initial determination of whether such a plan can work for your organization. Basically, you should do your homework before you seek support.

Financial Resources

Funding is a key consideration. If you don't have the financial resources to establish a fund for health plan costs, don't even start. You can determine roughly how much you will need by assuming an amount equal to your current annual health insurance cost. It's not every business that has the funds to pay a year's worth of premiums up front. In some cases, when a stable, reliable cash flow business wants to self-fund, the amount allocated to begin the fund is limited to three months in advance. This reduces the cash-flow demand on the organization's resources; however, it shouldn't be undertaken unless funding is readily available from reserves or income throughout the year.

Most self-funded plans realize a cash-flow advantage the first year, but the funds that are captured as a result should be dedicated to claims payments in the future. The apparent cash-flow savings are the result of diminished claims payments for services provided but not yet billed. These outstanding liabilities result in a chronic two- to three-month lag for the self-funded plan. These liabilities will have to be paid as run-off or lag claims if the self-funded plan is terminated or you transfer back to an insured plan.

Self-funding is not an exact science, and monthly needs for capital fluctuate, sometimes widely. It's a normal occurrence in the self-funded plan. Some months you will have relatively few inpatient hospital stays, and other months they will be numerous. A few high-cost claims can throw your "normal" expenses out of whack for several months or longer. In self-funding, this fluctuating need for funds reflects what we call "blips" in experience. As peaks and valleys occur, you should plan to have a constant fund cover costs and not expect operating capital to meet monthly costs that rise and fall with the vagaries of utilization.

Additional expenses for administration, plan advisers, and stop-loss insurance can be covered separately from operating expenses, or you can include them in the health plan fund. You should make monthly payments for these services and budget accordingly.

External Resources

You should be aware of the resources needed for a self-funded plan, and, before you self-fund, you should know whether plan administrators, advisers, stop-loss carriers, and other specialists are readily available to your organization. These are necessary outside resources who will make the difference in whether your plan operates efficiently.

You may be in an area where there are few or no such services. You should take the time to identify potential advisers by contacting large consulting firms, your yellow pages, and insurance professionals who serve your organization. There are fees and charges for these services that need to be considered in your total budget for a self-funded plan. You will need to coordinate the time frames for evaluation, recommendation, and implementation that are required by each of your advisors and plan services. Plan management, facilitated by your work with outside advisers, is your major responsibility for a self-funded plan. You should give their selection and relationship to one another your primary attention if you decide to self-fund.

■ THE LONG HAUL

If, as you read the characteristics listed in the previous section, you concluded that self-funding needs seem to match your organization, you may be a good candidate to sponsor a self-funded health plan. Keep in mind that the goals of self-funding take several years to be realized. A self-funded health plan requires a sizable investment from your organization of both staff and money. You need to establish a fund, prepare communications, adopt administrative procedures, and contract with various services and advisers.

Although you will experience short-term cash flow savings, the real advantages will vary year to year and be most evident over the long term. It will take three to five years to develop a pattern of reduced cost and to compare the self-funded plan with others to measure its relative merits. As with any variable program, your self-funded plan will have some years that are outstanding and some that are marginal or disappointing. The key is to understand the long-term nature of this financing method and to track its performance over time.

Self-funding is a long-term, not a short-term, commitment.

■ HOW TO IMPLEMENT A SELF-FUNDED PLAN

My goal in this section is to give you an outline of action that starts with your plan benefits and moves on, step by step, to the startup of a self-funded plan for your organization.

You should have a reasonable timetable for implementation. As a general rule, the process will require sixty to ninety days from when you have selected your administrator, which should occur about sixty to ninety days after you have decided to self-fund. Totally, you are looking at four to six months for implementation.

How to implement a self-funded plan is the subject of volumes of books and writings, and this is not meant to be a complete, detailed text. You can be guided by the discussion, checklists, and illustrations presented, but if you need more detail, there are several excellent resources for further information listed in the Appendix.

■ BENEFITS UNDER A SELF-FUNDED PLAN

You have the same three areas of concern in a self-funded plan that exist with any plan design: coverage, procedures for administration, and providers. If your goal is to keep coverage or benefits exactly the same but to realize the cash-flow and cost-saving aspects of a self-funded plan, there is no need to make any changes in benefits.

Once the decision has been made to keep benefits the same, your implementation should include:

1. *Selection of a plan administrator and plan adviser.* Follow the procedure outlined in Chapter 4.

2. *Internal training and communication.* You need to alert your staff, other managers, and your employees about the change. The process of decision should have resulted in

some activity and cooperation on the part of your staff and other managers, such as their natural involvement in the selection process of a plan adviser and administrator. Ongoing updates, memorandums, and reports on progress and on implementation are good ways to keep everyone in the loop.

You should prioritize internal training of benefits staff. Your plan administrator and adviser can assist with on-site training and review and provide off-site support through telephone contact, by fax, and written materials. Training is required for enrollment and eligibility procedures to be implemented by your staff. The original census of plan members is provided by your staff to the administrator in advance, and monthly updates are furnished to reflect those who are added or deleted from the plan each month. The other responsibilities of your benefits staff will be to send notices to employees on COBRA, FMLA, disability and Medicare eligibility, termination rights, and claims appeals. Some of these responsibilities can be delegated to your plan administrator, and some are a continuation of staff's current duties with your insured health plan.

Communication to all employees should include distribution of plan materials at the onset of the plan. You can provide advance notice in announcements and memorandums, depending on your employee relations and your time frame.

3. *Plan materials.* Plan documents, most often furnished by the plan administrator, are reviewed and possibly amended by your plan adviser or health insurance professional. These include:

- User-ready plan booklets, personalized for your organization.
- Individual identification cards printed with each member's name, ID number, and plan information on penalties and restrictions.
- Claim forms to be provided directly to plan members, to personnel offices, and to other employee offices to make a supply readily available as needed.
- Enrollment forms and new employee packets to be kept on hand in the benefits or personnel office. You may opt to reenroll all employees when you implement a self-funded plan. The enrollment forms will update information on dependents and employees so that eligibility is verified and coordination of benefits with other plans is facilitated.
- Marketing materials to encourage enrollment in the plan. These may be provided by the administrator or your plan adviser or developed by your staff. They may be announcements or brochures that describe special services or features of your self-funded plan. Exhibit 12-7 is a sample marketing brochure used to describe a point of service option added to a self-funded plan.
- Network provider listing. A listing of providers, by specialty, geographic location, and alphabetical order, is usually provided to plan members to identify participating providers they are encouraged to use. If an outside network is used, it may furnish you with the listing and marketing material about the network for distribution to your employees. If your plan administrator provides the network, these materials may come from it. If you develop your own network, the network listing and description of its use should be developed and provided by you with the help of your plan adviser and plan administrator. Exhibit 12-8 shows a section of a provider listing from a self-funded plan where the network is provided by the plan administrator.

4. *Voluntary services.* You should have available and distribute any descriptions, claim forms, and procedural guides on voluntary services such as mail-order drug programs, prescription drug cards, case management, nurse call centers, wellness discounts, and clinic services. These are in addition to your benefit booklet, ID card, and standard enrollment and claim form.

We've Got You Covered...

With All the Basics, Plus!

We cover your doctor:

Freedom of Choice
- ❖ No need to ask for permission to see a doctor of your choice
- ❖ Self-referral when you want it
- ❖ All local, out of area, and specialty doctors covered

We cover your specialists:

Specialty Services include
- ❖ Chiropractic
- ❖ Outpatient Mental Health visits
- ❖ Well Child Care in network
- ❖ All immunizations
- ❖ Patient Advocacy available for chronic and catastrophic illness
- ❖ Hospice Care
- ❖ At-Home Care
- ❖ All medical/surgical specialists
- ❖ Specialized therapies

We cover your lab and testing needs:

- ❖ Low cost to you for quality testing and lab work
- ❖ Select lab or testing services of your choice
- ❖ All local, out of area and specialty services covered

We cover your hospital costs—anywhere:

- ❖ Full hospitalization at local and out of area hospitals
- ❖ Specialty hospitals covered
- ❖ No restriction on choice of hospitals
- ❖ Advance notification required
- ❖ Patient Advocacy service available for inpatients.
- ❖ Discharge planning assistance
- ❖ Same-day surgery

We cover you for prescription drugs:

Convenient Rx drugs by mail
- ❖ Receive up to a 90-day supply
- ❖ Prompt delivery for chronic and long-term drugs
- ❖ Copayment of $3/generic for up to a 3-month supply
- ❖ Toll free number for service
- ❖ Pharmacist on call to answer questions

Rx drugs at the pharmacy:
- ❖ Drug card for pharmacies nationwide
- ❖ Low copayment $3/generic and $5 or $8 for brand drugs
- ❖ Over 95% of local and out of area pharmacies included
- ❖ Convenient prescription services where, and when you need them

EXHIBIT 12-7. Sample marketing brochure for employees. (Sources: Halo Associates and Dutchess County Office of Risk Management, Poughkeepsie, NY.)

When Benefits Change

If you want to change the benefits or have negotiated a change to be implemented with the self-funded plan, additional activities are needed. They include the following:

1. Check that plan booklets, ID cards, claim forms, and enrollment forms reflect any changes in procedures, coverage, or eligibility. Any new penalties, such as preadmission certification or discharge planning requirements, should be plainly stated and noticeable.
2. Be sure to include summaries of material modifications on every change if your plan booklet is not reprinted and to add the change to your one-sheet comparison of coverage used in open enrollment.

DERMATOPATHOLOGY

**Dermatopathology Associates
of New York**
1634 Hering Avenue
Bronx, NY 10461
(212) 829-2045

DIABETES

James Hellerman, MD
200 South Broadway
Tarrytown, NY 10591
(914) 631-9300

Cecil S. Kim, MD
Medical Arts Building
450 Gidney Avenue
Newburgh, NY 12550
(914) 562-2323

Jerry Kleinbaum, MD
1985 Crompond Road
Yorktown Heights, NY 10566
(914) 736-1100

**Middletown Community
Health Center**
27 West Main Street
Middletown, NY 10940
(914) 343-7614

Poughkeepsie Medical Group
375 Hooker Avenue
PO Box 3050
Poughkeepsie, NY 12603
(914) 454-5005

Daniel A. Sherber, MD, FACP
140 Lockwood Avenue
New Rochelle, NY 10801
(914) 636-5110

DURABLE MEDICAL EQUIPMENT

Ortho Bracing Systems Ltd.
3549 James Street
Shrub Oak, NY 10588
(914) 245-3112

EMERGENCY MED/INTENSIVE CARE

Danny Abbruzzese, MD
Arden Hill Hospital
Goshen, NY 10924
(914) 245-8935

Nora Varsano Aharon, MD
12 Greenridge Avenue
White Plains, NY 10601
(914) 682-0777

Luis F. Villamon, MD
222 Fishkill Avenue
Beacon, NY 12506
(914) 831-6100

FAMILY PRACTICE

Mohammad Ansari, MD
North Avenue
PO Box 678
Pleasant Valley, NY 12569
(914) 635-8789

Elio Argenziano, MD
65 South Highland Avenue
Ossining, NY 10562
(914) 941-3822

Peter Geigley, MD
Arden Hill Hospital
Goshen, NY 10924
(914) 245-8935

Health First Medical Care
375 White Plains Road
Eastchester, NY 10709
(914) 793-3300

Anne Lee, MD
Health First Medical Care
375 White Plains Road
Eastchester, NY 10709
(914) 793-3300

Thomas A. Arminio, MD
100 South Highland Avenue
Ossining, NY 10562
(914) 941-6262

Robert James Athans, MD
21 Meadow Avenue
Bronxville, NY 10708
(914) 337-5410

Pasquale D. Baratta, MD
Route 371, PO Box 14
Damascus, PA 18415
(717) 224-4181

Saul Blecher, MD
6 Pelton Street
Monticello, NY 12701
(914) 794-6100

John D. Cahill, MD
4000 Seton Avenue
Bronx, NY 10466
(212) 324-5408

ENDOCRINOLOGY & METABOLISM

Alfredo D'Ascanio, MD
1 South Greeley Avenue
Chappaqua, NY 10514
(914) 238-0801

James Hellerman, MD
200 South Broadway
Tarrytown, NY 10591
(914) 631-9300

Daniel P. Hoffman, MD
375 Hooker Avenue
Poughkeepsie, NY 12603
(914) 454-5000

Alan B. Kantor, MD
1974 Maplehill Street
Yorktown Heights, NY 10598
(914) 245-1111

Marc J. Condren, MD
Somers Family Health Care
Route 100, Box 367
Somers, NY 10589
(914) 277-8271

D*O*C*S
2001 Central Park Avenue
Yonkers, NY 10710
(914) 793-0001

Richard J. Daboul, MD
Professional Bldg., Route 97
PO Box 190
Barryville, NY 12719
(914) 557-6411

Robert H. Ezerman, MD
66A Pearl Street
Essex Junction, VT 05452
(802) 879-1234

EXHIBIT 12-8. Sample list of network providers. (Source: Halo Associates.)

3. Train your staff about the change and discuss how it affects their work and how it affects plan members. If you aren't sure, have your plan administrator or adviser present the change to your staff and to answer questions.
4. Convey all changes to your plan administrator in writing, with the request that the claims processors and customer service representatives, who deal with your employees, be advised of the change and its impact on plan members.
5. If provider access has changed or you have a different network, be sure to have sufficient quantities of provider listings available. If the procedure for using the network has changed, convey that to plan members with the new listing.

The underlying concept of implementation in a self-funded plan is to keep everyone informed. There should be a seamless continuum of service to your employees from your staff and from those who service your plan. Once you establish good lines of communication, it is your job to keep them open and functional. Exhibit 12-9 is an implementation checklist that covers the myriad small details you need to address when you start a self-funded plan.

In advance of following this list for plan implementation, you should have already moved forward with a self-funded plan by completing these activities:

- Select vendors, including administration firm(s), plan advisers.
- Alert benefit and support staff to timetable.
- Meet with vendors and develop a checklist of activities for them and for you.
- Negotiate and sign contracts with administrative and advisory vendors.

Three months prior to implementation:
1. Establish effective date for plan startup.
2. List contact persons, telephone, addresses for plan vendors, and provide them with relevant information about your staff and organization.
3. Enrollment checklist:
   a. Method for initial and subsequent enrollment (i.e., cards, computer tape)
   b. Information provided with enrollment data, preferably copy of census and current enrollment forms
   c. Codes needed for enrollment record (i.e., locations, divisions, bargaining units)
   d. Target date for enrollment process, including dates on which you require plan materials to be delivered
   e. Miscellaneous enrollment needs
4. Identification cards:
   a. Group name and number to appear on cards
   b. Managed care and/or PPO component and language for ID cards
   c. Target date for completion
   d. To be shipped to _____
5. Claim forms checklist:
   a. Type of form to be used, from variety available
   b. Colors to be used in printing
   c. Target date for delivery and to whom
6. Summary Plan Description (SPD) checklist:
   a. Content of basic text for benefits under the plan
   b. Current coverage and managed care incentives or restrictions
   c. Special provisions for coverage, financial penalties or copayments
   d. Plan changes and how they are to be included; modifications during the plan year and the procedure for notification and amendments
   e. Target date for approval of SPD and printing/delivery dates, including who has final approval, the approval process, and deadlines for delivery

(*continues*)

EXHIBIT 12-9. List of start-up activities for a self-funded plan. (Source: Halo Associates.)

7. Financial Procedures checklist:
   a. Client liaison for expenditure reporting, including the contact name(s), telephone, address, and fax
   b. Bank arrangements, including name of bank, account if available, and any terms or conditions related to the bank used
   c. Account specifications and signature, including who signs checks and the appropriate procedure to open the account
   d. Check reconciliation procedure, including the timing and manner in which records are forwarded, reviewed, and approved
   e. Target date for check printing and procedure to be followed for approvals
8. Claim History and Deductibles checklist:
   a. Current administrator, name, contact, address, telephone
   b. Required data and format
      __ Date, Employee, Social Security Number, Patient, Charge, Amount Paid, Date of Service, Provider, Diagnosis or CPT Code
      __ Deductible for Individual and Family for plan year
      __ Carry-Over Deductible (from _____ to _____)
      __ Out-Of-Pocket Costs (specify below if more than one type)
   c. Target date for transmittal of data to new administrator, including who is responsible to follow up that it is transmitted
9. Claims Transition checklist:
   a. Date present administrator will cease paying claims
   b. Target date for forwarding of claims to new administrator
   c. Time required for input of deductibles and other out-of-pocket provisions
   d. Target date for new administrator to pay claims
10. Notification to major providers checklist:
    a. Provider names and addresses (copy of latest 1099 if available)
    b. Target date for such notification, including who should be responsible for preparation and distribution of such notification
11. Stop-Loss Insurance checklist:
    a. Specific excess insurance terms and deductible. Include any census, claims history, high-cost claim reports, or other details to be furnished to stop-loss carrier by new administrator throughout the plan year
    b. Aggregate excess insurance terms and attachment point. Include any reports or tracking required by the carrier throughout the year. Clarify the notification process to the carrier and who is responsible for same.
    c. Premium transmittal and payment agreement, including binder amount and subsequent payments, if applicable. (This is relevant if the new administrator is the agent or broker for the stop-loss coverage to be bought for the plan.)
12. Specific administrative activity checklist:
    a. Flexible spending accounts, including MSAs, Flex 125, etc.
    b. COBRA implementation and responsibility
    c. Disability and leave of absence notification and coverage, including how notification is made to administrator, and responsibilities for collection of premium, verification of continued coverage, etc.
    d. FMLA responsibilities
    e. HIPAA responsibilities
    f. 800 # services required of administrator, including managed care counseling.
    g. Prescription drug card, mail order drug plan, and other coverage that may be provided by a different vendor with whom the administrator needs to coordinate claims payment, money transfers, or reporting
13. Installation and administration fee transmittal
    a. Set up fee or advance payments required for expenses or installation, such as printing costs, bank fees, service fees, etc. and whether they are to be deducted from the plan's fund and reported by the administrator, or billed and paid separately by the plan sponsor.
    b. Administrative fees, including how frequently they are billed, and under what terms, to clarify payment cycles, and when additional fees are appropriate, including the procedure to bill and collect payment for same.

EXHIBIT 12-9. Continued

■ ADMINISTRATIVE AND ADVISORY SERVICES

You should establish a specific timetable for implementation when you hire an administrative or advisory firm for your self-funded plan. These professionals should assist you with each step and be held accountable for plan materials, training, and implementation activities. To work most effectively with them, you should:

- Establish a regular meeting schedule, at least weekly with your plan adviser or administrator. This is your opportunity to ask questions, approve materials, make suggestions, transmit documents, and develop a working relationship.
- Require your review and written approval for any plan documents to be delivered. This will protect you from costly printed mistakes that reflect on your organization and that can cause a delay in your delivery of printed materials.

You must take some specific actions to implement administration:

- Prepare a contractual agreement, in keeping with your specifications and including any performance standards on which you have agreed. This sometimes requires more time than you think and should be pursued to completion before the plan is implemented.
- Prepare other agreements with ancillary vendors or providers, including networks, consultants, and other services needed for the plan (e.g., a prescription drug administrator, case management firm). The various professionals who work on your plan will coordinate their efforts through you, since each is contracted directly with you. Some plans delegate ancillary services, and subcontracting for them, to the plan administrator. These services are then selected and supervised outside your direct control.
- Decide on funding and finance procedures and mechanisms. Selecting a bank, printing checks, and establishing a procedure for replenishment of your health plan fund— these are the nuts and bolts of a self-funded plan.

You may want the administrator to do it all and to keep your involvement to responding to requests for more funds and reviewing plan financial reports, or you may want to have the administrator use a local bank of your choice, arrange to print the checks through them, and send benefit checks to you for signature. You should require a check register and accounting review prior to approval of requests for funds. The exact procedure you follow will depend on your organization's philosophy and staffing. It will also reflect your management style—more or less restrictive.

Administrative Control

When there are multiple administrators and plan services, some may be subcontracted to your plan administrator, and some may be accountable directly to you. This bears discussion, because it has a lot to do with your ability to monitor performance and to manage effectively.

The role of the plan administrator can be narrow or broad. It is not uncommon for the plan administrator to broker the stop-loss insurance, to provide an outside actuary for premium projection and valuation, to provide a legal specialist in benefits when needed, and to provide medical peer review of claims decisions. There are also plan administrators who have competent health benefits consultants on staff and who normally provide all consulting services to plans they administer. Some administrators provide claims appeal review and claims auditing services. It is increasingly common to see plan administrators who include preadmission certification, utilization review, and discharge planning among their services. Some provide case management and network referral services.

If you can one-stop shop, why not? In some cases, it's a good idea. For example, if you are a small organization for whom it is marginal to be self-funded, the additional work of coordinating multiple administrators and advisers may not be for you. When you rely solely on one administrator, though, it is vital that your selection process and supervision be thorough. It's as if you put all your eggs in one basket, so watch that basket.

If you are a mid-sized organization or have in-house expertise in benefits, you may want to have more control over your self-funded health plan. For some aspects of health plan management, transferring total control to an outside administrator is like having the fox watch the hen house. I recommend that you keep some functions separate from your administrator, including these:

- Claims audit to determine accuracy and appropriateness of claims processing and payments. Industry standard calls for 97–99 percent accuracy in adjudication and payments
- Case management services to negotiate discounts, counsel patients on necessary services, and coordinate care with several medical providers
- Actuarial review of plan costs, trends, and projection of premiums
- Claim appeals when the payment of a claim is in dispute
- Consulting services to determine if the plan is performing properly and efficiently

There are other administrative services that should automatically be part of the claims processing and reporting activity included in a contract when an administrator is hired. Some of these are:

- Legal benefits advice, within reason
- Consulting when it determines cash-flow needs and claims payments that the administrator does as part of daily work
- Medical peer review of questionable claims or disputed claims for which the administrator decision must be justified
- Referrals to participating providers and provider relations to resolve problems with fee payments
- Preadmission certification, utilization review, and discharge planning when they are part of the notification or coverage requirements of your plan

I expect that your contract and scope of services for a health plan administrator will include the basics of paying claims and providing reports but also the related services that will keep your plan running efficiently. This is different from having one firm run the show singlehandedly. You should balance the administrator's role, your ability to supervise and manage, and ancillary services.

Although most administrators know a lot about self-funded health plans and the problems that occur, I don't think it's good business to have your health plan managed completely by a single, subjective viewpoint. It will limit your possibilities for new ideas and improved services, and it will result in fewer checks and balances. The administrator, for example, will approach a problem of whether to expand a network from the perspective of how it will affect administrative services, not how it will enhance the plan for members or improve your employee relations. The administrator may have ongoing relationships with certain networks or earn commissions from certain networks that can affect its objectivity. I worked with one administrator who refused to work with a large hospital network. Every time we checked on hospital discounts from the network, we found that the administrator had negotiated directly for higher payments rather than going through the network.

When it comes to high-cost claims, it's difficult if not impossible for the administrator to have a case-management approach toward coordinating services and providing patient advocacy. Remember, the administrator has a mission to scrutinize claims costs and to reduce and eliminate services. In one instance, the focus is on the claim; in the other, it is on the patient and the patient's welfare. They are not mutually exclusive, since most case management nurses also reduce cost and unnecessary utilization. It is a matter of perspective and goals.

Insurance Safeguards

Depending on your claims experience, which you should review before deciding to self-fund, you may be prudent to purchase certain types of insurance when you self-fund. There are different methods to safeguard your organization's assets from catastrophic health plan losses.

Limited Self-Funding

You can limit the amount and scope of your self-funded plan to only some benefits. For instance, you can self-fund only major medical and purchase an insured plan for drug coverage and hospitalization. If your experience shows that your major medical costs are moderate, this should save you substantial money and yet provide you with a comprehensive health plan.

Another combination of self-funding and insurance is a self-funded employer deductible. In this plan, the employer assumes a deductible, on top of the member's deductible, thereby reducing the health plan premium. For instance, if your employees have a $200 deductible annually and you assume an employer deductible up to the first $2,000 of claims, you will pay up to $1,800 each year for a plan member after the patient deductible is met. In exchange, the insurance company will cover all claims higher than $2,000 a year for a greatly reduced premium. A small client of mine in New York City arranged this program and saved almost 60 percent of the health plan premium. Unfortunately, as the workforce aged, the program was not viable. It is suitable for a healthy, younger group where few higher cost claims occur.

Catastrophic Insurance

You can insure almost anything, and this insurance proves that maxim. Stop-loss insurance is the primary type of insurance purchased by self-funded plans to safeguard against catastrophic loss. There are two types, aggregate and specific stop-loss, and a plan sponsor can purchase one or the other, or neither of them. They are sold by carriers approved by each state, under terms established by the state. The regulatory body for this type of insurance is the state insurance department.

Specific Stop Loss. Specific stop-loss insurance places a maximum limit on each plan member, beyond which the stop-loss insurance pays for all claims for the year. The limit is called an attachment point, being the dollar amount at which the stop-loss insurance begins to pay. Once claims exceed that amount, the stop-loss carrier and not the self-funded plan pays the balance.

When you want to purchase stop-loss insurance, your plan administrator must provide high-cost claim data for the previous three years, such as the simple report shown in Exhibit 12-10. This, with the diagnosis and prognosis, has to be furnished to the stop-loss carrier for review before a premium is quoted. There may be an "actively at work" provision to the policy so that it only covers employees who are at work and not those on disability or sick leave at the time the policy takes effect.

You will also be asked to furnish the stop-loss carrier a complete census, or listing of your plan members and covered dependents, and three years of plan experience in addition to high-cost claims, and a copy of your benefit booklet describing coverage. The cost of your stop-loss policy will be based on your health plan experience, the demographics of your workforce, and the attachment point and coverage level you specify. When there is a higher probability of loss, the stop-loss carrier will quote a higher premium; when a loss seems unlikely or limited, the premium will be lower.

Stop-loss policies are written to cover losses if a claim is incurred during the twelve months of coverage. Payment above the attachment point will then be made to the stop-loss limit. Think about the feasibility of collecting on this basis. Many catastrophic conditions, such as heart disease requiring a transplant, take a long time to diagnose, to identify, to schedule medical services, and to obtain patient consent. Sometimes, the delay is due to availability of services, as in transplants. For many high-cost procedures, it is unlikely that the patient will incur the cost during twelve months of coverage. You might think the patient can collect in the next year. Not always so, with stop-loss coverage.

The insurer tracks high-cost claims throughout the year through reports of all claims over a certain dollar amount, such as $25,000. These reports show the diagnosis, recommended treatment, and prognosis for each high-cost claim. If a covered member is diagnosed and recommended for a high-cost service that is not provided during the stop-loss year, the person can be "carved out" of coverage for subsequent years. Some stop-loss coverage is written on a 12–15 basis, meaning that the member can be diagnosed during the twelve months of the insured year and file claims over a fifteen-month period, allowing an extra three months after the plan year to cover the cost. This makes it more likely that the plan will collect from the stop-loss carrier, but it is still not a lot of time for catastrophic conditions.

Once a patient who requires expensive treatment is carved out of a stop-loss policy, the person becomes the full responsibility of your self-funded plan, subject to your terms of coverage. There are some conditions, such as end-stage renal disease and other disabling conditions, for which government programs such as Medicare and Social Security provide coverage after a time period. You should be aware of these alternatives.

Aggregate Stop-Loss. This type of insurance sets a limit for the group expenses as a whole, after which the stop-loss carrier will pay. A typical limit is 125 percent of anticipated claims cost, although higher limits are available. The higher limit or attachment point you set, the lower your premium.

With aggregate stop loss at 125 percent limit, if your self-funded plan of 100 employees expects to have claims of $200,000 for a year, the stop-loss carrier will pay for all claims after the plan has paid for $250,000 of claims. There is also an upper limit on payment, usually between $1 million and $5 million. Stop-loss carriers call these "layers" of coverage, since the carrier provides coverage from one limit to another, or by layers.

Stop-loss carriers agree to accept your risk of loss, as any insurance carrier does, in return for a premium payment. Underwriting, or analysis of your probability of loss based on your workforce, claims history, and other factors, is a refined art in the stop-loss business.

				ICD-9	
		Claims Paid in Excess of $25,000 for 01/01/9X–11/30/9X			
Claim#	Draft#	Draft Date	Draft Amount	Code	Diagnosis
050634	022734	08/18/93	$52.00CR	721	Musculoskeletal disorder
	021679	01/05/93	$100.20	174	Breast cancer
	021680	01/05/93	$49.00	174	Breast cancer
	022165	01/07/93	$177.90	174	Breast cancer
	022166	01/07/93	$235.00	354	Nervous system disorder
	022733	01/28/93	$50.10	174	Breast cancer
	022734	01/28/93	$101.00	721	Musculoskeletal disorder
	022735	01/28/93	$3,089.00	174	Breast cancer
	023060	02/11/93	$150.40	722	
	023061	02/11/93	$744.50	174	Breast cancer
	023062	02/11/93	$68.80	174	Breast cancer
	023063	02/11/93	$40.00	721	Musculoskeletal disorder
	023064	02/11/93	$40.00	461	
	023415	02/25/93	$1,007.00	174	Breast cancer
	023416	02/25/93	$760.00	723	
	023417	02/25/93	$39.20	174	Breast cancer
	023697	03/11/93	$965.50	789	
	024074	03/25/93	$50.45	285	
	024075	03/25/93	$24.00	285	
	024076	03/25/93	$104.00	722	
	024206	04/08/93	$1,593.00	756	
	024207	04/08/93	$6,776.10	722	
	024437	04/15/93	$12,624.00	721	Musculoskeletal disorder
	024572	04/22/93	$110.00	721	Musculoskeletal disorder
	024722	05/06/93	$53.00	354	Nervous system disorder
	024902	05/13/93	$110.00	721	Musculoskeletal disorder
	024903	05/13/93	$1,377.90	721	Musculoskeletal disorder
	025105	05/27/93	$1,539.50	354	Nervous system disorder
	025106	05/27/93	$55.00	311	
	025317	06/10/93	$40.00	311	
	025318	06/10/93	$590.00	354	Nervous system disorder
	025554	06/24/93	$46.00	174	Breast cancer
	025858	07/08/93	$81.55	611	
	026016	07/22/93	$2,201.95	354	Nervous system disorder
	026017	07/22/93	$198.00	727	
	026018	07/22/93	$52.00	174	Breast cancer

EXHIBIT 12-10. Sample claims record for stop-loss insurance. (Source: Halo Associates.)

Stop-loss pays high commissions, ranging from 10–30 percent of premium. It is sold by brokers, agents, plan advisers, and plan administrators. When you solicit stop-loss bids from your plan advisers and specialists, they should advise you of their commission on the insurance.

Stop-Loss Reserve Fund.   Another safeguard is a home-grown version of stop-loss that I find useful when a self-funded plan is large enough and has adequate resources. The establishment of a stop-loss reserve fund can operate under stop-loss rules to replenish plan funds when a large claim occurs. If such a reserve fund is built up over the first five years of a self-funded plan's operation, it eliminates the necessity for stop-loss coverage. Eventually it will reduce your operating expense, while safeguarding against unforeseen catastrophic claims. For the development of an appropriate reserve amount and the mechanism to create your own stop-loss fund, I suggest you seek the help of a benefits consultant and an actuary.

■ IMPLEMENTATION AND YOUR STAFF

When you implement a self-funded plan, your staff will be directly involved in the daily operation and ongoing plan management activities. Even when plan administration is outsourced, your staff will be more directly involved with claims, plan reports, and confidential information. I recommend that you use a confidentiality agreement as part of your training and management of staff. This will impress upon them the seriousness of member privacy and their responsibility to protect it. Standard language to use for such an agreement is presented in Exhibit 12-11. You should review the language with your legal adviser and amend it to serve the needs of your organization and your health plan. Signed agreements should be kept in your plan management file. Be clear about your intention and the importance of following privacy guidelines in day-to-day plan activities. Your philosophy and commitment to employee privacy and confidentiality will permeate your office and trickle down to employees who are plan members and who may be concerned about this issue.

You should review the following implementation list with your staff and assign duties to them according to their responsibilities and capability. The differences between a self-funded plan and a regular health plan, from your staff's point of view, will be minimal. Changes may involve the following:

1. A full census will be provided at startup to the plan administrator, and the normal monthly updated census will be provided to other carriers or MCOs.
2. ID cards, claim forms, and enrollment forms will be distributed to all employees, rather than those who choose to switch plans at open enrollment. The volume of enrollment records and paperwork is higher.
3. New benefit booklets and plan descriptions have to be reviewed and understood so that employee questions can be answered.
4. New sales and service staff from the self-funded plan will replace the former service staff for the carrier or MCO. You may continue to offer MCO or carrier coverage, so your staff will work with more plan representatives and staff than before.
5. Close communication with plan advisers, administrators, and other vendors will have to be maintained, especially during the first three months to iron out any problems.

I, _____, do hereby acknowledge that I am a staff member (committee member) for the XYZ Organization's self-funded plan and that, in the course of performing various work and attending meetings, I may have access to, or may receive from time to time, certain confidential documents, material, or other information. Among the types of information that I understand are confidential and not to be released are any description of the employee or plan member's medical condition, physical or mental conditions, diseases, medications, or other forms of treatment, and hospitalization, and I hereby agree not to divulge any such information, except to those persons duly authorized by law to receive the same, and/or as I am required under legal process.

I recognize and understand that this information is privileged and confidential. In performing any of my duties as a staff person (committee member) to the plan, I acknowledge my responsibility to keep this information at all times secure and confidential and agree at no time shall I release to anyone the contents of that information by any means of communication.

Dated _____   Signed _____

EXHIBIT 12-11. Sample staff confidentiality agreement. (Source: Halo Associates.)

Most of the implementation activities will be part of the training and the decision making and should come as no surprise to your staff. If possible, allow for additional staff and cooperative support by other employees during the startup phase of a new plan.

Your employees may learn about a self-funded plan gradually through your newsletter, work-site meetings, flyers, or employee representatives, or your organization may inform them after the fact by sending out the startup packet of booklet, enrollment form, announcement, and claim form. You should arrange for employee feedback and ongoing communication as described in Chapter 7.

You will need to decide whether to require reenrollment in order to update employee records for dependent coverage and coordination of benefits. This is an important point, since in a self-funded plan your funds are at stake. Another issue is how to comply with federal regulations such as COBRA, Medicare, and the Family Medical Leave Act, which require you to provide employees with notices and forms. You can opt to have the plan administrator or adviser set up the systems and procedures or provide the services for you. If you send out the notifications, collect COBRA payments, and maintain records on FMLA and others, you need clear lines of responsibility and accountability.

You also need to decide on waiting periods, retiree coverage, cash buyouts, and coverage for disabled employees and those on leave, transferring employees, and status changes. Your self-funded plan may institute new policies for some or all of these situations.

■ HOW TO MONITOR A SELF-FUNDED PLAN

There is nothing more important to plan management than the function of monitoring. Its goal is to make appropriate adjustments that will keep your plan on track. Your timing, focus, and management activities to monitor a self-funded plan are based on the unique qualities of your organization.

How often should you review plan finances? When should you compare costs and report findings to management? What's the best time to have committee meetings, and how long should they last? Your answers will depend on the size of your organization, the availability of resources, the scope of your plan, and your organizational structure

If you are an employer of 200 employees who manufactures on a twenty-four-hour schedule, with minimal inhouse management staff, you will most likely examine your health plan performance and costs infrequently. Rather than setting yourself up for a fall, you should realistically appraise your needs. In this case, I'd recommend that you hold a quarterly meeting with your plan adviser, plan administrator, finance officer, and any other key management staff. Your meeting should have an agenda of under two hours and consist of a presentation by your health plan professionals on plan performance, based on reports provided to you in advance. Their goal should be to inform you about costs, utilization, any red flags that require management action, and projected changes they recommend.

On the other hand, if you are the plan manager for an organization of 2,500 employees that offers four health plan options, the largest of which is your self-funded plan, which covers 1,800 employees, and your organization provides financial services and includes primarily white-collar employees in an urban area, with a sizable benefits staff and no unions, reviews should occur no less than monthly, with weekly claims registers reviewed briefly by your assistant and perhaps tracked into a computer report that you receive on weekly and monthly activity. Your plan management meeting will include your plan adviser, plan administrator, team of staff and management representatives, and possibly ancillary vendors when specific items are in question. In a meeting of three hours or so you will cover cost comparisons month to month and year to year, network and other discounts, cost savings from case management and other services, employee satisfaction issues, member communications, and high-cost claims. Every six months you will review recommendations from your plan adviser, administrator, and others, and receive an update on current trends in the medical benefits industry.

Focus

Focus is important in your monitoring efforts. Your organization has its own focus related to the health plan. When you self-funded your plan, you established goals, which you now need to keep in sight. These may be altered or replaced by new goals that reflect changes in your organization, your workforce, or your health plan.

Cost

You may be expected to reduce cost with the self-funded plan, in which case you will always address cost issues when you monitor the plan. A portion of every meeting with a plan adviser, administrator, or other professional will be devoted to discussion of cost, how to implement cost-saving features and then to measure their results. Your perspective on recommendations and plan activity will be focused on cost impact as a first priority.

Providers

On the other hand, your mission may be to improve access to physicians and use of network services. If this is the case, you will ask for feedback from advisers, employees, and staff on how to inform employees and encourage network use. Your focus will be on reports that summarize the providers used, any changes in volume or percentage, and any improvements in network scope.

Benefits

Your focus may be to review a certain aspect of benefits. For instance, you may spend some time on retiree benefits as an issue of high cost and philosophical concern to your organization. Or you may identify high-cost areas of use such as fertility treatments, outpatient psychiatric services, or prescription drug utilization, which you want to address through education and, perhaps, plan changes,. You may find that some benefits are underutilized and need to be dropped or changed. Your focus will be on specific benefit studies, evaluations, and plan design recommendations. This process will take time, as you gather facts and prioritize potential actions.

Management Style

Are you the type of manager who relies upon staff and delegates? If so, you may want to have a key person assigned to assist you with the self-funded plan. This staff person can prepare for periodic health plan meetings, gather and assemble the appropriate reports for distribution and discussion, and provide a thumbnail sketch of each topic.

Are you understaffed and expected to do everything yourself? If so, you will want a good plan adviser, administrator, or health professional to make you look good and to assist you with plan monitoring. You may not have time for a regular committee meeting. As a substitute and to limit meetings, you can have draft reports submitted to you by your plan administrator for review and editing. Then it is a simpler task to prepare and distribute them.

You can limit your reports to two a month, with periodic special reports to read. I recommend a comprehensive monthly, bimonthly, or quarterly report to show plan costs by benefit category. Your special reports might include a lag report to measure the amount of claims that will be filed late and into the next plan year, or you may get a quarterly or semiannual report on your drug benefit.

The message is simply this: adapt how you monitor your self-funded health plan to your management style and to the available staff and resources at your disposal. Monitoring in general is facilitated by reports and feedback.

For a self-funded plan, reports and monitoring are essential. Unlike insured plans, where your control over costs and benefits is minimal, the self-funded plan relies on fine-tuning throughout the year to keep costs in line and to respond to coverage issues. For example, a network report is used in a self-funded plan to trigger an employee mailing and announcements on network expansion and then to monitor the response by tracking network use thereafter. You can measure the impact of management actions faster and more accurately in a self-funded plan.

■ HEALTH PLAN COMMITTEE

A plan management committee is a useful way to monitor the performance of a self-funded plan for several reasons. Whether you are a small or mid-sized organization, there is a certain amount of importance attached to the creation of a committee and its function. The establishment of a committee implies a serious commitment to the plan. Practically, it will encourage regular meetings and improve plan management just by its existence.

You should develop agendas and a procedure to prepare and distribute minutes and to review and discuss reports. Such a committee is helpful for gathering feedback on your health plan. Exhibit 12-12 is an agenda for a health plan committee meeting.

As a result of the . . . meeting of the subcommittee, the following recommendations are made:

1. Two-party checks. Recommendation: That this payment system be implemented as soon as possible. An estimated savings of $183,850 based on 1997 hospital costs, and for the first four months of 1998, a savings of $68,120 would have occurred if this system had been in place already.

2. Discharge planning requirement with penalty. Recommendation: Requirement for discharge planning with a $300 penalty for noncompliance. An extension of other managed-care provisions (i.e., preadmission certification), this would allow the plan administrator to work closely with plan participants after hospitalization.

3. Nonurgent emergency room coverage. Recommendation: No coverage. These visits totaled 99 for 1997, at a cost of $13,189.01 for emergency services only. The cost does not reflect other services rendered.

4. Private-duty nursing services. Recommendation: Limit coverage by managed-care approval and review by administrator, based on medical necessity and physician justification.

EXHIBIT 12-12. Sample health plan committee agenda. (Source: Halo Associates.)

Selection of committee members should follow some basic guidelines:

- They should represent various departments and facilities in your organization.
- They should come from various disciplines or backgrounds.
- They should be enthusiastic, communicate well, and preferably be open-minded.

You can ask that appointments be made by top management, although committee members should be recommended by you. If you are unionized or have employee representatives, it is a good idea to include their recommendations for the committee. The more senior management on the committee, the more clout it will be perceived to have. Your role should be to guide and coordinate committee activities. The committee's mission is to provide feedback, evaluation, recommendations, and support to health plan activity.

■ WORKING WITH OUTSIDE ADVISERS

Although there is a complete chapter on this topic, in a self-funded plan your relationship with a health plan adviser is so vital, I thought it best to recap it here. Consultants and advisers evaluate plan performance, monitor the impact of adjustments and changes, help the plan comply with regulations, and provide special communication and employee relations services. Your job is made easier when you have a competent adviser who understands your needs and provides expertise and support. Exhibit 12-13 shows the simplicity of the bottom line—what should be done next. The art of consulting and advising is to suggest things that will make a measurable difference and that can realistically be done.

a) Continue with an annual claims review audit of Plan Administrator by an outside consultant.

b) Stop-loss insurance should be put out to bid annually to available markets to ensure the lowest cost. A change in the terms and conditions from a 12/12 policy to a 12/15 should be bid. The possibility of becoming self-insured for Stop-Loss should be studied for feasibility.

c) The administrator should prepare and provide a regular drug utilization and cost report to the District. A quarterly managed care report to describe activity and cost savings should also be provided.

d) Drug Utilization Review with the use of electronic edits should be used to reduce inappropriate prescription fills.

e) The Mail Order Drug Program should be offered to retirees on the same basis (reimbursement) that they now receive prescription coverage.

f) The concept of a PPO of local pharmacies for drug coverage should be explored—either with other area employers or alone.

g) Electronic billings direct to the administrator from medical providers should be explored to improve service and streamline the claims filing process.

h) The plan should work toward increased discounts from medical providers with no impact on benefits or services to plan participants.

i) The two-party check system should continue to be monitored for cost savings.

j) Language should be developed for our Plan to prevent dependents and spouses from waiving coverage elsewhere (i.e., through but-outs or coinsurance clauses) and selecting our Plan as primary. This will help eliminate cost-shifting from other Plans to our Plan.

EXHIBIT 12-13. Sample adviser's recommendations. (Source: Halo Associates.)

■ WORKING WITH YOUR PLAN ADMINISTRATOR

You should keep your monitoring activities somewhat aloof from the administration firm. Carriers and administrators are both claims payors, and, for a self-funded plan, they both have the same perspective. Since they are paid either on a per capita basis, as a flat amount per month per plan member, or on a percentage of claims paid, neither has a primary focus of reducing the cost of claims. You can alter this viewpoint by a performance clause that relates a portion of the fee, or fee increases, to claim costs. Although your plan administrator is a specialist and is aware of trends and regulations that affect self-funded plans, it is removed from your need to evaluate and monitor the health plan for several reasons.

First, the administrator is in the operations and not the design end of your plan. Some large carriers have departments that work on plan design and may be able to furnish you with information generated from that department. You should rely on recommendations for services and procedures raised by your administrator or carrier; you should also recognize their limitations. Exhibit 12-14 is a sample of a third-party administrator's suggestions for a self-funded plan. It's interesting to note, however, that more than half of the recommendations in this case were prohibited by employee contracts, and another quarter were prohibited by state law. The ideas on operations and plan service recommendations are the most valuable recommendations from administration firms.

September 25, 1998

Ms. Mary Smith
Benefits Manager
XYZ Company

Dear Ms. Smith:

In response to your request of August 15, 1998, we have reviewed your self-funded plan utilization and costs and are sending along these recommendations for your consideration. They are divided into those that are administrative, and those that will require amendments to your plan.

Administrative Recommendations

1. Conduct a reenrollment of all plan members when open enrollment and option transfer is conducted in November of this year. An updated file will help us to maximize savings to your plan through coordination of benefits with other coverage available to your plan members and their covered dependents.

2. Furnish an enrollment census monthly, rather than bimonthly to eliminate those situations where a covered member is terminated and continues to receive services under the plan beyond what is allowed by the coverage due to tardy notice.

3. Allow us to implement the HIPAA requirement for a certificate of coverage so that it can be generated and tracked as part of our reporting to you. There is a slight fee for this service, but it will improve the efficiency of compliance and in the long run reduce the administrative burden and cost to internal staff.

Coverage and Eligibility Recommendations

1. Increase the plan deductible to $300/individual and maximum $900/family from the current level of $220/individual and $500/family. Your current levels are well below the going rate for your geographic area.

2. Eliminate retiree coverage, except for reimbursement of the Medicare Part B premium. Your current coverage allows reimbursement for Medicare Part B, plus what is essentially Medicare gap coverage, which supplements Medicare and covers retirees for the prescription drug benefit and additional services not provided by Medicare. The cost of retirees in your plan currently represents 24 percent of plan year cost, but retirees account for only 11 percent of plan members. We will work with your benefit consultant to project potential savings, if you wish to pursue this recommendation.

3. Increase your copayment for network providers from $8/visit to $15/visit in keeping with the two HMO plans you offer. We are seeing copayment levels of $10/visit to $15/visit in other self-funded plans we administer.

4. Institute a 120-day waiting period for new hires before they are eligible for health benefits. This would help eliminate the need for higher administrative costs we are charging, based on your current turnover rate.

Please contact me with any questions about these recommendations. We will be happy to assist you in their further evaluation and to work with your benefits consultant if you wish to project their cost impact.

Very truly your,

ABC Administration Firm

EXHIBIT 12-14. Sample administrator's recommendations. (Source: Halo Associates.)

■ PAYING ATTENTION TO BENEFITS STAFF

Your benefits staff can be a valuable resource in the monitoring and oversight of a health plan. They are the first line of contact for plan members, whether employees, retirees, or family members. If your staff understands the health plan, has ready access to the administrator's service staff, can easily order and distribute plan materials, and is trained to refer troublesome issues promptly for action, you are on your way to a smoothly run plan. The burden on your staff is increased with a self-funded plan, despite assistance from plan advisers, administrators, and insurance professionals. There's more to do, and each responsibility has a direct impact on your employees.

Institute a few routines with your staff to make their job easier. Establish morning catchup sessions on benefit issues or questions. Implement the use of written logs and notes on problem calls. Provide calendars to diary report-due dates and to document fund transfers. Encourage a system of standard letters and forms for required mailings. With some encouragement, your staff can provide you with meaningful input on plan performance. They should be given the opportunity to suggest how to improve service and simplify work.

When you are self-funded, the responsibility for costs, plan performance, and employee satisfaction rests on your shoulders. Although self-funding is not a new concept, it is one that requires your organization to assume risk. You are expected to set the pace and the mission for your self-funded plan and to use staff and outside professionals to accomplish your goals of reducing cost and maintaining or improving plan services.

■ SUMMARY

The climate for health plans in the United States has changed dramatically in the past ten years. We are now in a situation where more than 70 percent of all health plans restrict services through managed care and where the goals are to reduce or eliminate retiree health benefits and to shift cost to employees and to government programs. We are concerned that our Medicare system may be underfunded, just when our population needs it most, with the aging of the baby boomers. Although our economy is currently strong, health care costs are starting on an upward spiral. The field of medicine is more and more a business, with doctors and hospitals increasingly in the insurance business, accepting risk for patients.

With all of these changes, self-funding is thriving. It allows you the chance to be a master of your destiny, at least with regard to your health plan. Not only can you control the benefits, provider access, and services, but you can better control the cost. Self-funding, however, is not a piece of cake. It requires work, expertise, and careful attention. But, when it suits you, it offers much in return.

CHAPTER 13

Opportunities for the Smaller Organization

Are there problems unique to the small organization during health plan review? How can you negotiate reduced cost with carriers and MCOs? What should you ask about a health plan? Is self-funding appropriate? How should you evaluate an association plan or other pool? As a small organization, you have limited resources and less influence, which make management strategies crucial to improving the value and services of your health plan.

Two relevant and commonly known facts should be foremost in our minds as we discuss small business and health coverage. First, more than 70 percent of all health coverage for the nonelderly is provided through employer-sponsored health plans; second, more than 40 percent of all employees in the United States are self-employed or work for small employers. Small organizations create more new jobs than large employers, according to the Employee Benefit Research Institute Issue Brief No. 172 for April 1996, which reports that in the five years between 1987 and 1992, companies with fewer than 100 employees created 16.9 million new jobs, while those with 1,000 or more employees created only 5.1 million.

Given the importance of employer-sponsored plans and the market share of small organizations, it's no surprise that government and regulatory attention has increasingly been given to the small, employer-sponsored health plan. Nor is it a surprise when new employees ask about the health coverage you provide. Health benefits were the most sought-after employment benefit in a 1998 study by the National Association of Colleges and employers of recent college graduates. You need to be prepared with a cost-effective and competitive health plan to attract and keep valued employees.

■ SMALL AND SMALLER

For the purpose of our discussion, a small organization is one with fewer than 100 employees. For some employee benefit options, such as self-funding, 100–500 employees is a more realistic threshold. Organizational size relates to your region of the country, whether you are in an urban or rural setting, and to your industry. For an effective health plan, you need to allocate time, staff, and money and to develop or identify the expertise needed to effectively manage the plan. Size relates to the availability of these resources, which, in turn, affects your ability to offer a health plan and to maintain it.

Exhibit 13-1 presents a breakdown of the percentage of all employees by size of their employer, from two employees to more than fifty employees. Exhibit 13-2 shows the percentage of businesses according to their staff size. Together, these illustrate the importance of small employers with regard to employee health plans. Only 5 percent of the

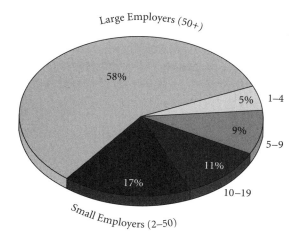

EXHIBIT 13-1. Distribution of workers by size of employer. (Source: Based on U.S. government statistics for 1994.)

businesses in the United States employ fifty-one or more employees. With 55 percent of businesses employing between one and four employees and another 20 percent employing between five and nine employees, the strategies such small businesses use to select, implement, and monitor their health plans and their costs have an impact on vast numbers of employees and on the business community.

The likelihood that your organization sponsors an employee health plan is directly related to its size. Only 12 percent of those who are self-employed, and 26 percent of those in companies with fewer than ten employees participate in a health plan at work. This percentage increases with size. The limited number of small organizations that provide health plans contributes to the growing number of uninsured and underinsured persons in our population.

Some solutions proposed by government and some market trends anticipate a further decrease in employer-sponsored plans. Some of the reasons given for the drop in participation in employer health plans over the past ten years are the increase in government programs, which fulfill a need for many employees, and rising employee cost sharing. Employees pay more for copays, premium contributions, deductibles, and uncovered expenses than previously. As recently reported, out-of-pocket health costs rank third among annual consumer expenses. In addition, 30 percent of American families spend more than 10 percent of their income on health care.

According to a report published in 1998 by the University of California with KPMG Peat Marwick and funded by the Henry Kaiser Family Foundation, more companies now offer health plans, but fewer employees enroll. The percentage of companies with between three and nine employees offering health insurance increased during the past ten

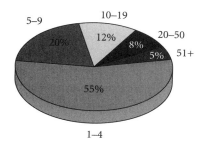

EXHIBIT 13-2. Distribution of businesses by number of employees. (Source: Based on U.S. government statistics for 1994.)

years from 43 percent to 51 percent, and those with ten to twenty-four workers that offered health benefits increased from 72 percent to 78 percent. However, for both of these categories, participation in the health plans dropped. The same report noted that in 1987, 13.3 percent of workers at companies with 100 to 499 employees were uninsured, compared to 15.3 percent uninsured in 1995. Reasons given for this decrease in enrollment were rising costs and eligibility restrictions on employees. Employee contributions during this period doubled on average for employers surveyed in the report, according to a synopsis of this report published in *National Underwriter* for July 13, 1998.

Government programs over the years have included the expansion of Medicare and Medicaid, with new programs for children and the disabled, as well as for the elderly. In most cases, Congress exempts organizations with fewer than fifteen, twenty-five, or fifty employees, depending on the legislation. In some cases, smaller employers are given tax breaks and other incentives to offer employee programs. Often, there is a phased-in timetable for such legislation, which allows the smaller organization more time to comply with the law.

Some states offer subsidized insurance plans, guaranteed rate plans, and pools for smaller employers. For instance, New York State has an insurance partnership that subsidizes 50 percent of the cost of a health plan for a small employer, subject to income and other requirements. These initiatives are structured to encourage employer-sponsored plans. It's not in the public interest to rely only on tax-supported programs to insure growing numbers of Americans. Our tradition has been to encourage employment-based health coverage so that government does not become the sole health plan provider. We have seen gradual changes to this tradition over the years, including cost shifting from the employer to the employee and from the employer to government-sponsored programs.

■ INDIVIDUAL ISSUES FOR SMALLER ORGANIZATIONS

Chronic and Catastrophic Illness

The fewer employees you have, the greater the impact of high-cost claims on your health plan (see Exhibit 13-3). What can you do as a small organization to reduce the severity of high cost claims and their impact on your health plan?

Organizational Changes

First and foremost, you can encourage healthier lifestyles in the way you manage your organization. Some steps you can take are the following:

- You can have a no-smoking policy that discourages smoking and cuts down on the negative effect of passive smoking on nonsmokers.
- You can select healthier choices for vending machines and cafeteria menus that encourage better nutrition habits among employees.
- You can create a healthier organizational culture, with lunch and break times that are taken in low-stress settings away from work.
- You can institute a walking program at work.
- You can adopt procedures and identify resources to provide support and counseling when employees need it. Traditional employee assistance programs and staff are one approach; a more informal service might be available from existing personnel staff, or an outside counselor who is available to see employees on site in groups or individually as part of in-service training in stress management.

Number of Workers	Total Cost of Health Benefits (average cost = $2,000 per employee per yr.)	Average Per-Employee Cost of Health Benefits If One Enrollee Is Costly (130% of average enrollee)
2	$ 4,000	$2,300
10	20,000	2,060
20	40,000	2,030
50	100,000	2,012
75	150,000	2,008
100	200,000	2,006
200	400,000	2,003

EXHIBIT 13-3. Impact of a costly employee on premiums. (Source: U.S. General Accounting Office, June 1998. From *Medical Benefits*, vol. 15, no. 14, July 30, 1998, p. 9; copyright © Aspen Publishers Inc.)

Outside Resources

Wellness and preventive health programs have expanded in recent years and are increasingly available to smaller organizations. There are mobile services for early diagnosis of specific chronic and catastrophic illness, such as breast cancer, diabetes and cardiac disease, prostate cancer, skin cancer, osteoporosis, and general physicals to screen for multiple conditions. Many of these are provided at no direct cost to your organization, because the medical services are billed to the employee's health plan. The Appendix lists wellness resources that include nonprofit organizations that provide seminars, telephonic support, and literature on specific illnesses and intervention services. In addition, your local hospital may offer services that make it easier and less costly for employees to receive services and support for chronic illness.

Often, there are public programs available through your county health department, such as flu shots, hospice care, or checkups provided free of charge or on a sliding scale based on income. Keep literature from your local hospice organization and other support agencies handy, and make them available to employees.

Finally, be aware of when disability coverage, Medicare, or Medicaid coverage begins and advise employees to apply when appropriate.

Each of these activities can help you reduce the cost of seriously ill employees, and may offer some opportunities for your employees to reduce out-of-pocket costs, too.

Limits on Your Control

When you are a smaller organization, you have limited ability to design your health plan and to have an impact on its administration. Your primary focus is on enrollment and eligibility and on monitoring your plan for cost and employee satisfaction. You should be fully aware of the choices available to you and of industry standards of service. Your health plan adviser can assist you in these areas and counsel you as you select and manage your health plan.

Benefit Design

Benefit designs for coverage for from three to fifty workers are standard, and your flexibility is limited to selecting out-of-pocket expenses such as copays, deductible limits, coinsurance, and network choices. Your cost is directly related to the choices you make for cost sharing.

Some of the questions you should ask about a health plan option are:

- Is there an out-of-pocket maximum, beyond which a covered member has no further expense, and the plan pays 100 percent? This is typically $2,500 per family contract.
- Does the coverage include comprehensive major medical, hospitalization, and drugs?
- Is there access to a reasonable number of physicians, hospitals, and other facilities in your geographic area?
- Are the policies for referrals and specialist access restrictive or reasonable?
- Does the insurance plan pay a reasonable and customary fee to providers that is realistic for your area?
- What is the lifetime maximum limit for the plan? Typically this might be $1 million as a total, and there may be other lifetime limits on specific coverage, such as mental health.
- Is there a coinsurance for specific coverage that can mean a hardship, such as expensive drug therapies, mental health, and organ transplants?

You should be aware of the advantages and disadvantages of each health plan you consider. A quick comparison of coverage descriptions can help you identify potential problem areas. The reputation and track record of the carrier or MCO is also an indicator. If claims payment is slow, inaccurate, or complex, you will have dissatisfied employees. If many of the physicians and hospitals in your area are not part of the plan's network, your employees will not have access to services when they need them.

Exhibit 13-4 is a checklist for small-group health insurance. You can use it as a guide when you are comparing health plans for your organization. As with any other standard guide, you can adapt it to meet your needs. Be sure to review it with your health plan adviser.

■ NEGOTIATING WITH YOUR CARRIER OR MCO

There are some standards you can apply to your insurance plan so that the plan administrator reduces cost or increases benefits or services at no additional cost. This type of negotiation can include:

- Expanded network with a guarantee of a specific number of providers of a certain type in your geographic area within a time period, subject to financial penalties or reduced premium
- Patient advocacy services, on-site mobile services, and case management services for your employees
- Multiyear rate guarantees to keep premium increases stable, with a cap on increases and the possibility of no increase, subject to your annual approval
- Stop-loss reserve subject to a percentage refund, based on limited or no high-cost claims
- Guaranteed stop-loss premium for multiyear contract
- A grant for your work site wellness program from your carrier or MCO

The Plan

1. Are needed medical services covered?

___ Inpatient hospital services
___ Outpatient facility
___ Doctors and specialists
___ Psychiatric
___ Skilled nursing care
___ Home health-care visits
___ Rehabilitation facility
___ Hospice
___ Prescription drugs
___ Preventive, wellness services

2. What services are excluded from coverage?

3. What restrictions or limitations are placed on catastrophic medical claims, preexisting conditions, inpatient hospital stays, etc.?

4. Are there quality and peer review procedures to ensure quality of care and handle claims appeals?

5. Does the plan offer disease management and other high-cost claim services, such as high-risk maternity, diabetic management, and asthma programs?

6. What are the out-of-pocket expenses to employees and other covered members, including lifetime and annual maximums?

7. Are the premiums competitive for individual and family coverage?

8. For how long is the premium guaranteed? What is the track record of premium increases over the past three years?

Insurance Carrier or MCO

1. How long has the company sold small-group health plans?

2. What percentage of the company's business is devoted to small-group health plans?

3. What is the financial rating of the company, in A.M. Best or from other rating sources?

Plan Services

1. Who will administer the plan, and how long have they been administering health plans for small groups?

2. Is there dedicated customer service staff and a toll-free number to give your employees easy access?

3. How is claims processing done, and where?

4. How long will it take to process claims?

5. What are the channels for service to you and support materials provided to you, as the employer?

6. When will your application be processed by the underwriter, and when will coverage begin?

7. How often, and when, will you be billed? Is there a minimum premium or other payment plan available to meet your needs?

Note: Sales materials should give you some of these answers, especially for coverage and its limitations. Your sales representative, broker, agent, or plan adviser can provide other information.

EXHIBIT 13-4. Health insurance checklist for small organizations. (Source: Halo Associates.)

- Consulting services for plan design, employee survey, or other need that doesn't conflict with your review of administrative and plan services

These are examples of the type of agreements that a carrier or MCO may find acceptable and that can help you reduce your cost and improve health plan services.

■ GEOGRAPHIC DIFFERENCES AND THEIR IMPACT

There are differences by region and by state in the number of employers who offer health plans and how many employees enroll. Some of the variations are related to the cost sharing allowed and the coverage mandated by state regulations, and some may have to do with the rural or urban nature of the locale. This difference in availability is, in turn, related to the expectations of employees in a given state, and that also affects you when you hire or recruit employees.

In addition to availability, you should examine the statewide rankings to determine the average health status of a state's residents. This speaks to the issue of regional disparity in the quality of health care, measured by standard outcomes. It also addresses public policy, demographic influences on health, and public attitude about health. States with higher rankings offer preventive health services, regulate seat belt use, encourage safety standards, have lower suicide rates, and have greater numbers of providers and services available. Each of forty-six individual measures are included in the scoring for the rankings in Exhibit 13-5. As a result, the ranking can identify those states most supportive of healthier lifestyles and with lower death rates from preventable causes. These regional differences in the health of the general population are important to you if you do business in a location that is less healthy. You can advocate for more services from government and other agencies and expect that your health plan costs may be higher than need be. If you are in a healthier state, you may have an easier time self-funding, with less likelihood of catastrophic loss that can be prevented.

There are differences in what you can expect to pay for health plan premiums according to geographic locale, as shown in Exhibit 13-6. The cities with the least expensive and most expensive premiums for HMO membership are presented for comparison to the average annual HMO premium of $3,610 for a family. Competition and regional differ-

State	Rank	Score	State	Rank	Score
Hawaii	1	117.7	Maryland	27	103.0
Minnesota	2	117.5	Michigan	28	102.1
New Hampshire	3	116.0	California	29	101.9
North Dakota	4	113.3	Indiana	30	101.8
Wisconsin	5	112.1	Delaware	31	100.2
Massachusetts	6	111.6	National average		100.0
Maine	7	110.5	New York	32	98.7
Connecticut	8	110.1	Idaho	33	97.8
Nebraska	9	109.6	North Carolina	34	97.6
South Dakota	10	108.7	Missouri	35	97.1
Washington	11	108.6	Georgia	36	96.7
Alaska	12	108.0	Florida	37	96.1
Utah	13	107.9	West Virginia	38	95.9
Virginia	13	107.9	Arizona	39	94.0
Iowa	15	107.5	Texas	39	94.0
Vermont	16	107.4	Kentucky	41	92.7
Colorado	17	107.0	South Carolina	42	92.0
Montana	18	106.4	New Mexico	43	91.2
Wyoming	19	105.9	Tennessee	44	90.6
Rhode Island	20	105.7	Oklahoma	45	89.9
New Jersey	21	104.8	Nevada	46	89.1
Kansas	22	104.7	Alabama	47	89.0
Ohio	23	104.6	Arkansas	48	88.7
Oregon	24	104.2	Mississippi	49	84.3
Illinois	25	103.6	Louisiana	50	82.0
Pennsylvania	26	103.1			

EXHIBIT 13-5. Overall state health rankings. (Source: Institute for Healthcare Quality, April 23, 1998. From *Medical Benefits*, vol. 15, no. 10, May 30, 1998, p. 10; copyright © Aspen Publishers Inc.)

Cost per employee for HMO plan, by market			
National average	$3,610		

Least expensive		Most expensive	
San Diego	$2,789	Toledo, Ohio	$4,946
Los Angeles	$2,922	Madison, Wis.	$4,590
Seattle	$2,987	Fairfield, Conn.	$4,256
Orlando, Fla.	$3,051	Northern N.J.	$4,227

EXHIBIT 13-6. Cost for family HMO premium by city. (Source: Hewett Health Value Initiative™, May 1998.)

ences in coverage have an impact on these costs. If you have several locations for your business, variations in cost can affect your organization's health plan budget.

■ YOUR INDUSTRY

Certain industries pay more for health care for employees, according to a Hewitt Health Value Initiative study reprinted in *On Managed Care* for July 1998. Your organization will be driven by what the competition does and by what is common within your industry, so it's helpful to note that wide differences exist and to consider why. Exhibit 13-7 presents health care premiums by industry.

■ TURNOVER AND YOUR HEALTH PLAN

New employees will ask about benefits, and specifically your health plan, before they are hired. Your goal when hiring is to select employees who can do the job and who will stay with your organization. This reduces not only your cost of hiring and recruiting but your training expenses. It also lowers your health plan administrative costs; enrolling, dropping, reenrolling, and changing plan members frequently raises costs.

Which industries pay the most per employee* for health care?

Top and bottom three industries:

Manufacturing	**$5,389**
Chemicals	**$5,233**
Utilities (gas, elec.)	**$5,183**
Health care	**$3,739**
Professional services	**$3,375**
Retail	**$3,147**

*Per employee cost represents employee claims and administration or insured premium, including managed care (HMO, POS, PPO) and indemnity.

EXHIBIT 13-7. Health care premiums by industry. (Source: Hewett Health Value Initiative™, May 1998.)

What can you do to increase the number of years that employees work for you? This is an employee relations question, and your health plan is a significant part of it. When managing your health plan, you need to have a clear policy about health coverage and communicate it to current and new employees. Cost sharing, coverage, and enrollment and eligibility information about your health plan should be readily available to all staff. You should train your benefits personnel regarding each of these issues and in the procedures for enrollment, changes, continuation of coverage, and other administrative duties. A smoothly operating plan is one that complies with the law, is understood by employees, provides needed coverage, and maintains accurate records.

Employees tend to stay at a job, once they are there over five years. A recent Employee Benefits Research Institute Issue Brief reports that 20 percent of employees were at their job between five and nine years, and another 17 percent were there for fifteen or more years. The highest turnover rate of employees was during the first four years of employment. Turnover is an important consideration for the smaller organization, and you can discourage turnover by making your health plan attractive to those who work for your organization longer than a year but less than five years. For example, you can adopt a lower contribution rate for plan years 2–5 or add benefits in those years. In this way, you might reduce turnover. Turnover needs to be considered when you select a health plan, develop a cost-sharing philosophy, and communicate with employees.

There should be a win-win goal to your health plan. To attain that, you need to project how your health plan is of value to employees and track whether it helps you attract and keep employees. Make a list of the positive features of your plan, including the cost to your organization. Employees should be aware of this expense, since it affects other benefits and, possibly, salary increases. When health plan costs rise, the smaller organization may not be able to offer salary increases and continue to pay for the health plan. Employees who don't have the information to make this connection may feel undervalued and leave the organization. Periodic communications about your health plan and its costs and efforts to involve employees in health plan review committees can help avoid this type of turnover. At exit interviews, be sure to ask about the effect of your health plan on the employee's decision to leave.

Employee Choice and Turnover

Many employers have moved to offering multiple choices to employees as another way to improve satisfaction with the health plan. This has the potential to backfire, unless there is effective communication about each option and what it offers. Frequently, plan information is developed by a carrier or MCO for marketing purposes and stresses only the positive points. You should fully understand the differences between the options you offer to employees and provide them with a clear-cut comparison.

You can ask your broker, agent, or health plan adviser to prepare a plan comparison sheet for you or prepare it yourself from the one-page description of coverage provided by each health plan. Ask several staff members to read it before it is distributed to make sure it is easy to understand. It should be a supplement to complete plan materials available to all employees when they are given health plan options during an open-enrollment period.

■ CASH BUYOUT

In my opinion, a cash buyout is not helpful in the long term to control costs. However, if you have a workforce where most employees have a working spouse with health coverage elsewhere, and you are fully insured, it may make sense for you. The "ifs" relate to the need to be assured that coverage exists somewhere for the employee who opts out of your health plan in exchange for a cash payment of a portion of the premium you would have paid.

Usually the cash payment equals half the premium that applies. For instance, a person who is eligible for individual coverage that costs $2,000 per year could waive the right to coverage for a payment of $1,000, usually payable in quarterly installments in advance of each quarter; you would pay the employee $250 on January 1, April 1, July 1, and October 1 for a plan year. The decision to opt out is made on an annual basis, and might be subject to filing a waiver that indicates the employee has coverage elsewhere.

Even with a cash buyout, your employee will have the right to reenroll in your plan during the plan year, subject to the same eligibility requirements as anyone else. You should design this option, if you choose to make it available, so that the reenrollment period and your payment period for installments coincide. For example, once an employee receives a quarterly payment, there would be a three-month waiting period for reenrollment, if the plan requires it. This eliminates the possibility of the employee's having to repay your advance buyout payment.

The potential for loss exists if employees leave employment during the buyout term covered by your payment to them. You should consider this possibility for loss when you project cost savings from the buyout option. You can limit this loss by restricting the buyout to those who have worked for your organization a specified number of years.

■ COST AND SIMPLICITY

The top concerns for larger organizations when selecting a health plan are cost and quality of coverage, while smaller organizations focus on cost and ease of administration. After all, a smaller organization has limited benefits staff and resources to deal with administrative duties. You should aim for "the simpler, the better" so that your health plan is not an administrative burden.

Some tips to follow that will help you keep things simple:

1. Offer only one option, carefully selected, with varying eligibility and cost-sharing choices. This will limit your communication to one level of coverage and yet offer flexibility to employees who may not choose to enroll or who wish to enroll when cost sharing is lowest. For instance, offer health plan enrollment after ninety days of employment, subject to a 50 percent cost sharing of premium and after one year, subject to a 30 percent cost sharing of premium.

2. Consider a Flex 125 plan, with records kept by your plan administrator. This will allow your employees to set aside, tax-free, a portion of their wages from which they can pay medical costs and out-of-pocket expenses. For instance, a Flex 125 plan enables employees to set aside pretax dollars to pay for premium contributions. This arrangement lowers your employer contribution for FICA and other payroll deductions and lowers the cost to employees, too.

3. Have all claims filed directly with the plan administrator. This will remove your staff from the administrative function, except for enrollment and eligibility.

4. Establish a one-enrollment period each year after the initial enrollment period has passed for new employees. This will limit your involvement in reenrollment and plan communications.

5. Require your broker or agent to assist with open enrollment and plan enrollment for newly hired employees, to relieve your staff of most of the burden. Commissions are paid to these health advisers, and they expect to provide such services to your account.

■ POOLING AND ASSOCIATION HEALTH PLANS

You probably belong to a business association or an industry organization that offers a group health plan to members. Some of these plans are individually rated so that your premiums reflect your employee health care costs during the year. Others are group rated so that premiums are based on the health care costs of the entire plan (risk-sharing plans). Each organization that joins will rely upon the group as a whole to have lower costs than it might have individually.

The Law of Large Numbers, discussed in Chapter 2, and underwriting are related to the concept of pooling or association plans. If you are a good risk, the probability of your causing a group plan premium to rise is less likely than if you are a bad risk. Your risk level is determined by the age, gender, ethnicity, and health status of your employees. It is also affected by the availability of health services and the education level and income level of your employees.

Adverse selection, you may remember, is the tendency for higher-risk individuals to enroll in a plan, causing costs to rise disproportionately. Association and pooled plans try to avoid this by two methods:

1. They require enrollment of all, or nearly all, of your employees in the plan.
2. They review the past claim expenses of your employees.

Both of these help the association plan or pool prevent a negative impact on its cost and utilization. There is no fail-safe method, of course.

Association plans are so-called because members of an association or other organization, generally of employers in a like industry, are eligible for plan enrollment. The administrator and other plan services are selected by the association, as are benefit levels and administrative policies for enrollment and eligibility. Your control and options under an association plan are very limited. In exchange, you receive the advantage of lower costs than you might have otherwise.

There is less personalization, and sometimes less employer service, than in other plans. On the other hand, the association itself provides certain added member services. The burden of communication is relieved because the association or pool generally provides all plan materials. Plan reports and monitoring plan performance are also the responsibility of the sponsoring association. This doesn't mean you are unaware of costs but that you have transferred the responsibility for managing the plan to another entity. This is all well and good as long as services and coverage meet your expectations and your employees are satisfied. If your costs are competitive or lower and the plan operates at a quality level that is acceptable, your association plan or pool can be the best choice you have. However, when services, health care providers, claims payments, or other features of your plan are unacceptable, there is little you can do, other than to leave the plan.

These are some questions to ask if you are considering an association plan or pool for your employee health plan:

1. How long has the pool or association plan been in existence, and who are the other members? You should be careful about joining a plan unless it has five or more years of

experience. Check to see if there are a substantial number of other members similar to your organization, by size and industry.

2. Where is the pool or association plan based, and what geographic area does it service? Remember, health care is still regional in the way it is provided, so an association plan located across the country may not have providers and services to meet the needs of your employees. If it is national, are there regional services provided for claims payment, customer representatives, provider networks, pharmacy benefits, and inpatient hospital stays?

3. What administrative and member services are provided? Many of these plans excel in member services. Often you will receive regular newsletters, notices, and circulars for distribution to employees on benefit and service topics. Sometimes these are personalized for your organization. Ask for a sample enrollment packet before you decide on the plan, to see the type and quality of plan materials provided.

4. Is there an 800 number for employee calls and for your needs as the employer? Ask about the availability of staff, dedicated personnel, and their training. Some of these issues are covered under health plan selection in Chapter 4. You should be as careful with an association plan as you are with a carrier or MCO plan under review.

5. What about claims appeals and peer reviews for any approvals required for service? Read the plan materials related to restrictions on coverage and the approval process, and have any questions answered.

6. What is the plan's history of premium increases and decreases? Some association plans and pools have a long history of minimal premium changes and perform well below national averages for health care costs due to their larger numbers and their careful underwriting policies. You can judge whether or not the plan is a good buy for the long term if it has a published premium that compares favorably with your own premium history over a period of three to five years.

7. What changes in coverage or service have been made during the previous two to three years? Some plans have improved, while others have reduced coverage and services to control costs and to attract members. Ask for a synopsis of any changes so that you can see the trend in the plan you are considering. It's better to know in advance if the plan is in the midst of a multiyear plan redesign or is instituting service cutbacks.

As with any selection, you should review plan contracts and service providers. Exhibit 13-8 shows a typical pooling clause related to benefit changes that can typically be instituted by the plan administrator who is the plan sponsor.

8. What special provisions for excess losses does the plan require? In other words, if you exceed anticipated expenses for your group, because of higher-than-projected employee health care costs, will you be assessed or expected to pay them and under what conditions? Exhibit 13-9 presents a typical pool provision to hold you accountable for excess costs. Review these provisions, and decide whether they are acceptable to you and whether you can afford to take on the risk that they imply.

Some pools require an upfront deposit; others may assess you retrospectively for fees and charges. You may be asked to make a multiyear commitment to the plan. Each of these variations should be considered in light of your needs, the plan's ability to meet them, and your comfort level with the information you have about the plan. Your health plan adviser should provide you with written recommendations that list the plan's advantages and disadvantages.

ARTICLE V

Powers of Administrator

Section 2. The Administrator will form an advisory group with representatives from each municipality, Department of Personnel, and chaired by the Administrator or his designee. This group will advise on all rate increases, terminations or additions of members and benefits changes. The committee will also review any complaints of Plan members. Said advisory group shall meet at least annually upon call of the Administrator or his designee.

EXHIBIT 13-8. Sample pooling clause on benefit changes. (Source: Halo Associates.)

Section 3. The Administrator shall have the right to levy assessments upon Members when, in its judgment, such assessments are necessary to effectuate the purposes of this agreement.

(a) Members whose loss ratio exceeds the average group loss by 25 percent for two consecutive twelve-month periods will repay 50 percent of their average excess loss on a monthly basis to be paid in full within twelve months.

This method of recouping excess loss is subject to review in five (5) years

EXHIBIT 13-9. Typical pooling clause on excess charges. (Source: Halo Associates.)

The broad powers and responsibilities of the plan sponsor or association for plan coverage, administration, and services is a two-edged sword. It is helpful to you, because it can limit your responsibility and activity; it can be troublesome when the benefits or services do not meet your needs. As with other plan choices, you need to carefully review the reputation, track record, and references provided.

■ SELF-FUNDING FOR THE SMALLER EMPLOYER

As a smaller organization, your concerns about self-funding have a unique focus. In Chapter 12 the concept, implementation, and features of a self-funded health plan are discussed in detail. In this chapter, we address the particular concerns of a smaller organization. Exhibit 13-10 lists items you should review when you consider self-funding your health plan. It's not an option open to every organization.

When should you consider self-funding? Is there a limit of size, or of resources? What differences are there between an insured and a self-funded plan for the smaller organization? What variables should you consider as a smaller organization before self-funding? These are some of the questions you need to answer before you proceed.

Your Number of Employees

Size is primary. If you have fewer than 100 employees, the viability of your being self-funded is dependent on some specific demographics and claims history parameters. If

Size

Self funding is recommended, most often for larger employers, with a minimum threshold of 100 employees. Consult your plan adviser if you have less than 100 employees.

___ >500 employees	3	Probably good risk for self-funding
___ >100 but <500 employees	2	Possibly good risk for self-funding
___ <100 employees	0	Probably poor risk for self-funding

Assets and Capital

An initial lump sum and adequate cash flow are needed to properly finance a self-funded plan. A quick calculation of total lump sum is one-year plan expenses, based on previous year premium plus 10 percent.

___ 100% of health plan expenses available	3	Probably good risk
___ 50–100% of health plan expenses available	2	Possibly good risk
___ 25–50% of health plan expenses available	1	Marginal risk
___ <25% of health plan expenses available	0	Poor risk
___ Cash flow steady and ample	3	Probably good risk
___ Cash flow ample, not steady	2	Possibly good risk
___ Cash flow steady, not ample	1	Marginal risk
___ Cash flow inadequate	0	Poor risk

Demographics

___ Average age <35 years	3	Probably good risk
___ Average age <45 years	2	Possibly good risk
___ Average age >45 years	0	Poor risk
___ Average salary >$30,000	3	Probably good risk
___ Average education >14 years	3	Probably good risk
___ Close to 50/50 distribution of males/females	3	Probably good risk
___ No known chronic or catastrophic illnesses	3	Probably good risk
___ No retiree coverage covered by plan directly	3	Probably good risk

Health Plan History

___ Premiums have stayed the same or decreased	3	Probably good risk
___ Premiums have increased 1–5 percent	2	Possibly good risk
___ Premiums have increased >5 percent in past 3 years	1	Marginal risk
___ Plan has remained the same for 3 years	3	Probably good risk
___ Plan has changed once in 3 years	2	Possibly good risk
___ Plan has changed every year in past 3 years	0	Poor risk
___ Plan design moderate, not expansive in benefits	3	Probably good risk
___ Plan design moderate, cost sharing in place	3	Probably good risk
___ Plan design enriched, cost sharing in place	2	Possibly good risk
___ Plan design moderate, no cost sharing	1	Marginal risk
___ Plan design enriched, no cost sharing	0	Poor risk
___ Plan design fluctuating	0	Poor risk
___ No utilization data available from current plan	0	Poor risk

Organizational Structure

___ Centralized, clear lines of authority	3	Probably good risk
___ Decentralized, clear lines of authority	2	Possibly good risk
___ Decentralized or centralized, lacking structure	0	Poor risk
___ Benefits, personnel, in-house staff in place	3	Probably good risk
___ Support of top management	3	Probably good risk
___ Communication good with employees	3	Probably good risk
___ Employees supportive of self-funding	3	Probably good risk
___ Adequate computerization and record keeping	3	Probably good risk
___ Positive employee relations exist	3	Probably good risk

(*continues*)

EXHIBIT 13-10. Self-funding checklist for small organizations. (Source: Halo Associates.)

Location

Where your organization does business and the health care environment of the area are key elements to the success of a self-funded plan. They are hard to measure, though, and your health plan adviser should be enlisted to help you with this section. Check only one.

___ Rural setting, adequate health care services	3	Probably good risk
___ Urban setting, quality medical services	3	Probably good risk
___ Suburban setting, adjacent to city services	2	Possibly good risk
___ Urban setting, competitive health services	2	Possibly good risk
___ Rural setting, limited health services	0	Poor risk
___ City/suburban setting, limited health services	0	Poor risk

Philosophy about Risk

Your organization will be responsible for costs and plan administration in a self-funded plan. You should assess the propensity for and willingness to assume risk before you self-fund.

___ Organization is risk taking	3	Probably good risk
___ Organization takes moderate risks	2	Possibly good risk
___ Organization avoids risk	0	Poor risk
___ Management is risk taking	3	Probably good risk
___ Management limits risk to moderate	2	Possibly good risk
___ Management avoids risk	0	Poor risk

How to Score Your Organization:

The purpose of this checklist is to help you consider self-funding in a general way. A detailed evaluation is urged once you understand the pros and cons of self-funding for your organization. The higher the score you receive on this checklist, the more likely self-funding is an option you should consider. The areas in which you scored low should be looked at carefully to determine whether they are of sufficient importance to stop you from going forward.

Total score available is 66. The closer you are to that number, the lower your risk with a self-funded plan.

EXHIBIT 13-10. Continued

you have more than 100 employees, it is more feasible for you to self-fund, although size is not the only characteristic to consider.

Assets and Capital

The next question is money. If you don't have resources to establish a reserve fund that will pay three to four months of claims at a moment's notice, don't self-fund. This has implications for the smaller organization. Cash-flow needs, operating expenses, and capital budgets are all things to consider. Evaluate your organization in this regard, and do not consider self-funding:

- If your cash flow is sporadic, or unstable
- If your operating expenses are not uniform each month and cannot be projected
- If you expect to expand, build a facility, invest heavily in materials or fixed equipment, or have other short-term need for available capital
- If you have inadequate reserve funds available (if you can't prefund all plan costs for six months, including stop-loss and professional fees)

Your Workforce

Demographics are as important as size and your current assets and capital. As a smaller organization, you will be more affected by a few high-cost claims, so it is important to project their probability when you consider self-funding.

There are three basic characteristics for you to review:

1. Is your work force young? "Young" is not a relative term. It means, is your workforce below the age when chronic and catastrophic disease begins to manifest itself (age 45). The younger the age of your workforce, the better.

2. Are your employees mostly female, or mostly of one ethnic background? If you have a preponderance of women below age 35, you should consider the costs of premature infants and possible problem pregnancies. If your workforce is primarily of one ethnic group, such as African American or Hispanic, consider the higher incidence of diabetes, prostate cancer, and hypertension among these groups.

3. Do you have a lower-paid, less-educated workforce? The cost for workers with less than a high school education, and for those who make less money, is proportionately higher as you move down the socioeconomic scale. Those who are higher paid, with more education, tend to receive earlier diagnosis and more consistent health care, which helps keep cost down.

Another consideration, somewhat related to the demographic of age, is whether your health plan offers extensive retiree benefits. You should think about the long-term cost and consider adjustments to coverage so that your self-funded plan can survive when employees reach retirement. Your health plan is a long-term commitment that should offer appropriate benefits to your employees over their employment careers. One option for retiree coverage is to limit it to reimbursement for Medicare, whether the retiree selects Part B or the new Medicare Part C with comprehensive managed-care choices. Your out-of-pocket expense then will be limited, and the more costly retiree will be removed from your self-funded plan.

Your cost history is not as good an indicator of future cost as demographics when you are a small organization. You may have had several very good years, but as employees age, one or two catastrophic claims can bankrupt your self-funded plan. You should be ultracautious in your projections of cost and in your budgeting. Review your health plan costs over the previous three years. Are they are consistently 20 percent lower than the premiums you paid, counting all administrative fees and retention? On top of this comparison, you should add another 10 percent of the total as a margin, before you even consider self-funding.

Organizational Characteristics

Relevant characteristics include your structure, how your organization operates, and the availability of staff and resources. If your organization is scattered, with a few employees in each location, it will be difficult for you to self-fund, even if you have 100 to 500 or more employees. A self-funded plan demands more in the way of employee communications, which is complicated by a widespread workforce with no cohesive central structure. However, if you have multiple division offices with a tight organizational structure, self-funding is more plausible. A central organization is appropriate, and the most logical type to self-fund, when lines of communication and decision are clear-cut. Reflect on how your organization handles major change and whether it is change-friendly before you decide to self-fund.

Consider whether you have needed organizational resources, such as a personnel or benefits office, expert staff, communication network, suitable computerization for electronic enrollment and reporting, and adequate support staff for finance and legal issues that arise with self-funded plans. Although a self-funded plan should have cost reductions in the long run, there are short-term costs for your organization to fund.

Rural, Urban, or Suburban Location

Location can determine success. If you are located in an urban area, you may be less likely to control costs than a larger employer in the same area. Your ability to negotiate discounts and compete with insurance carriers and MCOs will be limited by your size. You will be more likely in an urban area to work through a network that charges a fee for use of its discounted arrangements. Because of size, you may be limited in your choice of case management companies and others who negotiate for larger employers to reduce costs. The company you select may not have as much success with your negotiations because you are not big enough for the provider to worry about.

If you are in a rural area, you may be one of the larger employers around. As such, you may be able to negotiate for discounts effectively and to better control the providers covered by your plan. The limits of the rural setting make it more important that you establish good provider relations, and this can result in limits on discounted fees. Providers tend to be more independent and less likely to negotiate in rural settings, since competition is not the issue. Quality medical care may be a concern for you, and accessibility of specialty care may be, too. For instance, the absence of the "best" obstetrician in a rural area from a plan's network is devastating, where in a more populated area there will be several top specialists from whom to choose. The auditing of provider bills, case management coordination of services, and other typical cost-containing services may be frowned upon by rural providers, who, typically, have more control.

Even plan features, such as mail-order drug programs and generic drug substitutions, can be difficult in a rural setting. Local pharmacists are important to the services your plan members get and may balk at a plan that sends business outside the area or limits their discretion in filling a prescription. As another example, elimination of nonurgent emergency room visits may not work if there are few providers with evening or weekend hours. The hospital emergency room may be the only place to receive medical care when the condition is not life-threatening but requires attention.

Your location may be suburban, with a higher socioeconomic level and higher employee expectations for services, including specialists. It is common for employees to seek city-based specialists for catastrophic care, thus driving up plan costs. Local suburban hospitals, in order to compete, often join a consortium or network of area hospitals to maintain higher rates and market share. For your self-funded plan, this can mean less opportunity to negotiate discounts.

The problems of location are more significant for small organizations than for larger ones, because your plan will be more sensitive to market forces and more reliant on discounts to be cost-effective. In the larger plans, the Law of Large Numbers applies, and high-cost claims are absorbed more easily. The smaller self-funded plan has to operate more cost-effectively within its environment.

Employee Relations

You should assess how receptive your employees are to self-funding their health plan. If you have conducted a brief, written survey or informally surveyed employees, you will have an idea of their response. You should poll employees in some manner before making a change. Poll responses will give you useful feedback and can help you avoid miscommunication that can occur in small organizations. Word-of-mouth is almost instantaneous because of the size of your organization; it's difficult to keep management decisions quiet. Consequently, you should advise employees, seek their input, and include them in monitoring plan changes as they are made.

■ ADVANTAGES AND DISADVANTAGES OF SELF-FUNDING

If you have realistically appraised your organization and self-funding seems workable for you, you will have these rewards:

- More control over your benefits and the quality of care
- More administrative services for your staff and plan members
- Better cost containment and bang for your buck
- Reduced administrative and other costs
- Improved communication, most often personalized for your organization
- Closer management of your health plan, with greater understanding of its use

These are a few of the advantages of self-funding for the smaller organization. The disadvantages are these:

- The risk of loss from excessive claims
- Greater responsibility for plan communications and employee relations
- The need for more effort from you and your staff to manage your health plan
- Increased activity to control high-cost claims and utilization

I would rather err on the side of caution when it comes to discussing a self-funded plan with employers who have fewer than 500 employees. Your health plan is a high-cost liability for your organization, and the added risk of a self-funded plan is to be carefully evaluated. I have spent the past twenty years working on self-funded plans of different sizes and find that, just when you think everything is under control, something happens. You might say, "Well, that's life," and so it is. But when it comes to your health plan, you have to have a tolerance for risk to self-fund.

More than two-thirds of all employees covered by employer plans are in self-funded plans today. That speaks to their success and to employer satisfaction with them. Self-funding is not the only option you have as a small organization to reduce your cost, but it can be the best way to control your health plan, and to guide its services.

■ SUMMARY

When you explore health plan options as a small organization, review the essentials of your organization's size, demographics, location, organization, stability, assets and capital, employee relations, and future plans. Recognize that the choices available to you may be limited by the industry you are in, by your management team, or by your propensity for risk. Keep in mind that you are in the majority of employers in the United States and that the health and well-being of small business is a focus of federal and state government and vital to our economy. As a result, there are many support organizations and public resources that can provide low-cost free advice about your health plan.

Resources

Books

The Handbook of Employee Benefits, Second Edition, Jerry S. Rosenbloom, editor, Dow-Jones-Irwin, Homewood, IL 1985. This is a must-have reference book that covers everything from soup-to-nuts about employee benefits, including pensions and health plans. It's technical, but covers each subject in detail. An invaluable guide to health insurance, it is aimed at professionals rather than the self-funded group or the smaller organization.

HIAA Source Book of Health Insurance Data, 1997–98. Health Insurance Association of America, Washington, DC. This reference guide is packed with information about all health plans, regardless of type. Data, tables, graphs, and charts show you at a glance the comparable costs by region, utilization trends, and retiree and active employee information. You can use it at negotiations to compare costs, if you are a national company interested in regional variations, and if you require background information to consider change.

The Managed Care Yearbook, 1998, American Business Publishing, Wall Township, NJ. Although poorly printed, this publication has wonderful information, including graphs and charts to help you understand the use of benefits and their costs, and the role of managed care plans and activities in reducing costs. A summary of current legislation is included that can assist you with compliance. Because it's produced each year, it's timely.

Guidebooks to Medicare, COBRA, FMLA, and so on, Thompson Publishing Group, New York. These are useful workbooks, with ready-to-use forms and sample letters that allow you to implement procedures for COBRA, FMLA, etc. Easy-to-follow guidelines and forms can be reproduced or personalized to minimize your cost for outside administration of these regulations.

Health at Home, American Institute of Preventive Health, Farmington Hills, MI. In the large or small versions, these are the best self-care guides available. They come in Spanish and low literacy versions, and other titles cover specific issues, such as women's health, children, and seniors. Easy to follow and use as references, these guides help reduce cost and can enable your employees to take care of simple, minor medical needs at home.

Self-Funding of Health Care Benefits, Carlton Harker, International Foundation of Employee Benefit Plans, Brookfield, WI. The best overall handbook on self-funding available, with comprehensive discussions on funding, legal, and administration issues. It includes a large appendix with standard forms reproduced and explained.

Periodicals

Business Insurance, New York or Chicago. This weekly publication is the last word in the insurance industry on all insurance issues. The focus on health plans can be occasional or scattered, although there are three editions each year that include directories of great value: the third-party administration directory, a broker/consultant's directory, a utilization directory, and case management directory. There are overview articles on major health coverage issues in each edition, and summaries of how industry and market forces affect health care costs.

On Managed Care, Aspen Publishers, New York. This bimonthly publication is written and designed with a busy person in mind. It is comprehensive in the range of information about managed care plans and the industry, and how these affect bottom-line costs and service. Quick stats and facts are presented in brief charts, graphs, and newsletter-style articles. Easy to read and well edited, it's worth getting if you have or are considering a managed care health plan.

Business & Health, Montvale, NJ. This monthly publication has expanded over the past few years, and yet retains its flavor of readability and news-at-a-glance. Lots of in-depth articles on specific health program topics, by well-versed professionals, feature graphs and charts that make it easy to follow. Timely articles on hot topics and interpretation by experts make this publication helpful if you manage your health plan and want to follow industry and economic trends easily.

National Underwriter, Cincinnati, OH. This is a format like *Business Insurance*, but it is not as comprehensive. It covers the insurance industry and has good health articles, written by solid writers, but not consistently. The focus is more on property/casualty, liability, and workers compensation. If you are responsible for these programs, as well as your health plan, it may be worthwhile for you to subscribe.

Medical Benefits, Aspen Publishers, New York. This is my favorite biweekly publication for keeping up with trends, fast-breaking changes, and long-term impact of the marketplace, legislation, and the industry. Recently, a focus on managing chronic illness, wellness, and state/federal legislation shows a shift to the hot topics of the day, and updated overviews of surveys/studies as well as new sources of information to flesh out how the hotter trends affect costs, employee satisfaction, and health plan performance.

MANAGING BENEFIT PLANS

Insurance Advocate, Mt. Vernon, NY. This publication has a great directory to guide you to health plan articles, and it has a section on legislation that affects health plans in each edition. It's dry, but direct, and has a focus on actions that will affect costs and compliance requirements.

Emphasis, Tillinghast-Towers Perrin, New York. This magazine-format benefits quarterly is developed by a large consultant broker firm, and covers four to six topics in each issue, one of which is usually health insurance. Timely, in-depth articles provide expertise on a specific benefit issue. It often includes graphs and charts, and is usually easy to read.

Segal Executive Letter, The Segal Company, New York. This is one of a few newsletter-format publications provided by this consulting firm. Timely topics are discussed with the employer viewpoint in mind—whether on comparison of HMOs, impact of Medicare+Choice on retiree health costs, or medical spending accounts.

Eli Medicare Risk, Chapel Hill, NC. This low-cost publication provides down-and-dirty quick news on the managed care industry, covering mergers and legislation that will affect how service can be provided and whether costs will be affected. It is helpful to identify trends, especially if you manage a health plan that is national or covers several geographic areas.

Inside Preventive Health, Arlington, VA. This publication focuses on trends and development in wellness and health promotion programs, with specific articles on new concepts and established activities. It isn't a compilation of data, nor are studies usually published, but it is a hands-on approach to explain how these programs work.

Managing Flexible Benefit Plans, New York. This low-cost publication is for those who have a flex plan and want to track how it compares with others, and to follow trends in this area.

Benefits Quarterly, International Foundation of Employee Benefits, Brookfield, WI. This is a useful publication that covers a range of benefit topics that are timely, well researched, and both technical and well written. It's for the health plan manager looking for professional, high quality information.

American Journal of Health Promotion, Keego Harbor, MI. This publication is my favorite for new ideas and to follow program results for wellness, health promotion, and chronic disease management. It's a blue-blood publication that offers you the best in new research outcomes and scientific results for programs that affect the health and well-being of employees.

The Medicare News Brief, Washington, DC. This publication is distributed by the Health Care Financing Administration and is publicly funded. It includes the latest rate information and Medicare rules and regulations about treatments, diagnosis, and billing, as well as changes to Medicare coverage. I recommend it only for those who are self-funded and have a need to follow Medicare because retirees are covered by the health plan, supplemental to Medicare.

Organizations

International Foundation of Employee Benefit Plans, Brookfield, WI. This is the most comprehensive organization, covering all sizes and types of organizations with an interest in employee health plan costs and activities. In addition to conferences, continuing education, a library, and an electronic resource site, this organization offers publications and updates on specific and general health plan issues.

Society for Certified Employee Benefit Specialists, Brookfield, WI. This organization is for those who have attained the CEBS degree from the Wharton School program. Publications, conferences, and collegial exchange are part of CEBS membership.

Employee Benefit Research Institute, Washington, DC. This organization devotes itself to research and publications related to health program topics and analysis of current trends.

American Society of Actuaries, Washington, DC. This organization is composed of those who are certified actuaries, indicating that they have completed and passed ten standardized tests, given nationally.

Washington Business Group on Health, Washington, DC. This organization provides research information, conducts studies, and works with business and government on legislation and other initiatives to track and to improve employer sponsored health plans.

Public Risk Insurance Management Association, Washington, DC. This organization is composed of public sector risk managers, health plan managers, and those who serve this population. In addition to annual and periodic conferences, PRIMA offers publications, electronic access to resources, a staff to assist with plan questions and referrals, and annual recognition awards.

Self Insured Association of America, Santa Ana, CA. This organization provides for exchange of information, publications, and conferences for those who are self-insured for health and other programs.

Health Insurance Association of America, Washington, DC. This organization provides definitive publications, a resource available for purchase for pricing and cost information, and a range of studies and findings on issues related to health insurance.

Risk and Insurance Management Association, Washington, DC. This national organization hosts a conference and provides literature and publications on general insurance matters, focused on property/casualty and liability issues.

National Safety Council, Washington, DC. This organization sells posters, literature, and publications, and provides some training and conference materials to promote safer work sites and safer driving.

National Wellness Institute, Stevens Point, WI. This organization offers membership to vendors and organizations that encourage and provide wellness and preventive health at work sites.

Federal Sources

Health and Human Services. Many divisions of this federal department deal with health plans. The Health Care Financing Administration and many others, such as Social Security are under the auspices of this department.

Centers for Disease Control and Prevention. This federal agency has national and regional offices, and is responsible for research and monitoring of health risks, disease, and treatment outcomes related to the control of preventable and other diseases in the United States.

Health Care Finance Administration. This national organization has responsibility for the funding, claims payment, and administration of federal health plans and programs, such as Medicare and Medicaid, and those for children, the blind, and the disabled. Voluminous data and information is printed by HCFA each year to track utilization and costs for these programs and for health care in general in the United States.

Social Security Administration. This national organization is responsible for enrollment in Medicare, as well as for the government sponsored pension plan known as Society Security.

Department of Labor. This national department is responsible for ERISA compliance by employers with regard to communicating about your health plan with employees, among other responsibilities related to wages, labor standards, and so on.

Note: You can use "keyword" on your computer, if you have Internet access, to go to websites sponsored by each of these federal agencies. Just type in the name as shown.

State Sources

Department of Insurance

Department of Health

Note: These are the two main agencies of state government that handle health plan issues. Most states have websites for these departments. Using "keyword" on your computer, type in the name of the state and then go to the department name.

Local Sources

County Health Department

Independent Agents Association

Note: Look in your telephone directory under "Health Insurance Brokers, Consultants, Agents."

Websites

http://www.health.gov   Consumer information on health programs and health insurance, and guidance on access to government sponsored programs.

http://www.hcfa.gov/pubforms/pubpti.htm   Data and updates on Medicare and other government health programs.

http://www.intellectualcapital.com/index.html   Think-tank articles and perspective on health issues, governmental policy, and trends.

http://www.aahp.org   American Association of Health Plans site; primarily on managed care health plans and news about developments in this industry, cost trends, and policy positions.

http://www.nbch.org   National Business Coalition on Health site; a membership organization to advise, lobby elected officials, and inform business owners about health care issues.

http://www.allhealth.org/pub/pub.htm   Alliance for Health Reform site; updates on legal and legislative initiatives and issues that affect health plans and their cost.

http://www.hiaa.org   Health Insurance Association of America site; regular updates and annual reports on cost trends, utilization, and projections of changes in both.

http://medpro.frontierhealthcare.net/links.html   A listing of the membership of physician and other provider organizations such as the American Medical Association, American Association of Physician Specialists, etc.

http://www2.milliman.com/milliman/

Glossary

1099 reports   Annual earnings reports required by the IRS to be sent to independent contractors who have been paid fees for services. Doctors and other professionals who have been paid more than $600 receive such a report from each source of income. A report of 1099 payments can be provided by your administrator, if you are self-funded, to identify medical professionals used by your employees in your health plan.

5500 reports   Annual reports required of benefit plans, both health insurance and pensions, by the IRS and filed by the administrator to report the fiscal condition, membership, and activity of the plan to the IRS.

access to care   Ease with which plan members can receive services from medical professionals, the opposite of barriers to care. Cost, geographic proximity, approval restrictions, lack of hours, services, or staff can limit access to care.

active employee   An employee at work, not retired or disabled.

actuarial assumptions   Factors considered in projecting future costs and activity of a health plan, including basic information about the group such as numbers, gender, family and individual status of plan membership, retired and active status, projected cost increases, projected utilization changes, time period for plan operation, and past plan performance.

actuarial balance   The difference between the income rate and the expense rate of your health plan as projected by the actuary for a specific time period, usually a plan year.

actuary   A financial specialist trained to evaluate costs and the financial methods and operation of a health plan, including the computing of premiums, losses, reserves, cash flow, and lags. A certified actuary is usually a member of the Society of Actuaries.

administration, internal   Benefits staff, legal advisers, claims processors, and managers who provide administration of a health plan from within the sponsoring organization. Most often found in very large employer plans, pools, and union welfare plans. Not to be confused with internal support staff who monitor, select, and implement health plan eligibility and enrollment while the actual administration of the plan is provided by outside professionals.

administration, plan   Four general functions are covered by plan administration, which include transactions such as claims payments, benefits management such as coordination of benefits, selling and marketing such as stop-loss and open enrollment, and regulatory compliance services.

alternative therapies   Medical and health promotion services that are not traditionally covered by all health plans but that are credentialed and accepted to various degrees by the medical profession as beneficial to health. Examples are nutritionists, acupuncturists, herbalists, and massage therapists.

Americans with Disabilities Act   Federal legislation that afforded safeguards to disabled and handicapped persons for employment and benefit opportunities and rights.

annual maximum   A dollar limit placed on how much will be spent each plan year for health care services provided to your company and separately to each dependent covered by your health plan as specified by your plan. Often this limit is $1,000,000.

Association Plan   A health plan that is a pool of smaller employers or organizations that wish to combine forces to purchase insurance or to pool risk to self-insure to reduce cost and improve services to members.

benefits   The covered services and advantages provided under your employment contract with employees or as a business policy, including sick days, vacation time, a health plan, tuition reimbursement, and moving expenses.

benefits communications   Information about your health plan and other benefits that is provided to plan members and employees, some of which is required by law.

benefits consultant   A health plan professional, trained formally or informally, with experience in how health plans work, capable of advising and counseling on issues of coverage, financing, enrollment and eligibility, and provider relations.

benefit levels   The amount of coverage or benefit allowed by a health plan, including the deductible or other out-of-pocket, the number of days of hospital stays allowed, the degree of coverage for outpatient services, access to services, and the basis of payment to providers.

binder   Legal document used by insurance salespeople and carriers to signify your approval of the plan and premium quoted and your intention to purchase coverage.

brand-name drugs   Drugs for which there is no generic substitute or that are manufactured by the drug company that received a patent and FDA approval for distribution. Sometimes there is only one manufacturer; then the drug is referred to as single source.

capitation   A system or method by which to charge for services; in a health plan, a monthly fee per member, based on estimates of services to be provided. Used by hospitals, MCOs, carriers, administrators, and others who offer services on a capitated basis.

case management   Coordination of care, selection of services, referral to appropriate services, and reporting on the activity of a patient who requires complex medical services. Usually provided by carriers, MCOs, specialty companies for self-funded plans, and others who have an interest in the efficient and wise use of medical resources.

catastrophic claims   Large claims that exceed a normal amount and for which excessive cost and utilization is anticipated. Examples are cancer claims, transplants, and open heart surgery.

charges   The amount of fee generally published or routinely billed for medical services rendered, without application of any discount or negotiated reduction.

chronic drugs   Generally medications that are prescribed for consecutive, long-term use, usually more than sixty days.

chronic illness   Conditions and disease that are ongoing, often for a person's lifetime, and for which medical services, medications, and support services are expected to be needed on a long-term basis.

claims appeal process   A specific procedure, spelled out in a plan booklet, by which a plan member can ask for outside review of a nonpayment or reduced payment for services received.

claims review   Examination of a health claim by an insurance or health professional to ascertain issues of medical necessity, appropriateness of care, cost, and frequency. Often done to determine whether payment of the claim should be made.

COBRA rate   The amount of premium charged to individual and family plan members who continue coverage in an employer health plan after termination under federal COBRA legislation. The law limits the amount of premium to be paid by COBRA enrollees to 102 percent of premium charged for others in the plan.

cohort   A group of individuals separated from the whole number looked at for some common trait or characteristic. A cohort can be those employees or plan members in a group from age 18 to age 25 or those retirees between ages 55 and 65.

coinsurance   The percentage of a covered medical fee or charge for which the plan member or employee is responsible. A cost-shifting technique, the coinsurance doesn't specify a specific amount but rather a percentage, commonly 20 percent once an amount is approved.

collective bargaining agreement   Also called an employment contract, union contract, or employee agreement, this document can set forth the terms and conditions of an employee health plan, as well as other benefits provided by an employer.

collective bargaining unit   This refers to an organized group of employees whose wages and benefits are negotiated by representatives, typically elected by them annually.

commissions   The percentage of premium payable to salespeople and others by the carrier or MCO in exchange for writing the business and providing services to the client or plan sponsor. Commissions are often split among several entities when a health plan is sold.

community rating   A system of developing cost of health plan premiums based on the average utilization and cost in a geographic area. Its purpose is to ensure smaller employers of reasonable rates for health plans, although in high-cost areas, the employer with better-than-average costs will pay more if plans are community rated.

competitive bidding   The practice of soliciting bids in an impartial, objective manner, and then comparing the resulting proposals without favor to one bidder, on the basis of cost and services proposed.

complaint ratio   A rating published by each state insurance department for carriers and MCOs to indicate member satisfaction, by number and outcome of complaints, with coverage and services.

concurrent review   Services provided by monitoring health professionals, and insurance professionals when treatment or an inpatient stay is under way for a plan member. The purpose of the review is to work with the treating physician or other provider to ensure quality of care and to monitor the duration and cost of services.

consortium   A group of public sector employers who pool for health benefits, or other employee benefits, in an organization designed for that purpose, governed by legislated rules and procedures and generally not risk sharing.

consumer price index (CPI)   A published index that serves as a basis for measuring inflation and price changes over time, produced by the federal government.

continuation coverage   Plan provisions that allow for terminating members to purchase or continue coverage, subject to payment and enrollment requirements. This type of coverage is now being replaced under COBRA and HIPAA (see legislation).

coordination of benefits   Assessment, during processing of a health claim, by the administrator of other coverage that may pay for some or all of the claim. For example, a dependent child may be covered by both parents' plans when one parent's plan is primary and pays 80 percent, and the other parent's plan pays 80 percent of the remaining 20 percent. Coverage is thus coordinated between the two plans. Its purpose is to ensure that claims are not paid at a higher rate than actual charges, or excessively.

copayment   The amount paid by the plan member, usually at the time of service, to the medical provider directly, as required by the plan. It is an example of cost sharing and generally replaces the deductible and is used with provider networks. It can limit member out-of-pocket to a reasonable amount and yet shift costs to those who need and use medical services.

cost avoidance   Elimination of a previously covered cost, or a cost that is reasonable to expect. For example, when coverage is changed to eliminate certain types, such as emergency room visits, the cost has been avoided. Similarly, when a work-site wellness program results in early detection of breast cancer, the catastrophic costs of later detection are avoided.

cost containment   The practice of holding cost to a minimal increase or slowing increases below former rates or below an average. Typical cost containment is negotiated discounts used for medical providers, thus holding down increased doctor or hospital costs.

cost shifting   The practice of causing another entity or person to pay for health care services that might normally be covered by the benefits provided. For example, when the federal government requires that active employees of any age be covered by their employer first, not Medicare, it is shifting the cost of those age 65 and older who are still at work back to the employer. Or, when an employer stops retiree coverage, the cost is shifted back to Medicare or to another source. This applies, also, when an employer requires a higher deductible, copayment, or coinsurance, thus shifting cost to the plan member, who pays more out of pocket when services are needed.

cost-of-living adjustment (COLA)   A national, published percentage of increase in living expenses that is computed annually and on the basis of which contributions to health plans, and sometimes variable deductibles are calculated.

coverage   The actual terms and conditions of the health plan and what it provides. This can be specific as to a fee schedule, more general as to services, limited to a range of acceptable fees and charges, and expansive or restricted in where services can be obtained.

CPT codes These are published procedure codes, used by physicians and hospitals in billing as a uniform description of what medical service was provided. They are linked, by insurance carriers, MCOs, and self-funded plans, with a range of cost based on the geographic area in which they were provided.

dedicated funds Some states require that self-funded plans establish a fund for the health plan that is held separately from other organizational funds. This helps ensure that the money to pay claims will be there when it is needed. It is generally not allowed to be commingled, or mixed, with other moneys or to be used for other purposes.

deductible The dollar amount that a plan member must pay each plan year for medical services before the health plan begins to pay. Often this is used for nonnetwork services where a copayment is used in network. Deductibles are usually fixed for individuals, with the dependents meeting a deductible, too, and a maximum of three deductibles required for each family in the plan. This limits the deductible a family of more than three must pay in a year.

demand management This catchall phrase is used when plan member initiate services, such as case management, counseling, or coordination of discharge planning and at-home services or requests patient education or referral information or help with accessing and understanding health care services. It is often delegated to a professional medical firm to provide the demand management services that help with chronic, catastrophic, or urgent health care needs.

demographics The traits or characteristics of a group, such as gender, sex, ethnicity, age, employment status, income level, and socioeconomic level.

dependent A person who is eligible for health plan membership, based on a relationship to the employee-member, for example, a spouse, child, adopted child, or a child for whom the member is a legal guardian, as described in the plan booklet. It does not apply to parents or others who live in the person's household and may be dependents for tax purposes.

dependent student A dependent of a plan member who is eligible for coverage based on status as a full-time student, verified annually by the plan. Usually, dependent students are covered up to age 25.

disability leave Absence from work due to medical or other disability, for a time period allowed by the employer and subject to any waiver of coverage, direct pay, or other conditions that may apply.

disclosure A term made famous by ERISA, this refers to the responsibility of the employer who sponsors a health plan to inform employees and plan members about plan activities, including eligibility and enrollment conditions and other required information.

discounted fee schedule A published schedule that has been accepted as payment in full for medical services by providers in a network or who have a special contractual relationship to the health plan.

disease management Specifically refers to protocols and interventions by medical professionals with patients and their families for the purpose of assisting with treatment options and services needed for chronic or catastrophic condition or disability. The goal of these services is to improve outcomes, coordinate patient needs, educate and counsel the family, and in the process help to reduce cost to the plan and the patient by making full use of appropriate services.

early diagnosis Diagnosis of a disease or condition before its symptoms cause severe limitations or pain and before it requires intensive treatment with few options.

eligibility Health plan rules about who can join the plan and under what conditions.

employee assistance program Employer-sponsored services for employees, often at the work site and sometimes provided by internal staff, such as substance abuse or spousal violence counseling, legal referral, financial counseling, and psychiatric counseling and referral. These services are confidential and provided to improve productivity and morale and to help employees handle personal and family issues that keep them from working.

end-stage renal disease Kidney disease that requires dialysis services on an ongoing basis and results in premature death. The number of Americans with this disease and the cost of treatment has led Medicare to cover treatment of ESRD as a social program.

enrollees Employees and others covered by a health plan who have enrolled in it. Often we refer to HMO members and Medicare or Medicaid beneficiaries as enrollees.

enrollment   The process of signing up for a health plan so that you can become eligible for the benefits and coverage it provides. Enrollment for dependents may require separate enrollment.

excess insurance   Another name for stop-loss insurance, which covers excessive claims.

exclusions   Those benefits and services specifically left out of a plan.

experience   The track record of your health plan for costs, enrollment, and utilization.

experience rating   Premium calculation based on how much your claims have cost and your utilization history. If you have had low losses, for example, your experience rating will show that you should be charged a lower premium than if you had higher losses.

fee for service   A payment basis that relies upon use, where payment is made at an agreed-upon amount based on the services provided. This differs from capitation, which pays per month regardless of use. It will reflect the up-and-down cycle of use of services and is thought to cost more over the long run because there is no incentive to the provider to control use.

fee splitting   Practice prohibited by state laws that providers cannot share fees for medical services, or refer to one another or to themselves for certain services.

fees, capitated   Per member per month charges for services, such as administrative fees that are paid regardless of claim volume or services provided.

fees, incentive-based   Another fee method based on standards to be met by the administrator, consultant, or other plan vendor. The goal can be established to meet a time deadline, to accomplish a certain project, such as the development of a network, and other specific goals. Payment is linked to meeting the standard or goal established.

fees, percentage-of-claims   Some health plan administrators, carriers, and others charge for services based on the total amount of claims. This method provides no incentive for reduced cost since the higher the cost of claims, the higher the fees charged.

fees, percentage-of-savings   Sometimes used by consultants, often used by network administrators who feel confident that savings will arise from their services. The cost basis is established clearly, at the outset, and then lower-than-anticipated costs result in a savings to the health plan, and form the fee basis for the consultant or network administrator.

fees, performance-based   Consulting, administrative, and network services based on performance. Work or outcomes are tied to time deadlines, cost parameters, or discounts.

fees, retrospective   A payment method to allow for lower payments during the plan year and a catch-up payment thereafter based on claims paid, volume or amount of claims processed, and, for a health plan, the amount paid out on behalf of plan members.

fiduciary   A person or firm who provides management, administration, consulting, or policy-making services to a health plan is deemed a fiduciary of the plan and is held by law to a high standard of conduct with regard to plan activities and decisions.

frivolous utilization   Medical services that are not needed for the health and well-being of the person or that do not provide meaningful services to further treatment or to correct a condition.

generic drugs   Look-alike drugs, approved as a substitute for brand-name drugs and available at lower cost for many reasons, including the reduced cost of their development and often their lower-cost ingredients.

going to market   An insurance term used to describe the process of having a consultant or insurance professional seek bids for coverage or services you require for your health plan. It refers, specifically, to the insurance market and so does not apply to hiring a consultant, for example.

grievance procedure   Union and employee agreements usually provide a procedure to allow plan members to file a grievance against the employer if the health plan does not comply with union or employee contracts. This can be due to enrollment, eligibility, claims payment, or processing disputes. The procedure relies upon the collective bargaining process of filing a complaint, scheduling a hearing with labor and management representation, and coming to a finding based on evidence presented.

group practice association (GPA)   One type of Health Maintenance Organization (HMO), the GPA is also called a staff model where many specialists and medical providers are housed in one facility, generally owned by the HMO, and provide care there to members in a clinic setting. This type of HMO is less popular and restricts plan member more often to limited GPA physicians.

health decision support   A new discipline, this term refers to pharmacist and medical adviser support for patient treatment options, often drug therapy versus surgery or more invasive procedures. For example, it could refer to a decision about the pros and cons of assisted living centers versus a nursing home setting; or chemotherapy for prostate cancer versus radiation and medication alone.

health maintenance organization (HMO)   An entity supported by enabling federal legislation, licensed by each state, and then certified by county. Regional and localized in nature, the HMO has begun to spread out into larger networks in some cases. A capitated system of managed care, the HMO relies upon limited costs per member, restrictions to the physicians and hospitals where they have discounts, and control of care in general.

health risk assessment   A tool to measure the health risks of those completing an information form or responding to questions about their health history and lifestyle. There are computerized and written versions used to identify high-risk individuals who require further services. Every time a doctor or health professional reviews your medical history, he or she is conducting a health risk assessment.

high-cost claims   Medical claims that cost more than an arbitrary limit, such as $5,000, which indicates a catastrophic, chronic, or disabling condition. Often claims that are for certain diagnoses, such as head injury or fracture, are assigned as high-cost claims because of the long-term rehabilitation and other services anticipated.

high risk   Refers to a plan member who, by virtue of lifestyle issues such as smoking or obesity, or a family history of a condition, or personal symptoms or health history from which a predisposition to one or more diseases or conditions seems likely. For instance, someone who smokes, is obese, has hypertension, and whose father died at age 40 from a heart attack is predisposed to cardiac disease.

home health care   The fastest growing type of medical care in the United States, this refers to care for the homebound, disabled, and chronically ill where services of nurses, therapists, and other medical professionals are routinely provided in the home. Services may be to assist the patient with daily living activities or to administer medications or other treatment.

hospital discounts   Fee reductions granted by hospitals in exchange for volume business or prompt payment, to reduce their usual fees and charges for medical services, as when hospitals contract with HMOs and other carriers or with self-funded plans or large employers. Hospitals are in a competitive environment, and these arrangements help them to capture a market share.

hospital provider organization   There are many names for this type of organization, including PSN (provider service network) and PSO (provider service organization). A hospital is the organizing force behind a network of providers who then offer medical services on a capitated basis, with some reserves built in for out-of-network referrals and services.

hospitalization   Health plan coverage for inpatient hospital stays and care. This coverage is typically for 365 days of care in most typical plans. Medicare pays up to 120 days, and the patient is required to pay a deductible that decreases per day, based on the length of stay. Basic insurance covers hospitalization as a primary category of benefits, and inpatient stays are a traditional benefit from when insurance was created to cover high costs that the average person didn't have resources to cover.

individual practice association (IPA)   A type of HMO that includes numerous, sometimes thousands, of individual practices, some with several doctors, where each doctor is contracted to the HMO directly. Payment for primary care physicians in the HMO network is on a capitated basis usually, a flat amount per month for those HMO members who select a doctor to be their PCP, with specialists and other facilities being paid on a fee-for-service basis. Hospitals have direct contracts with the HMO and may be paid on a mixed capitated and fee basis.

inpatient   Patient admitted to the hospital, usually for an overnight stay.

insurance agent   A representative of the insurance carrier who is contracted to write business with the carrier or MCO directly on behalf of individuals, businesses, and brokers. Primarily works with brokers who bring multiple accounts to the agent. The agent is the intermediary with the carrier and generally writes substantial business with the carrier. Agents are often limited in the number of carriers with whom they do business.

insurance broker   The broker is a smaller business than an agent, usually, and writes direct business for individuals and smaller organizations, which is placed through agents or directly with carriers and MCOs. The broker provides hands-on service to the organization and usually writes several types of insurance with the client, such as property, liability, and workers compensation, as well as health insurance.

insurance carrier   Offers insurance products to buyers, which are underwritten by the carrier's assets, and approved by the state insurance department through which the carrier is licensed.

insurance commissioner   The head of a state insurance department who sets policies, conducts hearings, approves rate increases, examines fund and asset balances of carrier and MCOs, and implements legislation enacted by state legislatures.

insurance department   The state regulatory body that governs and supervises the insurance industry.

insurance market, hard   Times when premiums and the cost of insurance are high, usually because there is less available money to underwrite losses; times when losses are high or the economy is poor.

insurance market, soft   Periods when premiums and the cost of insurance is lower, usually because there is a surplus of money available to underwrite insurance; times when the economy is good, and losses may be lower than expected.

integrated care   The concept of combining various types of health service in a coordinated manner. For instance, workers compensation and disability care may overlap. Integration of multiple services needed through the use of disease management or case management coordination and education.

intervention   The interaction between a patient and health plan or medical provider. For instance, case management intervenes with a seriously ill patient to counsel and guide care and to assist with coordination. A medical professional intervenes with a woman with diabetes when the disease is diagnosed and treatment options are suggested. Intervention can be by telephone, in person, in writing, or by third party.

investment strategy   For a self-funded plan, it is vital to understand the importance of asset management and to adopt an investment strategy to safeguard the health plan fund. Taft-Hartley funds, managed by labor management committees, are institutional investors with major assets in the stock market, and where investment strategy is vital to the well-being of the plan run for members.

labor-management committee   For some plans, this body is informal and appointed by management and employee representatives; for others it is the plan management committee that controls and decides plan coverage, financing, administrative and procedural issues.

lag   The time between when services are performed and the claim is filed and paid by the administrator. The lag is an advantage to the funding agency, whether a self-funded sponsor or an insurance carrier.

large employer   Employers for whom the number of employees is large enough so that individual cases of catastrophic conditions can be more easily absorbed due to the large pool of plan members covered by the health plan. As a result, such loss will not usually have a direct effect on plan costs for these employer groups. Generally, an employer of 5,000 employees or more.

Law of Large Numbers   An insurance term meaning the theory and concept of spreading risk among a large pool or group of individual risks (persons, organizations, entities) to lessen the impact of loss on all. It is the basis of insurance that not all of those insured will collect as much as they pay in premium so that the excess can be used to cover those who suffer losses. Insurance is sold on the basis that coverage will be there when you need it.

leave of absence   Unpaid time away from work, although the employee is still considered an active employee. Leaves are used for sabbaticals in the teaching field, for instance, and now family leaves are part of employee rights under the law for most organizations, and disability leaves are also permitted. Health insurance rules apply to each situation.

legislation   State, federal, and local laws that are passed to regulate or mandate (require) insurance terms and conditions of employer-sponsored and other health plans available for purchase by individuals and groups.

ADA (Americans with Disabilities Act)   This federal law prohibits discrimination by employers against the disabled in many areas, including provision of health insurance and other benefits.

COBRA (Consolidated Omnibus Budget Reconciliation Act)   Federal legislation that requires a continuation of coverage for employees and dependents who lose coverage due to a change such as termination of employment, loss of dependent status due to divorce, or completion of schooling, or for other reasons. It provides for from eighteen to thirty-six months of coverage, depending on the specific situation.

ERISA (Employee Retirement and Income Security Act)   Landmark federal legislation that requires reporting and disclosure and strict adherence to standards for fiduciaries of employer-sponsored health plans. ERISA plans include self-funded health plans and labor-management (union) pension and health benefit funds.

FMLA   The federal Family Medical Leave Act requires that employers allow employees to take family leave within limits for the care of children, elders, spouses, or themselves during the year and further that they continue health coverage in such cases. This law ensures an employee's right to take a leave for medical needs of family members and guarantees that their health coverage will continue to be provided, under specified conditions.

HMO Protection   Federal legislation passed in 1985 to protect health maintenance organizations by requiring that employers of a certain size allow both models of such plans, the staff model and the individual practice model, to be offered to employees as an option if the HMO petitions the employer to do so and if the HMO is licensed to provide service in the area. This affords HMOs several marketing and organizational advantages and helps them grow.

Medicare Act   Landmark legislation that created a system of health coverage for the aged, some disabled citizens, and those with end-stage renal disease, provided in two categories, Part A, hospitalization, and Part B, major medical. It is funded by payroll contributions of employers and employees and by the general fund of the United States. About 25 percent of the Part B health coverage is funded by premiums collected from those enrolled for Part B. A new coverage, dubbed Part C, was enacted in 1998 and allows for Medicare-eligible persons to select a managed-care option for Medicare coverage. Various HMOs, other MCOs, and insurance carriers offer a range of programs that follow rules of preapprovals, primary care physician oversight of all services, restricted access to services without approvals, and sometimes added benefits, including coverage for prescription drugs.

Patient Rights Act   Federal legislation that ensures access to specialists, provides liability recourse if the managed-care organization denies care and the patient's health is affected, and guarantees the right of patients to information about services and providers covered by the health plan offered.

Portability Act (Health Insurance Portability and Access Act, or HIPAA)   Recent federal legislation that requires health plans, whether sponsored by an employer or by insurance company, to limit pre-existing-condition clauses and to extend both coverage and the right to plan enrollment so that fewer workers are without insurance when they change jobs or are between jobs.

Social Security Act   Provided pension income for retired workers, based on contributions by employers and employees over the working lifetime. This federal legislation has been expanded to provide SSI or Supplemental Income, which covers the disabled who require specific care.

Taft-Hartley Act   Major federal legislation that created the union pension and welfare funds, run by labor-management committees and trustees to provide health coverage to eligible union members and their families.

TEFRA (Tax Equity and Finance Reconciliation Act)   Expands the coverage of older workers by employer-sponsored plans so that Medicare doesn't cover workers or their spouses age 65 and older until they retire.

mail-order drugs   Also known as a maintenance drug or chronic drug program, this is usually an added service to a prescription drug card for the drug benefit. The advantages, lowered cost of the drugs and reduced fees to dispense the drugs, make a mail-order service useful for self-funded plans. They are sometimes used for prescription fills of drugs that need to be taken over a long time, such as sixty, ninety, or 120 days or longer, and not for urgent drugs, most often prescribed for thirty days or less.

major medical   A main category of coverage in a health plan that usually includes doctor and specialist services, outpatient testing and treatment, and services connected with outpatient care.

managed care   Several versions of managed care exist, but the most common is the managed-care organization, which requires care to be managed by one physician, sometimes called the gatekeeper or primary care physician. Other versions include plan provisions that require an approval of some sort before services are covered, such as preadmission certification or discharge planning.

managed care approval   Permission required before certain services can be covered, from a primary care physician, an insurance company department, an outside, objective medical person, or a claims administrator. The purpose is to reduce unnecessary or excessive services, thereby reducing cost, and to monitor health care services provided to plan members, sometimes allowing for advance discounts to be negotiated.

market forces   Economic forces, such as the availability of capital, interest rates, unemployment, inflationary trends, losses, and underwriting errors which relate to profitability, and to competition among insurance companies and others who offer health plans. These market forces combine to affect the cost of coverage and services provided.

maximum, annual   A fixed amount payable for all claims of each plan member during one plan year. Often this applies only to major medical coverage, although it can apply to drug coverage or any other specified benefit, or to all benefits provided by the plan. For instance, a $100,000 annual maximum for major medical means that all major medical claims, combined for each member, for a plan year will not be paid by the plan after they total $100,000.

maximum, lifetime   A fixed amount beyond which the plan will not pay for all covered claims for each plan member for all types of coverage, combined, for the person's lifetime. For instance, a $1,000,000 lifetime maximum means that the plan will pay up to $1,000,000 total for one member's claims, no matter how long the member is covered by the plan and subject to all terms and conditions of the plan.

maximum benefit   Some benefits are restricted for coverage and have their own maximums. A commonly restricted benefit has been chiropractic care, which often is limited to a certain number of visits or a total dollar amount for each member for each plan year. Another often restricted benefit is dental coverage or a prescription drug benefit. Most benefits subject to a maximum are not connected with urgent care or high cost, which has traditionally been the focus of health insurance plans.

Medicaid   A federal program, administered by the states and county government, subject to mandates (requirements) for services, which provides coverage to people in need and health care services to women and children. Doctors and other providers are part of a Medicaid network, which makes payment at a greatly reduced rate for the care provided. This program is funded by the general fund of the United States.

medical necessity   Need for a particular kind of treatment. Payment of health claims rests on whether or not the service provided was medically necessary or required to improve or stabilize a person's health, in the opinion of the ordering physician and based on the patient's condition and health history. In theory, this definition is applied to reduce abuse of services and unnecessary procedures and services to be billed to the health plan.

Medigap insurance   Supplemental insurance programs bought by those eligible for Medicare, or provided by employer plans for retirees as a coordination with Medicare coverage, where payment is made only for services not provided by Medicare or for the out-of-pocket expense required by Medicare, such as a deductible.

members   Those eligible for, and enrolled in, a health plan.

mid-sized employer   An employer who employs more than 500 and fewer than 5,000 employees.

minimum premium plan   A negotiated premium plan in which an employer pays less than the anticipated amount of claims and administrative expense, calculated and based on the number of plan members and the history of claims cost. This type of arrangement may help an employer with cash flow. Typically, there is a catchup payment required at the end of the plan year, periodically during the year, or some payment in advance, minimum premiums paid during the year, and another payment made at the end of the plan year based on the actual costs.

morbidity   Rates of death and illness, which affect a health plan, especially whether they occur more often than an average or fluctuate outside the average, up or down. A morbidity factor and its impact on claims cost and utilization is usually developed by an actuary.

negotiated fee for service   A fee schedule or range of fees to be paid for specific services that has been negotiated with one or more providers of health services to plan members. Payment depends on the number of services, and the negotiated fee may be 10–50 percent lower than the doctor or facility's going rate.

network   A group of contracted providers who agree to provide services on some reduced cost basis, subject to acceptance by the network, and with the understanding that participation will increase or maintain their volume of services provided to health plan members who are eligible to use the network. Some networks are developed by carriers or MCOs, and others are developed separately and then contracted to health plans.

nonnetwork providers   Those who are not participating in a network. Such status will limit coverage of services from these providers and may increase the member's out-of-pocket expense.

notification   Written or verbal communication that alerts a health plan, or a plan member, to a relevant fact or situation that triggers the need to communicate, such as notification to a plan that a member is scheduled for a hospital admission or is continuing a course of treatment that requires notification periodically. Another example is notification to a plan member of new rights, diminished rights, or changes in coverage made in response to the member's situation or condition, such as notification of the right to continuation of coverage under COBRA, the Family Medical Leave Act, or HIPAA.

notification requirements   Rules established by the health plan, in compliance with any state or federal regulations, by which notification to a plan or to a member must be made in order for the condition or situation to be routinely handled under the plan.

nurse advice line   A telephone service, usually an 800 number, where patients and plan members call for information about health topics, nurse counseling and patient education, guidance with obtaining medical services, referrals to network providers, and general assistance with health care needs. Some services track member calls and report data to plan sponsors, who usually pay for the service through premiums or a monthly fee based on the number of members eligible to call.

nurse practitioner   A licensed nurse, with advanced training, who works under a doctor's supervision but is allowed to dispense prescriptions and to provide specific services that were formerly reserved to medical doctors.

nurse, practical   A licensed nurse with less training than a registered nurse but who has met standards set by each state for practical experience and training.

nurse, registered   A licensed nurse who has completed course work and passed a standardized test that enables the nurse to work with acutely ill patients in hospital and other settings.

open enrollment   A set time period, usually one month, during a health plan year when members can choose between health plan options offered by the employer or organization.

out-of-pocket costs   Costs that, under the plan, are paid by members. This includes deductibles, copayments, coinsurance, and expenses incurred beyond annual and other maximums.

outpatient care   Healthcare services provided to members who are not hospitalized overnight to receive them and that are not billed by the hospital as in hospital care.

over-the-counter medications   Substances, supplements, most vitamins, and other extracts that can be purchased without a doctor's prescription. These can include some alternative substances such as herbs and other treatments and standard tablets, liquids, creams, or ointments used by the average person as a home remedy or treatment. Examples are calamine lotion, aspirin, some eye drops, vitamin C, iodine extract, cold compresses, food supplements, and herbal teas.

participants   Those who join a plan, network, or other health care service. Most often, these are medical providers who join a group to provide services, contractually, at a discount. They can also be employees who participate in optional services offered, sometimes at a fee to them.

participating provider organization (PPO)   A group of providers, often doctors, hospitals, and other facilities, that agree contractually to provide services through a separate organization that sells those discounted services for a fee to health plans. Sometimes the PPO itself offers coverage to health plans on a premium basis, much the same as an insurance company.

patient education   Counseling and information provided to a patient on request or as directed that is specific to a health condition, medical need, or inquiry. This is often provided by a nurse or nurse call center at the patient's instigation, although it can be provided in a doctor's office, at a group setting, or by another health care facility.

per diem   Fees charged on a daily basis for services. This refers to inpatient hospital stays, which are computed daily and based on complex formulas that take all hospital costs, direct and indirect, into account. Consultants and other shorter-term health plan advisers may also have a per diem or daily rate for services.

per member per month   A common payment method used to charge for health plan premiums, PPO services, nurse call lines, administrative services, and most ancillary services to health plans. This method is useful, since plan membership is computed monthly as members join or leave health plans.

physician autonomy   The freedom of a doctor to decide appropriate services for a patient, without seeking outside approval from an insurance company, MCO, or other doctor.

physician's assistant   A medical provider with specialized training who is allowed to provide nearly all of the services provided by a doctor, but under a doctor's supervision and responsibility.

plan amendment   An addition or change to the plan that has been approved. Notice of such amendments is required to be made to plan members and, depending on their nature, to various government agencies.

plan design   The terms, conditions, special features, and coverage of a health plan.

plan documents   All materials that relate to the plan, including a summary plan description, any summaries of material modifications, claim forms, enrollment forms, contracts with insurance carriers, MCOs, administrators, consultants, union or employee contracts related to the health plan, financial summary and annual report, all forms required by state, federal, or local government, and the establishment and termination documents for the health plan.

plan management   A system to monitor and guide the health plan's activities, including claims payment, enrollment and eligibility, employee relations, administration, financial performance, investment of assets and payment of plan costs, plan communications, health plan design, selection of vendors and providers, and relationship with networks and providers. All aspects of a health plan that require management skills of planning, implementation, monitoring, and adjusting.

plan performance   Measurement of plan activities against standards and goals that determine whether the health plan is effective for the sponsoring organization.

plan provision   Each item in a plan that governs the terms, conditions, special features, and coverage provided or required by it.

plan sponsor   The organization that offers the health plan to members. Often, it is the employer, a union, or an association.

point-of-service plan   A health plan that requires out-of-pocket payment and decision about which provider to use when a service is needed. Usually such a plan has a network of providers attached to it, for whom the patient's out-of-pocket is limited or capped. Some plans allow the member total freedom in selection of a provider at a higher out-of-pocket cost.

pool   A group of organizations or a sponsoring organization where members are employers who can join the group and receive reduced health plan costs, additional services, and a fixed level of benefits, subject to terms and conditions set by the pool for enrollment, eligibility, and plan use.

pooling charge   A fee charged by most carriers and health plans as part of their premium, sometimes required by the regulating state, which becomes a fund to pay catastrophic or unexpected claims. This charge is expected to help stabilize premium for those who contribute to it. This fee is used to offset unexpected morbidity levels.

preadmission certification   Plans may require, as a term of coverage, that the plan be notified before a service is provided to a plan member, most often hospitalization, and that the plan certify the admission in order for it to be covered. Questions of the diagnosis, the doctor, the name of the hospital, the length of stay expected, and the condition of the patient, including whether or not the patient is a covered member, will be asked by the plan before certification is made.

preexisting condition   Illness, or a medical condition, that exists before a member is covered by the health plan. Some plans exclude services and claims for such conditions for a spell of time, and some federal guidelines now limit how such exclusion can be made.

premium   The amount of money charged on a monthly or annual basis for each covered member in a health plan. Usually there is a separate amount for individual coverage (the member only) and for family coverage (the member and eligible dependents). Other categories may exist for the plan, too.

premium equivalent   The amount of money charged on a monthly or annual basis for each covered member of a self-funded plan. Established for individual and family enrollments, and perhaps for other categories, such as Medicare-eligible (when retirees are covered) or two-person families.

premium illustration   A document that shows the plan sponsor what fees and charges, including retention or profit, and all taxes, administrative fees, and anticipated claims or other costs are added to calculate the premium quoted. Since premiums are quoted in advance, much of the premium illustration will be based on projections by the carrier or MCO, except for the fees they will be receiving.

premium tax A state charge for fully insured health plans (1–4 percent of premium), paid by the plan sponsor (usually the employer) as part of the premium charged by the insurance carrier or MCO. This charge is avoided by self-funded plans.

prescription drug card program A convenient, widespread program where a card, similar to a credit card is provided to plan members, who can use it at participating pharmacies to receive prescription drugs subject to the terms of the plan for deductible, limits, or coinsurance and copayments. This method of drug coverage replaced an earlier method of reimbursement where the member paid for the drug and then sought reimbursement from the plan for covered drug expenses.

prescription drugs Medications and drugs that require a doctor's prescription in order to purchase them, divided into urgent medications (seven to twenty-one days' supply) and chronic or maintenance medications, which are required over the long term to control or treat an illness or condition.

preventive health program An organized and integrated system of services, often brought to a work site or facility that encourage healthier lifestyles among health plan members, provide early diagnosis, patient education, and interventions to promote appropriate care, and offer plan sponsor-supported services to improve health and decrease health plan costs. There are embryonic programs and highly sophisticated and successful programs that strive toward this goal.

primary care physician (PCP) A medical doctor, usually an internist, family practice specialist, or OB/Gyn, who has been identified by the insurance carrier or MCO as someone qualified to manage the health care needs of plan members. Plan members must consult with and gain approval from this physician for all medical services, subject to plan provisions, before they receive services. Most often, a written permission or referral is required. This physician is usually paid on a capitated basis. Payment is made whether or not the person visits the physician.

projections Estimates or educated guesses about cost and utilization in the future that are made by a self-funded plan, health plan advisers, actuaries, insurance carriers, and MCOs based on what costs and utilization patterns have been in the past.

protocols Step-by-step guides to how services are provided. These are used by physicians as they model their care of patients to existing treatment protocols, amending them to meet the specific needs or condition of the patient and their reactions. They are used by case management nurses and other health professionals who follow guidelines in providing medical services. The purpose of such guidelines is to establish logical and minimum standards for services, not to be followed by rote in every instance.

provider A medical doctor, nurse, nurse practitioner, dentist, optician, pharmacist, home care aide, physician's assistant, specialist, case management nurse, hospital, diagnostic facility, radiation treatment facility, and other medical suppliers and providers who render care to patients.

quality of care Linked to outcomes, or the success of various treatments and services to improve and maintain the health of patients, quality is dependent on the training, credentialing, and track record of medical providers. Measurements for quality include preventive services, death rates, surgery rates, outcomes of services, inpatient stays, outpatient utilization, use of drug therapies, survival rates for catastrophic illness, and so forth.

referrals, medical A permission slip to receive services and have them covered by your health plan. The referral system depends upon a medical provider, health plan administrator, or another approval source, to agree that the service is medically necessary and that it should be provided by the medical provider identified in the referral.

report, budget Report that tracks how close to a budgeted amount your costs are. This is important to a self-funded plan and to plans that are based on minimum premium where additional moneys may be needed at year end, based on costs. Keeping a running balance of plan payments and costs compared to budget is a prudent way to have advance notice of any problems with meeting plan expenses.

report, cost savings Periodic and annual measurement of administrative savings, such as coordination of benefits, subrogation recoveries, elimination of noneligible plan members, and claims adjudication savings. Other savings include the savings from a network (whether PPO, POS, HMO, or MCO plan) compared to nonnetwork; any negotiated fees on a case-by-case or planwide basis, and reduced cost of drug, dental, or other services as a result of changes to the plan or to the payment method used.

report, lag   A projection of claims that will be sent in over a certain time period, based on estimated utilization and a report of actual claims paid from an earlier time period in the current time period are both lag reports. For instance, if a December claim is paid in January, and you have a lag report from January, it will explain how many claims, and how much in claims dollars was spent in January on December claims. Also, the estimated "lag" of unpaid, but incurred claims is calculated to plan for their payment when they are submitted.

report, providers   Report on which providers are used by your plan and what sorts of services they are ordering and providing. The cost of services, frequency of visits, and outcomes for each provider is important to monitor. Network providers and nonnetwork are tracked separately, as are relative costs and use of each type of provider.

report, utilization   Report on which services are used and how often by which plan members and in what patterns. The overall look at how plan coverage and services are meeting, or not meeting, the needs of your employees and plan members.

reporting plan   Reporting is vital to efficient management and includes the need to report certain information to plan members, by law. Management of your health plan relates to its use, cost, enrollment, and any problems. Your plan members are entitled to know what is paid on their behalf for each claim and annually and how the plan is doing financially and administratively.

retiree   A former employee who is now retired from work with the employer-sponsor of the health plan and eligible for retiree benefits. If not eligible, the term is "former employee." A retiree can be actively working at another organization and covered by that health plan or may be fully retired and not working.

retrospective rating plan   A plan for which a final payment is made on the basis of costs for claims and administrative services after the end of the plan year, usually when all claims have been received (three to six months after the end of the plan year). These plans reduce the cost during the year to a minimum premium and are available mainly to those plan sponsors with adequate capital and assets to ensure payment when due.

retrospective review   Review of a claim after the service has been rendered, and before or after payment has been made, with a goal of determining accuracy of charge or payment. This is conducted often by a trained nurse or other health professional, or by a plan adviser or financial expert.

risk factors   These are characteristics, some genetic, some medical, and some lifestyle related, that are recognized to have an impact on the health status of an individual and that correlate to the known incidence of certain illness or conditions. For example, a risk factor for cancer is cigarette smoking; for diabetes, obesity; for cardiac arrest, high blood cholesterol.

safety program   A system of communication, training, management commitment and reports to encourage and reduce frequency and severity of accidents and injuries at the workplace.

second surgical opinion   Consultation with another physician or specialist with regard to a diagnosis, condition, or treatment by a patient. This is sometimes required for surgery that is common and sometimes optional. Some plans require a second opinion from a special panel paid by the plan to monitor such surgery or services.

segregated funds   Health plan moneys that are kept separate to pay for plan costs. This concept of a separate fund is an assurance to plan members that the plan sponsor intends the health plan to stay solvent if it is self-funded, and, if insured, that its costs will be paid.

self-care   An approach to health care services that provides patient education and assistance when a health condition arises so that care can be rendered at home or by the patient. Examples are the home remedies used for simple sprains or self-medication with aspirin and rest or antihistamines for colds and flu.

self-funding   Use of a fund to pay health claims and cost, with moneys deposited to the fund by the plan sponsor. It is another term for self-insurance and includes the elements of risk and offsetting risk with stop-loss coverage.

self-insurance   Establishment and maintenance of a fund and program to provide a health plan with the plan sponsor's assumption of the risk for losses. Often, this risk is subcontracted to stop-loss carriers and others in exchange for an insurance policy for a certain level of loss.

set-up fees   Service fees charged by providers, most often third-party administrators or carriers and MCOs, to establish or modify your health plan or to initiate new services.

single-source drugs   Prescription drugs manufactured, under copyright, by one manufacturer. They tend to be substantially higher-priced than other types of drugs.

social programs   Publicly supported programs that provide benefits to individuals and families as legislated by local, state, or federal government.

Social Security Income   Designed for the disabled and for dependent children of deceased workers, this legislation has grown in importance with the increase in the disabled population. This income-based program is supplemented by other Medicare benefits.

specifications   Detailed requirements published and distributed to companies and individuals invited to bid on providing health plan services.

stop-loss insurance   This insurance accepts a layer of risk from the health plan sponsor in exchange for a premium calculated on the likelihood that the company will have to pay. Claims history, demographics of the covered members, and the extent of coverage are among the factors considered by the carrier as premium is developed.

stop-loss insurance, aggregate   This is standard insurance, approved by each state, provided by an insurance company for a premium to cover health plan losses that rise above an agreed-upon level for the plan year. This insurance covers the health plan as a whole, not individual health plan members. The level after which payment is made is called the attachment point and is often calculated at 25 percent to 150 percent of the projected, or anticipated, cost of the plan for the year.

stop-loss insurance, specific   This insurance, also licensed and regulated by each state and provided by an insurance carrier, covers the health plan for each individual member whose claims exceed a specific amount for the plan year. Often this amount is set at $75,000 to $100,000 for the year.

subrogation   Recovery of medical expenses from those who have been injured where a lawsuit pays for their medical costs based on a requirement that they repay health-plan payments made. The purpose of this plan provision is so that moneys can be recovered when a settlement or payment results from the lawsuit.

summary of material modifications   Plan amendments or changes that need to be communicated to plan members, especially if they occur during the plan year, or as a supplement to the summary plan description. A readable explanation of the change and how plan members are affected is required to be distributed to all plan members.

summary plan description   A full explanation of the eligibility, enrollment, coverage levels, out-of-pocket expenses, plan administration, procedures for participating in the plan and for filing or appealing claims, and a long list of plan-related information included in a user-friendly booklet that is distributed to all plan members. It is meant to alert them to the benefits to which they are entitled and to explain any limitations, terms or conditions, that apply to them.

surviving spouse   When a plan member dies and has a dependent spouse who is covered under the plan, the surviving spouse must receive a notice of any change in status, what to do to remain in the plan and any costs, and how to exercise any available options for coverage.

tenure   A requirement of some health plans that each enrollee, after a set number of years, be entitled to lifetime membership in the plan, subject to its terms and conditions. For many this means that the plan will cover the member in retirement at reduced or no cost, and for others it means that the plan will allow the member to remain as long as the premium is paid within a set time limit.

termination   End of an employee's stay with an employer, either by choice or when fired or for some other reason. For a health plan member in an employer-sponsored plan, termination results in limited or no coverage under the plan or COBRA- and HIPAA-required coverage.

tiered benefits   Some plans create different standards for eligibility and coverage for groups of employees or plan members based on bargaining unit, employee agreement, or years of service. For example, for new hires benefits may start after six months, compared to long-term workers, who were covered within thirty days. Coverage can be at a different level, too, with longer-term employees receiving a higher level of benefits and new hires covered at lower annual maximums or higher deductibles. Benefits at different levels, or tiers, develop when plan sponsors make adjustments to a health plan based on costs and organizational needs over time.

trend   Patterns in health care. Components are used to compute and project likely increases or decreases by percentage of health care costs. Medical inflation, utilization rates of high-cost procedures, new technology, are all part of the measurement.

twenty-four hour care   A concept that includes disability, workers compensation, and health coverage as one complete set of benefits for employees. Advocates say that it will eliminate duplication and unnecessary expense. Others argue that they are different types of coverage with different goals and purposes and should be kept separate.

underwriting   A method for calculating risk and its cost, used by the insurance industry and provided by actuarial and finance experts who consider a wide range of factors to conclude likely losses for particular groups and larger entities.

union welfare funds (also known as **Taft-Hartley Funds**)   Pools that gather payments from various employers for union workers. The union manages the fund, its benefits, and its administration on behalf of members. These funds are huge and account for more than 50 percent of all investments in the U.S. stock markets.

usual, customary, and reasonable (UCR or UC)   Standard fees for medical procedures, by geographic region. Charges made by hospitals and other providers are tracked by insurance companies, and by specific organizations, which develop standardized fee levels by procedure in a given geographic area. National companies sell these schedules to guide self-funded plans, third-party administrators, and others on appropriate payments to doctors, specialists, and other providers for specific services. Each doctor has a profile, which is added to others in the area to create a composite fee that is acceptable to most health plans.

utilization   The use of services, as measured by industry norms of inpatient stays, outpatient services and treatments, and including the demographics and established history of use of the group examined.

utilization review   Trained examination of services provided, taking into account the condition or diagnosis of the patient, health history, treatment pattern and previous treatment, to determine if the services provided were appropriate, within medical necessity guidelines, in keeping with accepted protocols, and helpful to the patient.

vesting   Attainment by an employee of a required number of years of service, which earns a percentage of permanent rights in a benefit provided. For instance, after ten years some health plans "vest" employees with the right to health plan participation whether or not they remain employees.

waiting period   The time required before an employee or potential plan member is eligible to enroll for coverage under the health plan. Longer waiting periods are more common today, with three to six months usual.

wellness program   A series of services and activities offered at the work site or other facility that promote and encourage well-being and good health.

Workers Compensation   A required coverage, regulated by each state, to allow for wage replacement and medical costs for those injured while at work. This coverage can be fully insured or self-funded and is often high cost for hazardous positions, and those where employees are exposed to danger from bloodborne or airborne pathogens.

work-hardening program   A system to provide rehabilitation and counseling services to the disabled and those injured on the job. The focus and goal are to have the employee return to some level of work in a reasonable time period. It is a humane and cost-effective method to help those who may function in a reduced capacity to return as valued, productive employees.

Bibliography and Suggested Readings

General Reading Tips

Certain publications focus on cost containment, others on background material and concepts, still others on specific interest areas such as wellness, case management, HMOs, traditional coverage, small group insurance, and issues. Other publications provide data and information without editorial context or guidance. My suggestions for reading material and its use are included in the Appendix.

Chapter One

"Average Health Costs 1998," *Segal Report*, The Segal Company, New York, May 1998, p. 3.

Changing Demographics and the World of Work, Issue Brief No. 172, Employee Benefit Research Institute, Washington, DC, April 1996.

Employee Benefit Planning, Jerry S. Rosenbloom and G. Victor Hallman, Prentice-Hall, Englewood Cliffs, NJ, 1981, pp. 1–18.

"Employers Step Up Healthcare Quality Initiative in Private Market," *The Executive Report on Managed Care*, vol. 11, no. 8, p. 4, 1997.

Federal Cost Shifting: A Continuing Trend, Harvey C. Sigelbaum, Amalgamated Life Insurance Company, New York, 1989, pp. 3–6.

Fundamentals of Employee Benefit Programs, Employee Benefit Research Institute, Washington, DC, 1990, pp. 177–185.

"Health Care Payers' Coalition Urging N.J. Powers to Preserve Charity Funding of Blues," *Insurance Advocate*, Dec. 15, 1997, p. 35.

HHS News, Anne Verano, U.S. Dept. of Health and Human Services, Health Care Financing Administration, Office of the Actuary, Washington, DC, Nov. 22, 1994, pp. 1–3, figure 1.

"In Search of Value—An International Comparison of Cost, Access, and Outcomes," *Medical Benefits*, vol. 15, no. 1, p. 8, 1998.

"The National Health Care Dollar, 1995," *Source Book of Health Insurance Data 1997–1998*, Health Insurance Association of America, Washington, DC, 1998, p. 90.

"National Health Expenditure Projections, 1994–2005," Sally T. Burner and Daniel R. Waldo, Data View, *Health Care Financing Review*, vol. 16, no. 4, pp. 221–225, Summer 1995.

"National Health Expenditures, 1994 & 1995," *Source Book of Health Insurance Data 1997–1998*, Health Insurance Association of America, Washington, DC, 1998, p. 102.

National Hospital Panel Survey, Trend Analysis Group, American Hospital Association, *Monthly Reports for January 1991–June 1996*, April 1998, tables 1, 2.

"A New Alliance: Between Physicians and Hospitals," *Emphasis* (Tillinghast-Towers Perrin, New York), vol. 1, pp. 6–9, 1998.

"N.J. Investigations Chief Reports 65% of Fraud At Blue Cross Committed by Medical Providers," Vincent R. Zarate, *Insurance Advocate*, Nov. 2, 1996, p. 5.

Percentage of Plans by Type That Include Coverage for Infertility Treatment, by Region, St. Anthony's Health Care Risk Contracting Report, March 1998, p. 6.

"Personal Consumption Expenditures for Medical Care, 1995," *Source Book of Health Insurance Data 1997–1998*, Health Insurance Association of America, Washington, DC, 1998, p. 93.

"Providers of Group Medical Expense Coverage," *Employee Benefits*, 2nd ed., Burton T. Beam, Jr., and John J. McFadden, Irwin, Homewood, IL, 1988, pp. 144–160.

Retiree Medical Coverage—Let's Talk Expensive, Newsbriefs, International Society of Certified Employee Benefit Specialists, Brookfield, WI, 1991, pp. 3–5.

Segal Trend Survey, The Segal Company, New York, January 1998, pp. 1–5.

Sources of Health Insurance and Characteristics of the Uninsured, Issue Brief No. 192, Employee Benefit Research Institute, Washington, DC, Dec. 1997.

"Steady Health Plan Costs Seen," *National Underwriter*, Nov. 11, 1998, pp. 21, 25.

"Suspected Fraud Cases Investigated by Health Insurers, by Type and Method of Fraud and by Perpetrator, 1993–1995," *Source Book of Health Insurance Data 1997–1998*, Health Insurance Association of America, Washington, DC, 1998, p. 185.

"Trends in Health Insurance Coverage," Netscape, IC Policy Online, May 8, 1997, Employee Benefits Research Institute, Washington, DC.

Websites

http://www.health.gov   Consumer information on health programs and health insurance, and guidance on access to government sponsored programs.

http://www.hcfa.gov/pubforms/pubpti.htm   Data and updates on Medicare and other government health programs.

http://www.intellectualcapital.com/index.html   Think-tank articles and perspective on health issues, governmental policy, and trends.

http://www.aahp.org   American Association of Health Plans site; primarily on managed care health plans and news about developments in this industry, cost trends, and policy positions.

http://www.nbch.org   National Business Coalition on Health site; a membership organization to advise, lobby elected officials, and inform business owners about health care issues.

http://www.allhealth.org/pub/pub.htm   Alliance for Health Reform site; updates on legal and legislative initiatives and issues that affect health plans and their cost.

http://www.hiaa.org   Health Insurance Association of America site; regular updates and annual reports on cost trends, utilization, and projections of changes in both.

http://medpro.frontierhealthcare.net/links.html   A listing of the membership of physician and other provider organizations such as the American Medical Association, American Association of Physician Specialists, etc.

Chapter Two

Annual Health Insurer Complaint Rankings, Health Maintenance Organizations, New York State Insurance Department, Albany, NY, 1997.

Cancer Facts & Figures—1997, American Cancer Society, Atlanta, GA, 1997, p. 19.

Consumers' Guide to New York's Managed Care Bill of Rights, The Public Policy and Education Fund of New York, Albany, NY, April 1, 1997.

"Consumers Rate HMOs above FFS," *On Managed Care*, Aug. 1998, p. 5.

"Designing Medical Care Expense Plans," Charles P. Hall, *The Handbook of Employee Benefits*, 2nd ed., Jerry S. Rosenbloom, editor, Dow Jones-Irwin, Homewood, IL, 1985, pp. 117–130.

"Distribution of Health Plans in the Market, 1997," *Source Book of Health Insurance Data 1997–1998*, Health Insurance Association of America, Washington, DC, 1998, p. 58.

"Firms Assess Value of Cost Control Tools," Jerry Geisel, *Business Insurance*, February 5, 1990, pp. 1, 23.

Fundamentals of Employee Benefit Programs, Employee Benefit Research Institute, Washington, DC, 1990, pp. 209–222.

"Greater Recognition of Need For Intervention/Support for Chronic Medical Conditions Is Now Developing," Barbara A. Morris, *Insurance Advocate*, Dec. 14, 1996, p. 35.

"Health Plan Report Cards Are Not Helping Consumers," *The Executive Report on Managed Care*, vol. 11, no. 8, pp. 2–3, 1998.

"Key Health Insurance Statistics, 1990–1995," *Source Book of Health Insurance Data 1997–1998*, Health Insurance Association of America, Washington, DC, 1998, p. 10.

"Quality Management and Improvement Under the Health Security Act," *Executive Letter*, The Segal Company, New York, vol. 17, no. 10/11, p. 7, 1993.

"Report on MEDSTAT Quality Catalyst Program," *BW Healthwire*, Oct. 16, 1997.

Website

Milliman & Robertson, actuarial and consulting firm for underwriting and cost projection data: www2 .milliman.com/milliman/

Chapter Three

"Developing Plan Specifications," David R. Klock and Sharon S. Graham, *The Handbook of Employee Benefits*, 2nd ed., Jerry S. Rosenbloom, editor, Dow Jones-Irwin, Homewood, IL, 1985, pp. 877–889.

"Employee Benefits: Company Actions to Limit Retiree Health Costs," U.S. General Accounting Office, *The Sourcebook on Postretirement Health Care Benefits*, Diane M. Disney, editor, Panel Publishers, New York, 1990, pp. 45–52.

"Implementing and Reviewing Employee Benefit Plans," Joseph D. Young, *The Handbook of Employee Benefits*, 2nd ed., Jerry S. Rosenbloom, editor, Dow Jones-Irwin, Homewood, IL, 1985, pp. 916–925.

"New Hospital Reimbursement System Enacted in N.Y.," Muriel Gibbons, *Insurance Advocate*, July 20, 1996, pp. 28–29.

"New Mandate Need Not Sink Mental Health Benefits," editorial, *National Underwriter*, Oct. 7, 1996, p. 26.

Chapter Four

"Developing Plan Specifications," David R. Klock and Sharon S. Graham, *The Handbook of Employee Benefits*, 2nd ed., Jerry S. Rosenbloom, editor, Dow Jones-Irwin, Homewood, IL, 1985, pp. 877–902.

"Principles of Administration," Edward E. Mack, Jr. and Mary A. Carroll, *The Handbook of Employee Benefits*, 2nd ed., Jerry S. Rosenbloom, editor, Dow Jones-Irwin, Homewood, IL, 1985, pp. 866–876.

"Providers of Group Medical Expense Coverage," *Employee Benefits*, 2nd ed., Burton T. Beam, Jr. and John J. McFadden, Irwin, Homewood, IL, 1988, pp. 144–160.

Chapter Five

"Benefit Changes Anticipated by Industry Type," *The Sourcebook on Postretirement Health Care Benefits*, Diane M. Disney, editor, Aspen Publishers, New York, 1990, p. 11.

"Capital Gains, Is Your HMO Ok—Or Not?" Jane Bryant-Quinn, *Newsweek*, Feb. 10, 1997, p. 52.

Changing Demographics and the World of Work, EBRI Issue Brief No. 172, Employee Benefit Research Institute, Washington, DC, April 1996.

"Consumer/Provider Coalition Announces 'Sound Off' to Document Managed Care 'Abuses' Via Internet WWW," *Insurance Advocate*, March 2, 1996, p. 23, 26.

"Covered Benefits in Group Health Plans," *Business & Health*, January 1993, p. 33 (reprint from *Databook on Employee Benefits, 1992*, Employee Benefits Research Institute, Washington, DC, 1992).

"CPI Detailed Report," U.S. Dept. of Labor, Bureau of Labor Statistics, Washington, DC, *Monthly Reports for January 1992–June, 1996*, April 1998, tables 8, 9.

The Dartmouth Atlas of Health Care, John E. Wennberg, American Hospital Association, Washington, DC, 1996.

"Designing the Retiree Health Plan," *Retiree Health Benefits in the 1990s*, Mercer, New York, 1991, p. 406.

"The Face of Health Insurance in 2000: 'Indistinct'," Phil Zinkewicz, *Insurance Advocate*, Nov. 16, 1996, p. 6.

"Factors Affecting NHE Growth," *Health Care Financing Review*, vol. 16, no. 4, pp. 224–233, Summer 1995.

"Full Flexible Benefits—3-D Flex Programs," *Executive Letter*, The Segal Company, New York, vol. 19, no. 4/5, 1995.

"Health Benefits in 1998," *Medical Benefits*, vol. 15, no. 14, p. 1, 1998.

"Health Care Cost Survey," *Medical Benefits*, Feb. 15, 1998, pp. 2–3.

"Health Care Costs to Climb, but Not Yet," *On Managed Care*, August 1998, p. 4.

"Health Care Worries," *On Managed Care*, May 1998, p. 4.

"HMOs Can and Do Hold Their Own on Quality," *Managing Benefits Plans*, Institute of Management and Administration, New York, August 1998, pp. 1, 6.

"HMOs, to Sue or Not to Sue?" Ellyn E. Spragins, *Newsweek*, Dec. 9, 1996, p. 50.

"HMO-PPO Digest, 1996," Hoechst Marion Roussel, *Medical Benefits*, Jan. 30, 1997, p. 6.

"Improved Prognosis, Pricing Should Bring Better Year for HMOs," Judy Greenwald, *Business Insurance*, April 7, 1997, pp. 2, 32.

"Managed Care, Bound and Gagged," Michael Meyer, *Newsweek*, March 17, 1997, p. 45

Managing Flexible Benefits Plans, Institute of Management and Administration, New York, June 1994, p. 10.

Mohawk Valley Physicians Health Plan, Coverage Comparison, 1998.

"National Survey of Employer-Sponsored Health Plans," *Medical Benefits*, Feb. 15, 1998, pp. 1–2.

"NY Health Care Act Called 'Unprecedented System'," *Insurance Advocate*, July 20, 1996, pp. 28–29.

"New York State Legislative Update," *Empire News for Groups*, Empire Blue Cross Blue Shield, NY, April 1998, p. 1.

"1997 Employer Survey on Managed Care," *Medical Benefits*, vol. 15, no. 10, pp. 1–2, May 30, 1998.

"Outpatient Surgery Trends, 1980–1990," *Medical Benefits*, May 30, 1992, p. 4.

"PSOs Are Coming to Rural America," Scott C. Keyes, *Emphasis*, vol. 2, pp. 10–13, 1998.

"Pulling Together," *Business & Health*, April 1994, p. 56.

"Retiree Health Benefits: An Era of Uncertainty," *Healthcare Trends Report*, KPMG Peat Marwick, Chevy Chase, MD, May 1993, p. 4.

"Satisfaction Differences Among Plan Types," based on 1997 CareData Commercial Health Plan Member Survey, *PRNewswire*, Oct. 22, 1997.

Chapter Six

"Alternative Insurance Company Arrangements," Richard L. Tewksbury, Jr., *The Handbook of Employee Benefits*, 2nd ed., Jerry S. Rosenbloom, editor, Dow Jones-Irwin, Homewood, IL, 1985, pp. 384–417.

Changing Demographics and the World of Work, EBRI Issue Brief No. 172, Employee Benefit Research Institute, Washington, DC, April 1996.

"Employee Benefits, 1997 Edition," *Medical Benefits*, Jan. 15, 1998, pp. 1–2.

Employers' Accounting for Postretirement Benefits Other Than Pensions, Federal Accounting Standards Board Statement No. 106, FASB, Washington, DC, 1990.

Expanding Health Insurance Coverage for Children: Examining the Alternatives, EBRI Issue Brief No. 187, Employee Benefit Research Institute, Washington, DC, July 1997.

"Exploring the Determinants of Employer Health Insurance Coverage," *Medical Benefits*, vol. 15, no. 7, p. 3, 1998.

"Final Physician Incentive Plans Rule . . . ," *Eli Medicare Risk*, Dec. 31, 1996, p. 185.

Flexible Benefits for the Small Organization, The Segal Company, New York, Aug. 1993, pp. 19–25.

"Funding of Employee Benefit Plans," *Employee Benefit Planning*, Jerry S. Rosenbloom and G. Victor Hallman, Prentice-Hall, Englewood Cliffs, NJ, 1981, pp. 393–406.

"Going It Alone: Direct Provider Negotiations," *Integrated Health Plans: Managed Care in the 90s*, Mercer, New York, 1990, p. 11.

"Health Care Cost Increases for 1999? Pick a Number," *Managing Benefits Plans*, Institute of Management and Administration, New York, Aug. 1998, p. 10.

"Health Care Cost Survey," *Medical Benefits*, Feb. 15, 1998, pp. 2–3.

"HMOs Face Conflicts in Workers' Comp," Joseph Paduda, *National Underwriter*, Feb. 9, 1998, p. 21.

"Local Governments Use Self Insurance to Cut Cost," Gregory Berg, *National Underwriter*, Nov. 18, 1993, p. 11.

"Managing Care vs. Managing Costs," *On Managed Care*, vol. 3, no. 7, p. 1, July 1998.

"Managing Health Care Costs," *Fundamentals of Employee Benefit Programs*, Employee Benefit Research Institute, Washington, DC, 1990, pp. 201–208.

"Medical Inflation to Hit Double Digits in 1999," *Medical Benefits*, June 30, 1998, p. 4.

"Methods of Cost Containment," *The 1997 Managed Care Yearbook*, American Business Publishing, Wall Township, NJ, p. 114.

"1997 Employer Survey on Managed Care," *Medical Benefits*, vol. 15, no. 10, p. 1 (figure 1: performance standards), May 30, 1998.

"Percentage of Increase in Health Insurance Premiums, by Plan Type, 1991–1996," *Medical Benefits*, Nov. 15, 1996, p. 1.

"Prevalence of Benefits Practices," *Medical Benefits*, Nov. 15, 1996, p. 3.

"The Prevalence of Cost Containment Approaches, 1980–1991," *Medical Benefits*, June 30, 1992, p. 2.

Retiree Health Benefits: What the Changes May Mean for Future Benefits, EBRI Issue Brief No. 175, Employee Benefit Research Institute, Washington, DC, July 1996.

Segal Trend Survey, The Segal Company, New York, January 1998, pp. 1–4.

"Setting Actuarial Assumptions," *Retiree Health Benefits in the 1990s*, Mercer, New York, 1991, p. 15.

"Survey Report on Employee Benefits," *Medical Benefits*, vol. 15, no. 14, p. 8, 1998.

"Taking a Look at Healthcare: The Employer's Perspective," *The Executive Report on Managed Care*, vol. 11, no. 4, p. 7, 1997.

"Top 50: A Survey of Retiree Benefits . . . ," *Medical Benefits*, vol. 11, no. 18, p. 3, 1998.

Trends in Health Insurance Coverage, EBRI Issue Brief No. 185, Employee Benefit Research Institute, Washington, DC, May 1997.

"Waviers of Subrogation Principles and Strategy," Jack L. Cohen, *Insurance Advocate*, July 6, 1991, p. 16.

"What to Look for in a Retrospective Rating Plan," *The Insurance Buyer's Handbook*, The John Liner Organization, Boston, MA, 1988, pp. 95–104.

Chapter Seven

"Communication and Disclosure of Employee Benefit Plans," Thomas Martinez and Robert V. Nally, *The Handbook of Employee Benefits*, 2nd ed., Jerry S. Rosenbloom, editor, Dow Jones-Irwin, Homewood, IL, 1985, pp. 926–946.

Health Maintenance Organization Enrollment by County, Hudson Valley Health Systems Agency, New York, Dec. 31, 1992, Table HMO-5.

"Hidden from View: The Growing Burden of Health Care Costs, Consumers Should Ask," Gail Shearer, *Medical Benefits*, vol. 15, no. 7, p. 7, 1998.

"New ERISA Disclosure Rules for Health Plans," *Bulletin*, The Segal Company, New York, May 1997, pp. 1–5.

"New Regulation Gives Medicare Managed Care Enrollees Appeal Rights," *The Executive Report on Integrated Care and Capitation*, vol. 1, no. 4, p. 8, 1998.

"New York State HMOs Report Growth and Successful Operations," *Hudson Valley Business Journal*, Feb. 16, 1998, p. 24.

"Picking a Health Care Plan: A Consumer's Guide," Richard J. Newman, *U.S. News & World Report*, Sept. 27, 1993.

"Using Health Plan Satisfaction Information," *Managing Employee Health Benefits*, Spring 1996 (with reference to *Care Data Reports*, New York, 1996, p. 71).

"Your Health Benefits Plan Cost-Effectiveness Self-Test," *Medical Benefits*, Jan. 15, 1993, p. 6.

"Your Right to Information About Your Health Plan," *Consumers' Guide to New York's Managed Care Bill of Rights*, The Public Policy and Education Fund of New York, Albany, NY, April 1, 1997, p. 1.

Chapter Eight

"Alternative Therapies Expanding," *On Managed Care*, May 1998, p. 7.

"Asthma Programs Benefiting Employers with Aspirations to Reap Savings," Joanne Wojcik, *Business Insurance*, Feb. 3, 1997, pp. 3, 13.

"Benefits of Prevention Outweigh Costs: Experts," Christopher Dauer, *National Underwriter*, April 18, 1994, pp. 13, 18.

Bottom Line, Wellness Works, State of New York, Department of Health, Albany, 1990.

"California Agencies Test Wellness Program Waters," Robert Kazel, *Business Insurance*, March 31, 1997, p. 4.

Cancer Facts & Figures—1997, American Cancer Society, Atlanta, GA, 1997.

"Cardiovascular Risk Factors," *The Complete Guide to Family Health*, Masters Publishers, Pittsburgh, PA, 1998.

"Care Costs More in Some Regions," Gina Kolata, *New York Times*, Jan. 30, 1996.

Changing for Good, James O. Prochaska, et al., William Morrow & Co., New York, 1994.

"Characteristics of High Cost Patients and the Percent They Consume of All Costs," Michael Von Korff and Jean Marshall, *HMO Practice*, vol. 6, no. 1, 1992.

"Chronic Care in America," Ellen Freudenheim and Paul Tarini, *Advances*, Issue 4, 1996.

"Comparison of Average Medical Claims Costs According to Health Risk Levels," Louis Tze-Ching Yen, *American Journal of Health Promotion*, Sept./Oct. 1992.

"Corporate Fitness Program," William B. Braun, et al., *Journal of Occupational Medicine*, vol. 28, no. 1, pp. 19–22, Jan. 1986.

"Demand Management: Health Promotion Through Preventive and Self-Care Programs," *The Executive Report on Integrated Care and Capitation*, vol. 1, no. 4, pp. 8–9, 1995.

"Disease Self-Management Program Under Way in New Jersey," *On Managed Care*, October 1997, p. 6.

"The DuPont Study," *Healthy, Wealthy & Wise*, Wellness Councils of America, p. 25, 1993.

"Early Data Support Ounce of Prevention," *Benefits Insight*, Fall 1994, pp. 1–3.

"Employee Assistance and Health Promotion Programs," *Fundamentals of Employee Benefit Programs*, Employee Benefit Research Institute, Washington, DC, 1990, pp. 223–227.

"Employees Who Self-Care When Sick Cut Health Costs by Nearly 25%," *Employee Health & Fitness*, Dec. 1995, p. 134.

"Employer-Sponsored Managed Care Health Promotion Initiatives, 1993–95," *Source Book of Health Insurance Data*, Health Insurance Association of America, Washington, DC, 1997–98, p. 99.

"Employers with Onsite Screening Finding Programs Successful," Deborah Shalowitz-Cowans, *Business Insurance*, Feb. 24, 1997, pp. 3, 11.

"Firms Assess Value of Cost Control Tools," Jerry Geisel, *Business Insurance*, Feb. 5, 1990, pp. 1, 23.

"Greater Recognition of Need for Intervention/Support for Chronic Medical Conditions Is Now Developing," Barbara A. Morris, *Insurance Advocate*, Dec. 14, 1996, p. 35.

"Health Benefit Cost Containment: What Really Works?" *Public Risk*, Nov./Dec. 1989, pp. 11–14.

"Health Care Reform May Boost Wellness Plans," Bruce C. Kelley, *National Underwriter*, April 18, 1994, pp. 15, 65.

"Health Habits, Health Care Use and Costs in a Sample of Retirees," J. Paul Leigh and James F. Fries, *Medical Benefits*, May 15, 1992, p. 5.

Health Objectives for the Year 2000, Hennipen County Community Health Dept., Minneapolis, MN, Spring 1992, p. 18.

Health Promotion and Disease Prevention: A Look at Demand Management Programs, EBRI Issue Brief No. 177, Employee Benefit Research Institute, Washington, DC, Sept. 1996.

"Health Promotion Information or Activities Offered by Subject, 1985 and 1992," *Healthy, Wealthy & Wise*, Wellness Councils of America, p. 22.

Healthstyle: A Self-Test, National Health Information Clearinghouse, Washington, DC, 1990.

HealthyLife Self-Care Guide, American Institute for Preventive Medicine, Farmington Hills, MI, 1997, pp. 50–51.

"Heart Attacks," *The Complete Guide to Family Health*, Masters Publishers, Pittsburgh, PA, 1998.

"Heidis 3.0 Reporting, Special Insert," *Inside Preventive Health*, Oct. 1996.

"House Prepares Decoy Legislation," *Legislative Update, Campaign for Tobacco-Free Kids*, Washington, DC, July 15, 1998, pp. 1, 7.

"Hyperlipidemia Control Program Helps HMO Members Avoid Bypasses and Angioplasty," Steve Larose, editor, *Inside Preventive Care*, Oct. 1996, pp. 1–3.

Judging the Effectiveness of Medical Case Management, Jackie Mazoway, Intracorp, Atlanta, GA, 1992, p. 1.

Large Case Management, Group Health Incorporated, New York, 1990.

"Leading Causes of Death," *Business & Health Special Report*, Oct. 1998, p. 7.

"Link Probed Between Health Care Costs, Employee Education," Diane West, *National Underwriter*, March 2, 1998, pp. 9–10.

"Managed Care Still Leads the List of Health Care Cost-Cutting Techniques," *What's New in Benefits & Compensation*, July 24, 1997, p. 3.

Managing Prescription Drug Costs: A Case Study, Robert W. DuBois and Priscilla E. Feinberg, Public Information Office, New York State Dept. of Civil Service, Albany, NY, June 1994.

"The Nation's Health Risks," *Alto.* Rugo von Mering, Inc., Partners in Health 2000, ARM Inc., April 27, 1992.

Negotiating Health Benefits, the Union Perspective, Irving Perlman and Michael Harren, New York State Bar Association, Albany, NY, Spring 1993.

"A New Look at Wellness Plans," Edward R. Stasica, *Business Insurance*, Feb. 18, 1991, p. 4.

1998 Heart and Stroke, Statistical Update, American Heart Association, Dallas, TX, pp. 11, 22, 24, 25.

"Novartis Pharmacy Benefit Report," *Medical Benefits*, Jan. 15, 1998, pp. 2–3.

"Obesity and Absenteeism: An Epidemiologic Study," Larry A. Tucker and Glenn M. Friedman, *Medical Benefits*, Feb. 15, 1998, p. 8.

Reduced Health Care Costs, American Corporate Health Programs, Inc., 1994.

"Reducing Health Care Costs by Reducing the Need and Demand for Medical Services," James F. Fries, et al., *The Health Project Consortium (Washington, DC) Special Articles*, vol. 329, no. 5, July 29, 1993.

"Risky Behaviors . . . Near $40B," *Insurance Advocate*, April 5, 1997, p. 30.

"Statistically, 100 People," *Healthy, Wealthy & Wise*, Wellness Councils of America, Stevens Point, WI, p. 26.

Survey on American Attitude About Health and Medicine, Reuters, Washington, DC, Dec. 11, 1997.

"Tabloid Brags About Successful Results of Employee Health Test Program," *Blue Note*, Feb. 1990, p. 8.

"24-Hour Plan Covers Health, Disability, WC," Linda Koco, *National Underwriter*, March 9, 1998, p. 21.

"Wellness Program Guidelines," *Benefits Quarterly*, First Quarter 1992, pp. 45–48.

"Wellness Programs Not Reaching All Employees," *Wellness Program Management Advisor*, vol. 1, no. 11, pp. 1–2, 1996.

"Wellness Programs That Work," Nancy Coe-Bailey, *Business & Health*, Nov. 1990, pp. 28–40.

Women's Health, Report of the Interagency Work Group on Women's Health, State of New York, Office of the Governor, May 1994, p. 31.

"Work/Family Programs Could Lead to Backlash," *What's New in Benefits & Compensation*, Sept. 25, 1997, p. 8.

Chapter Nine

"Implementing and Reviewing Employee Benefit Plans," Joseph D. Young, *The Handbook of Employee Benefits*, 2nd ed., Jerry S. Rosenbloom, editor, Dow Jones-Irwin, Homewood, IL, 1985, pp. 921–923.

Chapter Ten

"The ADA and Employee Benefits," Robert Storch, *The Risk & Benefits Journal*, Summer 1993, pp. 32–35.

"Americans with Disabilities Act Bars Discrimination Based on HIV . . . ," *Bulletin*, The Segal Company, New York, July 1998.

"Aspects of Disability Management," *Segal Executive Letter*, The Segal Company, New York, vol. 19, no. 1, 1995.

"Bill Mandates Unlimited Hospital Stay Insurance Coverage Where Needed," *Insurance Advocate*, Feb. 8, 1997, p. 31.

"Budget Proposal Calls for Changes to Medicare Risk HMOs," Jerry Geisel, *Business Insurance*, Feb. 10, 1997, p. 21.

"Child Health Plus Expanded," *The Bulletin*, State of New York, Department of Insurance, Albany, vol. 37, no. 3, pp. 1–2.

COBRA: A Cross-Examination, Census of Certified Employee Benefit Specialists, Brookfield, WI, Nov. 1991.

"The Coming Revolution in Medicare: What Medicare+Choice Means for Health Plans That Cover Retirees," *Segal Special Report*, The Segal Company, New York, April 1998.

"Comparison of 1996–1997 Aged Part A and Part B Monthly AAPCC Rates for the Top 100 HMO-Enrolled Counties," *HFCA Statistics, 1996—Expenditures*, Health Care Financing Administration, Washington, DC, 1997.

"Contracting Risks," *Pennsylvania Municipal Liability Pooling News*, H.A. Thomson Company, Exton, PA, Summer 1992, p. 1.

"Corporate Decision Makers Agree Health Care Costs Is Top Issue But Vary on Control, New Survey Finds," *Insurance Advocate*, vol. 107, no. 30, p. 23, Aug. 3, 1996.

DOL Regulations and Court Cases, Newsletter, Pellerino Consulting Services, Marine City, MI, September 1998.

Enrollment and Incurred Reimbursement for End-Stage Renal Disease (Table II.F9), Health Care Financing Administration, Office of the Actuary, Washington, DC, April 1997.

Estimated Operations of the HI Trust Fund Under Intermediate Assumptions, Calendar Years 1997–2007, (Table 1.E1), Health Care Financing Administration, Washington, DC, April 1998.

"Family & Medical Leave Act," *State Trends, Keep Up to Date On Payroll*, Progressive Business Publications, Malvern, PA, July 17, 1998, p. 8.

"The FASB Exposure Draft: Issues and Implications," Joel G. Siegel, *The Sourcebook on Postretirement Health Care Benefits*, Diane M. Disney, editor, A Panel Publication, New York, 1990, pp. 165–167.

Federal Cost Shifting: A Continuing Trend, Harvey C. Sigelbaum, Amalgamated Life Insurance Company, New York, May 1992.

"Foundation to Purchase HSI in Latest Managed Care Mega Merger," David McGuire, *Managed Care Outlook*, vol. 9, no. 20, pp. 1–3, Oct. 4, 1996.

"Frequency of Permissible Enrollment/Disenrollment Under Medicare+Choice," *Executive Newsletter*, The Segal Company, New York, October 1998, p. 2.

"Getting Beyond the Managed Care Backlash," Tom Miller, *On Managed Care*, vol. 3, no. 8, p. 7, Aug. 1998.

"HCFA Regs Help Employers Shift to Secondary Payer Role," *Employee Benefit News*, April 1994, p. 12.

HCFA Statistics, 1996—Expenditures, Health Care Financing Administration, Washington, DC, 1998, table 26: Program Outlays/Trends, table 27: Benefit Outlays by Program, table 28: Regional Expenses Medicare/Medicaid—U.S., table 29: Medicare/Trust Fund Projections, table 32: Medicaid/Type of Service, table 33: Attributed Expenditures to Secondary Payors, table 34: Medicaid/Payments by Eligibility Status.

"Health Care Bill of Rights," Deborah Zabarenko, *Reuters News Service*, Nov. 20, 1997.

"Health Care Reform Battle Heating Up Again in Congress," Mary Jane Fisher, *National Underwriter*, March 30, 1998, p. 15.

Health Insurance Portability: COBRA Expansions and Job Mobility, EBRI Issue Brief No. 194, Employee Benefit Research Institute, Washington, DC, Feb. 1998.

"Health Insurance Portability and Accountability Act," *The Medicare News Brief*, Health Care Financing Administration, Washington, DC, MNB-98-4, April 1998, p. 15.

"Health Insurance Portability Reform Legislation . . . Freeing Employees from 'Job Lock'—Good or Bad?" *Insurance Advocate*, vol. 106, no. 44, pp. 28–29, Nov. 11, 1995.

"Health Insurance Standards: New Federal Law Creates Challenges for Consumers, Insurers, Regulators," *Medical Benefits*, vol. 15, no. 7, p. 4, 1998.

"HIPAA HIPAA Hooray for Employees," Steele R. Stewart, *Emphasis* (Tillinghast-Towers Perrin, New York), vol. 4, p. 18–21, 1997.

"HMOs Dissected to Check Liability Status: Article Reviews Types and How They Have Fared in Lawsuits," *Insurance Advocate*, vol. 107, no. 16, pp. 17–18, April 20, 1996.

Implications of ERISA for Health Benefits and the Number of Self-Funded ERISA Plans, EBRI Issue Brief No. 193, Employee Benefit Research Institute, Washington, DC, Jan. 1998.

Information About Medicaid Managed Care, #3315, State of New York, Department of Health, Albany, 1998.

"Jae L. Wittlich Named Chairman of Health Insurance Assn.," *Insurance Advocate*, vol. 107, no. 50, p. 30, Dec. 28, 1996.

"Kaiser Restructures Following Two Surprise Purchase Decisions," *Managed Care Outlook*, vol. 9, no. 18, pp. 1, 5–7, Sept. 6, 1996.

"Legislative Action Follows Complaints; 33 States Enact Laws Regulating Managed Care," *Insurance Advocate*, vol. 107, no. 29, pp. 37–38.

"Legislative Update 1997—Part II, Conforming to Federal Health Insurance Requirements," *The Bulletin*, New York State, Department of Insurance, vol. 35, nos. 11&12, pp. 3–4.

"Long Term Budgetary Pressures and Policy Options," *Medical Benefits*, vol. 15, no. 12, pp. 1–2, June 30, 1998.

"Managing Care vs. Managing Costs," *On Managed Care*, vol. 3, no. 7, July 1998, p. 1, table 1: Provisions Related to Denial-of-Treatment Issues.

"Managing the Managers: Health Insurance Bill of Rights," Robert Kazel, *Business Insurance*, March 3, 1997, pp. 1, 31.

"Massachusetts Uncompensated Care Act Takes Effect," *Group Administrator Update*, Empire Blue Cross Blue Shield, New York, April 1998.

"Medical Privacy Bill Introduced," Mary Jane Fisher, *National Underwriter*, April 13, 1998, pp. 4, 31.

Medical Savings Account High Deductible Health Insurance Policies, Circular Letter No. 23, State of New York, Department of Insurance, Albany, Sept. 28, 1998.

"Medical Savings Accounts Today," *Segal Executive Letter*, The Segal Company, New York, vol. 19, no. 2/3, 1995.

"Medicare as Secondary Payer: The Provisions, The Problems . . . ," Cynthia J. Drinkwater, *Benefits Quarterly*, Third Quarter 1991, pp. 1–2.

"Medicare HMOs Not Protecting Appeals Rights OIG Charges," *Eli Medicare Risk Report*, vol. 3, no. 2, pp. 13–14, 1997.

Medicare Payments, by Type of Benefit, 1995–1997, Data Compendium, Health Care Financing Administration, Washington, DC, 1996.

"Medicare Risk Enrollment Jumps 31% in 1996," *Eli Medicare Risk Report*, vol. 3, no. 1, Jan. 15, 1997.

"Medicare Risk Plan Information Problems Prompting Legislation," *Eli Medicare Risk Report*, vol. 3, no. 7, p. 51, April 15, 1997.

"Medicare Risk Plans Escape Payment Freeze Under Republican Reforms," *Eli Medicare Risk*, vol. 3, no. 10, pp. 73–77.

"Meeting Retirees' Demand for Information," *Segal Executive Letter*, The Segal Company, New York, vol. 22, no. 4/5, 1995.

"National Health Expenditure Amounts, Percent Distribution, and Average Annual Percent Growth by Source of Funds: Selected Calendar Years 1980–2005, Table 1," *Health Care Financing Review*, vol. 16, no. 4, p. 234, Summer 1995.

"NCQA Updates Rules for Evaluating HMOs," Allison Bell, *National Underwriter*, May 18, 1998, p. 32.

"Nearly 25 Percent of Plans Submitting HEDIS Data Will Undergo On-Site Audits," *Eli Medicare Risk Report*, vol. 3, no. 9, pp. 65–66, 1997.

New Focus on Retiree Medical Benefits, Mercer, New York, 1991, pp. 1, 4–5, 10, 17.

"New Hampshire Cited as Healthiest State in US," Matthew P. Schwartz, *National Underwriter*, Nov. 27, 1995, p. 13.

"New Health-Care Law Includes Inducement for Purchase of Long Term Care Insurance," *Insurance Advocate*, vol. 107, no. 33, pp. 1, 30, Aug. 24, 1996.

"New Tax Ruling on Retiree Health Plans," *Compensation & Benefits Manager's Report*, Oct. 21, 1994, p. 8.

"NY Bill Seeks to End HMO Freedom from Malpractice Suits Dropped in MD Laps," *Insurance Advocate*, vol. 107, no. 13, p. 21, March 30, 1996.

"New York State Legislative Update," *Group Administrator Update*, Empire Blue Cross Blue Shield, New York, April 1998.

"1998 Annual Health Insurer Complaint Rankings: Health Maintenance Organizations," State of New York, Department of Insurance, Albany, 1999.

"1998 Medicare Deductible and Coinsurance Amounts," *Looking Forward*, Rockland County Office for the Aging, Pomona, NY, vol. 23, no. 1, p. 1, 1998.

Notice of Changes to COBRA Requirements Implemented by the Health Insurance Portability and Accountability Act of 1996, Thompson Publishing Group, October 1996, table 1300, pp. 47, 48, 48.1, 48.2.

"Official HIPAA Guidance on Reports for Former Participants," *Bulletin*, The Segal Company, New York, April 1997.

"Ombudsman Program to Provide Consumers with Outlet," *Managed Care Outlook*, vol. 9, no. 18, p. 3, Sept. 6, 1996.

Personal Health Care/Payment Source, Medicare charts, Health Care Financing Administration, Office of the Actuary, Data from the Office of National Health Statistics, Washington, DC, 1998.

"Preemption of State Hospital Reimbursement Law," Katherine A. Hesse, esq., *Benefits Quarterly*, First Quarter 1994, pp. 80–81.

Providers Are Key to Preventing Medicare Disenrollment, Public Sector Contracting Report, National Health Information, Marietta, GA, May 1997, pp. 65–67, 75.

"The Quest Goes On: Health Care Interest Groups Offer Strong, But Separate, Views on Medicare Reform . . . ," *Insurance Advocate*, vol. 108, no. 11, pp. 1, 37, March 15, 1997.

"Reasonable Rules Key in Portability Bill," Terry Humo, *Business Insurance*, March 24, 1997, p. 18.

"SMI—B. Highlights," *HCFA News Release*, Health Care Financing Administration, Washington, DC, April 29, 1998.

"Social Security and Medicare," Robert J. Myers, *The Handbook of Employee Benefits*, 2nd ed., Jerry S. Rosenbloom, editor, Dow-Jones Irwin, Homewood, IL, 1985, pp. 71–75.

"States Race to Set Up Kids' Health Plans," Allison Bell, *National Underwriter*, May 18, 1998, pp. 41–42.

"U.S. Supreme Court Rules That Former Employees May Take COBRA Even If They Have Other Coverage," *Bulletin*, The Segal Company, New York, July 1998.

"What a Medicaid HMO Looks Like," *On Managed Care*, vol. 3, no. 8, p. 7, August 1998.

Your Rights under the Family and Medical Leave Act of 1993, Publication 1420, U.S. Department of Labor, Employment Standards Administration, Wage and Hour Division, Washington, DC, June 1993.

Chapter Eleven

"Applying HEDIS 2.0: Segal SelectNet," *Segal Executive Letter*, The Segal Company, New York, vol. 18, no. 5, 1994.

"Evaluating a Benefit Program," *Employee Benefit Planning*, Jerry S. Rosenbloom and G. Victor Hallman, Prentice Hall, Englewood Cliffs, NJ, 1981, pp. 462–466.

Executive Summary, Strategic Plan, NYS Health Insurance Plan, New York State Department of Civil Service, Albany, NY, 1995, p. 13.

"Guidance on Evaluating an Employee Benefit Package," *Fundamentals of Employee Benefit Programs*, 4th ed., Employee Benefit Research Institute, Washington, DC, 1990, pp. 279–290.

"How to Choose an Agent or Broker," *The Insurance Buyer's Handbook*, The John Liner Organization, Boston, MA, 1988, pp. 31–40.

"Implementing and Reviewing Employee Benefit Plans," Joseph D. Young, *The Handbook of Employee Benefits*, 2nd ed., Jerry S. Rosenbloom, editor, Dow-Jones Irwin, Homewood, IL, 1985, pp. 916–925.

"Managed Care Reform: House Passes Patient Protection Act . . . ," *Bulletin*, The Segal Company, New York, Sept. 1, 1998.

1997 Managed Care Yearbook, American Business Publishing, Wall Township, NJ, 1998.

"Northeast Region Result Highlights (Table 4)," *Annual Benefit Summary*, Foster Higgins, New York, 1995.

"Regional Health Care Price Index, Last 12 Months," *Health Care Price Index*, vol. 1, no. 10, Dec. 18, 1992.

Chapter Twelve

"Alternative Funding Methods," Burton T. Beam, Jr., and John J. McFadden, *Employee Benefits*, 2nd ed., Irwin, Homewood, IL, 1988, pp. 237–250.

Employer-Sponsored Health Insurance, State and National Estimates, Centers for Disease Control and Prevention, National Center for Health Statistics, Washington, DC, December 1997.

"Funding of Employee Benefit Plans," *Employee Benefit Planning*, Jerry S. Rosenbloom and G. Victor Hallman, Prentice Hall, Englewood Cliffs, NJ, 1981, pp. 393–406.

"Health Care Cost Containment Techniques," William G. Williams, *The Handbook of Employee Benefits*, 2nd ed., Jerry S. Rosenbloom, editor, Dow-Jones Irwin, Homewood, IL, 1985, pp. 238–258.

"Managing Health Care Costs," *Fundamentals of Employee Benefit Programs*, Employee Benefit Research Institute, Washington, DC, 1990, pp. 201–208.

"Medicare Changes: . . . Medicare Recovery and Preventive Benefits," *Segal Special Report*, The Segal Company, New York, April 1998.

"The Move to Self Funding," *On Managed Care*, vol. 3, no. 5, May 1998, p. 4.

"Noninsured Approaches to Funding Health Care Benefits," Carlton Harker, *The Handbook of Employee Benefits*, 2nd ed., Jerry S. Rosenbloom, editor, Dow-Jones Irwin, Homewood, IL, 1985, pp. 418–531.

"Partner Strategy Has Long-Term Reward," *On Managed Care*, vol. 3, no. 5, May 1998, p. 3.

"Pharmacy Benefit Report: Trends & Forecasts, 1998 Edition," *Medical Benefits*, vol. 15, no. 14, p. 5, 1998.

"Retiree Medical-Care Obligations for 1997," *Medical Benefits*, vol. 15, no. 14, p. 10, July 30, 1998.

"Roundup of State Managed Care Laws," *On Managed Care*, vol. 2, no. 10, October 1997.

"With Potential for Higher Rates, More Employers May Self-Insure," Robert Kazel, *Business Insurance*, Feb. 17, 1997, pp. 3, 14.

Chapter Thirteen

"The American Express 'Everyday Spending' Index," *Medical Benefits*, vol. 15, no. 7, p. 11, 1998.

"A Benchmark for Measuring Healthcare Quality," *Medical Benefits*, vol. 15, no. 10, p. 10, 1998.

Blue Choice: HMO/POS Benefit Summary, for Groups with 3–50 Contracts, Empire Blue Cross Blue Shield, New York, Sept. 1995.

Changing Demographics and the World of Work, EBRI Issue Brief No. 172, Employee Benefit Research Institute, Washington, DC, April 1996.

"Declining Employer Coverage May Affect Access for 55 to 64-Year-Olds," *Medical Benefits*, vol. 15, no. 14, p. 9, 1998.

"Do Employers/Employees Still Need Employee Benefits?" Christopher R. Conte, *Medical Benefits*, vol. 15, no. 7, pp. 2–3, April 15, 1998.

"Employment-Based Health Benefits," *Medical Benefits*, vol. 11, no. 18, p. 2, Sept. 30, 1994.

"Hidden from View: The Growing Burden of Health Care Costs," Gail Shearer, *Medical Benefits*, vol. 15, no. 7, p. 6, 1998.

"National Survey of Employer-Sponsored Health Plans," *Medical Benefits*, vol. 15, no. 3, pp. 1–2, 1998.

"Nonprofit Association Sponsored Insurance Plans," Gary K. Stone, *The Handbook of Employee Benefits*, 2nd ed., Jerry S. Rosenbloom, editor, Dow-Jones Irwin, Homewood, IL, 1985, pp. 1087–1107.

Percentage of Employees Eligible and Enrolled in Employer's Health Plan, by State, Centers for Disease Control and Prevention, National Center for Health Statistics, Washington, DC, 1997.

"Small-Group Health Insurance Checklist," *The Nation's Business*, October 1990, p. 29.

"Study Finds Fewer Workers in Health Plans," Joseph D'Allegro, *National Underwriter*, July 13, 1998, p. 25.

"Switching to Managed Care in the Small Employer Market," Michael A. Morrisey and Gail A. Jensen, *Medical Benefits*, vol. 15, no. 1, table 2: Percentage of Insured Workers in Small Firms, by Plan Type, p. 4, 1998.

"10 Ways to Cut Your Health-Care Costs Now," Roger Thompson, *The Nation's Business*, October 1990, pp. 20–29.

"Third Annual Survey on Purchasing Value in Health Care," *Medical Benefits*, vol. 15, no. 14, p. 2, 1998.

"What Benefits Do New Graduates Want?", *Medical Benefits*, vol. 15, no. 10, p. 11, 1998.

"Where to Get the Most HMO Value," *On Managed Care*, vol. 3, no. 7, p. 4, July 1998.

Index